Violence at work

Violence at work

Third edition

Duncan Chappell and Vittorio Di Martino

INTERNATIONAL LABOUR OFFICE • GENEVA

Chappell, D.; Di Martino, V.
Violence at work. Third edition.
Geneva, International Labour Office, 2006

Workplace violence, occupational safety, developed countries, developing countries.
13.04.5
ISBN 92-2-117948-6 / 978-92-2-117948-1
                                        ILO Cataloguing in Publication Data

ILO publications can be obtained through major booksellers or ILO local offices in many countries, or direct from ILO Publications, International Labour Office, CH-1211 Geneva 22, Switzerland. Catalogues or lists of new publications are available free of charge from the above address or by email: pubvente@ilo.org

Visit our website: www.ilo.org/publns

Typeset by Magheross Graphics, France & Ireland *www.magheross.com*
Printed in Switzerland   ATA

PREFACE

Dialogue, discussions and disagreements form a regular part of the interactions in many work environments. As a result, most workers and managers are confronted with personal, work-related and client/customer challenges on a daily basis, including the anxieties and frustration of co-workers, personality clashes, organizational and production difficulties, diminished resources, increasing production/output demands, aggressive intruders from outside the business, and problematic relations with clients and members of the public. Despite this, dialogue usually prevails over confrontation, and most people manage to organize efficient and productive activities within the workplace. There are cases, however, where dialogue fails to develop in a positive way, relationships between workers, managers, clients or the public deteriorate, and the objectives of working efficiently and achieving productive results are negatively affected. Thus violence may emerge in work environments and turn a previously benign environment into a hostile and hazardous setting.

Contemporary community awareness about the issue of violence at work has been magnified by several recent tragic workplace killings perpetrated by disturbed individuals and fanatical groups armed with powerful weapons. For example, since the first edition of this book appeared in 1998, terrorist attacks on a number of workplaces, public transport facilities, and hotel and residential compounds have resulted in significant loss of life around the world. While media attention has generally concentrated on the victims of these attacks – and sometimes the risks faced by criminal justice system workers tracking the perpetrators – it is frequently forgotten that many victims were either at work or travelling to or from their jobs. Similarly, media attention often focuses on single events with multiple victims, such as when an armed individual attacks a group of co-workers, perhaps after unresolved interpersonal or employment disagreements.

Yet many other workplace violence events occur out of sight of the general public, in one-to-one situations, result in emotional rather than physical injury to the victim, and produce extensive costs for both the employer and the recipient. Often the victims of these less-dramatic occurrences lack power in their employment relationship, have limited protection from unfair dismissal, and have few alternative job options. The end result is that victimized workers without support may resign from their jobs, be pushed out if they remonstrate, or accept low-level workplace violence or sexual harassment as the price to be paid for a job. Thus, the causes and consequences of workplace violence cannot be analysed independently of employment relationships.

In this book, the full range of aggressive acts that occur in workplaces are reviewed, including homicides, assaults, sexual harassment, threats, bullying, mobbing and verbal abuse. Part I (chapters 1 to 4) details evidence about the incidence and severity of workplace violence in different countries (including examination of some terrorist and mass murder events), identifies occupations and situations at particular risk, evaluates various causal explanations, and details some of the social and economic costs. In Part II (chapters 5 to 8), the potential benefits from different types of responses to workplace violence are evaluated, including regulatory innovations, policy interventions, workplace designs that may reduce the risks, collective agreements, and "best practice" options. In Part III (Chapter 9), international initiatives and recommendations for specific action are enunciated.

It is encouraging to note the increasing attention being paid to the extent and severity of all forms of workplace violence, including by workers, trade unions, employers, government authorities and experts across the world. The data and discussions in this book emphasize that workplace violence is not merely an episodic problem created by deranged persons, but a highly complex issue, rooted in wider economic, employment-relationship, organizational, gender-role and cultural factors. Thus instead of searching for simplistic, single solutions to deal with the entire problem, the full range of causes which generate violence must be analysed and a variety of intervention strategies applied. Recognition of the variety and complexity of the factors which contribute to workplace violence is a key precursor to the design and implementation of effective anti-violence control programmes.

Based on case studies, objective data and recent scientific publications, the contents of this book are intended to provide a basis for understanding the nature of workplace violence, and to enhance development and implementation of effective preventive interventions. The book stresses the importance of a systematic and targeted preventive response. For example, in many countries the scope of existing criminal, occupational safety and health, labour, environmental and allied law is being extended progressively and adapted to deal with the issue of workplace violence. In several countries, violence at work is emerging as a separate legal issue, with legislative and regulatory provisions making for a focused rather than a diffuse response.

Integrated within this book are reviews of numerous guidelines emerging from governments, trade unions, specialist study groups, workplace violence experts and employers' organizations, most of which contain blueprints for action. Despite different approaches, these guidelines reveal common themes: preventive action is possible and necessary; work organization and the working environment can provide important pointers to the causes and solutions; the participation of workers and their representatives is crucial both in identifying the risk factors and in implementing solutions; the interpersonal skills of management and workers alike must not be underrated; there cannot be one formula for action because the unique risk factors in each workplace situation must be addressed; and continued review of policies and programmes is essential to keep up with rapidly changing work environment scenarios.

The ILO has been in the vanguard in addressing protection of workers' dignity and equality in the workplace, including publications on occupational stress, sexual harassment and child labour, among others. The commitment of the ILO to reducing workplace violence is demonstrated through the publication, in 2004, of its code of practice *Workplace violence in services sectors and measures to combat this phenomenon.*

The third edition of this ILO publication is directed toward all those engaged in combating violence at work: policymakers in government agencies; employers' and workers' organizations; occupational health and safety professionals; human resources managers; trainers and workers. We hope this book will promote dialogue, policies and initiatives "to repudiate violence and remove it from the workplace now".

François Eyraud, Director
Conditions of Work and Employment Programme
ILO Social Protection Sector

William Salter, Senior Adviser
Conditions of Work and Employment Programme
ILO Social Protection Sector

CONTENTS

PART III   FUTURE ACTION

Figures

Tables

Boxes

ACKNOWLEDGEMENTS

This third edition of a book first prepared for publication more than a decade ago, includes invaluable contributions made by numerous individuals and organizations. As readers will quickly appreciate, this is a new edition containing fresh and updated material about issues which are now far more widely recognized and discussed on a global scale than was the case during the initial gestation period of the first edition.

There could not have been a third edition without the tireless effort and support provided by the Conditions of Work and Employment Programme of the ILO. The authors owe a special debt of gratitude to Bill Salter, who steered the venture around many shoals, and coped with the realities of dealing with two individuals living in different continents and time zones. We also owe a great deal to Claire Mayhew, whose technical editing, patience and collegiate spirit kept us refining and revising the text, and to Rosemary Beattie who pulled all of the disparate pieces together in order to produce the final printed version of the book. Bibliographic assistance was most ably provided by Karin Halldén.

Apart from those we can name in person, the authors also wish to extend their warm thanks to the individuals, governments, employers, trade unions, research institutes and other organizations that provided information, advice and comments on the grist of the material that is now contained in this book.

Duncan Chappell
Vittorio Di Martino

ABBREVIATIONS AND ACRONYMS

ADA	Americans with Disabilities Act
APWU	American Postal Workers' Union
A&E	Accident and emergency
BCS	British Crime Survey
BJS	Bureau of Justice Statistics (US)
BLS	Bureau of Labor Statistics (US)
BRC	British Retail Consortium
CAL/OSHA	California Occupational Safety and Health Administration
CCOHS	Canadian Centre for Occupational Health and Safety
CC.OO	Confederación Sindical de Comisiones Obreras
CCTV	Closed-circuit television/video system
CEDAW	Committee on the Elimination of Discrimination Against Women (UN)
CEEP	European Centre of Enterprises with Public Participation of Enterprises of General Economic Interest
CEO	Chief executive officer
CHSCT	Comité d'Hygiène, de Securité et des Conditions de Travail
CONICET	Consejo Nacional de Investigaciones y Técnicas
CPTED	Crime Prevention through Environmental Design
CSVR	Centre for the Study of Violence and Reconciliation (South Africa)
DOSH	Department of Occupational Safety and Health (Malaysia)
ETUC	European Trade Union Confederation
EUROFIET	European Branch of the International Federation of Commercial, Clinical, Professional and Technical Employees
EU	European Union
GPS	Global Positioning System
HAS	Health and Safety Authority (Ireland)
HSE	Health and Safety Executive (United Kingdom)

ICN	International Council of Nurses
ICFTU	International Confederation of Free Trade Unions
IFJ	International Federation of Journalists
ILO	International Labour Office/Organization
INAIL	Istituto Nazionale per l'Assicurazione contro gli Infortuni sul Lavoro (Italy)
ISPESL	Istituto Superiore per la Prevenzione e la Sicurezza (Italy)
ISTAT	Italian Studies of Statistics
LO	Norwegian Federation of Trade Unions/Danish Confederation of Trade Unions
MSF	Manufacturing Science and Finance union
MSP	Member of Scottish Parliament
MSPB	Merit Systems Protection Board (US)
NCV	Australian National Committee on Violence
NCVS	National Crime Victimization Survey
NGO	Non-governmental organization
NHO	Confederation of Norwegian Business and Industry
NHS	National Health Service (UK)
NIOSH	National Institute for Occupational Safety and Health (US)
NOHSC	National Occupational Health and Safety Commission (Australia)
NSW	New South Wales
OSH	Occupational safety and health
OSHA	Occupational Safety and Health Administration (US)
PSI	Public Services International
PTS	Patient transport services
RIDDOR	Reporting of Injuries, Disease and Dangerous Occurrences Regulations
SHRM	Society for Human Resource Management
SLA	South Lebanon Army
SOLVE	Stress, Tobacco, Alcohol and drugs, HIV/AIDS and Violence
UNVFT	United Nations Voluntary Fund for the Victims of Torture
UNICEF	United Nations Children's Fund
UEAPME	European Association of Craft, Small and Medium-sized Enterprises
UNICE	Union of Industrial and Employers' Confederations
UNDP	United Nations Development Programme
UNIFEM	United Nations Development Fund for Women
USS	Union of Swiss Trade Unions
VIF	Violent incident form (Sweden)
WHO	World Health Organization

PART I

UNDERSTANDING VIOLENCE AT WORK

INTRODUCTION: A CATALYST FOR ACTION

1

The face of workplace violence continues to change in our troubled world, with a range of aggressive acts inflicted on workers by diverse perpetrators. While a uniform definition of what constitutes workplace violence remains elusive, most commentators include homicide, assault, threats, mobbing and bullying on the job as forms of violence at work. Even the definition of a "workplace" is elusive as an increasing number of people earn their living in mobile sites and home-based offices, and via telework. While homicide on the job has historically been identified as the most severe form of workplace aggression, this perception is shifting as in the opening decade of the twenty-first century workers across the globe have been exposed to an increasing risk of becoming the victims of acts of terror. Brutal and often random terrorist attacks have cut a swathe of death and destruction in many countries in both the developed and developing world, including in workplaces. This book examines all forms of workplace violence, beginning with terrorism (box 1).

Terrorism in the workplace

Box 1	Tuesday 11 September 2001[1]
7:58 a.m.	United Airlines flight 175 to Los Angeles departs Boston, Massachusetts, with 56 passengers and nine crew on board.
7:59 a.m.	American Airlines flight 11 to Los Angeles leaves Logan Airport in Boston, with 81 passengers and 11 crew on board.
8:01 a.m.	United Airlines flight 93 to San Francisco takes off from Newark airport in New Jersey with 38 passengers and seven crew on board.
8:10 a.m.	American Airlines flight 77 to Los Angeles departs Washington DC's Dulles Airport with 58 passengers and six crew on board.

/cont'd

/cont'd

8:51 a.m.	Plane crashes into north World Trade Center tower.
9:06 a.m.	Second plane crashes into south World Trade Center tower.
9:25 a.m.	New York Stock Exchange delays trading. US Federal Aviation Administration orders all planes grounded.
9:27 a.m.	New York City airports closed.
9:30 a.m.	President George W. Bush calls crashes "apparent terrorism attack" in television comments from Florida.
9:41 a.m.	Plane crashes into the Pentagon in Arlington County, Virginia.
9:44 a.m.	White House, Pentagon evacuated.
9:48 a.m.	US Capitol evacuated.
10:00 a.m.	South World Trade Center tower collapses.
10:28 a.m.	North World Trade Center tower collapses.
10:40 a.m.	United Airlines flight 93 crashes southeast of Pittsburgh.
10:56 a.m.	Securities and Exchange Commission closes all US markets for the day.
11:25 a.m.	American Airlines confirms flights 11 and 77 were lost.
11:54 a.m.	United Airlines confirms two separate crashes of flights 93, 175.
Noon 12:00	US-Mexican border sealed.
1:04 p.m.	Bush, speaking from Barksdale Air Force Base in Louisiana, says that all appropriate security measures are being taken, including putting the US military on high alert worldwide. He asks for prayers for those killed or wounded in the attacks.
1:44 p.m.	The Pentagon says five warships and two aircraft carriers will leave the US Naval Station in Norfolk, Virginia, to protect the East Coast from further attack.
1:48 p.m.	Bush leaves Barksdale Air Force Base aboard Air Force One and flies to an Air Force base in Nebraska.
2:30 p.m.	The FAA announces there will be no US commercial air traffic until noon Wednesday at the earliest.
3:55 p.m.	Karen Hughes, a White House counsellor, says the President is at an undisclosed location, later revealed to be Offutt Air Force Base in Nebraska, and is conducting a National Security Council meeting by phone.

4:30 p.m.	The President leaves Offutt aboard Air Force One to return to Washington, DC.
5:20 p.m.	The 47-story Building 7 of the World Trade Center complex collapses.
6:00 p.m.	Explosions are heard in Kabul, Afghanistan, hours after the terrorist attacks in the United States. Afghanistan is believed to be where Osama bin Laden, whom US officials say is possibly behind Tuesday's deadly attacks, is located.
6:54 p.m.	Bush arrives back at the White House aboard Marine One. The President earlier landed at Andrews Air Force Base in Maryland with a three-fighter jet escort.
8:30 p.m.	Bush addresses the nation, saying "thousands of lives were suddenly ended by evil" and asks for prayers for the families and friends of Tuesday's victims.

Source: Adapted from Delawareonline: *The News Journal*, no date (see: http://www.delawareonline.com/newsjournal/local/2001/09/11terrortimeline400.html, accessed 27 Sep. 2005).

According to official statistics, 2001 saw an average of 20 workplace homicides weekly in the United States (US), one of the lowest figures recorded in the last 20 years.[2] However, these statistics do not take account of the victims of 11 September 2001. The total dead and missing numbered 2,996: 2,752 in New York City, 184 at the Pentagon, 40 in Pennsylvania, and 19 hijackers.[3] Many of the dead and missing were people at work: 319 firefighters, 50 police officers, 35 plane crew and 36 civilian employees at the Pentagon, as well as hundreds of people working for the many financial and commercial companies operating within the World Trade Center. If these figures are taken into account, 11 September appears as the most deadly act of violence at work ever, and 2001 the record year for the number of workplace homicides.

The following year in Indonesia, 202 people were killed and 309 injured on 12 October 2002, when two terrorist bombs ripped through the Sari nightclub and Paddy's Bar at Kuta Beach in Bali.[4] Those victimized in Bali came from 22 countries; hence the victims – and the subsequent investigative team – were a broad international mix of people from industrialized and developing countries. Subsequently, on 11 March 2004, a series of bomb blasts on the commuter rail network in the Spanish capital of Madrid left 191 dead and more than 1,800 wounded.[5] Again, the victims were an international mix, coming from 14 different countries. More recently, on 7 July 2005, 56 people were killed and 700 injured in London in a series of four bomb attacks at peak commuting time in the underground and on a bus.[6] In each of these tragedies, many of the casualties were workers, including transport workers, those travelling to work, and others working in the tourist trade.[7]

In some instances, terrorists have deliberately targeted specific groups of workers. In contemporary Iraq for example, members of that nation's new and fledgling police and military forces have been the victims of a rash of lethal bombings and shootings.[8] Foreign workers, including journalists[9] and those involved in assisting with the reconstruction of Iraq, have also been the subject of widely publicized kidnappings and murders. Horrific pictures of those captured by ruthless terrorist groups have been beamed into the living-rooms of countless millions through satellite television and the Internet.[10]

It must now be acknowledged that acts of terrorism are on many occasions also acts of workplace violence. While recognizing this linkage, a conscious decision has been taken in this new edition of *Violence at work*, as was the case with the two earlier editions, to focus attention upon the less extreme forms of this phenomenon. The roots of terrorism are usually deeply entwined with socio-political struggles that require separate and continued analysis beyond the scope of this book.[11] Where, however, certain occupational groups appear to be at greater risk of becoming victimized by terrorists, as in the case of aid workers, law enforcement officers or journalists, consideration will be given to this vulnerability in succeeding chapters.

Workplace tragedies

While terrorism is becoming an ever-increasing occupational risk for workers around the globe, other dramatic episodes of murderous violence continue to plague the workplace. These episodes differ from terrorism where the perpetrator is in most cases an expert in delivering violence and a complete stranger to the victims, and to the environments where most workplace violence is perpetrated. In "normal" workplace violence the perpetrator frequently appears as a person whom nobody would expect to commit homicide, and who may be a stranger to the working environment where violence is perpetrated and workers victimized. While the casualty lists for these episodes of violence may be smaller than those of the terrorist attacks described above, they generate great and long-lasting distress not only among the victims but also throughout the workplace and the community involved.

A murderous attack upon a school is an example of the intrusion of this type of violence into one workplace which most would have believed to be entirely safe and secure (box 2).

The damage inflicted by one lone individual, armed with powerful modern weapons, upon the young pupils and their teachers at this Scottish

Box 2   The shootings at Dunblane Primary School on 13 March 1996

The school day had started at 9 a.m. for all primary classes. The school had 640 pupils, making it one of the largest primary schools in Scotland. On 13 March all primary 1, 2 and 3 classes had attended assembly from 9.10 a.m. to 9.30 a.m. They consisted of a total of about 250 pupils, together with their teachers and the school chaplain. They included Primary 1/13, which was a class of 28 pupils, along with their teacher Mrs. [M]. This class had already changed for their gym lesson before attending assembly. 25 members of the class were 5 years of age and three were 6 years of age. Mrs. [M] was 47 years of age.

At the conclusion of assembly all those present had dispersed to their respective classrooms, with the exception of Primary 1/13 who with Mrs. [M] had made their way to the gymnasium. [Thomas Hamilton] entered the gym. He was wearing a dark jacket, black corduroy trousers and a woolly hat with ear defenders. He had a pistol in his hand. He advanced a couple of steps into the gym and fired indiscriminately and in rapid succession ...

Mrs.[M] and 15 children lay dead in the gym and one further child was close to death. They had sustained a total of 58 gunshot wounds; 26 of these wounds were of such a nature that individually they would have proved fatal. While it is not possible to be precise as to the times at which the shootings took place, it is likely that they occurred within a period of 3-4 minutes, starting between 9.35 a.m. and 9.40 a.m.

The survivors of the incident were taken to Stirling Royal Infirmary. They consisted of the remaining 12 members of the class; two pupils aged 11 who were elsewhere than in the gym when they were injured; and [three teachers] Mrs. [H], Mrs. [B] and Mrs. [T]. Thirteen of them had sustained gunshot wounds, 4 being serious, 6 very serious and 3 minor.

Source: This edited description of the events which took place at the Dunblane Primary School in Scotland has been taken from the official inquiry into the shootings by the Hon. Lord W. Douglas Cullen. The results of the inquiry were presented to Parliament by the Secretary of State for Scotland in October 1996. See Cullen, 1996 — *The Public Inquiry into the Shootings at Dunblane Primary School on 13 March 1996* (hereafter the Cullen Report), Ch. 3, pp. 11–13. This excerpt is crown copyright, reproduced with the permission of the Controller of Her Majesty's Stationery Office.

school came as a profound shock to the British nation. The shootings prompted an official inquiry, conducted by Lord Cullen.

The Cullen Report, as it has become known, was published in October 1996. Among the recommendations made by Lord Cullen were a number relating to the possession and use of firearms, as well as measures to enhance the security and safety of British schools.[12] The firearms recommendations led, ultimately, to a decision by the British Government to place a ban on the possession and use of handguns in the United Kingdom.[13] In regard to the health and safety of teaching staff and pupils, the British Government also acknowledged the need to prepare a safety strategy for the protection of the school population against violence, and to provide more comprehensive guidance to the school population as a whole about hazards arising in workplaces in the education sector.[14]

A tragedy like that occurring at Dunblane can on occasions act as a powerful catalyst for social action and reform. The ripples of anxiety and fear about the lethal reach of violence in this primary school have also spread far beyond the borders of Scotland and the United Kingdom. France had already been deeply affected by an incident in Neuilly-sur-Seine (Paris) in 1993, when a number of schoolchildren and their teachers were held hostage for several days by an armed man.[15]

More recently, schools have again been the scene of some of the most tragic episodes of violence. In the United States, in particular, shootings at Thurston High School, Oregon, in May 1998 and at Columbine High School in Littleton, Colorado, in April 1999 shocked Americans.[16] The Thurston High School incident, in which two pupils were killed and more than 20 injured in a shooting spree by an expelled student, prompted immediate action by the then United States President Bill Clinton. The United States Departments of Education and Justice were directed to develop a guide to help school personnel, parents, community members and others to identify early indicators of troubling and potentially dangerous student behaviour. Three months after the Thurston High School shooting, they jointly published *A guide to safe school* – see under "Published guidelines on violence: A selection", in Chapter 6.

It is not only United States and European schools which have experienced such tragedies. In Japan an attack by a deranged man at an elementary school in June 2001 caused widespread alarm in a society known for its low rates of violent crime (box 3).

Box 3   Japan executes man who killed eight schoolchildren

On 14 September 2004 a man convicted of stabbing to death eight elementary school children in a rampage that shocked the Japanese was hanged. Mamoru Takuma, 40, was executed less than a year after his death sentence was finalized for an attack at a school in western Japan in 2001.

Takuma, an unemployed man who had previously received treatment for mental illness, pleaded guilty to the killings and to injuring 13 other children and two teachers at Ikeda elementary school near Osaka.

Seven girls and a boy were killed when he burst into a classroom and began slashing at random with a long knife. One of the dead children was aged 6 and the rest were 7-year-olds.

Takuma, who at one point told a court hearing he wanted to pay for the crime with his life, had withdrawn an appeal filed by defense lawyers.

Source: ABC Radio Australia, 14 Sep. 2002. (See also People's Daily Online: http://english.people.com.cn/, accessed 16 June 2005.)

The school shootings at Neuilly, Dunblane, Thurston and Columbine had already been preceded by a number of other highly publicized workplace homicides in the United States dating from the mid-1980s onwards. Workplace mass murders apparently started with an attack by a lone gunman on an Oklahoma Post Office in 1986, which resulted in the deaths of 14 people and the wounding of six. The gunman, Patrick Henry Sherrill, had been suspended from work at the Edmond Post Office. Following this suspension, he returned to his place of employment to engage in a killing rampage before taking his own life. The incident, one of the worst mass murders committed by a single gunman in American history, has since become synonymous with the term "going postal", used to describe workplace homicides by disgruntled workers.[17] Since that time a series of further murderous attacks, mainly by disgruntled employees, has taken place in the United States (box 4), and elsewhere in the world.

Box 4   Seven die in Chicago warehouse shooting

S.T. returned to the Windy City Core Supply warehouse where he had been fired six months ago and killed six of his former co-workers, police said Wednesday. Tapia, 36, was then shot and killed in the last of three gun battles with police, said acting police superintendent Phil Cline.

"It appears he went throughout the supply warehouse shooting them. They weren't all in one section, they were in different sections of the warehouse", Cline said.

Most of the victims were in an office near the front door. Police tried to enter the building but Tapia came out and fired three shots at police, Cline said. Fire was returned. One minute later, Tapia came back outside the building and shot at police again. Finally, after considering the injured victims inside, the Hostage Barricade and Terrorist team was "ordered to make an assault on the building".

Tapia was found with a Walther PP .380-caliber semiautomatic pistol and at least one extra clip of ammunition.

Tapia was fired for being "a poor employee", Cline said. He was late to work and often missed entire days. Cline said Tapia had at least a few telephone conversations with his former boss after he was fired. It's unclear whether he had returned to the job site since his termination or met with his boss in person. Tapia has been arrested 12 times, Cline said. He has an arrest record dating back to 1989, including counts of domestic battery, gun violations, aggravated assault and driving while intoxicated.

"The problem here is easy access to a firearm", Cline told reporters. "Here is someone who never should have had a gun that had a gun."

Source: CNN.com/US, Wed. 27 Aug. 2003 (see: http://www.cnn.com/2003/US/Midwest/08/27/chicago.shooting/, accessed 27 Sep. 2005). Courtesy of CNN.

Thus far examples have been provided of mass murders through terrorist attacks and homicides perpetrated by armed individuals from outside the organization and former employees. However, workplace violence events are not always fatal and, indeed, do not always result in a *physical* injury.

Violence in the everyday life of workplaces around the world

There is no doubt that a series of tragedies like those described above have helped to focus international attention on violence at work as an issue of significant concern. The question of just what does constitute violence at work remains a matter of some conjecture, and will be addressed in more detail in Chapter 2. Suffice it to note that debate continues to evolve about what is, and is not, appropriately included within definitional terms for workplace violence.

The ILO recently developed a definition that was subsequently included within its code of practice *Workplace violence in services sectors and measures to combat this phenomenon* (box 5).

The ILO definition shown below emphasizes the physical aspects of this type of behaviour. A somewhat broader definition, encompassing verbal abuse, threats, bullying and other forms of non-physical behaviour, is more typically adopted in many jurisdictions. In Australia, for example, the National Occupational Health and Safety Commission (NOHSC) describes such violence in the following way: "Occupational violence is the attempted or actual exercise by a person of any force so as to cause injury to a worker, including any threatening statement or behaviour which gives a worker reasonable cause to believe he or she is at risk."[18]

Box 5 Definition of workplace violence

Any action, incident or behaviour that departs from reasonable conduct in which a person is assaulted, threatened, harmed, injured in the course of, or as a direct result of,[1] his or her work:

- Internal workplace violence is that which takes place between workers, including managers and supervisors.

- External workplace violence is that which takes place between workers (and managers and supervisors) and any other person present at the workplace.

[1] The reference to "direct result" is understood to mean that there is a clear link with work, and that the action, incident or behaviour occurred within a reasonable period afterwards.

Source: ILO, 2004b, p. 4.

Historically most workplaces were viewed as relatively benign and violence-free environments where dialogue and debate form a part of the normal operating milieu. Yet workers and managers are confronted on a daily basis with their personal and work-related problems, possibly including the anxieties and frustration of co-workers, organizational and production difficulties, personality clashes, diminished resources, increasing production/ output demands, aggressive intruders from outside, and problematic relations with clients and the public. Despite this, dialogue usually prevails over confrontation and people manage to organize efficient and productive activities within the workplace. There are cases, however, where this course of events fails to develop in a positive way, when relationships between workers, managers, clients or the public deteriorate, and the objectives of working efficiently and achieving productive results are negatively affected. When this situation occurs, and it would seem to be occurring with increasing frequency, violence may enter the workplace and transform it into a hostile and hazardous setting.

Some brief examples can assist at this stage in illustrating the scope, dimension and type of violence associated with workplaces in various parts of the world.

Australia

In Australia, a series of empirical studies have been conducted in different industry sectors, using representative samples of working populations. During a one-to-one face-to-face interview, each respondent in each separate survey was requested to detail their experiences of workplace aggression in the previous 12-month period. In table 1, the different types of aggression at work are shown as a percentage of all interviewees in each industry sector study. The row totals sometimes exceed 100 per cent because some randomly selected interviewees had experienced more than one violent event over the 12-month period, and sometimes more than one form of aggression was used by a perpetrator; for example, both verbal abuse and assaults could occur simultaneously.

The data shown in table 1 indicate that:

• There are marked differences in patterns of occupational violence across different occupations and industry sectors.

• While verbal abuse and threats were common experiences in many jobs, the vast majority of aggressive events involved no physical attack on a worker. Assaults on the job were most commonly experienced by juvenile detention and health workers.

• Jobs that involved close face-to-face contact with clients/customers (for example, taxi drivers) appear to be at increased risk.

Table 1 Workplace violence experiences over a 12-month period by industry
sector, Australia (percentage of interviewees)

Industry sector		Verbal abuse	Threats	Assault	Bullying	Other	Total
Juvenile justice	(n=50)	68	36	17	12	13	76
Tertiary education	(n=100)	50	39	1	65	25	80
Health care	(n=400)	67	33	12	10.5	11	67
Seafaring	(n=108)	19	5.5	1	–	1	27
Long-haul transport	(n=300)	33	8	1	–	21	–
Fast-food	(n=304)	48	8	1	–	2	–
Taxi	(n=100)	81	17	10	–	–	–

Note: Each of the studies summarized in table 1 (except tertiary education) were based on randomly selected representative samples of the working population in that industry sector. The tertiary education workers had previously taken part in an electronic survey of all staff members of a multi-campus university. The responses of those who also volunteered to take part in a face-to-face interview appear in table 1; thus they are likely to over-represent workers victimized by bullying.

Source: Mayhew, 2005b, p. 387.

France

The available evidence for different occupational groups working in the transport sector indicates that acts of violence have been on the rise, including for public transport workers and taxicab drivers. One study indicated that the total number of acts of aggression towards urban transport staff had increased from 3,051 in 2001 to 3,185 in 2002.[19] The steadily increasing incidence over the longer time-period 1997–2002 can be clearly seen in figure 1.

Figure 1 Assaults on personnel in the transport sector, France, 1997–2002[1]

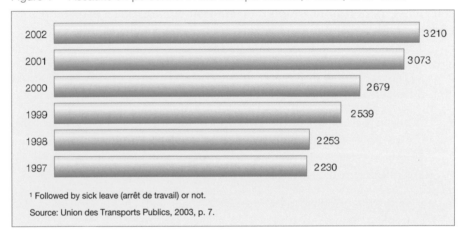

Year	Value
2002	3210
2001	3073
2000	2679
1999	2539
1998	2253
1997	2230

[1] Followed by sick leave (arrêt de travail) or not.

Source: Union des Transports Publics, 2003, p. 7.

Germany

A 2002 representative study on the phenomenon of mobbing (bullying) in western Germany showed that more than 800,000 workers were victims of this form of violence.[20] Similarly, a 2002 survey conducted across the then 15 EU Member States cited a range of forms of workplace violence during the previous 12-month period: harassment (7 per cent); physical violence (2 per cent from colleagues and 4 per cent from people external to the organization); sexual harassment (2 per cent); and intimidation and bullying (9 per cent).[21] In other words, bullying, harassment and intimidation (forms of aggression that frequently overlap) are widespread in the EU Member States.

Japan

In Japan more and more disputes concerning violence at work are brought to the courts for conciliation or decision. The number of cases brought before court counsellors totalled 625,572 in the period from April 2002 to March 2003. Of these, 5.1 per cent, or almost 32,000, were related to harassment and bullying.[22] Between April and September 2003 a total of 51,444 consultation requests were made, of which 9.6 per cent concerned bullying and harassment.[23] In other words, the number of these disputes appears to be growing over time, resulting in the Tokyo Labor Bureau setting up labour consultation centres at 21 locations in Tokyo to provide information on methods of resolving disputes and on how to contact dispute-settlement institutions. These non-physical forms of workplace violence appear to have significant negative emotional/psychological consequences (box 6).

Box 6	Bullying categorized as *rosai* (industrial injury): Employees suffer clinical depression after being denied work

According to a Kyodo News Agency report, two male individuals, aged 35 and 36, working at a health food manufacturing/sales company based in Yokohama City, applied for the categorization of having suffered *rosai*, or "industrial injury", claiming that they became clinically depressed after being intentionally given no work to do. The West Yokohama Labour Standards Inspection Office determined in August that the cases had indeed corresponded to *rosai*.

The majority of clinical depression cases which are categorized as *rosai* are caused by overwork. The lawyer who assisted these two employees' application for *rosai* approval hailed the ruling as a major breakthrough, since *rosai* has never been approved because of "not being given any work to do". The two employees were ordered to transfer to a subsidiary in April 2001, but refused to comply. The following month, they were

/cont'd

/cont'd

transferred to the Personnel Department but given absolutely no work to do. Several months later, they were ordered to sit at a desk that was physically separated from the rest of the office by a partition and to do nothing all day long.

Both men complained of headache, nausea and other symptoms, and were diagnosed with clinical depression. In July 2001, they applied for *rosai* categorization, alleging that the depression was caused by the company's work environment that included in-house bullying. In January 2002, they demanded compensation for damage from the company and filed a lawsuit to the Yokohama District Court.

Source: *Japan Labor Flash*, 2003.

South Africa

In South Africa, a study was undertaken as part of an ILO/ICN/WHO/PSI consultative programme.[24] Workers in the health sector were found to be subject to all kinds of workplace violence. Over a 12-month period, 9 per cent of those employed in the private health sector and up to 17 per cent of those in the public sector experienced physical violence; 52 per cent in the private sector (60.1 per cent in the public sector) suffered verbal abuse; and 20.6 per cent, bullying/mobbing in the combined private and the public sectors.[25]

The public sector appears particularly vulnerable to violence with more crime-related incidents such as robberies, criminals hiding in big hospitals, gang wars being continued in the hospitals, patients with firearms and convicted criminals attacking the staff. At the same time it also has the highest levels of overcrowding, staff shortages plus long waiting times, less resources for training and human resources development, shortage of beds and resources, budget cuts and inadequate or old equipment. It comes as no surprise, then, that almost a third of all respondents in the public sector indicated that they are "very worried" about this situation.[26]

Spain

A recent study on mobbing in the Spanish public administration indicated that 22 per cent of officials had been subjected to this form of violence and that 9.5 per cent suffered burnout.[27] By contrast, a 2002 Spanish study reported a bullying prevalence ratio of 16 per cent.[28] Similarly, 5 per cent were subjected to "intimidation".[29] Nevertheless, the proportion of Spanish workers experiencing physical violence appears to have fallen from 2 per cent in 1995 to 1 per cent in 2000.[30] There are also a few studies that separate out victimization ratios in particular industry sectors, for example, public administration.[31]

United Kingdom

The British Crime Survey (BCS) estimated that there were 849,000 workplace violence events in England and Wales in 2002/03, comprising 431,000 physical assaults and 418,000 threats. In total, 378,000 workers had experienced at least one incident of violence at work (figure 2).[32] The incidence appears to have declined markedly since the 1999/2000 survey which cited 1,288,000 workplace violence events (comprising 634,000 assaults and 654,000 threats) reported by 604,000 workers.[33]

Figure 2   Number of victims and incidents of violence at work, 2002/03 BCS interviews (in thousands)[1]

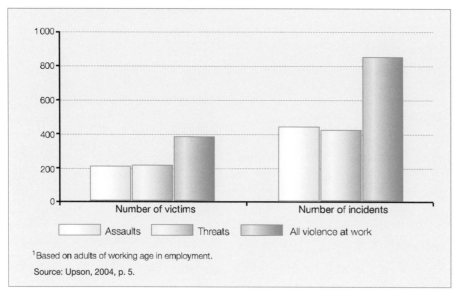

[1] Based on adults of working age in employment.

Source: Upson, 2004, p. 5.

United States

Homicide is the most dramatic and serious aspect of workplace violence. In the United States, official statistics show that homicide, despite a recent decline, is still the third leading cause of occupational death overall.[34] (These statistics are reviewed in more detail in Chapter 2.)

Data and vignettes from particular events of workplace violence occurring in different countries around the globe suggest that this issue truly transcends the boundaries of particular countries, industry sectors and occupational groups. No country, work setting or occupation can claim realistically to be entirely free of any form of workplace violence although some countries, like some workplaces and occupations, are undoubtedly at higher risk than others.

The changing profile of violence at work

The variety of behaviours which may be covered under the general rubric of violence at work is so large, the borderline with acceptable behaviours is often so vague, and the perception in different contexts and cultures of what constitutes violence is so diverse, that defining the workplace violence phenomenon is a significant challenge. In practice, violence in the workplace may include a wide range of behaviours, often continuing or overlapping, as exemplified in box 7.

The state of our knowledge about current patterns and trends in violence at work is reviewed in the following chapters. However, there does appear to be evidence that both the incidence and severity of workplace violence are

Box 7	Examples of violent behaviours at work	
— homicide	— bullying
— rape	— mobbing
— robbery	— victimizing
— wounding	— intimidation
— battering	— threats
— physical attacks	— ostracism
— kicking	— leaving offensive messages
— biting	— aggressive posturing
— punching	— rude gestures
— spitting	— interfering with work tools and equipment
— scratching	— hostile behaviour
— squeezing, pinching and related actions	
— swearing	— shouting
— stalking	— name-calling
— harassment, including sexual and racial abuse	
— innuendo	— deliberate silence

increasing in many jurisdictions. This trend may well reflect a growing community awareness and condemnation leading to increased reporting of incidents, as well as an actual rise in the total number of workplace violence events being committed in certain jurisdictions.

A similar trend has been observed in recent years in the arena of family and domestic violence, where a "hidden issue" has rapidly become a very public one, and the subject of extensive attention and action. As a result, the real magnitude of domestic violence is only now being disclosed, as is its potential to have a negative "spillover" impact on the workplace through the transfer of family conflicts to a work setting. It is also becoming clear that violence has a disproportionate impact on women, children and young people, as well as socially and economically deprived groups, both in developing and industrialized countries. The vulnerability to job loss and insecurity of a growing number of precariously employed workers seems also to be mirrored by an increase in their victimization through workplace violence.[35] Even in those countries and workplaces where violence still appears to be a "hidden issue", it is likely to reveal itself immediately upon closer analysis and investigation. Nevertheless, non-fatal events remain largely under-reported.

From physical to psychological

Attention has traditionally been focused on physical violence, and the typical profile of violence at work which has emerged has been largely one of isolated, major incidents of the kind referred to at the start of this chapter. In more recent years, however, new evidence has been emerging of the impact and harm caused by non-physical violence, often referred to as **psychological violence**. "Psychological" violence can include diverse aggressive tactics, all of which have the potential to cause significant emotional injury among those victimized. It is often considered to include bullying, mobbing, coercion, verbal abuse and sexual harassment. Many of these forms of workplace violence are **repeated** by the perpetrators and while one-off events may be relatively minor, the cumulative impact on the recipients results in very serious consequences[36] (often with a greater impact than that from physical violence), for example following repeated acts of **sexual harassment, bullying** or **mobbing**. Some of the different forms of psychological violence are briefly reviewed below.

Sexual harassment

Although a single incident can constitute sexual harassment, it often consists of repeated unwelcome, unreciprocated and imposed action which may have a devastating effect on the victim. Because the perpetrators in workplaces are

Box 8   Forms of sexual harassment

Physical

- deliberate and unsolicited physical contact;
- unnecessarily close physical proximity; and
- stalking, for example, repeatedly following in an insistent but often unobtrusive way.

Verbal

- repeated sexually oriented comments or gestures about a person's body, appearance or life-style;
- offensive phone calls;
- questions or insinuations about a person's private life;
- sexually explicit jokes or propositions;
- persistent invitations to social activities after a person has made it clear they are not welcome;
- unwanted compliments with sexual content;
- sexually coloured remarks, bantering or innuendo;
- name-calling;
- playing games with a person's name; and
- reference to sexual orientation.

Gestures

- repeated sexually oriented gestures about a person's body, appearance or life-style;
- nods, winks, gestures with the hands, fingers, legs or arms, signs and other offensive behaviour which is sexually suggestive; and
- persistent leering at the person or at part of his/her body.

Written

- Offensive, letters or e-mail messages.

Coercive behaviour

- overt or covert behaviour used to control, influence or affect a person's job, career or status;
- explicit/implicit promise of career advancement in exchange of sexual favours;
- explicit/implicit promise of recruitment in exchange of sexual favours;
- threatening of dismissal if sexual favours are not granted; and
- making work difficult if sexual favours are not granted.   /cont'd

Hostile environment

- showing or displaying sexually explicit graphics, cartoons, pictures, photographs or Internet images;

- offensive jokes of a sexual nature;

- display of pornographic material, graffiti, pin-ups etc;

- exposure of intimate parts of the body; and

- use of obscene language.

Source: Di Martino, 2002a.

frequently in a supervisory or more powerful work role than the recipient of sexual harassment, victims may be frightened to object or formally lodge complaints.

The following extract from European Directive 2002/73/EC provides a definition of sexual harassment: "Where any form of unwanted verbal, non-verbal or physical conduct of a sexual nature occurs, with the purpose or effect of violating the dignity of a person, in particular when creating an intimidating, hostile, degrading, humiliating or offensive environment."[37]

Sexual harassment can take many forms and the terms used to describe these behaviours, as well as the situations involved, may overlap, as they often do in real life (box 8).

The findings of a survey on violence at work carried out by the European Union are presented in box 9.

Box 9   Survey on violence at work in the European Union

The findings from the questionnaire suggested the following situation:

- There is a considerable difference in awareness of the issue of violence in the context of health and safety between countries.

- The legislative position, with the exception of the Netherlands, is that violence at work is generally covered by both framework type health and safety legislation and by the civil and criminal codes.

- Research into the issue of violence appears to be a relatively recent phenomenon where it occurs. Research seems to be concentrated in the more developed countries in Europe.

- The implementation of legislation was generally reported to take place, both within the general implementation of the requirements of health and safety legislation, and to some extent, using the criminal and civil codes.

/cont'd

- Significant barriers to the implementation in many countries include lack of awareness, difficulties in implementing legislation in SMEs [small and medium-sized enterprises], and limited resources for enforcement of legislation.

The overall impression from the data supplied by the respondents to the survey is that there is limited awareness of the issue of violence at work in many countries, but that legislative provisions appear to exist in general terms and are generally implemented. However, there are grounds for questioning this impression.

Firstly, a major finding from reviewing the literature is that the extent of the problem is usually underestimated. In the absence of specific and comprehensive research on the prevalence and extent of workplace violence, it is difficult to believe that the problem is being adequately dealt with.

Secondly, the existence of guidelines to deal with violence is not uniform across the EU. In their absence, it is unlikely that consistent and comprehensive management of the issue actually takes place.

Thirdly, the situation with regard to the implementation of legislation must be questioned. While the respondents to the survey generally reported good levels of implementation, the precise nature of implementation is, at best, unclear. While there is no doubt that the appropriate agencies dealing with health and safety carry out their duties with regard to the range of health and safety issues, they do so only in the context of the resources provided to them. In practice, this often means that they have limited resources available to them for enforcement, and that SMEs in particular tend not to be subject to high levels of enforcement. Furthermore, in the context of limited awareness of the problem, the extent of actual management activity within enterprises must be questioned.

For these reasons, it is likely that the operation of legislation in the area is somewhat less than optimal.

A final issue of concern is that despite the apparently positive situation in many countries, some countries reported low levels of concern and activity with regard to violence at work. Without wishing to single out specific countries, it is evident both by some of the comments made, and by the absence of response from some countries that there is considerable room for improvement in the management of this issue at all levels.

Source: Wynne et al., 1997, pp. 28–29.

Bullying

Workplace bullying constitutes **repeated** offensive behaviour through vindictive, cruel, malicious or humiliating attempts to undermine an individual or group of employees. Bullying is frequently **covert** and occurs out of sight of potential witnesses. However, the behaviours usually **escalate** in intensity over time.[38] These persistently negative attacks on the personal and professional performance of victims are typically unpredictable, irrational and unfair.

Bullying can occur in a number of different ways, as illustrated below. Some are obvious and easy to identify, while others are subtle and difficult to unequivocally distinguish.

Bullying at work means harassing, offending, socially excluding someone or negatively affecting someone's work tasks. In order for the label bullying (or mobbing) to be applied to a particular activity, interaction or process it has to occur repeatedly and regularly (e.g. weekly) and over a period of time (e.g. about six months). Bullying is an escalating process in the course of which the person confronted ends up in an inferior position and becomes the target of systematic negative social acts. A conflict cannot be called bullying if the incident is an isolated event or if two parties of approximately equal "strength" are in conflict.[39]

Bullying behaviours may include:

- making life difficult for those who have the potential to do the bully's job better than the bully;

- punishing others for being too competent by constant criticism or by removing their responsibilities, often giving them trivial tasks to do instead;

- refusing to delegate because bullies feel they can't trust anyone else;

- shouting at staff to get things done;

- persistently picking on people in front of others or in private;

- insisting that a way of doing things is always right;

- keeping individuals in their place by blocking their promotion;

- if someone challenges a bully's authority, overloading them with work and reducing the deadlines, hoping that they will fail at what they do; and

- feeling envious of another's professional or social ability, so setting out to make them appear incompetent, or make their lives miserable, in the hope of getting them dismissed or making them resign.[40]

Mobbing

In recent years, another form of systematic collective violence has been reported to be on the increase in countries such as Australia, Austria, Denmark, Germany, Sweden, the United Kingdom and the United States. In Europe this collective violence has often been referred to as "mobbing". Even in countries with their own terms (such as *harcèlement moral* in France, *acoso* or *maltrato psicológico* in Spain, *coacção moral* in Portugal or *molestie psicologiche* in Italy), mobbing is becoming increasingly recognized.

Box 10   Mobbing in a Norwegian factory

Leif worked in a large Norwegian factory. His job, as a repairman, was to keep the machine park running. He was a skilled worker, earning a high salary. He came originally from Denmark and his workmates often made fun of him as he spoke Norwegian with a Danish accent. This happened so often that his personal relations became seriously disturbed – he became isolated. On one occasion he became so irritated that he thumped the table with his fist and demanded an end to all further jokes about his accent. From that point, things became worse. His workmates intensified and widened the range of "jokes", one being to send him to machines which did not need repairing. In this way Leif gradually gained the reputation of being "The Mad Dane".

At the beginning, many workers and foremen did not know that his sudden appearances were the results of "jokes". His social contact network broke down, and more and more workmates joined in the hunt. Wherever he appeared, jokes and taunts flew around. His feeling of aggression grew and this drew the attention of management. It was their impression that Leif was at fault and that, in general, he was a low-performance worker (which he gradually became). He was admonished. His anxiety increased and he developed psychosomatic problems and began to take sick leave. His employers reassigned him to less skilled work without discussing his problems; this Leif felt as unjust. He considered himself blameless.

The situation gradually brought about serious psychosomatic disorders and longer periods of sick leave. Leif lost his job and could not find another, as his medical history was indicated in his job applications. There was nowhere in society where he could turn for help. He became totally unemployable – an outcast.

Source: Leymann, 1990, p. 119. Used by permission from Springer Publishing Company, Inc., New York, 10012.

Mobbing typically involves a group of workers ganging up on a target employee and subjecting that person to psychological harassment (box 10). Mobbing includes behaviours such as making continuous negative remarks about a person or criticizing them constantly; isolating a person by leaving them without social contacts; gossiping or spreading false information about a person; or ridiculing a person constantly. The impact upon a person of what might appear on the surface to be minor single actions of this type can be devastating. It has been estimated, for instance, that about 10–15 per cent of the total number of suicides in Sweden each year have this type of background.[41]

The original conceptual distinction between bullying (primarily referring to situations of individual harassment) and mobbing (primarily covering situations of collective harassment) is now giving way to a conceptual assimilation of these two terms. Most researchers now make no distinction between bullying and mobbing with regard to the number of perpetrators or targets involved. One may argue that, even if a distinction was accepted, the psychological processes – and the considerable impact on the recipient involved – appear to be the same.

The new profile of violence at work that emerges is one which gives equal emphasis to inappropriate physical and psychological behaviour, and full recognition to the significance of non-physical workplace violence. It is also a profile that recognizes that violence at work is not limited to a specified workplace, like an office, factory or retail establishment. There is a risk of violence during commuting and in non-traditional workplaces such as homes, satellite centres and mobile locations that are being used increasingly as a result of the spread of new information technologies.[42]

Given the rising levels of awareness and increased reporting, it is not surprising that increasing concern is now being expressed by workers, trade unions, employers, public bodies and experts on a broad international front about the extent of violence at work. This concern is being matched by calls for action to prevent such violence and/or, when it occurs, to deal with it in a way which alleviates the enormous social, economic and allied costs to the victims, their families, employers and the community at large. However, questions remain as to the nature and direction of the action that should be taken, and the identity of those who should be held responsible for the implementation of preventive interventions.

From awareness to action

With consensus emerging on a broad definition of violence at work that includes both physical and psychological elements, there would also seem to be widespread awareness that this form of violence is:

- a major although still under-recognized problem;

- not limited to individual instances of mass homicide, but extends to a much wider range of apparently minor but often devastating behaviours;

- an extremely costly burden for the worker, the enterprise and the community;

- not just an episodic, individual problem but a structural, strategic problem rooted in wider social, economic, organizational, gender role and cultural factors;

- detrimental to the functionality of the workplace, and any action taken against such violence is an integral part of the organizational development of a sound enterprise; and

- a problem which has to be tackled, and tackled now.

In responding to the problem of workplace violence, it is now realized to an increasing degree that violence in any form can no longer be accepted as a normal part of any job, even where it would seem to be an occupational hazard, such as in law enforcement. As in the case of hazardous manufacturing and allied occupations, where risk management strategies are put in place to reduce the level of uncertainty and possibility of injury, so too should these strategies be adopted to minimize the possibility of assault, harassment and abuse to employees in the workplace.

There is also a growing recognition that in confronting violence it is important to think comprehensively. This means that instead of searching for the simplistic "single solution" for any problem or situation, the full range of causes that generate violence should be identified and analysed, and a variety of intervention strategies applied. These strategies should seek to implant a broad preventive approach to the problem, which addresses the organizational, managerial and interpersonal roots of violence at the workplace. Preventive interventions should also increase the security of workers through worksite redesign and organizational interventions, and provide rehabilitation and psychological counselling, when necessary, to help victims to cope with the aftermath of violence.

The scope of this book

This book is intended to constitute a stimulus for future action in this area. It is centred around the analysis of scientific literature, data and information. While not claiming to be exhaustive in this regard, the authors have deliberately avoided the more "sensational" presentations of violent events (although vignettes of some of these are provided) to concentrate on the objective data, experiences and scientific publications which best help to explain and interpret the roots of violence at work, and to promote proactive initiatives in this field.

The book has a worldwide coverage because workplace violence is to be found in both developing and industrialized countries. Although the information from developing countries about this violence is frequently limited, episodic and ill-defined, it is becoming increasingly relevant and better documented. Improved data from a broad range of nation States has made it possible to include a special section in Chapter 2 devoted to violence in developing countries.

As already suggested, the underlying causes of violence at work are rooted in much wider social, cultural, economic, gender role and related areas. There is a vast literature available on the causes of violence at large. However, this material is so extensive and far-reaching that, for the purpose of this book, it cannot be treated in detail. Instead, Chapter 4 reviews the principal explanations of violence found in the literature as they relate to the specific issue of violence at work.

In order to avoid duplication of effort, only limited attention is paid in this book to issues already covered by extensive and specific ILO action, such as those to address occupational stress, alcohol and drug abuse, as well as others such as child labour[43] and migrant workers. Certain technical issues, such as violence associated with military action, are also excluded from the scope of this report, as is any detailed review of the issues associated with the overreaching problem of international terrorism referred to at the beginning of this chapter.

The book is intended to provide a basis for understanding the nature of violence at work, and to suggest ways of preventing this in the future. The discussions therefore highlight best-practice successful methods of prevention, illustrating the positive lessons to be drawn from such experience. The book is directed towards all those engaged in combating violence at work: policy makers in government agencies; employers' and workers' organizations; health and safety professionals; consultants; trainers; and management and workers' representatives.

The book is structured in **three parts**:

Part I is devoted to the **understanding of violence at work**. It covers the growing body of scientific evidence regarding this phenomenon and the changing profile of violence (Chapter 1). Part I also includes an analysis of data patterns and trends in both industrialized and developing countries (Chapter 2) and of the situations at special risk (Chapter 3). It concludes with an examination of the various causal explanations for violence at work, and of the social and economic costs for individuals, the enterprise and the community (Chapter 4).

Part II examines **different types of response** to violence at work and identifies the best solutions. Included in this part is an analysis of legislative and regulatory interventions and the emergence of specific legislation; growing attention to prevention strategies; and new collective agreements to combat workplace violence (Chapter 5). Part II also includes an analysis of policies and guidelines; their main messages about how to tackle violence at work effectively; and guidance for specific occupations and for particular types of violence (Chapter 6). Best-practice interventions are dealt with in Chapter 7. Finally, the growing international concern about violence at work and the initiatives undertaken in this area are considered (Chapter 8).

Part III (Chapter 9) considers the key lessons to be drawn from the preceding analysis, highlights the main messages to be delivered and **suggests specific and practical action** based on successful experience.

Notes

[1] For a detailed description and analysis of the above events, see *The 9/11 Commission Report*, Final Report of the National Commission on Terrorist Attacks upon the United States, 22 July 2004. The Commission closed on 21 August 2004 (see: http://www.9-11commission.gov/report/911Report.pdf, accessed 27 Sep. 2005).

[2] Loomis et al., 2001, pp. 410–417.

[3] Infoplease. No date. "Terrorist attacks (within the United States or against Americans abroad): September 11, 2001 victims".

[4] Australian Federal Police, no date.

[5] Wikipedia, 11 Mar. 2004, "Madrid train bombings".

[6] Ibid., 4 Oct. 2005, "West London bombings".

[7] Iraq Body Count. "A dossier of civilian casualties", 2003–2005.

[8] Ibid.

[9] Regular updates on media casualties are produced by the International Federation of Journalists, for example, "Journalists and media staff killed in 2003" (see: www.ifj.org/pdfs/killreport2003.pdf, accessed 27 Sep. 2005).

[10] CBS News Online. 2005. "Indepth: Iraq: Foreign hostages in Iraq", 15 May.

[11] See, for example, A. O'Neill, 2005, pp. 377–391. See also electronic publications on possible health effects from bioterrorism: Schwid et al., 2002.

[12] These recommendations are summarized in Ch. 12 of the Cullen Report. An official Government Response to each of the recommendations was provided at the time of the publication of the Report. See Scottish Office, 1996 – *The Public Inquiry into the Shootings at Dunblane Primary School on 13 March 1996: The Government Response*.

[13] See Cullen Report (Cullen, 1996), Ch. 9, and the Government Response (Scottish Office, 1996, pp. 5-6). In 1997 a new law banned handguns over 22-calibre. In 1998, the ban was further extended to include smaller calibre handguns (see: "Gun Law Campaign", http://www.crimelibrary.com/notorious%5Fmurders/mass/dunblane%5Fmassacre, accessed 27 Sep. 2005).

[14] Government Response (Edinburgh, Scottish Office, 1996, pp. 6–7). In 1997 the British Health and Safety Executive (HSE) via its Education Service Advisory Committee issued *Violence in the education sector* (London, HMSO, 1997c), which provides advice to managers and staff in the education service on identifying potential risks of violence; formulating an action plan and statement of intent; recording incidents; elaborating preventive strategies; supporting staff who are victims of violence; and the role of the police.

[15] This incident prompted a major review of the security and safety of French schools. See: "Les dix-neuf mesures arrêtés. Le plan de prévention de la violence à l'école se présente en trois grands axes et dix-neuf mesures", in *Le Figaro*, 21 Mar. 1996, p. 9.

[16] *Liberty Internet Magazine*, "Courage at Columbine High School", July 1999 (see: http://www.doctor liberty.com/columbine.html). This incident has also been the subject of an award-winning documentary film "Bowling for Columbine" (2000), directed by Michael Moore, which received widespread screening in the United States and elsewhere.

[17] The US Postal Service, stung by criticism of its failure to prevent this and later homicides at postal premises, commissioned a study to examine the prevalence of this type of workplace violence within the service. The study indicated that, contrary to popular belief, the incidence of workplace assaults and homicides in the Postal Service was far below the national average. According to the United States Department of Labor, Bureau of Statistics, "postal work is one of the safest occupations in the job pool. Postal workers are not even a blip on the Department of Labor's scale of occupational fatalities, no matter how the statistics are compiled, by job related accident or homicide", in US Postal Service, 1998, p. 2 (see: "Going Postal", http://www.crimelibrary.com/notorious murders/mass/work homicide/4.html?sect=8, accessed 27 Sep. 2005). See also: *MMR Weekly*, 1994).

[18] National Occupational Health and Safety Committee (NOHSC), 1999.

[19] Union des Transports Publics, France, 2003, p. 7.

[20] Meschkutat, Stackelbeck and Langenhoff, 2002.

[21] Paoli and Parent-Thirion, 2003, p. 63.

[22] Ministry of Health, Labour and Welfare, Japan, 2003.

[23] *Japan Labor Flash*, 2003.

[24] Di Martino, 2002b.

[25] Ibid., p. 25. It is important to recognize that while the results reported are based upon standardized quantitative and qualitative methodologies and instruments, they are only case studies relating to a specific geographic area and should therefore be interpreted with some caution. See also ibid., p. ix.

[26] Ibid.

[27] CISNEROS V, "Mobbing in Spanish public administrations" report. Courtesy of Iñaki Piñuel to the authors, 18 Sep. 2004.

[28] Piñuel and Zabala, 2002.

[29] Di Martino, Hoel, and Cooper, 2003, p. 42.

[30] Ibid, p. 39.

[31] For public administration see Scialpi, 2004.

[32] Upson, 2004.

[33] Budd, 2001, p. 3.

[34] Santana and Fisher, 2002, pp. 90–113. See also Fisher et al., 1998, pp. 65–82.

[35] Mayhew and Quinlan, 1999, pp. 183–205. See also Mayhew, 2003, pp. 203–219.

[36] See, for example, Mayhew et al., 2004, pp. 117–134.

[37] European Parliament, 2002a.

[38] McCarthy and Mayhew, 2004. See also Mayhew, 2000a.

[39] Einarsen et al., 2003b, p. 15.

[40] UNISON, 1996.

[41] Leymann, 1990, p. 122. Used by permission from Springer Publishing Company, Inc., New York, 10012. See also Einarsen and Mikkelsen, 2003a, pp. 127–144.

[42] On the spreading of telework, and associated risks of violence, see Di Martino, 2001. See also idem, 2005.

[43] In June 1999, the International Labour Conference adopted the Worst Forms of Child Labour Convention (No. 182), and Recommendation (No. 190), by which ratifying member States must "take immediate and effective measures to secure the prohibition and elimination of the worst forms of child labour as a matter of urgency". These comprise: "(a) all forms of slavery or practices similar to slavery, such as the sale and trafficking of children, debt bondage and serfdom and forced or compulsory labour, including forced or compulsory recruitment of children for use in armed conflict; (b) the use, procuring or offering of a child for prostitution, for the production of pornography or for pornographic performances; (c) the use, procuring or offering of a child for illicit activities, in particular for the production and trafficking of drugs as defined in the relevant international treaties; and (d) work which, by its nature or the circumstances in which it is carried out, is likely to harm the health, safety or morals of children".

PATTERNS AND TRENDS

2

This chapter presents and analyses data about the extent of workplace violence experienced in different countries. Wherever possible, reliable government statistics are provided to enhance understandings of patterns of risk. Nevertheless, cross-country comparisons are fraught with difficulty and interpretations drawn from the data must be made with caution. For example, difficulties are always encountered when data from one country are compared with those from another because of variable definitions about the different forms of workplace violence, and variations in coding criteria adopted by different authorities, as well as distinctive cultural interpretations across nation States.

The discussions in this chapter begin with some internationally accepted definitions of workplace violence, followed by a detailed review of the extant data in Europe and the United States. The data provided include workplace violence in the form of homicide, assault, bullying, sexual harassment and other forms of aggression. A series of case studies is then presented detailing the experiences of some victimized workers in various developing countries, including the risks faced by some trade union members, migrant workers, child labourers, and the particular risks of sexual harassment and violence. The chapter concludes with a review of the differential level of exposure to workplace violence between male and female workers, and the particular risks faced by young workers.

Definitions

A significant challenge to any analysis of this issue arises from a lack of agreement regarding the definitions of **violence, work** or the **workplace**. A recent comprehensive and authoritative *WHO World Report on Violence and Health* defines violence as: "The intentional use of physical force or power, threatened or actual, against oneself, another person, or against a group or community, that either results in or has a high likelihood of resulting in injury, death, psychological harm, maldevelopment or deprivation."[1] A general definition of **violence at work** has yet to be agreed in the international arena. A first concerted effort towards reaching a common understanding in this area was made at an Expert Meeting organized by the European Commission in Dublin in May 1994, where the following definition was proposed: "Incidents where persons are abused, threatened or assaulted in circumstances related to their work, involving an explicit or implicit challenge to their safety, well-being and health."[2]

- Abuse is used to indicate all behaviours which depart from reasonable conduct and involve the misuse of physical or psychological strength.

- Threats encompass the menace of death, or the announcement of an intention to harm a person or damage their property.

- Assault generally includes any attempt at physical injury or attack on a person including actual physical harm.

In real situations these behaviours often overlap, making any attempt to categorize different forms of violence very difficult. The emphasis on the impact of incidents on the safety, health and well-being of a person, although important, appears primarily to be a reflection of the special concern of the experts who participated in the meeting.

Along similar lines, the ILO code of practice *Workplace violence in services sectors and measures to combat this phenomenon*, adopted in 2003 by a Meeting of Experts of the Governing Body of the ILO, provides the following definition of workplace violence: "Any action, incident or behaviour that departs from reasonable conduct in which a person is assaulted, threatened, harmed, injured in the course of, or as a direct result of, his or her work."[3]

Within this general definition the code distinguishes between internal and external violence:

- Internal workplace violence is that which takes place between workers, including managers and supervisors.

- External workplace violence is that which takes place between workers (and managers and supervisors) and any other person present at the workplace.[4]

Other types of workplace violence are excluded from these definitions and from the scope of this book. For example, violence against property is not considered, even although it does represent a significant issue in workplaces in the retail sector. Similarly workplace crime in a broad sense is excluded, to the extent that the term includes non-violent crimes like theft, fraud and embezzlement. It is probably important to note that the incidence and prevalence of these types of non-violent crime are significantly higher than violent events in workplaces (just as they are in the wider community). Workplace conflicts, which can sometimes degenerate into violent behaviours, are also excluded with the important exceptions of bullying, intimidation and sexual harassment.

The definition of **work** or the **workplace** is also fraught with problems. When official crime statistics do make a link with occupational data and provide information about the location at which incidents of criminal violence occur, they tend to adopt a quite constrained definition of these terms. Data may be provided about violent offences committed in offices, commercial premises such as banks, schools or other physical settings. This construction of the workplace does not however allow for mobile or geographically diverse occupational activities such as those conducted by law enforcement officials,[5] taxi drivers or journalists, nor does it take account of occupational groups whose work takes them to people's homes, like meter readers, plumbers and postal officials, or those who use their own homes as their workplace. The latter category of employment is becoming far more prevalent as new technologies make many traditional workplaces redundant.

Trying to meet these concerns, the ILO code of practice *Workplace violence in services sectors and measures to combat this phenomenon* provides, for the first time, clarification on the relationship between violence and work, and on what is to be considered a workplace. It specifies that: "The reference to a 'direct result [of work]' is to be understood to mean that there is a clear link with work, and that the action, incident or behaviour occurred within a reasonable period afterward."[6]

It also provides the following definition of workplace: "All places where workers need to be or to go by reason of their work and which are under the direct or indirect control of the employer."[7]

Regional and national data on workplace violence

Attention is now turned to selected regional and national data relating to patterns and trends in violence at work. It is neither the intention nor purpose of this book to provide an exhaustive account of the nature and extent of such violence in each country and region of the world. Indeed, such an account would for most practical purposes be quite meaningless, since in many jurisdictions the data about this issue are of very limited quality and quantity. As an authoritative review of this data in European countries, conducted for the European Commission, has stated:

The prevalence of workplace-related violence is difficult to estimate because of the general absence of either national level or occupational level data on this issue. Specific barriers exist in relation to acquiring this information. These include:

- In many countries, incidents involving violence at work fall outside the scope of health and safety requirements, e.g. reporting requirements for accidents at work.

- Where data is collected, it is often only gathered on the fatal outcomes of violence. This data tends to focus on incidents involving extreme violence, e.g. physical assaults which involve the use of weapons.

- Employers do not generally have in place appropriate mechanisms and procedures to either record or deal effectively with the problem of violence to their employees.

- There are several problems with procedures used to record incidents of violence in workplaces. In many cases records are collected on accident forms, thereby making it difficult to assess the true number of incidents in which violence is involved. Also, reporting procedures do not record the emotional or psychological conditions caused by threats of violence or exposure to threatening behaviour.

- Certain categories of violence, e.g. threats of violence, fights between employees and vandalism may not be reported outside of the organization where the incident occurs.[8]

Within these limitations, what follows is an attempt to provide some impressions of the more significant patterns and trends in workplace violence which emerge from the published data.[9] While specific trend data are in very short supply, the scale and severity of workplace violence would appear to be both recognized and documented with greatest detail in Europe and North America.

Europe

Longitudinal data for the European Union (EU) are available from the European Foundation for the Improvement of Living and Working Conditions (European Foundation). The European Foundation's Third European Survey on Working Conditions, carried out in 2000, was based on 21,703 interviews with workers throughout the then 15 EU Member States. However, an important caveat is that the 1995/96 and 2000 European Working Conditions surveys asked about experiences of violence and harassment in slightly different ways. Hence the changes in survey methodologies have made comparisons between the survey findings a little difficult.

The European Foundation's Third European Survey findings indicate that in 2000 around 6 per cent of workers were subjected to physical violence (4 per cent from other people and 1.5 per cent from co-workers), 2 per cent to sexual harassment, and 9 per cent to intimidation/bullying over the previous 12-month period. However, the risk of exposure to workplace violence was not homogenous across industry sectors and occupational groups:[10]

> Physical violence seems to be experienced most in the health care and educational sectors throughout the European Union ... in 2000, 11% of employees in health care and education had experienced physical violence... 1.5% of all employed people in the EU had been subjected to violence from colleagues, while 4.1% reported having been subjected to violence from people from outside their workplace. This indicates that the problem of increasing physical violence concerns mostly occupations that require dealing with difficult customers.[11]

While figure 3 indicates a decline in physical violence and a slight rise in intimidation/bullying over time, other European Foundation publications report a more consistent rise in reported levels of violence, intimidation and sexual harassment for both males and females over the period 1996–2000.[12] Thus, caution needs to be exercised in interpreting short-term trends since the increase may well be partially linked to enhanced publicity and improved reporting in more recent years, rather than to an actual growth in these forms of workplace violence.

Figure 3   Violence at work in the European Union, 1996 and 2000 (percentage of cases reported)

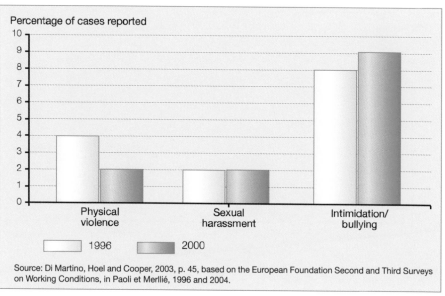

Source: Di Martino, Hoel and Cooper, 2003, p. 45, based on the European Foundation Second and Third Surveys on Working Conditions, in Paoli et Merllié, 1996 and 2004.

Figure 4   Workers subjected to physical violence over the past 12 months,
            acceding countries and EU Member States (percentages)

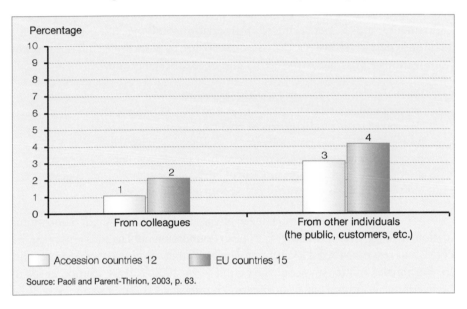

Source: Paoli and Parent-Thirion, 2003, p. 63.

Figure 5   Levels of intimidation and sexual harassment over the past 12 months,
            acceding countries and EU Member States (percentages)

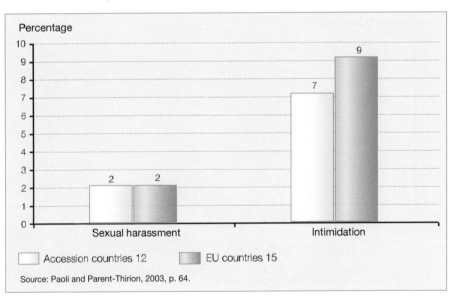

Source: Paoli and Parent-Thirion, 2003, p. 64.

In 2003 the European Foundation published the results of an extension of the research to the 12 acceding and candidate countries (Cyprus, Czech Republic, Estonia, Hungary, Latvia, Lithuania, Malta, Poland, Romania, Slovenia, and Slovakia).[13] The survey revealed roughly similar proportions between the EU and the acceding and candidate countries for various forms of workplace violence, as indicated in figures 4 and 5.[14]

While the workplace violence figures shown in figures 4 and 5 may seem relatively low, it should be remembered that the 7 per cent of workers amount to many victimized workers. In total, those who reported that they were the victims of harassment at work over the previous 12 months represented between three and four million people.

Physical violence

Similarly, even though a decline appears to have occurred in reported cases of physical violence, the European Foundation's survey findings in 2000 still suggest that as many as 3 million of the EU's 130 million workers were subjected to physical violence over the 12-month period.[15] In figure 6, the proportion of workers subjected to physical violence over the previous 12 months is displayed for each of the 15 Member States of the EU in 1996 and 2000.

The findings shown in figure 6 were drawn from the European Foundation's face-to-face interviews with employees. The survey findings reveal considerable

Figure 6   Workers subjected to physical violence over the previous 12 months in the 15 EU Member States, 1996 and 2000 (percentages)

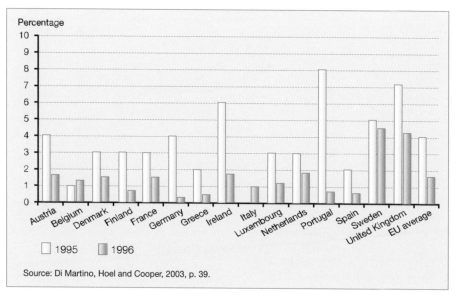

Source: Di Martino, Hoel and Cooper, 2003, p. 39.

variations between countries, with the highest levels of violence occurring in 2000 in Sweden and the United Kingdom, and the lowest in certain southern European nations.

In their comprehensive appraisal of the EU data patterns and trends in workplace violence, Di Martino et al. (2003) warn of the risks associated with making comparisons between countries. As they state: "Strictly speaking, only studies using the same or at least similar methodologies are fully comparable. As a result, only a few studies provide comparative data across EU countries. These studies are especially valuable ... [as they are] longitudinal studies, which may provide the most reliable information with regard to changing trends."[16]

After assessing the available studies, Di Martino et al. identified several which met rigorous methodological standards in five EU countries. These studies are shown in table 2. They suggest a considerable discrepancy in the risk of exposure to physical violence between countries.[17]

The various studies displayed in table 2 report an incidence ratio ranging from 2.5 per cent to 71 per cent. It is of concern that a significant proportion of respondents to these European surveys had been victimized on more than one occasion during the study period.

The most comprehensive data gathered on a longitudinal basis about workplace violence in a single European country is to be found in the United Kingdom. The findings on this subject from the British Crime Survey are shown in figure 7.

Figure 7   Number of incidents of violence at work, United Kingdom, 1991–2003 (thousands)

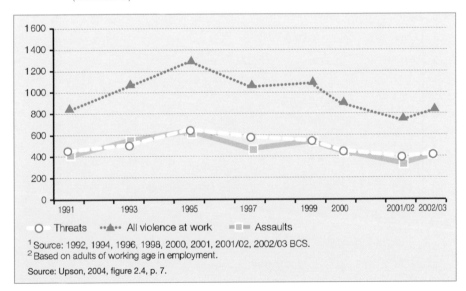

O   Threats   ··▲·· All violence at work   ■■■ Assaults

[1] Source: 1992, 1994, 1996, 1998, 2000, 2001, 2001/02, 2002/03 BCS.
[2] Based on adults of working age in employment.
Source: Upson, 2004, figure 2.4, p. 7.

Table 2   Studies of physical violence in selected EU Member States

Country	Sample	N	Method	Risk of violence	Reference
Denmark	National representative sample of union members	1 989	Survey	7% (within last 12 months)	FTF, 2001
	National representative sample	4 000	Household survey	7.5%	Hogh and Dofradottir, 2001
Finland	National representative sample	–	Survey	5% of workers	Saarela, 2002
	National representative sample	2 972	Survey	14% of workers	Haapanlemi and Kinnunen, 1997
	Representative sample of teachers	2 038	Survey	9% victims of violence by pupils	Hakanen, 2002
Sweden	Random national sample	14 234	Survey	14% reporting violence/threats (17% women, 10% men)	Statistiska Centralbyrån (Statistics Sweden), 1999
	Random sample of nurses	720	Survey (comparative study)	59% 60% several times	Nolan et al., 2001
Norway	Representative sample of social workers	854	Survey	21%	Skarpaas and Hetle, 1996
United Kingdom	National representative sample	19 411	Household survey	2.5% report at least one incident (1.2% physically assaulted, 1.4% threatened)	British Crime Survey, 2000
	Random sample of nurses	720	Survey (comparative study)	71% 60% several times	Nolan et al., 2001
	Retail outlets	17 000	Member survey	5% of outlets	British Retail Consortium 1999/2000

– = not available.

Source: Di Martino, Hoel and Cooper, 2003, p. 41, adapted from Hoel, Rayner and Cooper, 1999, and Zapf et al., 2003.

The data for this ten-year period show that: (a) threats and assaults occur at a similar frequency; and (b) a peak in incidence occurred in 1995 which subsequently fell (although there was a slight rise in the most recent 2002/03 survey period). Overall, these findings suggest that the incidence of workplace violence has remained relatively stable in the United Kingdom during the past decade. The picture is somewhat different for the intimidation and bullying form of workplace violence.

Intimidation and bullying

A sharp rise has occurred over recent years in the number of surveys conducted on harassment and bullying in the workplace. Whereas in the past most studies were confined mainly to Nordic countries, they now extend to most EU countries. Some of these studies focus on a particular occupational group, such as the military and particular professional groups, while others extend to cross-sections of the general population.[18]

According to the European Foundation survey in 2000, intimidation/ bullying was reported by more than 13 million workers, or almost one in ten, over the previous 12-month period, with the highest exposure among services/ sales workers (13 per cent).[19] Employees (9 per cent) were more prone to intimidation than the self-employed (5 per cent) and women more than men (10 per cent as against 7 per cent).[20]

Other research, conducted by Hoel and Cooper in the United Kingdom,[21] involved analysis of 5,300 questionnaires. The responses have been collated in figure 8, which shows how frequently respondents felt bullied.

The studies reveal a wide variation in the prevalence of bullying, dependent in large part upon the applied measurement strategy, occupation, sector or country involved. Table 3 provides an overview of some of these studies.

Figure 8   Frequency of bullying experienced, as cited by 5,300 British workers

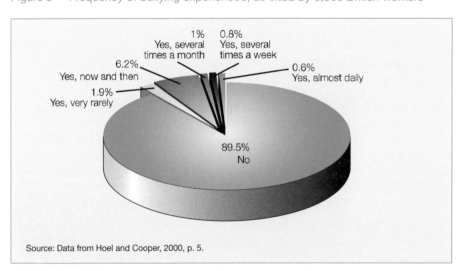

Source: Data from Hoel and Cooper, 2000, p. 5.

Table 3   European studies on the prevalence of bullying

Country	Reference	Target population	No	Findings
Austria	Niedl, 1995	Hospital employees	368	26%
		Research Institute employees	63	8%
Denmark	Hogh and	Random sample	1 857	2%
	Dofradottir, 2001	Students from the Royal		
	Mikkelsen and	Danish School of Educational		
	Einarsen, 2001	Studies	99	2%/14%
	Agervold, 2002	Hospital employees	236	3%/16%
	FTF, 2001	Manufacturing company		
		employees	224	4%/8%
		Department store employees	215	1%/25%
		Rural local authority, state		
		agencies, social pedagogues	1 613	4%
		Trade union members	–	18%
Finland	Björkqvist et al.,1994	University employees	338	17%
	Salin, 2001	Random sample of business		
		professionals	385	9%/24%
	Vartia, 1996	Local authority employees	949	10%
	Vartia and	Prison officers	896	11% men;
	Hyyti, 2002			17% women
	Haapanlemi and	Random and representative		
	Kinunen, 1997	sample	2 956	3%
	(Finnish Quality			
	of Life Survey)			
	Kivimaki et al., 2000	Hospital employees	–	5%
Germany	Mackensen von			
	Astfeld, 2000	Administrative employees	1 989	3%
	Meschkutat et al., 2002	Representative sample	1 317	3%–6%
Ireland	O'Moore, 2000	Random national sample	1 009	17%
	HSA, 2001	Random national sample		
		(telephone interviews)	5 252	7%
Netherlands	Hubert et al., 2001	Mixed production – office		
		business	427	4%
	Hubert et al., 2001	Financial institution		
		employees; stacked sample	3 011	1%
	Hubert and van	Mixed sample across 14		
	Veldhoven, 2001	industrial sectors	66 764	2%[1]

/cont'd

Table 3   European studies on the prevalence of bullying (/cont'd)

Country	Reference	Target population	No	Findings
Norway	Einarsen and Skogstad, 1996	14 different random sector-specific samples	7 787	9%
	Matthiesen et al., 1989	Nurses and assistant nurses	99	10.3%
		Teachers	84	6%
Spain	Piñuel y Zabala, 2002	Representative sample of general working population and representative sample of tourism sector	2 410	16%
Portugal	Cowie et al., 2000	Large multinational organization	221	34%
Sweden	Leymann, 1992	Representative sample of employed except self-employed	2 438	4%
	Lindroth and Leymann, 1993	Nursery school teachers	230	6%
	Voss et al., 2001	Postal employees	3 470	8% for women
United Kingdom	Rayner, 1997	Part-time students	581	53%
	UNISON, 1997	Public sector union members	736	18%
	Quine, 1999	National Health Service employees	1 100	38%
	Cowie et al., 2000	International organization employees	386	15%
	Hoel et al., 2001a	Nationwide representative sample	5 288	11%

Note: Where two percentages are given divided by a slash (/), the second figure refers to bullying at least weekly.
[1] Figure referring to mean of four items of aggressive and unpleasant situations often or always.

Source: Di Martino, Hoel and Cooper, 2003, p. 41.

Each of the studies listed in table 3 identified bullying in the sampled populations, with the highest reported incidence 53 per cent (in the British study by Rayner, 1997). Obviously, the methodologies adopted varied significantly across the different studies, making comparisons difficult. As Di Martino et al. have commented:

When bullying is measured by means of a precise definition and refers to a regular experience on a weekly basis, less than 5 per cent of the population were found to have been bullied. When we include experiences of occasional bullying, a figure of around 10 per cent is often reached. By contrast, in cases where respondents were considered bullied if they had experienced one or more negative behaviours associated with bullying, figures of between more than 10 per cent to nearly 40 per cent are achieved.[22]

A similar pattern of exposure to sexual violence and harassment has been identified. Again, the broad European Foundation surveys provide a benchmark.

Sexual violence and harassment

The European Foundation survey in 2000 reported that 2 per cent of interviewed workers stated that they had been subjected to sexual harassment, although the incidence varied between industry sectors.[23] These data are corroborated by national studies, although the percentages reported are frequently higher, for example, in the Czech Republic (4 per cent) and Romania (3 per cent).[24] Differences in the reported levels of exposure to sexual harassment may be a reflection of the gendered composition of the sample, the type of questions administered, variable pressures to report or under-report (which may be influenced by variable levels of power in different labour markets) and, most importantly, workers' perception of significance in different national and cultural contexts.

The European Commission reports[25] as follows:

• A high incidence of sexual harassment has been identified in national surveys carried out in Austria, Germany and Luxembourg, and in sectoral studies in Austria, Germany, Norway and the United Kingdom. These studies report exposure ratios of between 70 and 90 per cent.[26]

• A medium incidence ratio of between 25 to 60 per cent has been estimated in Dutch, Finnish and British studies, as well as in other sectoral studies.[27]

• A comparatively low incidence ratio of between 2 to 25 per cent has been reported in national and sectoral studies from Denmark, Finland, Sweden and the Netherlands.[28]

Other recent studies help complete this picture:

• A study of workers in a German call centre reported that 75 per cent of female employees had experienced sexually harassing telephone calls.[29]

• A stratified sample survey of 1,000 workers aged 16 years and over, conducted by the Spanish Comisiones Obreras (Workers' Commissions), reported that 18 per cent of women and 9 per cent of men had experienced sexual harassment during their lives.[30]

- In Sweden, 2.3 per cent of women, as compared to 0.9 per cent of men, reported having been sexually harassed by superiors or co-workers in the last 12 months.[31]

- In 2004, the Italian Institute of Statistics (ISTAT) issued a report on sexual violence and harassment, based on a survey carried out in 2002.[32] The workplace emerged from the survey as one of the places where women are most exposed to sexual violence, followed by means of transport and in the street. In total, 14.3 per cent of women interviewed reported attempted violence and 12.1 per cent physical harassment at the workplace and surroundings during their working life. Over the immediately previous three-year period, the incidence reported was 10.9 per cent for attempted violence and 15.1 per cent for physical harassment.[33] Colleagues, employers and supervisors were responsible for a substantial part of this sexual violence, particularly attempted violence. The detailed data are displayed in table 4.

According to the ISTAT survey, in total 373,000 (3.1 per cent) of women had been subject to sexual intimidation during their working life, including requests for sexual favours during recruitment (1.8 per cent) or for career advancement (1.8 per cent). More than half a million women (4.9 per cent) were subjected to more subtle forms of sexual intimidation directed at testing their "sexual availability" (*disponibilità sessuale*). (While there are some minor inconsistencies between "working lifetime" and "last three years" reports, these may well be explained through improved recall of more recent events.) Table 5 shows the frequency of such forms of intimidation.

The data displayed in tables 4 and 5 provide a substantial body of evidence detailing the sexual violence and harassment faced by Italian women workers (although, again in table 5, there are some minor inconsistencies between

Table 4   Sexual violence and harassment of women in the workplace, Italy, 2002 (percentages)

Experienced	Colleagues, employers, superiors		Workplace and surroundings	
	At least once in their lifetime	In the past three years	At least once in their lifetime	In the past three years
Violence/attempted violence	15.3	8.8	11.8	9.9
Of which: violence	4.4	3.9	1.6	3.9
Of which: attempted violence	17.9	9.6	14.3	10.9
Physical harassment	10.4	11.6	12.1	15.1

Source: Italian Institute of Statistics (ISTAT), 2004.

Table 5   Frequency of intimidation of women in the workplace, Italy, 2002
           (percentages)

Experienced	In their lifetime	In the last three years
Every day	35.3	27.6
A few times a week	26.8	26.7
Once a week	4.0	3.9
A few times a month	19.2	27.3
A few times a year/more rarely	12.1	11.7
No response	2.6	2.8

Source: ISTAT, 2004.

"working lifetime" and "last three years" reports). Indeed, workplace violence in the form of sexual harassment appears to be almost an endemic risk for Italian women.

United States

The picture that emerges about workplace violence experiences in other countries is somewhat different for working men and women. In the United States, for example, there are substantial reliable data on a range of forms of workplace violence. Much more detailed data are available on many aspects of violence at work. The data are broken down by severity in the discussion below, beginning with homicides at work.

Homicides

In the United States, the Bureau of Labor Statistics (BLS) National Census of Fatal Occupational Injuries traces workplace homicide on an annual basis. The BLS data show that homicide is the third leading cause of death at work. During a ten-year period from 1992 to 2001, almost 9,000 workplace homicides occurred in the United States.[34] Table 6 shows the annual number and rates of these homicides and of non-fatal assaults.

Because the size of the workforce varies in different years, the most important columns in table 6 are the "rate per 100,000 workers". As can be seen in table 6, workplace homicides have been in almost continuous decline in recent years, and a similar trend appears for non-fatal assaults. However, it is important to note that the events of 11 September 2001 (mentioned at the outset of this book) resulted in additional deaths of many innocent workers.

The nature of this trend is shown in more detail in figure 9, which charts the three most frequent work-related fatal events in the period 1992–2003.

Table 6   Fatal and non-fatal workplace assaults, United States, 1992–2001[1]

Year	Fatal assaults[2]		Nonfatal assaults[3]	
	No.	Rate per 100,000 workers	No.	Rate per 100,000 workers
1992	1 044	0.88	22 396	2.9
1993	1 074	0.90	21 254	2.7
1994	1 080	0.88	20 439	2.5
1995	1 036	0.82	22 956	2.8
1996	927	0.72	18 538	2.2
1997	860	0.65	21 329	2.5
1998	714	0.54	17 589	2.0
1999	651	0.48	16 644	1.8
2000	677	0.49	18 418	2.0
2001	639	0.47	17 215	1.9

[1] Self-inflicted injuries and animal assaults are excluded.

[2] Data on fatal assaults for 2001 are preliminary. Updated numbers for 2001 are scheduled for release in September 2003.

[3] Assaults to self-employed and government workers and assaults that did not result in days away from work are excluded.

Source: Richardson and Windau, 2003, pp. 673–689, especially p. 677.

Figure 9   The three most frequent work-related fatal events, United States, 1992–2003

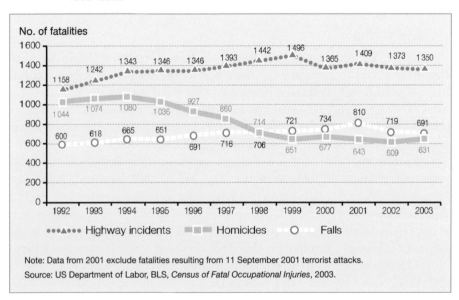

Note: Data from 2001 exclude fatalities resulting from 11 September 2001 terrorist attacks.
Source: US Department of Labor, BLS, *Census of Fatal Occupational Injuries*, 2003.

While there is a slight variation in numbers from the different sources used to construct table 6 and figure 9, the overall pattern is the same.

The data provided in figure 9 indicate that throughout the decade 1992–2003, the most frequent cause of work-related death was highway incidents; and since 1998 falls have surpassed homicides as the second most frequent fatal work-related event. The number of workplace homicides in 2003 at 631 was the lowest recorded and represented only 58.4 per cent of the high of 1,080 workplace homicides recorded in 1994.

The manner in which workplace fatalities occurred in 2003 in the United States is displayed in figure 10, showing that transport incidents are the major cause of death (and may not be recorded as work-related in all other databases).

As can be seen in figure 10, of the 5,559 fatalities recorded during 2003, 16 per cent were attributed to assaults and violent acts, with 11 per cent classified as homicides.

Tables 7 and 8 show the incidence of workplace homicides broken down by employment characteristics (table 7), and relative risk for homicide in selected occupations of the victims involved (table 8).

The data displayed in table 7 indicate that: (a) the risk of homicide is substantially higher for self-employed workers than for those employed on a wage and salary basis; and (b) workers in the transport (particularly taxi) and retail trade (specifically liquor stores and gasoline service stations) industry sectors were at greatest risk. A comparatively reduced level of risk is evident for workers in construction, manufacturing and federal and state public service.

Figure 10   The manner in which workplace fatalities occurred, US, 2003 (percentages)

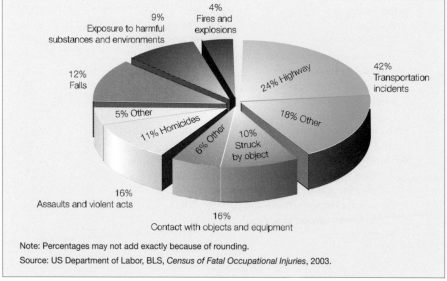

Note: Percentages may not add exactly because of rounding.

Source: US Department of Labor, BLS, *Census of Fatal Occupational Injuries*, 2003.

Table 7   Number, percentage and relative risk for workplace homicides by
            employment characteristics, United States, 1996–2000

Characteristics	No.	%	Rate per 100,000 workers	Relative risk
Employee status				
Wage and salary	2 806	73.3	0.46	0.80
Self-employed	1 023	26.7	1.95	3.40
Occupation				
Managerial and professional	730	19.1	0.37	0.65
Technical sales and administrative support	1 308	34.2	0.67	1.17
Service occupations	801	20.9	0.89	1.56
Farming, forestry and fishing	80	2.1	0.45	0.78
Precision production, craft and repair	187	4.9	0.26	0.46
Operators, fabricators and labourers	677	17.7	0.74	1.28
Industry				
Private industry	3 403	88.9	0.60	1.04
Agriculture, forestry and fishing	77	2.0	0.44	0.76
Construction	73	1.9	0.18	0.31
Manufacturing	172	4.5	0.17	0.29
Transportation and public utilities	399	10.2	1.01	1.75
Taxicab service	265	6.9	40.83	71.63
Trucking and warehousing	78	2.0	0.59	1.03
Trucking and courier services	63	1.6	0.51	0.89
Wholesale trade	108	2.8	0.42	0.74
Retail trade	1 693	44.2	1.52	2.67
Food stores	611	16.0	3.43	6.01
Grocery stores	571	14.9	3.69	6.48
Automotive dealers and service stations	175	4.6	1.56	2.73
Gasoline service stations	113	3.0	5.69	9.99
Eating and drinking places	499	13.0	1.48	2.59
Miscellaneous retail	271	7.1	1.43	2.50
Liquor stores	77	2.0	11.79	20.68
Finance, insurance and real estate	146	3.8	0.35	0.61
Real estate	75	2.0	0.68	1.20
Services	717	18.7	0.38	0.66
Business services	172	4.5	0.53	0.93
Detective and armoured car services	107	2.8	3.78	6.63
Automotive repair, services and parking	128	3.3	1.58	2.78
Automotive repair shops	77	2.0	1.28	2.25
Health services	58	1.5	0.07	0.12

/cont'd

Characteristics	No.	%	Rate per 100,000 workers	Relative risk
Government	424	11.1	0.43	0.75
Federal	47	1.2	0.21	0.36
State	83	2.2	0.31	0.55
Local	294	7.7	0.58	1.01
Public administration	255	6.7	2.12	3.72
Justice, public order and safety	228	6.0	2.86	5.02
Total	3 829	100.0	0.57	1.00

Source: Richardson and Windau, 2003, pp. 673–689, especially p. 683.

In table 8, workplace homicide data are provided, broken down by occupational groups. As can be seen, there are marked variations in risk between different occupational groups. When detailed occupational data were analysed, they clearly showed that taxi drivers and chauffeurs have the highest relative risk, followed by police and detectives, guards, and managers of food-serving and lodging establishments.[35] A similar pattern of risk for assault at work emerges from the data.

Table 8   Number, percentage of total and relative risk for workplace homicides by selected occupations, United States, 1996–2000

Occupation	No.	%	Rate per 100,000 workers	Relative risk
Sales supervisors and proprietors	619	16.2	2.61	4.6
Cashiers	308	8.0	2.08	3.6
Taxicab drivers and chauffeurs	265	6.9	20.78	36.3
Managers, food-serving and lodging establishments	252	6.6	3.51	6.1
Guards and police, except public service	193	5.0	5.24	9.1
Police and detectives, public services	184	4.8	6.29	11.0
Managers and administrators, not elsewhere classified	183	4.8	0.49	0.8
Truck drivers	105	2.7	0.69	1.2
Total	3 829	100.0	0.57	1.0

Source: Richardson and Windau, 2003, pp. 673–689.

47

Assaults

Two main sources are available to assist with estimation of the magnitude of workplace assaults in the United States. These data collations are produced annually, one by the BLS and the other by the Bureau of Justice Statistics (BJS).

The BLS *Annual Survey of Occupational Injuries and Illnesses* involves the surveying of about 250,000 private establishments. The BLS reported that about 24,000 workplace assaults and violent acts occurred in 2002; of these, around 18,000 were committed by individuals.[36] Females represented approximately 61 per cent of all victimized workers. This gender differential in exposure to the risk of workplace assault is undoubtedly partially determined by the sexual division of labour whereby women are concentrated in higher-risk jobs (see the discussion on gender distribution of risk in the discussion towards the end of this chapter, pp. 28ff.).

The majority of assaults were reported from workers in services and retail trade industry sectors. Figure 11 shows the different categories of **perpetrators** of assaults on workers.

The data displayed in figure 11 show that health-care patients perpetrated a significant proportion of assaults on workers. Given that the workforce in health care is disproportionately female, it is therefore unsurprising that women experience more workplace assaults in this industry sector.

Figure 11   Assaults and violent acts resulting in days away from work, by source of injury (perpetrator category), United States, 2001 (percentages)

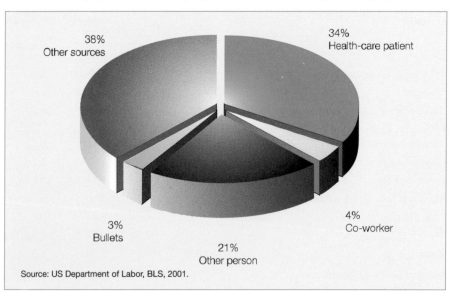

38% Other sources

34% Health-care patient

4% Co-worker

21% Other person

3% Bullets

Source: US Department of Labor, BLS, 2001.

Table 9   Average annual number, rate and percentage of workplace victimization by type of crime, United States, 1993–99

Crime category	Average annual workplace victimization	Rate per 1,000 persons in the workplace	% of workplace victimization
Homicide	900	0.01	0.1
Rape/sexual assault	36 500	0.3	2.1
Robbery	70 100	0.5	4.0
Aggravated assault	325 000	2.3	18.6
Simple assault	1 311 700	9.4	75.2
All violent crime	1 744 200	12.5	100

Note: Homicide data are obtained from the BLS Census of Fatal Occupational Injuries. Data on rape and sexual assault, robbery, aggravated assault and simple assault are obtained from the NCVS.

Source: Duhart, 2001, p. 2.

Another estimate of the number of non-fatal assaults occurring in American workplaces comes from the BJS National Crime Victimization Survey (NCVS) – a large-scale, annual nationwide, household-based study of more than 100,000 individuals aged 12 or older. The prevalence of different forms of workplace violence over the period 1993–99 is shown in table 9.

As shown in table 9, the BJS survey estimated an average annual incidence of 900 homicides, 36,500 rape/sexual assaults, 70,100 robberies, 325,000 aggravated assaults, and 1,311,700 simple assaults at United States workplaces. According to the NCVS:

> between 1993 and 1999 in the United States, an average of 1.7 million violent workplace victimizations per year were committed ... Rape and sexual assault, robbery, and homicide accounted for a small percentage (6%) of all workplace violent crime occurring between 1993 and 1999. The majority of workplace violent incidents, almost 19 of every 20, were aggravated or simple assaults.[37]

The incidence of workplace bullying is probably more difficult to estimate. Nevertheless, studies have also been conducted in the United States on this form of workplace violence.

Bullying (emotionally abusive behaviour)

According to the preliminary findings from a comprehensive survey of the prevalence of workplace bullying conducted by the authoritative US National Institute for Occupational Safety and Health (NIOSH), most incidents of bullying in the workplace appeared to be from one worker to another. Data was collected from key respondents at 516 private and public organizations across the United States.

Data reported from the survey indicate the following:

- 24.5 per cent of the companies surveyed reported that some degree of bullying had occurred there during the preceding year.

- In the most recent incident that had occurred, 39.2 per cent involved an employee as the aggressor, 24.5 per cent involved a customer, and 14.7 per cent a supervisor.

- In the most recent incident, 55.2 per cent involved the employee as the "victim", 10.5 per cent the customer and 7.7 per cent the supervisor.[38]

Again, the incidence ratio is of concern. Further, there is often a fine line between workplace bullying and sexual harassment on the job.

Sexual harassment

Some of the earliest systematic surveys of sexual harassment were conducted by the US Merit Systems Protection Board (MSPB), which used scientifically selected samples of Federal workers from across the United States. The operational definition of sexual harassment adopted in these surveys was "uninvited and unwanted sexual attention on the job". Respondents were asked to indicate the frequency with which they had experienced several kinds of "unwanted sexual attention" in the past 24 months. Surveys of Federal workers were conducted for the years 1980, 1987 and 1994. The 1994 survey added "stalking" to the list of unwanted behaviours. Remarkably, these three surveys found very similar incidence ratios. A breakdown of the percentages of women and men reporting each of the specific behaviours is presented in table 10.

The surveys of the US MSPB still remain a benchmark in research on sexual harassment.[39] More recent research findings confirm the magnitude of the sexual harassment detected by these earlier surveys. For example, in studies of sexual harassment in American companies, psychologist Louise Fitzgerald discovered that around half of women experienced some form of harassing behaviour over a two-year period.[40] Again, the definition adopted for sexual harassment and violence was of crucial importance:

> ... Although not all such experiences meet legal criteria for sexual harassment, they nonetheless lead to depression, anxiety and stress-related physical problems, particularly when the harassment is frequent and intense ... First published in 1988 and since revised, the 18-item SEQ [Sexual Experiences Questionnaire] measures harassment in what Fitzgerald has defined as the behavioural categories of gender

harassment, unwanted sexual attention and sexual coercion. Gender harassment includes crude words, acts and gestures conveying hostile, misogynist attitudes. Along with gender harassment, unwanted sexual attention is characteristic of the legally defined "hostile working environment". By comparison, sexual coercion is akin to the legal concept of quid pro quo harassment, meaning job rewards in exchange for sexual favours. Unlike legal inquiries, the SEQ gauges the psychological anguish harassment victims experience – whether, for example, the harassment made them feel incompetent. It also measures outcomes such as anxiety, depression, job satisfaction and work withdrawal ... Her research suggests that most women avoid disclosing harassment for fear of losing their jobs and sabotaging their careers. Although the number appears to be rising, historically less than 5 percent of women dared to reveal their experiences of it, she says. Those with a lot to lose – single mothers, for example – are especially leery of blowing the whistle... [41]

Table 10   Women and men reporting sexual harassment experiences from the 1980, 1987 and 1994 US Merit Systems Protection Board surveys of Federal workers (percentages)

Women	1980	1987	1994
Sexual teasing, jokes, remarks	33	35	37
Sexual looks, gestures	28	28	29
Deliberate touching, cornering	26	26	24
Pressure for dates	15	15	13
Suggestive letters, calls, materials	9	12	10
Pressure for sexual favours	9	9	7
Stalking	n.a.	n.a.	7
Actual/attempted rape, assault	1	0.8	4
Any type	42	42	44

Men	1980	1987	1994
Sexual teasing, jokes, remarks	10	12	14
Sexual looks, gestures	8	9	9
Deliberate touching, cornering	7	8	8
Pressure for dates	3	4	4
Suggestive letters, calls, materials	3	4	4
Pressure for sexual favours	2	3	2
Stalking	n.a.	n.a.	2
Actual/attempted rape, assault	0.3	0.3	2
Any type	15	14	19

Source: Pryor and Fitzgerald, 2003, p. 79.

In 2000 Palmieri et al. reported that 53 per cent of the women in their study on the military service had experienced sexual harassment.[42] Similarly, a cross-sectional survey of 558 women veterans who had served in Viet Nam reported extensive exposure to different forms of workplace violence: sexual harassment (79 per cent), unwanted sexual contact (54 per cent), and threatened or completed physical assault (36 per cent) during military service.[43] Nevertheless, it is likely that only a limited number of cases of sexual harassment are reported.

The findings from these studies have been used extensively in contemporary sexual harassment litigation in the United States. As a result, the number of harassment charges filed with the Equal Employment Opportunity Commission and the state fair employment practices agencies has risen significantly from 10,532 in fiscal year 1992 to 13,136 in fiscal year 2004. This increase reflects an increase in either the experience of sexual harassment or the willingness to report such conduct.[44]

Thus far, the discussions in this chapter have focused on the available data on different forms of workplace violence in Europe and the United States. The authors believe that it is also important to recognize the vulnerability of workers to violence on the job in developing countries.

Developing countries

In earlier editions of this book it has been stressed how limited are the data available about patterns and trends in workplace violence in developing countries. This situation is now beginning to change as workplace violence emerges as an issue of priority and concern. While evidence is still limited and fragmented, and often anecdotal, sufficient evidence is appearing to reveal the importance of the phenomenon of workplace violence in all countries, both developing and industrialized.

As will be seen in more detail below, much of the existing published data regarding workplace violence in developing countries is embedded in more general literature discussing human rights issues, and especially rights associated with trade union activities and the exercise of the freedom of association, the securing of safe working conditions and the prevention of the exploitation of workers (box 11). Another related literature stream concerns the rights of migrant workers who represent a much marginalized and exploited group, both in developing and developed nations. A third and substantial source of information is to be found in the literature on the rights of workers, including freedom from sexual abuse and exploitation.

The available evidence on workplace violence in developing countries is most probably only the tip of the iceberg. Incidents of workplace violence are frequently hidden by other critical problems that may divert attention away from this specific area. As a result, widespread under-reporting of incidents of workplace violence seems to be the norm rather than the exception.

Varying perceptions and cultural backgrounds can also contribute to a different understanding and evaluation of the relative importance of situations described as workplace violence in a society. Behaviours that would not be condoned in one country may be accepted or tolerated in another. Such differences in approach can lead to distorted representations of reality. Thus countries with a better awareness of the problem may be "penalized" statistically vis-à-vis countries which give more limited attention to the phenomenon of workplace violence.

Although concepts and definitions are loaded with cultural significance, and despite the fact that they may be perceived in different ways in developing countries, it would appear that a common understanding of workplace violence is emerging. The term "workplace violence" now seems able to capture a series of work events, including physical, psychological and sexual violence at work that is relevant for both the developing and the industrialized world.

In addition, special attention is often given in developing countries to behaviours consisting of unjust or grossly unfair treatment at work. Such treatment results in serious offence to the dignity and decency of employment and the life of the workers and their families. Different examples of this kind of treatment, referred to as institutional or societal violence, are given by commentators according to their different perceptions. These range from quite extreme cases, for example concerning forced labour or forcing someone to perform more than his or her regular work assignment without payment; to systemic examples such as providing comparatively low salaries in the public and private employment sectors; to examples of poor or indecent workplace practices such as making an employee do what he or she has no capacity to do; and perpetuating indecent work conditions or the coexistence of multiple types of work contracts for performing the same work for different salaries. Problems with gaining access to justice, and the fear of reprisals for complaining about abusive work conditions, would further exacerbate this kind of violence.

Whether all the above behaviours can be included in the notion of violence at work or should be referred to a broader notion of injustice and poor working conditions is a matter of debate. These broader unjust working condition issues remain, in any case, outside the scope of this report. A brief review of scenarios of workplace violence experienced in developing countries is provided below.

Physical violence

As the situation described in Colombia illustrates, members of trade unions who seek to exercise their rights in certain countries face the risk of life-threatening violence (box 11). In its Annual Survey of Violations of Trade

Box 11   War against Colombian trade unionists continues; 45 murdered in first
          three months of 2002

The wholesale murder of Colombia's trade unionists shows no signs of abating in 2002.
CUT [Central Unitaria de Trabajadores – Unitary Confederation of Workers], the country's
largest labour confederation, reported 45 union members murdered in 2002 as of 4 April.
Ten of the victims were leaders, including members of local executive committees as well
as three union presidents.

Enoc Samboni, a member of the local Executive Committee of CUT in the Department of
Cauca, was executed by a paramilitary death squad on 12 January. Eight paramilitary
members detained him at 1.30 pm at a fake police roadblock they had set up in La
Chorrera, Cauca. After forcing him out of his car, they took him to his home, where they
stole his cell phone and his personal agenda. They then took him to a site near the
Tupacinca River where they shot him three times in the head. The Interamerican Human
Rights Commission of the Organisation of American States (OAS) had ordered the
Colombian Government to provide protection for him, and in fact he was included in the
Interior Department's Protection Program at the time of his murder.

Source: US/LEAP, 2002, p. 1.

Union Rights, the ICFTU monitors and documents the conditions under
which trade unions operate within most nations of the world. In its 2004
report, detailing the conditions in 2003, the ICFTU indicated that Colombia
remains the most dangerous place on earth for trade unionists. In 2003 a total
of 94 people were killed for their trade union activity, and more than three
times that number received credible death threats.[45]

At its 292nd session held in March 2005 the ILO Governing Body
approved the 336th report of the ILO Committee on Freedom of Association,
which examined 30 cases.[46] The Committee drew special attention to the case
of Nepal concerning allegations of violent intervention in a demonstration
that resulted in the arrest and detention of trade unionists. The Committee
requested the Government to ensure that authorities resort to force only in
situations where law and order is seriously threatened and that the intervention should be in due proportion to the danger which the authorities are
attempting to control.[47]

In the case of Guatemala, the Committee examined serious allegations of
violence against trade unionists, dismissal of union leaders followed by
employer refusals to comply with reinstatement orders, and undue delays in
the proceedings. The Committee underlined the gravity of the allegations of
assaults, death threats and intimidation of trade union members, and the
attacks on trade union headquarters.[48]

The Committee also examined the case of Zimbabwe concerning
allegations of arbitrary arrests and detentions, anti-union intimidation and

harassment. It urged the Government to refrain from resorting to such measures. Referring to an atmosphere of intimidation and fear prejudicial to the normal development of trade union activities, the Committee expressed its overall deep concern with the extreme seriousness of the general trade union climate in Zimbabwe demonstrated by the number of cases of a similar nature which have recently been brought before it.[49]

The situations illustrated above are examples of the constant presence of physical violence, threats and other extreme forms of abuse affecting workers in developing countries. Physical violence and serious abuse at work persist in industrialized countries too, but in developing countries the magnitude of the phenomenon, especially in respect of the more vulnerable workers such as women, immigrants and children, is particularly relevant. The information that follows is merely indicative of the gravity of a problem that is present in many more countries than those mentioned below:

- Côte d'Ivoire is a destination for children trafficked to labour as plantation and other agricultural labourers, as mine workers, and as domestic servants, under conditions in some cases approaching involuntary servitude. Many of these children are trafficked from neighbouring countries such as Mali. An estimated 15,000 Malian children between the ages of 9 and 12 have been sold into forced labour on cotton, coffee, and cocoa farms in northern Côte d'Ivoire over the past few years; an even greater number have been pressed into domestic service. Organized networks of traffickers deceive the children and their families into believing that they will be given paid jobs outside their villages. They then are sold to plantation owners for sums ranging between US$20 and US$40 (14,500 and 29,000 CFA francs). The children reportedly are forced to work 12 hours per day without pay, and are often abused physically.[50]

- In Cairo, many immigrants from Sudan, Ethiopia, Eritrea, Nigeria and the Philippines work as domestic labourers and are either legally, or illegally, residing and working in this city. These people are often deprived of their rights as citizens and, fearing deportation, are often more vulnerable to violence. According to information received, African immigrants are harassed in the street on the basis of their appearance although many of them wear hijab or scarves in the street in an effort to appear more "Egyptian".[51]

- Some seven million foreigners work in Saudi Arabia, many of them from India, Egypt, Indonesia, Pakistan, the Philippines and Bangladesh. Conditions are particularly difficult for the estimated one million women who are employed as domestic workers, a job category not covered by the labour law. Over 19,000 women domestics fled from their employers in 2000, a Labour Ministry official acknowledged in April 2001, citing mistreatment, non-payment of wages and other grievances.[52]

Some graphic examples of the type of workplace violence and abuse from which women fled in Saudi Arabia are to be found in a report by the international human rights group, Human Rights Watch. One such example is the case of Fatima (box 12).

Box 12   An exploited domestic worker

Fatima, a 26-year-old Muslim woman from Mindanao province in the Philippines, told us that she had a fifth-grade education and was married at 14 years old in a union that her family arranged. When she travelled to Saudi Arabia in February 2003 on a two-year contract as a domestic worker, she left behind her husband and four children, aged 2 to 9 years old.

A manpower agency in Manila placed Fatima with a Saudi family in Dammam at a monthly salary of US$280. Fatima's work-day began at 5.30 a.m. and continued until 6.30 p.m., when she was allowed a 30-minute break. She then worked for another two hours until 9 p.m. She told us that she was fed one meal a day, typically rice and chicken, and any additional food was her own financial responsibility.

Fatima was not allowed to leave the house. Her male employer demanded her passport when he met her at the airport, and she was never provided with an *iqama*, the official residence permit that would have allowed her the freedom to move freely without the fear of arrest.

In addition to her long day of work, Fatima endured the shock and humiliation of three serious incidents of sexual harassment and one beating from her male employer. She told Human Rights Watch that twice he exposed himself to her and offered to pay her if she masturbated him. "I refused. I told him that I want money in the right way. I told him I am not a prostitute, but a married woman and a Muslim," she said. After these rejections, "he held a knife to my neck and threatened to kill me if I told the madame (his wife)".

Fatima had an opportunity to escape. Contact was made with the Philippines consulate, and a labour attaché agreed to meet Fatima. During her interview at the consulate later that day, "they told me that my employer was a rich man, and do not fight him". The diplomats sent Fatima to the local police, who were not concerned about her recent assault but with sending her back to the Philippines.

Back in the Philippines, Fatima's husband was not sympathetic to her situation. She telephoned him from the airport in Manila and explained everything that had happened to her. He did not provide the "moral support" that Fatima had anticipated: "He told me that it was stupid of me to return home, and that he hated me." At the time of her interview with Human Rights Watch, she was still in Manila, pressing a compensation claim against the manpower agency that recruited her. She said that she was unable to speak to her two youngest children because her husband denied her any form of communication with them.

Source: Adapted from Human Rights Watch, 2004a.

Human Rights Watch also reported that women migrants in Saudi Arabia suffered death and serious injury in attempts to escape from locked rooms and premises in which their employers had detained them. One of the country's largest hospitals reported in 2002 that two or three foreign female domestic workers were being admitted weekly suffering from serious bone fractures after jumping from upper storeys of their places of employment.[53]

Abuse of foreign domestic workers is also a growing problem in Indonesia and Malaysia, as illustrated by another recent report by Human Rights Watch.[54] The report provides a comprehensive account of the conditions faced by migrant domestic workers, detailing their experiences from initial recruitment in villages in Indonesia to their return home from Malaysia. The report was prompted by the case of Nivmala Bonat, a young Indonesian domestic worker in Malaysia, whose burned and battered body was displayed in the media across South-East Asia in May 2004. The Bonat case attracted international attention, it being alleged that Bonat's employer had brutally beaten and abused her.

The Human Rights Watch report documented a litany of abuse at every stage of the migration cycle, including physical violence, sexual assault and harassment. The report also emphasized how the current structure of the labour migration process between Malaysia and Indonesia leaves migrant workers in extreme vulnerability almost without any means of redress against those inflicting such violence.[55]

Serious abuses and physical violence are also widely experienced by street vendors in developing countries. The first International Congress of Streetnet International held in Seoul, Republic of Korea, in March 2004, reported:

- many of our members are facing constant harassment and government crack-downs, which continually interfere with their productivity and their ability to earn a decent livelihood;

- the harassment faced by street vendors takes many forms, including violent attacks, sexual harassment, bribery and extortion – sometimes perpetrated by authorities and sometimes perpetrated by thugs, gangsters and syndicates working hand-in-hand with the authorities;

- there are many types of gender-specific harassment, including different forms of gender-specific violence and sexual harassment, faced by women and children street vendors.[56]

In addition to the risk of homicide, assault and sexual harassment and violence, psychological violence is being reported. That is, more than one form of workplace violence can occur to the same person at different points in time, or multiple forms of aggression can be inflicted at the same time.

The emergence of psychological violence, together with physical violence in the health sector

Growing attention is being given to those industry sectors where workers are exposed to multiple different forms of violence, including physical, psychological, and all forms of harassment, bullying and mobbing. The health-care sector appears to be particularly at risk.

A path-breaking study of workers in the health sector across seven countries (Brazil, Bulgaria, Lebanon, Portugal, South Africa, Thailand and an affiliated Australian study), conducted in 2002, showed that psychological violence was more prevalent than physical violence.[57] While attention has traditionally been focused on physical violence, the new profile of workplace violence in the health sector emerging from these country studies emphasizes the importance of both psychological and physical violence in the developing world.

Physical violence was substantially present in most of the countries investigated. In Bulgaria, about 8 per cent of the respondents reported having been physically attacked in the previous year; in Brazil 6 per cent; in Lebanon 6 per cent; in Thailand 11 per cent; and in South Africa up to 17 per cent in the public sector.

The major new finding of the study was, however, the widespread presence of psychological violence in health sector workplaces, with **verbal abuse** at the top of the list. In Brazil, almost 40 per cent of the respondents had experienced verbal abuse in the last year; 32 per cent in Bulgaria; 60 per cent in South Africa; 48 per cent in Thailand; 41 per cent in Lebanon; and up to 67 per cent in Australia. The second main area of concern was that of **bullying and mobbing**, which had been experienced by almost 40 per cent in Bulgaria, 21 per cent in South Africa, 11 per cent in Thailand, 22 per cent in Lebanon, 10.5 per cent in Australia and 15 per cent in Brazil.

In the past, bullying or mobbing was virtually unknown (or at least not reported) in the developing world. The results of these country studies have unveiled for the first time the worrying dimension of these two forms of psychological violence both in the developed world and in countries in transition. The impact on the worker can be compounded if sexual harassment and violence are also occurring.

Sexual harassment and violence

With sexual harassment and violence, cultural perceptions and traditions can play a major role in describing and proscribing such behaviour. In many countries such behaviours in society and at the workplace are not only widespread, but in most cases associated with deeply ingrained stereotypes of conduct based on gender roles. Because of the traditional perception of women as objects of sexual desire, and their subordinate role in society and in the family, their sexual victimization is often seen as part of the "normal order" of things.

In a major review of actions taken against sexual harassment in Asia and the Pacific, the ILO has examined attitudes and perceptions towards this form of behaviour, and provides examples of sexual harassment across a diverse range of countries.[58] Four of these examples appear below (box 13).

As the ILO report stresses, significant differences often occur in the way sexual harassment is perceived by people at different levels in the work hierarchy, between men and women, and even between workers in variable age groups. Such harassment may also be viewed in some societies as an insignificant problem and yet in others it is accepted to be a serious issue. In

---

Box 13 Sexual harassment cases

"I am a secretary at a small firm. In the office there are only me and the president. Under the pretext of helping me learn my job, he keeps on harassing me by touching my breasts and rubbing his sexual organs against me. I cannot stand it any more. Because there are just the two of us in the office, I can't avoid him. Is there no way out of this except for resignation?"[1]

"... the production manager, who usually inspected the workers' performance every day, took many good-looking young women workers into his office. He proposed them administrative jobs in the office in exchange for his sexual desire ... many good-looking workers had to resign from their work due to his harassment and moved to other factories. But he still searched for them and when he knew where they stayed he would go to their rooms."[2]

"The Kangani (supervisor) has been continuously doing all kinds of things before this incident happened. He would make me work in a lonely block away from the rest of the workers, would carry my basket at the end of the day, or put an extra amount in my daily plucking load. The Kangani would keep telling me: "Ever since I saw your breasts when you were picking the fallen tea leaves, I wanted to have you. Sinna Dorai said that you have a nice body. But I will be the one who will first get you." (Mahaleswary, 19-year-old tea-plucker, Sri Lanka.)[3]

Several years after the plaintiff (woman employee) was hired and began working as an editor in a small publishing company, the company's male chief editor sought to concentrate on sales activities and his role as an editor declined. In the presence of other employees or business customers, the chief editor made comments about the plaintiff's private life, including her alleged promiscuity, unfitness as a role model for working women and so forth. He also informed the company's managing director that the plaintiff's relationship with men disrupted the company's business. As their relationship began to affect the operation of the enterprise, the managing director decided that one of the two should leave the company. After consulting with the plaintiff about the possibility of reconciliation with the chief editor, and the plaintiff's refusal and demand for an apology, the managing director told her that she should resign, which she did. (Case of sexual harassment in Fukuoka, Japan, 1992.)[4]

Sources: [1] Counselling case of Equaline, Inchon Women Workers Association, Republic of Korea, 1998, in Zaitun, 2001. [2] Interview with woman worker of the Par Garment Factory Labour Union on sexual harassment at the Par Garment Factory, Thailand, 1985, cited in Zaitun, 2001. [3] Wijayatitake and Zackariya, 2000. [4] Yamakawa, 2001.

studies cited from Sri Lanka and the Philippines, union officials were said to have belittled workplace sexual harassment as a matter requiring little attention in contrast to other more pressing labour issues.[59] Another problem is that reliable data and evidence are rarely available.

In relation to the incidence of sexual harassment in the regions under review, the ILO report noted that:

> The quality of official, empirical and anecdotal evidence and statistics on sexual harassment varies from country to country, depending on the levels of awareness and the type and quality of data collection. In some countries, statistics for sexual harassment in the workplace are sometimes compiled together with statistics of other kinds of violations such as breach of modesty, sexual assault and threats, so a true picture of workplace sexual harassment is difficult to garner.

> The research findings also vary according to the groups sampled, their size, level of awareness of the problem, and especially the precise questions asked. For example, a question that asks whether or not the respondent has experienced particular forms of unwelcome behaviour is more likely to elicit a positive answer than a question as to whether the person has been sexually harassed, because those questioned may differ in their understanding of what constitutes sexual harassment. For this reason, in countries where there have been a number of surveys on the incidence of sexual harassment, results can differ. Nevertheless, the overall majority of research findings show not only that sexual harassment at work exists but that it is a problem.[60]

The ILO report identified a number of high-risk sectors and occupations. These included domestic labourers and migrant workers, whose plight has already been considered earlier in this chapter; as well as young men and women at work or preparing for work in education and training institutions, workers in male-dominated occupations, or in situations where large numbers of women were supervised by a small number of men.[61]

It is not only the Asia and Pacific regions which encounter such behaviour. As the following examples indicate, this type of behaviour is commonplace throughout the entire developing world.

* A survey in Nigeria revealed that young female university graduates seeking employment are routinely required to grant sexual favours before their academic credentials can be evaluated.[62]

* According to a study of violence conducted by the Royal Malaysian Police, between 1997 and May 2001 there were 11,851 rape and molestation cases at the workplace (6,082 rape cases and 5,769 molestation cases).[63]

- In South Africa, in March 2001 Human Rights Watch released a report entitled *Scared at school: Sexual violence against girls in South African schools*, which documented widespread rape, sexual abuse, sexual harassment, and assaults of girls at school by teachers, students and other persons in the school community.[64]

- In Ukraine, women's groups reported widespread sexual harassment in the workplace, including coerced sex. Apart from the law that prohibits forced sex with a "materially dependent person" (which applies to employees), legal safeguards against harassment are reportedly inadequate.[65]

- In Kuwait, rape and sexual assault is of concern, particularly for foreign domestic servants, and perpetrated by male employers and co-workers. The local press devotes considerable attention to the problem, and both the police and the courts have taken action against employers when presented with evidence of serious abuse.[66]

- In Hong Kong, China, sexual harassment among women workers in domestic service is an area of major concern, according to a study carried out by the Asian Migrant Centre (AMC) in late 2000 (table 11).

Table 11   Extent of sexual harassment among migrant women workers in domestic service in Hong Kong, China, 2000

Type of sexual harassment/assault experienced	Sample group response rate (%)	Extrapolation over the 220,000 foreign domestic workers
Raped	0.2	440
Coerced to have sex or perform sexual acts	0.3	660
Employers asking them to do sexy things, e.g. dance, wear sexy dress	0.7	1 540
Employers watching them in a malicious manner or peeping at them in a toilet	0.9	1 980
Employers showing them or asking them to touch their bodies, walking naked or in underwear	1.1	2 420
Physical harassment (employers touching their body parts, making other sexual advances, kissing them)	1.3	2 860
Employers talking to them in explicit sexual language, showing them pornographic materials (books, videos, photos)	1.5	3 300

Source: Asian Migrant Centre (AMC), 2000, cited in Haspels et al., 2001, p. 59.

The data displayed in table 11 indicate that migrant women workers in Hong Kong, China, experience a range of forms of sexual harassment and violence. The authors' calculations showed that 440 of the estimated 220,000 foreign domestic workers had been raped.[67] Thus, it is clear that some forms of workplace violence pose a greater threat to women workers than to men.

Workplace violence by gender: Variations in exposure

Gender is an important dynamic in the workplace at large. Women have traditionally been relegated in many societies to lower-paid and lower-status employment than men. Equal opportunity initiatives have begun to redress this imbalance, but the effects of the sexual division of labour and gendered stereotypes remain all too prevalent in many sectors of industry and in many parts of the world.

These "realities" must be taken into account when examining the influence of gender upon experiences of workplace violence. While the majority of cases of aggression or violence overall are experienced by men, there are a range of differing explanations for the male–female gendered experience, including the sexual division of labour (for example, some groups of workers are at greater risk because particular jobs have increased levels of face-to-face contact); gendered socialization to behave in particular ways (for example, men may tend to meet aggression with aggression, while women may act to defuse or avoid aggressive incidents);[68] and/or the fact that women and other workers who are perceived to be "soft targets" may be victimized to a greater extent than men.

The most clear-cut and unambiguous example of workplace violence is homicide. In figure 12 all fatal traumatic workplace injuries in the United States are shown for the year 2002.

As shown in figure 12, the rate of exposure to workplace homicide is several times higher for women than for men. The data indicate that homicide accounts for 31 per cent of all traumatic occupational fatalities for women, compared with 9 per cent for men. By way of contrast, falls pose a greater risk for male workers, accounting for 13 per cent of male fatalities (as compared with 9 per cent for women); and exposure to harmful substances and environments accounts for 10 per cent (4 per cent for women).[69] Undoubtedly the gender division of labour in the United States has a primary influence on exposure to risk. Similar gender-based variations in risk of workplace violence are evident for other countries.

In Finland, exposure to mental violence (bullying) at the workplace poses a significant risk. There appear to be marked variations between male and female workers, as seen in table 12.

Figure 12 Fatal work injury incidents, men and women, United States, 2002
(percentages)

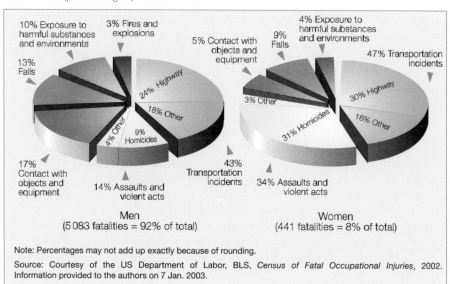

Men
(5 083 fatalities = 92% of total)

Women
(441 fatalities = 8% of total)

Note: Percentages may not add up exactly because of rounding.

Source: Courtesy of the US Department of Labor, BLS, *Census of Fatal Occupational Injuries*, 2002. Information provided to the authors on 7 Jan. 2003.

The data in table 12 indicate that exposure to mental violence (bullying) at the workplace is significantly higher for women than for men. This pattern of increased risk of experiencing bullying for women workers in Finland appears to be accentuating slightly over time.

Thus far workplace violence in many forms has been considered. However, in recent years emerging evidence suggests that domestic violence can "spill over" into workplaces with the potential for dramatic consequences for the victim, co-workers and employer.

The global impact of violence on women, both inside and outside the workplace, is dramatic.[70] Much of this violence occurs in the home and is typically labelled "domestic violence". It is now increasingly acknowledged

Table 12 Mental violence at the workplace by gender, Finland, 1997 and 2003
(percentages)

	1997			2003		
	Total	Men	Women	Total	Men	Women
Continuously	5	4	5	6	4	8
Occasionally	34	29	39	36	30	41
Never	60	65	55	58	66	50
Cannot say	1	1	1	–	–	–

Source: Statistics Finland, *Quality of Work Life Surveys* 1997 and 2003, special elaboration for the authors, 23 Mar. 2004.

that violence of this type can extend to the workplace, with the partners of working women intruding upon their place of employment to inflict physical or psychological aggression upon them. For employers, and for fellow employees, the challenge has become that of providing opportunities for abused women to resist such aggression and obtain refuge from their assailants. At the very least, without appropriate assistance women experiencing violence are likely to be less-productive workers and their physical and mental health placed in jeopardy.

For example, in Eastern Europe:

> domestic violence is the most widespread form of gender-based violence in all the surveyed countries. Across the region the legal systems do not properly address this issue: no specific provisions exist, nor are any restraining orders possible. There is also an insufficient understanding in society of what exactly domestic violence is and thus a failure to always recognize and name it. The lack of knowledge about the nature of domestic violence among women, and the absence of a support network in part explain why women themselves often downplay the seriousness of the abuse. There are no shelters for victims of domestic violence. It is very common for women to stay in an abusive marriage or relationship due to economic dependence on an abusive husband or male partner; at the same time, state authorities do either little or nothing to put an end to this situation. With regard to marital rape, although a few countries changed their legislation, making it an offence, in practice no cases have been decided by the courts.[71]

Why is so much violence perpetrated against women, particularly in the workplace? Evidence presented earlier in this chapter indicated that women are concentrated in many of the higher-risk occupations, essentially as teachers, social workers, nurses and other health-care workers, as well as bank and shop workers.[72] The continued segregation of women in low-paid and low status jobs, while men predominate in better-paid, higher status jobs and supervisory positions, also contributes to this problem.[73]

As shown in figure 13, exposure to sexual harassment among women in EU workplaces is above twice the average for the whole population. A similar increase in risk is experienced by precariously employed workers. The exposure to sexual harassment is even higher for young women workers in the service sector.

Although the percentages displayed in figure 13 cannot be simply added to one another, it is evident that a young woman on a short-term job in the hotel and catering sector can be at special risk of a range of forms of workplace violence. That is, individuals may experience multiple vulnerabilities.

Although it is overwhelmingly women who experience sexual harassment, this form of victimization is not exclusive to one sex. Men also experience harassment, sometimes in a substantial way, as emerging research is showing.

Figure 13   Exposure of women to sexual harassment in the European Union, 2000
(percentages)

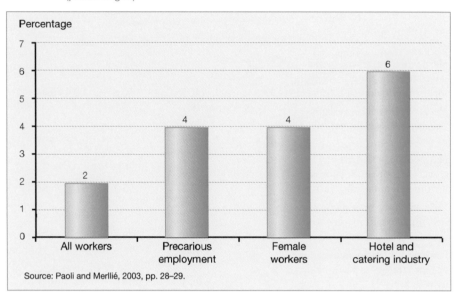

Source: Paoli and Merllié, 2003, pp. 28–29.

For example, a report was compiled for the European Commission on Sexual Harassment in Europe.[74] Other research from Portugal has found evidence that men in a health centre were more frequently victims of sexual harassment than women, which helps to highlight the danger of stereotypes.[75]

A study on sexual harassment in the health and social services sector was conducted in 1996 by the Social Science Research Institute at the University of Iceland.[76] As shown in table 13, the results of the "male and female exposure to sexual harassment" indicate how, depending on the type of question, percentages can change.

The data presented in table 13 indicate that the way questions are asked fundamentally influences the responses. Depending on the wording, sometimes women appear to be disproportionately victimized, at other times men and women experience similar levels of victimization, and occasionally men are victimized more than women. Probably the most surprising finding from the data displayed in table 13 is the relatively similar levels experienced by both men and women.

With bullying in particular, it is also possible that the differential levels of men and women reporting experiences of this form of workplace violence may be due to other factors, including:

• women may be more sensitive to bullying and less hesitant than men to label themselves as bullied;

Table 13   Results of the "Violence Against Nurses" study, Iceland, 1996 (percentages)

Question/sample (n)	Men			Women		
	No	Yes	Sample (n)	No	Yes	Sample (n)
Have you experienced verbal sexual harassment in your work for the past 6 months? (n = 785)	93.1	6.9	101	92.8	7.2	684
Have you ever been verbally sexually harassed in your work? (n = 767)	80.8	19.2	99	79.8	20.2	668
Have you experienced physical sexual harassment in your work for the past 6 months? (n = 786)	98	2	102	93.4	6.6	684
Have you ever been physically sexually harassed in your work? (n = 772)	86	14	100	79.8	20.2	672
Have you ever experienced rape or rape attempt in you work? (n = 771)	98	2	100	99.6	0.4	671

Source: University of Iceland, Social Science Research Institute, 1996.

- men may emphasize the role and responsibility of victims, whereas women may explain bullying by way of perpetrator characteristics or group dynamics;

- there may be a reduced willingness among men to label themselves as bullied;

- the employment of women may be concentrated in larger bureaucracies where dominant/subordinate positions are more common and where bullying can therefore thrive; and/or

- women may be concentrated in lower positions in hierarchies and hence be targeted more frequently by perpetrators of bullying.

The higher prevalence rates reported by women could thus be seen as the result of an interaction between both higher actual exposure rates to negative behaviours and less reluctance to classify these experiences as bullying.[77]

It is important to consider that, while women may be disproportionately victimized, this very fact does not justify a generalized statement such as "all men are perpetrators, all women are victims". In fact, although often to a lesser extent, women are also perpetrators of a range of forms of workplace violence. For example, research conducted by the Italian association Donne & Qualità della

Vita in more than 150 companies covering the entire Italian territory revealed that of 1,000 cases of mobbing, 38 per cent were perpetrated by female managers.[78]

Finally, it is important to recognize that other groups of workers can be marginalized. In particular, young and adolescent workers usually occupy jobs lower in the hierarchy, generally have fewer job skills and also tend to be disproportionately represented in precarious employment. As a result, young workers may also be vulnerable to workplace violence.

The vulnerability of young workers to workplace violence

Another common finding is the vulnerability of younger workers to violent victimization at the workplace. There are a range of reasons, including lack of experience in dealing with violent situations, inability to behave with self-confidence when confronted with aggression, vulnerability in the labour market, and/or lack of understanding of workers' protections enshrined in labour laws and regulations governing conditions of employment. Further, the job tasks assigned to young workers may expose them to increased levels of risk as, for example, if employed casually in a late night video store.

In the **United Kingdom**, for example, staff aged 18 to 30 working on the London Underground were found to have a higher probability of becoming victims of assault than older staff. As can be seen in figure 14, the risk for assaults decreases steadily with age.

Figure 14   Age profile of London Underground Ltd. (LUL), employees and staff assaulted, January 1993 to August 1996

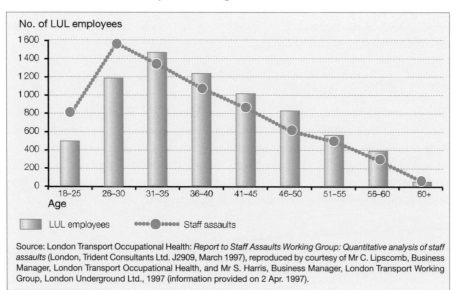

Source: London Transport Occupational Health: *Report to Staff Assaults Working Group: Quantitative analysis of staff assaults* (London, Trident Consultants Ltd. J2909, March 1997), reproduced by courtesy of Mr C. Lipscomb, Business Manager, London Transport Occupational Health, and Mr S. Harris, Business Manager, London Transport Working Group, London Underground Ltd., 1997 (information provided on 2 Apr. 1997).

Table 14   Employees reporting mobbing, by age, Germany, 2000 (percentages)

Age	% reporting mobbing
Under 25 years	3.7
25–34 years	2.6
35–44 years	2.6
44–54 years	2.2
55 years and above	2.9

Source: Meschkutat, Stackelbeck and Langenhoff, 2002, p. 28.

In the **United States**, the majority of workplace homicides during the period 1996–2000 occurred among male workers; almost half of these occurred to workers aged 25 to 44.[79]

In **Canada**, 25.9 per cent of all work accidents with at least one working day lost (including following acts of workplace violence) occurred to workers in the 15–29 age bracket.[80]

In **Germany**, it has been found that young workers (under 25 years) are at the greatest risk of being mobbed. These data are shown in table 14.

Thus, the available data indicate that around the industrialized world, young workers are at increased risk of exposure to workplace violence. Much of this increased vulnerability is undoubtedly due to the concentration of young workers in higher-risk jobs (such as those in the retail sector). However, it is also likely that their lack of power in the labour market results in a reduced willingness to speak out about inappropriate behaviour, a reluctance that has been demonstrated for other marginalized workers in the discussions earlier in this chapter.

From general to specific

The general patterns and trends of violence illustrated in this chapter confirm the global magnitude and the dramatic importance of the problem of workplace violence. Within this general context, a number of occupations and situations at special risk have been identified which deserve particular attention in order to focus research and action where most required. These occupations and situations are dealt with in Chapter 3.

Notes

[1] WHO, 2002b, p. 5.

[2] Wynne et al., 1997, p. 1.

[3] ILO, 2004b, p. 4, para. 1.3.1.

[4] Ibid.

[5] However, some official statistics may include information about crimes of violence committed against law enforcement officers in the course of their duties. Other vulnerable occupational groups such as taxi drivers and journalists are more likely to gather any such statistical data through their respective enterprises or trade union groups.

[6] ILO, 2004b, p. 4, para. 1.3.1, footnote 1.

[7] Ibid., p. 6, para. 1.3.3.

[8] Wynne et al., 1997, p. 5.

[9] In earlier editions of this book data obtained from the International Crime Victimization Survey (ICVS) have been considered. After consultations with members of the International Working Group which coordinates this survey (composed of representatives of the Ministry of Justice of the Netherlands, the United Nations Interregional Crime and Justice Research Institute (UNICRI) and the Home Office of the United Kingdom), it has been decided not to include data from the survey in this new edition of the book. This decision is based in part upon certain concerns about the past reliability and comparability of the information engendered by the survey, and especially that relating to sexual incidents, and to the non-availability of more current and comprehensive survey data than that already displayed in the first and second editions of this book, published respectively in 1998 and 2000.

[10] Paoli and Merllié, 2001, pp. 63–64.

[11] European Foundation for the Improvement of Living and Working Conditions, 2003, p. 4.

[12] Ibid.

[13] Since May 2004, Cyprus, Czech Republic, Estonia, Hungary, Latvia, Lithuania, Malta, Poland, Slovenia, Slovakia are Member States. Bulgaria and Romania hope to join by 2007.

[14] Paoli and Parent-Thirion, 2003, pp. 63 and 64.

[15] Di Martino, Hoel and Cooper, 2003, p. 39; European Foundation for the Improvement of Living and Working Conditions, 2003, p. 4.

[16] Di Martino, Hoel and Cooper, 2003, p. 36.

[17] Ibid.

[18] Ibid., p. 39. See also Sadler et al., 2001, pp. 325–334.

[19] European Foundation for the Improvement of Living and Working Conditions, 2003, p. 41.

[20] Paoli and Merllié, 2001, pp. 28–29. See also: European Commission, 2001, p. 11.

[21] Hoel and Cooper, Nov. 2000, cited in Rayner et al., 2002.

[22] Ibid., p. 41.

[23] Paoli and Parent-Thirion, 2003, p. 64.

[24] Ibid, p. 64.

[25] European Commission, 1998, p. 16.

[26] Di Martino, Hoel and Cooper, 2003, p. 28.

[27] Ibid.

[28] Ibid.

[29] Sczesny and Stahlberg, 2000, p. 127.

[30] Confederación Sindical de Comisiones Obreras (CO.OC), Spain, 2000, table 2, p. 28. See also Di Martino, Hoel and Cooper, 2003, p. 29.

[31] Statistics Sweden (Statistiska Centralbyrån), 1999, p. 24.

[32] Italian Institute of Statistics (ISTAT), 2004.

[33] Ibid.

[34] Richardson and Windau, 2003, pp. 673–689.

[35] Ibid.

[36] US Department of Labor, Bureau of Labor Statistics (BLS), 2002, table 5.

[37] Duhart, 2001, pp. 1–2.

[38] National Institute for Occupational Safety and Health (NIOSH), 2004, p. 1.

[39] US Merit Systems Protection Board, 1995.

[40] Fitzgerald and Shulman, 1993, cited in Murray, 1998, p. 1.

[41] Murray, 1998, pp. 1–2.

[42] Palmieri et al., 2003, p. 85.

[43] Sadler et al., 2001, pp. 325–334, especially p. 327.

[44] US Department of Labor, Equal Employment Opportunity Commission, 2002.

[45] International Confederation of Free Trade Unions (ICFTU), 2004, p. 2.

[46] ILO, 2005.

[47] Case No. 2341 (Nepal): Report in which the Committee requests to be kept informed of developments, paras. 631–654.

[48] Case No. 2203 (Guatemala): Interim report, paras. 405–465; case No. 2259 (Guatemala): Interim report, paras. 431–465; case No. 2295 (Guatemala): Interim report, paras. 466–478.

[49] Case No. 2328 (Zimbabwe): Report in which the Committee requests to be kept informed of developments, paras. 866–890; case No. 2365 (Zimbabwe): Interim report, paras. 891–914.

[50] United Nations, Commission of Human Rights, 2003, paras. 182 and 382.

[51] Ibid., para. 730.

[52] Ibid., para. 815.

[53] Human Rights Watch, 2004a, Part IV, p. 14.

[54] Idem, 2004b.

[55] Ibid.

[56] Streetnet International, 2004, Annexure 6.

[57] Di Martino, 2002b, p. 16.

[58] Haspels et al., 2001.

[59] Ibid., p. 16.

[60] Ibid., p. 58.

[61] Ibid., p. 60.

[62] Effah-Chukwuma and Osarenren, 2001, p. 93.

[63] Musri and Daud, 2002, pp. 10–12.

[64] Human Rights Watch, 2001.

[65] United Nations, Commission of Human Rights, 2003, para. 2142.

[66] Ibid., para. 763.

[67] AMC, 2000, cited in Haspels et al., 2001 p. 59.

[68] Suzy Lamplugh Trust, 1994b, pp. J:13:9:5–J:13:9:6.

[69] Courtesy of the US Department of Labor, BLS. Information provided to the authors on 7 Jan. 2003.

[70] US Bureau of Justice Statistics, 1998.

[71] United Nations, Commission of Human Rights, 2003, para. 1857.

[72] Aromaa, 1993, p. 145. See also chapters in VandenBos and Bulatao (eds.), 1996: Hurrell et al., 1996, pp. 163–170; and Lanza, 1996, pp. 189–198 respectively.

[73] Lim, L., 1996, p. 17.

[74] European Commission, Directorate-General for Employment, Industrial Relations and Social Affairs, 1998.

[75] Ferrinho et al., 2002. An overview of the findings from this survey has been incorporated into Di Martino, 2002b, p. 16.

[76] University of Iceland, Social Science Research Institute, 1996.

[77] Di Martino, Hoel and Cooper, 2003, p. 26.

[78] Donne & Qualità della Vita. No date.

[79] Richardson and Windau, 2003, pp. 673–689, especially p. 681.

[80] Développement Ressources Humaines Canada (DHRC), 2000, p. 48.

OCCUPATIONS AND SITUATIONS AT RISK

3

The available evidence on the general patterns of workplace violence, incidence ratios and severity estimates were elaborated in Chapter 2. As was identified, workers in a number of occupational groups and situations were at increased risk. These higher-risk scenarios are examined in detail in this chapter.

Although no occupation can be said to be entirely immune from some form of workplace violence, it is widely acknowledged that workers performing certain tasks are at special risk, as box 14 indicates. Journalists are not alone in confronting life-threatening violence as part of their working life. Policing

---

Box 14   Human Rights Day 2004: Media killings

The International Federation of Journalists (IFJ) today marked International Human Rights Day with a new call for governments to take urgent action to defend journalists and media staff whose rights have been routinely violated in a year that threatens to be the worst on record for the number of reporters and media staff killed.

"On this international human rights day journalists and media staff have little to celebrate", said Aidan White, IFJ General Secretary. "With more than 100 deaths, including targeted assassinations, and with growing evidence of callous disregard of media rights by governments, 2004 is turning into a year of brutality and abuse."

The IFJ has recorded 120 deaths so far this year. Many of the killings have been in Iraq, where 67 have died since the invasion of the country last year. One of the most dangerous regions this year has been the Philippines where 12 journalists have been murdered. In all 61 journalists have been killed since 1985, but not one of the killers has been brought to justice.

The IFJ and other media industry groups have responded to the ongoing crisis by establishing the International News Safety Institute, which is working to promote a culture of safety in journalism. Last month the INSI (International News Safety Institute) announced a new inquiry into the scope of international law and its capacity to protect journalists and media staff.

Source: International Federation of Journalists, 2004.

Box 15   Redfern Riots

On 15 February 2004 a riot broke out in Redfern, an inner city suburb of Sydney, Australia. The riot was sparked by the accidental death of a young Aboriginal boy [Thomas "TJ" Hickey]. The following is a description of several police officers' experiences of that occasion.

Sargent (Sgt) Baxter reported for duty at 6 a.m. on 15 February with little inkling of what his shift would bring. There was some tension following the death of Thomas "TJ" Hickey. Sgt Baxter went to the scene at 4.30 p.m.

There were reports of damage to civilian cars and of rocks being thrown at the railway station. The windscreens of police cars were also smashed. Police attempts to defuse the situation by holding a media conference to correct rumours blaming them for TJ's death didn't have the desired effect. Although due to knock off duty at 6.00 p.m., Sgt Baxter, along with the rest of the day shift, was kept back. After dark, he said, the situation "steadily escalated" with the rioters pursuing police back into the railway station at around 7.30 p.m. The main entrance of the railway station was closed after windows were smashed by the rock-throwing crowd. Six platforms of the station were also closed to civilians for safety reasons.

Despite attempts at negotiation by Redfern Commander Superintendent Dennis Smith, around 9.00 p.m. the situation worsened again. "A group ran up the street throwing rocks at police and jumping on vehicles. They were smashing the police cars and stealing the batons." At 9.04 p.m. Sgt Baxter deemed the situation so dangerous he called a signal one [a high priority alert].

Acting Sgt Greg Wright, who was part of the oncoming nightshift, said: "Without a doubt that's the most violent riot I've been involved in … I would liken that riot to the first 10 minutes of the movie *Saving Private Ryan*, when they got on that beach. We were getting hit with missiles but couldn't see where they were coming from."

Sgt Baxter suffered some bruising but other officers were not so lucky. "I noticed a few blokes knocked down, one was knocked out. Senior Constable Michael McGowan was knocked unconscious by a brick and required hospitalization for head injuries. He later described the riot as akin to British soccer riots. "I could see people bending down and picking up paving stones and throwing them directly at us … nothing in my training could prepare me for something that significant … About 40 police sustained injuries, eight requiring hospitalization for leg, knee and head injuries."

Source: Silva, 2004, pp. 7–9.

is another high-risk occupation where responding to violence often represents a routine hazard. Sometimes that hazard can prove to be extremely dangerous and distressing, as the account in box 15 illustrates.

Further indication of the occupations at greatest risk of workplace violence can be found among the comprehensive data generated by the British Crime Survey (BCS) and the British Health and Safety Executive's (HSE)

Reporting of Injuries, Disease and Dangerous Occurrences Regulations (RIDDOR). Estimates from the 2002/03 BCS show that the occupational grouping with the highest risk of assault was protective service occupations (such as police officer) at 12.6 per cent (12,600 per 100,000 workers), more than 14 times the average risk.[1] Several of the health-related occupational groups followed, including health and social welfare associate professionals (3.3 per cent, or 3,300 per 100,000 workers), and medical and dental practitioners (2.3 per cent).[2] RIDDOR figures[3] (which are calculated using narrower definitions of occupational groups) indicate that for the same period the highest estimated rates of fatal, major and over three-day injuries were found among prison officers (1,665 per 100,000 workers), police officers (541 per 100,000 workers), bus and coach drivers (360 per 100,000 workers) and care assistants (195 per 100,000 workers).[4]

It is now widely acknowledged that the magnitude of exposure to violence at work depends not only on a person's occupation, but also upon the circumstances or situations under which that person is performing a specific task or duty. These "situations at risk" include those associated with working alone; working with the public; working with valuables; working with people in distress; working in an environment increasingly open to violence; working in conditions of special vulnerability; working in military and paramilitary organizations; and working in zones of conflict. While each of these situations requires separate analysis and discussion, it needs to be emphasized that certain occupational groups may be exposed to a combination of these risk-related situations at any one time. For example, law enforcement officers are in frequent contact with members of the public and people in distress; taxi drivers with members of the public while handling valuables and working alone; and social workers with distressed people while also being alone.

Working alone

The number of people working alone is increasing. As automation spreads in factories and offices, often accompanied by processes of rationalization of production and reorganization of the workplace, solitary work becomes more frequent. This trend extends outside the traditional workplace into the growing practice of subcontracting, outplacement, teleworking, networking and "new" self-employment. The push towards increased mobility and the development of interactive communication technologies also favour one-person operations.

Working alone full time is only part of the picture. A much greater number of people work alone part of the time. In a survey among public employees in **Canada**, for example, nearly 84 per cent of respondents indicated

Box 16   Growing fears for safety of people working alone in the service sector:
Threat of violence more prevalent than in past years

A growing number of Finns work alone. This phenomenon has proliferated in the service industry in particular, with extensions to the opening hours of supermarkets and kiosks, and owners seeking to make even the quieter hours profitable.

In the public sector, such as in health care, the primary reason for lower staff numbers is a need to cut personnel expenses. The outsourcing of various tasks has also contributed to the number of people working alone.

According to the estimates of different organizations and authorities, there may already be 200,000 people in Finland who work alone for the majority of the time. This amount accounts for 10 per cent of the workforce.

Source: Talli, 2003.

that they **often** worked alone.[5] The same is true of a substantial percentage of service workers in **Finland** (box 16).

Solitary work does not automatically imply a higher risk of violence. It is generally understood, however, that working alone may increase the vulnerability of the workers concerned. This vulnerability level will depend on the type of situation in which the lone work is being carried out. For the lone worker, a short cut down a back street may be perfectly reasonable in broad daylight, but might be asking for trouble on a dark night. Mail delivery may be a dangerous activity in a crime-infested area, while being completely safe in a crime-free district.

People can find themselves working alone in a wide variety of situations.

Small shops, petrol stations and kiosks

Such workers are often seen as an "easy" target by aggressors, and are therefore particularly exposed to violence. In **South Africa**, an average of 60 per cent of some 426 petrol retailing sites surveyed in the 36 months prior to July 2002 had experienced violent crime.[6]

In **Australia**, recent research has shown that service stations (petrol retailing sites) are particularly vulnerable to attack. Since 1993 the proportion of all robberies occurring at service stations has increased substantially, with an overall rise being reported of 214 per cent in robberies at such premises between 1993 and 2000. Data from a national survey of small businesses, conducted in 1998–99, showed that 8 per cent of service stations reported at least one incident of robbery in the previous 12 months.[7] Further, 80 per cent of robberies occurred at service stations where only one staff member was on duty.

Working alone outside normal hours

Cleaners, maintenance and repair workers appear to be at special risk. For example, the cleaning sector, characterized by a large number of small enterprises and by precarious and unskilled work, is a typical case where women workers are frequently abused or harassed. These women are often migrant workers and, as such, particularly exposed to harassment and abuse both by superiors in the cleaning company and by someone in the client company.[8]

Taxi drivers

Taxi drivers are also usually sole operators. They have one of the highest levels of work-related homicide and serious assault in countries across the industrialized work.[9] In the **United States**, for example, taxi drivers face the highest risk for fatal assault – more than 30 times the risk of the average American worker.[10] The average annual rate of violent victimization over the period 1993–99 was 128.3 per 1,000 workers (the second most dangerous occupation after police officers).[11]

In **South Africa** the risks faced by taxi drivers are again very high. Between 1 January 1996 and 30 April 2000, 1,096 taxi killings were reported.[12] In South Africa there have also been reports of "taxi wars" in which gangster outfits literally shoot each other off the road; as a result thousands have died through bloody violence or in road crashes.[13]

In **Australia** three separate studies have focused on violence against taxi drivers in different states: Victoria, New South Wales and Queensland. While the studies were conducted by different researchers and the methodologies were slightly different, the findings were very similar. In each of the three studies taxi drivers were identified to be at significant risk of verbal abuse, threats, assaults and homicide. For example, in the Queensland-based study, 81 per cent had been verbally abused over the previous 12-month period, 17 per cent threatened and 10 per cent assaulted.[14]

Where sole operators also have repeated face-to-face contact with clients or customers, the risks are heightened. Indeed, evidence suggests that all workers with significant levels of client/customer interaction are at heightened risk of exposure to workplace violence.

Working in contact with the public

A wide variety of occupations and numerous working situations involve contact with the public. While in most circumstances this type of work can be generally agreeable, there are cases where exposure to the public can create a higher risk of violence.

Table 15   Occupations most at risk of assaults at work, 2001/02 and 2002/03
British Crime Survey interviews

% victims once or more	Assaults
Protective service occupations	12.6
Health and social welfare associate professionals	3.3
Transport and mobile machine drivers and operatives	1.9
Managers and proprietors in agriculture and services	1.8
Health professionals	1.4
Caring personal service occupations	1.3
Leisure and other personal service occupations	1.1
Teaching and research professionals	1.0
Elementary administration and service occupations	0.9
Corporate managers	0.8
All occupations	0.9

Source: Upson, 2004, p.10.

Table 15, based on responses from 100 union representatives in the **United Kingdom** covering a total of 90,000 workers, provides an overall – though subjective – impression of the magnitude of violent incidents across a number of commercial and service sectors where workers came into contact with the public during the course of their work.

The reasons for such violence are multiple, as has been suggested in Chapter 2. In very large organizations dealing with a large number of the general public, workers are likely to meet some individuals with a history of violence or dangerous mental illness, or who are intoxicated. This "random" aggression is very difficult to predict and can lead to very serious incidents.

In other cases, violent behaviour may be provoked by or result from a perceived or actual poor quality of service. Violence may also be triggered by dismissive and uncaring behaviour by the worker providing the service, or be a more general attack on the organization itself, based on a general non-fulfilment of the wishes and expectations of the customer, which has nothing to do directly with the actual conflict at a particular moment.

Bus, train and subway workers

These workers are often the easiest target of blame for any inadequacy regarding the standard of transport. Disputes over the cost of fares, hooliganism and traffic accidents increase the risk of aggression against transport workers, while aggression against other passengers and vandalism to property complete the picture.

Table 16   Recorded assaults on British railway workers, 1999–2004

1999	2000	2001	2002	2003	2004
1 479	1 720	2 261	3 017	3 640	3 847

Source: Rail Safety and Standards Board, 2004, p. 174.

In table 16, recorded assaults on British railway workers are provided. These data cover the period 1999–2004. As can be seen, assaults on railway workers have continued to rise over the six-year period. The report states:

> 53 per cent of assaults occur at stations (which also accounted for the small increase in 2004) and almost all the remainder are on board trains (which have the larger proportion of verbal assaults). The revenue protection function, platform staff and on-board staff are the groups most affected. The number of assaults related to fare evasion account for about 30 per cent of the total, although for the first time in recent years they remained broadly unchanged in 2004. Women report more non-physical assaults than men.[15]

A similar pattern is evident for workers on buses. Nearly 7,000 crimes were reported on London buses alone in 2001. These events included stabbings, graffiti, stone throwing and other serious incidents of violence.[16] However, attacks were not limited to bus workers in London: two of the largest bus companies in the north-east of England say that they together are short of 200 drivers. Rather, violence appears to be a widespread phenomenon, as the statements in box 17 indicate.

Violence is also perpetrated by passengers on aeroplanes. The reported incidence may vary marginally between short- and long-haul flights, between

Box 17   Attacks spark bus driver crisis

Rising violence against bus drivers has sparked a recruitment crisis which is threatening some services, it is claimed.

Two of the largest bus companies in the north-east of England say together they are short of about 200 drivers.

Alan Gray, regional organizer for the Transport and General Workers' Union (TGWU), blamed the crisis on an escalating number of attacks on drivers. Mr Gray called on the industry to do more to protect drivers ...

Several bus companies have introduced security measures in an effort to better protect drivers from attack.

Many buses now have CCTV cameras installed.

And in some areas undercover and uniformed police officers travel on buses at night in problem areas.

Source: BBC News: "Attacks spark bus driver crisis", 2003a.

different companies and for different occupational groups. For example, one study reported that 82.5 per cent of airport check-in workers had experienced verbal abuse, 17.4 per cent had been threatened and 4.5 per cent stated that they had been physically assaulted.[17] The risk factors appear to be similar for flight attendants.

Flight attendants

Flight attendants are another category of workers at major risk of violence. Air rage, extreme misbehaviour by unruly passengers exacerbated by excessive alcohol consumption, smoking bans, crowding and long flights is becoming a growing concern for airlines and their crews.[18] Violence on board also poses a serious threat to other passengers, as well as to flight safety.

It is difficult to obtain accurate statistics of the number of air rage incidents because airlines do not always keep or disclose records. However, it is known that the number of reports of aggressive and disruptive passengers and air rage has increased exponentially in recent years.[19] Unambiguous data are also difficult to obtain because there is also lack of agreement as to what constitutes air rage. British Airways recorded 266 incidents of disruptive behaviour on board aircraft in a 12-month period to the end of March 1998.[20] This number represented a 400 per cent increase since 1995. Similarly, American Airlines reported a 200 per cent increase in passenger interference with flight attendants' duties between 1994 and 1995. There were 450 similar incidents on board United Airlines flights in 1997. Thus, it is unsurprising that, according to the US Federal Aviation Administration, the number of incidents of passenger misconduct has more than doubled in the period 1995–2001, as shown in table 17. In 2002, figures for the full year were not available. Nevertheless, by 12 December, 216 incidents had been reported.

Table 17   US Federal Aviation Administration: Number of incidents of passenger misconduct, 1995–2001[1]

Year	No. of incidents
1995	146
1996	188
1997	321
1998	282
1999	310
2000	321
2001	321

[1] In 2002, figures for the full year were not available. Nevertheless, by 12 December, 216 incidents had been reported.

Source: Federal Aviation Administration, 2003.

These risks to workers in the transport industry subsectors are replicated among other groups which have significant levels of face-to-face contact with clients/customers. Indeed, some groups of workers face the additional risks of violence – or the threat of violence – during armed hold-ups, for example workers employed in the retail sector.

Shop workers in the retail sector

Shop workers can be exposed to violence from customers because of poor retail service or inferior products. Violence may also originate from customers who have grown impatient at checkouts, who try to pay with illegal credit cards or to exceed their cash limit, or during a hold-up. Drunken customers wanting to buy alcohol can also pose a problem to shop workers. The risks to staff are increased by late-night opening hours.[21] The British Retail Consortium (BRC) survey of losses in the retail industry showed that six employees in every 1,000 were victims of physical violence in 2002; an average of 18 staff per 1,000 were subjected to threats of violence; and 11 employees in every 1,000 suffered verbal abuse.[22] By 2003 violence against staff had risen by 17 per cent, with verbal abuse directed to staff more than doubling by 109 per cent and threats to staff soaring by 161 per cent.[23]

Workers providing social services

Violence may also be the final desperate act from extremely marginalized members of the public searching for a response to their pressing basic needs. Desperation does not automatically involve violence; however, it can pave the way for attitudes of revolt against what is felt to be unjust treatment, and eventually lead to abuse against the workers providing the service. In **Canada** for example, 61 per cent of social service and institutional workers in the province of Alberta reported having been verbally threatened, 42 per cent physically threatened and 30 per cent physically assaulted, according to a 1994 survey.[24]

In the **United Kingdom** 36 per cent of health and social welfare associate professionals (such as youth workers) reported being very or fairly worried about assaults at work. These findings were cited in the 2002/2003 British Crime Survey.[25] Similar findings have been reported from workers in the tourism and hospitality industry sectors.

Hotel, catering and restaurant staff

The relationship with the customer is often considered "personal", and any lack of commitment to the service, or insensitivity to the client's needs, may be perceived as a personal offence and lead to aggressive behaviour. Bar staff appear particularly exposed to assault by members of the public. A 1997 survey on the extent of violence in southern England's pubs revealed that 24 per cent of licensees felt "highly" at risk, and nearly another quarter felt themselves to be at risk "quite a lot".[26]

A 2000 survey of 274 students on a hospitality and catering course in a British higher education institution showed that 57 per cent had experienced some kind of unwanted sexual attention during periods of supervised work experience.[27] Most experiences involved verbal harassment such as suggestive remarks and abuse, followed by suggestive looks. The majority of the cases (88 per cent) involved a female student being harassed by a male. The perpetrators included colleagues, managers and customers.

Experiences of sexual harassment are also reported from the **United States** and from Asian countries, though to a substantially varying degree. In a comparative study of employees in restaurants in New Orleans (United States) and **Hong Kong, China**, 74.7 per cent and 25.3 per cent of employees respectively[28] responded positively to the question: "Have you ever felt that a customer, a manager or a co-worker was sexually harassing you?"

A 2002 Spanish survey on bullying of employees in the tourism sector concluded that 16 per cent had been exposed to psychological violence on a weekly or more frequent basis (measured as exposure to one or more negative behaviours associated with psychological violence during the past six months).[29] Among the respondents, 45 per cent had witnessed bullying taking place. According to the victims, the perpetrators were primarily bosses or managers (82 per cent), while colleagues accounted for 16 per cent of the incidents. In 47 per cent of cases, the violence had lasted more than one year, and in 30 per cent of cases, two years or more.[30] Looking at specific behaviours, the most commonly reported acts suffered were "giving meaningless work", "giving work below one's professional competencies", "putting under undue pressure" and "systematically devaluing the effort of the person" [author's translation from the original Spanish].

Dancers and other performing artists

Bullying appears to be particularly prevalent in the dance profession. From a nationwide survey of bullying in the **United Kingdom**, 14.1 per cent of respondents from the profession reported having been bullied in the previous six months and 29.6 per cent in the past five years, and 50 per cent reported having witnessed bullying in the previous five years.[31] Moreover, 75 per cent of perpetrators were identified as managers, 33 per cent as colleagues and 8.3 per cent as subordinates – some respondents identified perpetrators from more than one category. High levels of "unwanted sexual attention" are also reported in the dance profession (14.4 per cent) as compared to other professions; for example, the comparable figure for banking was 3.8 per cent.[32]

Some dancers, particularly those employed in "exotic dancing" such as stage dancing, table dancing and lap dancing, reported social disillusionment and increased health problems due to: costume and appearance restrictions; dirty work environments; coercion by management and customers to perform particular types of dance; sexual harassment; physical assault; forced sex; and the effects of stigmatization.[33] Their problems were compounded by allegations that the police failed to take any action, and accused victims of attracting trouble and being responsible for their own state of affairs ("victim blaming"). While some dancers might expect to be exposed to a certain level of harassment, this risk is probably not expected for library workers.

Librarians

While violence in the workplace is often associated with working in contact with the public, little consideration is usually given to the fact that librarians are also quite likely to experience an act of violence or aggression from members of the public during their working lives. Public librarians are more susceptible to violence than academic and other special librarians, as their open-door policy allows anyone to use the building. This can sometimes invite trouble from asocial citizens who can cause disruption and uneasiness, and even lead to acts of extreme violence. Several cases have been reported in the **United States** where guns have been used by robbers or members of the public harbouring extreme grievances against employees.[34] Some librarians have even been killed. If there are significant amounts of money or valuable goods on site, workers are generally exposed to an increased risk of violence, for example, violence associated with hold-ups.

Working with valuables and cash handling

Whenever valuables are, or seem to be, within "easy reach" there is a risk that crime, and increasingly violent crime, may be committed. Workers in many sectors are exposed to such a risk. At special risk of robbery-related violence are workers in shops, post offices, financial institutions, or anywhere people handle cash.

Shops

Low numbers of staff, a lack of training and poor security measures compound the risk of robbery-related violence. Small shops can be particularly vulnerable, especially at opening and closing times. So too can pharmacies, which are likely to be targeted for both cash and drugs.

In **Australia**, a national survey of small businesses has revealed that during 1998–99 11 per cent of pharmacies reported at least one incident of robbery in the previous 12 months.[35] A majority of these pharmacy robberies occurred while two or more staff were on duty. Repeat victimization was also a key factor in understanding the profile of robberies, with 5 per cent of all pharmacies in the sample accounting for nearly three-quarters of all reported robberies. Similar risks exist in other retail businesses.

Postal service

As noted earlier, postal work has been identified as a "high-risk" occupation for exposure to violence from co-workers, and the term "going postal" has become synonymous in the United States with severe acts of workplace violence such as homicide. However, the evidence does not support the belief that American postal workers are in fact more at risk of death and serious injury than other occupational groups.

The nature of postal work means that employees face the risk of violence emanating from people outside the work environment. For example, a series of bio-terrorism/anthrax cases occurred in the United States in 2001, where emergency precautions were taken in response to the threat. These events highlighted the omnipresent dangers that postal workers face while processing mass volumes of mail, and the need to remain particularly vigilant to suspect objects such as bombs and incendiary devices.

Postal workers also face the risk of hold-up related aggression from the public, as a result of being associated with handling cash and valuables in post offices, for example. These workers may also be at risk of heightened stress from organizational reforms, the impact of mergers and acquisitions, globalization, new technology, new work practices, audits of business performance and the like. In the United Kingdom, 14 per cent of a sample of postal workers saw the threat of violence as bad or very bad.[36]

Post office workers may be at particular risk of experiencing workplace bullying. In a British nationwide study on workplace bullying involving responses from 5,288 workers, it was estimated that approximately one in ten people had been bullied at work over the previous six-month period.[37] The highest incidence rates were reported in post and telecommunications (16 per cent and 27 per cent), the prison service (16 per cent in the past six months and 32 per cent in the previous five years), school teaching (15.5 per cent and 35 per cent) and dance professions (14 per cent and 28 per cent).[38]

These high reported ratios of workplace bullying have strained relationships between managers, employees and workers' organizations. They have also given rise to job insecurity, dissatisfaction and conflict among the workforce, and can lead to workers feeling unable to cope with the demands made upon them. According to an American Postal Workers Union (APWU) spokesperson:

"Better than 1 in 3 USPS [United States Postal Service] craft employees will be a victim of abuse or bullying during their career. This is higher than the national average. Most will never report it. Many will either be fired or will resign."[39]

High levels of job dissatisfaction, low morale and poor management–employee relations negatively impact on the behaviour of postal workers.[40] In the United States Postal Service, out of a total workforce of around 700,000 in the sector, postal worker grievances amount to approximately 150,000 a year, and around 69,000 postal workers face disciplinary hearings from management.[41] Nevertheless, hold-up related violence is most likely to result in a workplace homicide, and hold-ups are most likely in worksites that have large amounts of money on hand.

Financial institutions

Attacks upon financial institutions, and especially banks which are required as a part of their normal business operations to handle large sums of cash, have long represented a hazard for workers in the financial sector. While increased security measures have in recent years been successful in reducing the incidence of bank robberies, this type of crime remains a matter of concern. Table 18 illustrates the pattern of bank hold-ups in the United States. In 2001, there were more than 8,500 bank robberies, translating to approximately one robbery each hour (just under every 52 minutes) with a total loss of approximately US$70 million.

Table 18   Number of bank robbery incidents, United States, 1990–2001[1]

Year	BCS	Summary UCR
1990	8 042	9 589
1991	9 532	11 004
1992	9 540	11 432
1993	8 561	11 876
1994	7 081	8 663
1995	6 986	9 289
1996	8 362	10 741
1997	8 082	9 461
1998	7 711	8 486
1999	6 813	8 193
2000	7 310	8 565
2001	8 516	10 450

[1] Reported in Bank Crime Statistics database and the summary Uniform Crime Reporting Programme

Source: Federal Bureau of Investigation, United States, 2005.

Figure 15   Bank robberies by month, Australia, January 1998 to April 2002

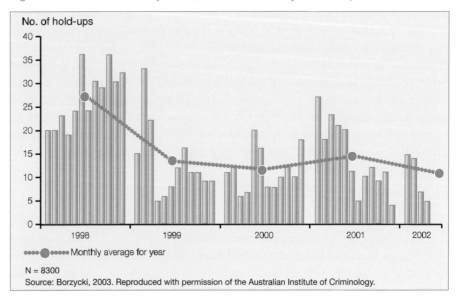

Longitudinal trend data indicate that the level of this type of crime has remained practically unchanged in the last decade.

There are cases, however, where heightened security adopted by banks and building societies has made them safer places in which to work. In South Africa, according to the Institute for Security Studies, the number of bank robberies has sharply declined, from 561 in the period April 1996–March 1997 to 127 in the period April 2002–March 2003.[42]

A similar trend is reported for Australia. In figure 15, bank robberies over the period January 1998 to April 2002 are displayed graphically. The monthly average of bank robberies has decreased over this five-year period. However, it may be that some of the hold-up related violence has merely been displaced to other, more vulnerable groups of workers handling money and valuables.

Private security industry employees

Mention has already been made of the risks of workplace violence experienced by police officers. A related occupational group which also experiences high rates of workplace violence is that of private security guards (also known as security officers). In many countries, guards are employed to protect vulnerable businesses against the threat of attack. Such businesses include not only banks but also jewellery stores, betting shops, gambling casinos and other work sites where large amounts of cash and valuables are located.

Although these workers usually receive special training to cope with violence, its prevalence and the pace of its growth are such that coping becomes more and more difficult. In the private security business, the cash-in-transit sector is possibly the most susceptible to attack, with ruthless criminal groups being prepared on occasions to kill guards protecting valuable items.

So far, this chapter has examined occupations at particular risk of workplace violence because staff work alone, have extensive face-to-face contact with members of the public, or have significant amounts of cash or valuables on site (an inducement to hold-up related violence). However, it is also probable that particular types of people are more likely to perpetrate acts of violence against workers. The discussion now turns to an examination of the characteristics of people who may have an increased proclivity to commit violence against workers.

Working with people in distress

People who are fearful, in distress, in pain or desperate may have an increased proclivity to commit violence. Workers in the health-care sector are quite likely to have face-to-face contact with such people, and as a result health workers are often victimized (box 18).

Box 18   Doctors and nurses want more protection from assault

Inadequate protection is being given to health care staff from violent attacks, it was claimed yesterday [19 December 2004].

The British Medical Association, Royal College of Nursing and the Royal College of Midwives claim that the Emergency Workers (Scotland) Bill, which makes it a specific offence to assault an emergency worker, has created anomalies.

The three organizations are calling on MSPs [Members of the Scottish Parliament] to support an amendment by the Nationalist MSP Stewart Stevenson during a debate in the Scottish Parliament on Wednesday. The amendment calls for all doctors, registered nurses and midwives to be given the same level of protection afforded to ambulance, fire and police personnel. The Bill makes it an offence to assault or impede police, fire or ambulance personnel at any time when they are on duty.

The NHS [National Health Service] Scotland Occupational Health and Safety Survey, published by the Scottish Executive last May, found that one in 10 staff suffers verbal or physical attacks in the course of a year and found that out of all NHS staff, nurses and midwives experience the greatest number of violent incidents.

Three-quarters of all occupational injuries experienced by nurses and midwives are violence-related. Nurses and midwives are second only to police officers as public sector workers most likely to be subjected to a violent assault while on duty. Almost one in three nurses report having been physically assaulted during their career.

Source: News Telegraph, "Doctors and nurses want more protection from assault", 2004.

Violence is so common among workers in contact with people in distress that it is often considered an inevitable part of the job. Frustration and anger arising out of illness and pain, older-age problems such as dementia, some psychiatric disorders, or intoxication with alcohol and substance abuse can affect behaviour and make people verbally or physically violent. Increasing poverty and marginalization in the community in which the aggressor lives, inadequacies in the environment where care activities are performed, or in the way these are organized, insufficient training and interpersonal skills of staff providing services to this population, and a general climate of stress and insecurity at the workplace can all contribute substantially to an increase in the level of workplace violence.

Health-care workers are at the forefront of this situation worldwide. Extensive cross-national research recently carried out in Brazil, Bulgaria, Lebanon, Portugal, South Africa, Thailand and an additional Australian study show that all workers in this profession are extensively exposed to the risks of both physical and psychological violence. (For a detailed presentation of data see discussions under "Developing countries" in Chapter 2).[43]

Just as no category of health workers appears immune from the risk of exposure to workplace violence, no work setting in the health-care sector is safe from workplace violence.[44] Nevertheless, risk is not homogeneous across health occupational groups. A range of different scenarios is provided below.

General hospitals

In the United States more than 5 million workers are employed in hospitals. They are exposed to many occupational health and safety hazards and risks, including violence: "According to estimates of the Bureau of Labor Statistics (BLS), 2,637 nonfatal assaults on hospital workers occurred in 1999 – a rate of 8.3 assaults per 10,000 workers. This rate is much higher than the rate of nonfatal assaults for all private-sector industries, which is 2 per 10,000 workers."[45]

Nevertheless, some groups of health workers are at greater risk than are others. Most at risk appear to be those working in emergency departments.

Health-care workers operating in emergency care units

Health-care workers providing emergency services appear to be at greater risk of violence, and especially from patients who are drunk or under the influence of illicit drugs. For example, 56 per cent of staff working in the emergency care unit of a major hospital in Barcelona (Spain) reported being exposed to verbal aggression by patients or their relatives.[46] An example of a recent attack upon staff working in an emergency care unit at a hospital in Scotland appears in the scenario described in box 19.

Box 19   Patient jailed for NHS violence

A disruptive patient who ran amok twice in a hospital casualty department has been jailed for nine months. JK, a drug addict and alcoholic, fought and hurled equipment at doctors and nurses at Perth Royal Infirmary earlier this year. Jailing him, Sheriff Derek Pyle said he wanted to send out the strongest possible message to violent patients. NHS Tayside is introducing a new policy on disruptive patients with a complete ban as the ultimate sanction. JK … admitted twice running riot at the hospital. He had been brought in drunk the first time after complaining of abdominal pain.

"His conduct was such that staff were unable to approach him and they just had to stand back out of harm's way. In the course of thrashing around he kicked out against the anaesthetic equipment on the wall and damaged a tube on the machine."

JK was later arrested by the police and removed from the hospital without treatment. On the second occasion, he was admitted after an accidental drug overdose and became verbally and physically abusive.

Source: BBC News, "Patient jailed for NHS violence", 2004.

Psychiatric hospital staff

In addition to staff in emergency departments in hospitals, health workers employed in psychiatric facilities are at risk. However, not all psychiatric patients are aggressive, although there are some mental health problems which have been identified as more commonly resulting in violence.

In psychiatric hospitals the majority of patients are usually not violent, and violent episodes in most cases do not result in a traumatic injury.[47] Nevertheless, in Sweden psychiatric nurses are five times more likely to experience violence, and three times more likely to be victimized through sexual harassment by patients, compared to nurses in other disciplines.[48] Some episodes of violence can be extremely severe, as the example in box 20 demonstrates.

Box 20   Incident at Rozelle Hospital, Sydney, Australia

TR's history prior to 6 April 1997

At the time of the incident TR was 26 years old, approximately six feet tall and weighing between 15 and 16 stone. He had a six-year history of schizo-affective disorder and had been admitted four times to Rozelle Hospital.

Incident: 6 April 1997

On Sunday, 6 April 1997 at about 7.30 p.m., TR, a patient at Rozelle Hospital returned from weekend leave. At about 9.30 p.m. TR was talking with staff and appeared to be

/cont'd

/cont'd

behaving appropriately. At about 9.45 p.m. in Ward 25, Nurse Mazoudier who was on the first floor of the ward, heard loud crashing footsteps and shouting. She went down the hallway to investigate the noise. Suddenly the door of dormitory 3 was slammed twice and TR emerged naked and shouting. One arm was raised; he was holding his genitals with his other hand and was shouting, "I've got to have sex". He then threw himself bodily at her and she fell against the hallway wall. She dropped the medication chart that she was holding, her keys and duress alarm. TR said he was going to kill her. Nurse Mazoudier pushed past him and shouted for help.

At that point Nurse Turner appeared at the bottom of the stairs and pressed her duress alarm. TR then proceeded to hit Nurse Turner around the head with closed fists. At the same time he was shouting sexual suggestions to Nurse Turner.

Another nurse, Nurse Walker began to shout at TR to stop hitting Nurse Turner. TR then attacked Nurse Walker, hitting her on the left temple. TR then ran down the corridor again hitting Nurse Walker and pushing her into the door jamb.

Nurse Carrick attended Ward 25 from the Observation Unit. He saw TR lying naked on the floor. TR was bleeding and there were splinters of glass all around the floor. TR stood up, grabbed Nurse Carrick in a headlock and rammed his head, running, into the exit door twice. TR then attacked Nurse Carrick again, throwing further punches. TR then grabbed him with one hand. In his other hand he had a large piece of broken mirror and said to Nurse Carrick that he was going to cut him. At that stage Nurse Carrick was able to say to him "No, no" and remove the glass from TR's hand.

Suddenly, TR appeared in the Nurses Station in Ward 25. He was naked and screaming with arms waving in the air. Nurse McLuckie was closest to TR as he entered the office. She grabbed his right arm and called out to surrounding staff to "bring him down", which was the taught method in Critical Incident Positive Outcome courses, known as CIPO. The patient was brought down and immobilized in the staff area of Ward 25.

As a result of the incident, Nurse Carrick sustained cuts to the back of his right hand, cuts to his right and left shoulder and bruising to the head. He experienced nightmares and received counselling. Nurse Mazoudier received bruising to the left thigh and soreness in the back and head. She also experienced difficulty sleeping following the incident. Nurse Turner suffered soft tissue damage to the head and neck, as well as headaches and psychological trauma. Nurse Walker suffered bruising to her forehead and cheek, and received counselling. All four nurses required some time off work as a result of the incident.

Source: WorkCover Authority of New South Wales (Inspector Pompili) v Central Sydney Area Health Service [2002] NSWIR Comm 44, pp. 10–12, IRC 1509 of 1999, Justice J. Schmidt. (See: www.aostlii.edu.au/cases/nsw/NSWIRComm/, accessed 28 Mar. 2002.)

However, violence is not committed solely by patients with mental health illnesses. Dementia is also frequently associated with aggression towards health workers.

Old-age care units

A study carried out in eight old-age nursing wards in **Sweden** in 1993 showed that 75 per cent of medical staff reported having been exposed to threats, 93 per cent to minor physical violence and 53 per cent to severe physical violence during the previous 12 months.[49] Similarly, a 1992 survey conducted in seven aged care facilities in the city of Adelaide in South Australia found that 91 per cent of all staff and 96 per cent of all personal care attendants in these nursing homes or hostels stated that they had experienced aggressive behaviour from a resident.[50]

More recent research in Sweden confirms that the situation remains extremely serious. A questionnaire was sent (December 1999–January 2000) to a stratified sample of 2,800 local government employees in the care and welfare sector, working mainly with the elderly or persons with developmental impairments. Seven occupational groups, including supervisors, specialists and other categories of carers, were included. In total this represented a population of more than 170,000 employees. The response rate was 85 per cent. The results indicated that up to 51 per cent of this population had been affected by threats/violence, either verbally or physically, over the previous year. Moreover, the results suggest that over 9 per cent of the employees in the care sector experienced acts of violence or threats on a daily basis, and 67 per cent several times a month. The most vulnerable groups were assistant nurses and direct carers. Verbal threats appeared more common (79 per cent). Subsequently staff reported feelings of anger (41 per cent) and helplessness (31 per cent), although minor physical injuries (18 per cent), were also frequent.[51] Organizational change in the workplace and a heavy workload appeared to be associated with increased risk.

Some idea of the overall spread and importance of violence towards health-care workers around the world is given in table 19. This table has been constructed from a series of country-specific surveys conducted on behalf of an International Labour Organization (ILO), International Council of Nurses (ICN), World Health Organization (WHO) and Public Services International (PSI) collaborative working group.

As can be seen from the data in table 19, in all seven countries where surveys were conducted a high incidence of verbal abuse, physical attack and bullying/mobbing was reported. The figures from **South Africa** are particularly disturbing. However, it is not just workers in the health industry sector who are increasingly reporting exposure to workplace violence. Other working environments with close and open contact with clients are also at risk, including education.

Table 19   Violence experienced by health care personnel in seven countries
(percentage of sample in previous 12 months)

Country	Physical attack	Verbal abuse	Bullying and mobbing
Australia	12.0	67.0	10.5
Brazil	6.4	39.5	15.2
Bulgaria	7.5	32.2	30.9
Lebanon	5.8	40.9	22.1
Portugal	3.0	51.0[1]	23.01[1]
		16.5[2]	16.5[2]
South Africa (private sector)	9.0	52.0	20.6
South Africa	17.0	60.1	–
Thailand	10.5	47.7	10.7

[1] In health-care complex. [2] In hospital. – = data not available.

Source: Table constructed from data provided in Di Martino, 2002b, p. 50.

Working in an environment increasingly "open" to violence

Working environments that traditionally have been relatively immune from violence are becoming progressively affected by workplace violence. This worrying trend seems to reflect a general growth in community violence and unrest, and the collapse of a number of societal values.

Teaching

Violence in schools is part of this trend. Teachers have been exposed to the risk of workplace violence for a long time. However, the level of risk to which they are now exposed in a number of countries is most disturbing. This risk is compounded in the United States (and elsewhere), where the possibility of mass shootings appears to be more common – as noted at the beginning of this book. There is also some evidence that a number of the school pupils responsible for such shootings were themselves the victim of bullying from other students. This is yet another example of shifting victim/perpetrator status; that is, where victims and perpetrators change roles. Box 21 provides some examples of this form of bullying and violence, and its potential consequences.

Bullying in schools is a widespread phenomenon worldwide. In many countries, bullying is the leading school safety problem, for example:

Box 21   Mass shootings: Bullying can be a factor

In a number of cases, bullying played a key role in the decision to attack. A number of attackers had experienced bullying and harassment that was long-standing and severe. In such cases, the experience of bullying appeared to play a major role in motivating an attack at school. Bullying was not a factor in every case, and clearly not every child who is bullied in school will pose a risk. However, in a number of cases, attackers described experiences of being bullied in terms that approached torment.

Attackers told of behaviours that, if they occurred in the workplace, would meet the legal definition of harassment. That bullying played a major role in a number of school shootings should strongly support ongoing efforts to combat bullying in American schools.

Two recent cases ... brought the issue of bullying to the nation's attention. One boy experienced the torment of other students burning their cigarette lighters and then pressing the hot metal against his neck. He was constantly picked on, even by his friends. To stop the daily taunting, he opened fire on his classmates, killing two.

In the second case, a girl had been the victim of such severe harassment that she frequently skipped school; and administrators threatened legal action if she did not begin to attend school regularly. Students called her names and threw stones at her as she walked home. Increasingly concerned, her parents transferred her to a small parochial school. The teasing continued. In an effort to stop the pain, the student planned to commit suicide in front of a classmate to whom she had revealed personal information. Instead of killing herself, she pointed the gun at her classmate and wounded her in the shoulder.

Source: US Department of Justice, 2002, pp. 10–15, especially p. 10.

- in **Norway**, 9 per cent of students are victims of bullying;[52]

- in **Great Britain**, the percentage of students who are bullied ranges from 4 to 10 per cent per year;[53]

- in **Spain**, 15 per cent of secondary school children are bullies or victims of bullying behaviour;[54]

- in **Australia**, during the 1990s, one in six or seven children indicated they were bullied on a weekly basis;[55]

- in **Germany**, between 4 and 12 per cent of students experienced frequent and persistent bullying;[56]

- in the **United States**, 20 per cent of 15-year-old students said they had been bullied in their current term in school.[57] A study of junior and high school students found that 77 per cent had been bullied in their school career.[58]

A WHO study of school-aged children in 27 countries reported that the majority of 13-year-olds in most of the countries surveyed had engaged in bullying at least some of the time.[59]

In **Canada**, violent situations in schools historically occurred infrequently, and tended to involve young people not attending school.[60] This situation has changed. An extensive 1993 survey of the Saskatchewan Teachers' Association showed that 66 per cent of teachers report having suffered abuse – either verbal insults, profane gestures, physical assaults or destruction of personal property – at the hands of students, parents, fellow teachers, administrators or others during their career. Sixty-five per cent of incidents reported for 1993 were verbal abuse or rude or obscene gestures; 18 per cent were physical abuse; and 17 per cent were damage to property. Seventy-eight per cent of teachers said they believed that school violence was growing. Seventy-one per cent stated that "the media contributes to the atmosphere which spawns abuse against teachers". Sixty per cent reported that teacher abuse was increasing in their school.[61]

More recent research indicates further escalation of the risk of violence in Canadian schools. In Quebec, 9 per cent of youth in schools were victims of extortion, and the figure was 15 per cent in Montreal.[62] In addition, 20 per cent of violent crime by 12- to 17-year-old urban youth occurred in school.[63]

In **Sweden**, there has been a 300 per cent increase in reports of school violence, although they all tended to be minor infractions that did not seem to have been reported in the past.[64]

In **South Africa**, a national survey found that 40 per cent of rapes and 43 per cent of indecent assaults were against girls under the age of 17, and often occurred at school.[65] Also, 62 per cent of school violence involved racial incidents and the sexual harassment of girls.[66]

In **France**, over the school year 2002–03, secondary schools reported some 13 incidents each on average. This worked out at slightly over two incidents per 100 pupils over the school year. The reported total of 72,000 incidents included 21,300 acts of physical violence without a weapon and 16,623 cases of verbal abuse or serious threats. Teachers were the victims in one incident out of six. The main victims – and perpetrators – of these acts were pupils.[67]

Violence is also increasingly reported in **Japanese** schools. The Ministry of Education, Culture, Sports, Science and Technology reported that in the 12-month period April 2002 to March 2003, 33,765 cases of violent acts occurred in public elementary, junior high and high schools. Of these, violence directed to teachers constituted 4,856 cases, or 14.4 per cent.[68] Bullying was also common in elementary and middle school, with students in the first year of middle school reporting high levels of bullying.[69] Occasionally, teachers are the perpetrators (box 22).

Box 22   Record violence among Japan's teachers

A record number of Japanese teachers were disciplined for committing "obscene acts" against students in the latest school year, an Education of Ministry survey found.

At the same time, teachers are facing extraordinary strains. Last year the same survey showed a record one-in-400 took a leave of absence citing mental anguish or stress.

Much has changed in Japan's once vaunted school system. What used to be a model of the country's success appears to have become a breeding ground for trouble. The problem has been blamed on a number of factors, including the enormous pressures students face to pass competitive exams.

The situation in Japan's schools mirrors what is happening across the country. Crime is rising nationwide, as are the levels of suicide and depression. Nearly all of the problems are attributed to Japan's decade of economic decline – a decline that shows no sign of ending.

Source: BBC News, 2001.

The risk appears similar in metropolitan and rural areas. The pattern of increased reports of violence in schools also appears to be similar across countries.

Schools in metropolitan areas

A study was conducted in Milan (Italy) in 2003 that involved a sample of 10,513 students. It was found that 64 per cent of students in primary schools and half of those in secondary schools reported having been either a victim or a perpetrator of bullying.[70]

Schools in rural areas

In Central America, women teachers, especially those working in marginal areas with a high delinquency rate, or in remote areas, are reported to be vulnerable to social and sexual violence. These teachers are also exposed to violence when commuting at night to attend training courses.[71]

School bullying and workplace victimization

Despite recognition of the rising risk of violence in schools, limited attention appears to have been given to its possible role as an antecedent to violence at the workplace. Recently, however, this issue has attracted growing attention.

Research in the **United Kingdom** involved analysis of 5,288 questionnaires completed by workers from various workplace venues.[72] The researchers found a significant (although modest) relationship between school bullying and experience of workplace victimization. In a different study, a high risk of workplace victimization was identified for those who had been bullies or victims of bullying at school, as shown in table 20.

Table 20   Risk of being bullied in the workplace for those victimized at school and bullies/victims at school, United Kingdom[1]

(a) Victimized at school (victims + bully/victims)

Victimized at school	Bullied at work in last six months		Bullied at work in last five years	
	Yes	No	Yes	No
Yes	309	2 285	753	1 832
No	237	2 357	529	2 070

(b) Bullies/victims at school

Victimized at school	Bullied at work in last six months		Bullied at work in last five years	
	Yes	No	Yes	No
Yes	118	426	271	1 011
No	765	3 877	609	3 293

[1] Risk of being bullied in the workplace in the past six months, and five years, for those (a) victimized at school and (b) bullies/victims at school.

Source: Smith et al., 2003, p. 182. Reproduced with permission from the British Journal of Psychology © The British Psychological Society.

The data in table 20 indicate that those most at risk of workplace bullying were those who had been bullies, or victims of bullying, at school. At greatest risk were bullies who had also been victims (bullies/victims), followed by those who were only victims.

Call centres

Another quite different group of workers at significant risk are those in call centres. Notably, while these workers do not have face-to-face contact with their clientele, constant telephone communications present the medium for transmission of verbal abuse and threats.

Call centres, often located offshore in developing countries in order to curb costs, are an increasingly familiar part of the global workplace. While in the view of many employers the concept of workplace violence does not and should not extend to such centres, there is no doubt that call centre workers experience substantial harassment and stress as a daily part of their employment. Working conditions in call centres can vary greatly, depending to a large extent on the type of work being performed. There is a considerable difference, for example, between the degree of work satisfaction and work pressure experienced by a highly trained call centre agent offering professional advice to callers on, say, legal or medical issues, and that experienced by low-paid, low-status workers handling routine enquiries and speaking only from a prepared script. Call centres which are dominated by the pressure to meet sales targets and/or to take new calls as quickly as possible can be particularly stressful environments.

ACD technology for forwarding incoming calls to available workers may be complemented in call centres by the use of predictive dialling techniques for outgoing calls; here calls are initiated automatically by technology, being passed to available agents only when callers pick up their phones. Both techniques mean that call centre workers are controlled by technology, rather than being able to control their own workload. The intense level of work can be further exacerbated by verbal abuse by angry customers and continuous technological monitoring.

In **Argentina**, a study from CONICET (Consejo Nacional de Investigaciones Científicas y Técnicas) reported that call centre workers are particularly at risk of experiencing work-related stress. This study reported that up to 20 per cent of such workers made use of tranquillizers.[73]

Call centre workers may also be at risk of sexual harassment over the telephone, which in itself can be stressful. In a German study of 106 staff working in call centres, three out of four women employees reported that they had experienced sexually harassing telephone calls.[74]

Sports

A quite different form of verbal abuse is directed to sports workers and athletes.

Violence is fast spreading among athletes and the public at sports events. In theory, sport encourages the emergence of team spirit, social inclusion, recognition of diversity, sharing of positive attitudes, healthy lifestyles, and increased participation and dialogue. In practice, violence can jeopardize the very values on which sport is based. For both amateur and professional athletes, and the elaborate network of sporting clubs and associations that support them, violence is increasingly being recognized as an occupational hazard. Major incidents of violence are reported on occasion at sport events, major competitions, and even on school playing-fields. Some have resulted in major tragedies.

For example, thousands of football fans went on the rampage in the centre of Moscow during the World Cup 2002, following the **Russian Federation's** defeat by Japan. As a result, two people died and about 50 people were hospitalized, including 20 police officers.[75]

A lack of respect for, and abuse of, sporting officials such as referees has been found to have had an effect on their willingness to participate in sporting events. In **Australia**, for example, a decline of 26 per cent was reported in the number of officials participating in sport between 1997 and 2001. Most of this decline was attributed to verbal abuse and harassment. The perpetrators were predominantly athletes (37 per cent), coaches (22 per cent), spectators (19 per cent) and parents (17 per cent).[76] When physical abuse was experienced, it most frequently involved hitting and/or kicking, throwing objects and spitting. Most harassment took place in community or local sport facilities, followed by district and state-wide sporting contests.

Thus far, the discussions have covered a wide range of occupations at particular risk, the specific problems for sole workers, worksite factors that may enhance the potential for workplace violence (such as cash or valuables), close contact with clients and customers, the risks associated with working with people in distress, individuals who may pose an increased risk to workers, and the particular problems associated with bullying and violence in educational settings. It is also important to recognize that some groups of workers are particularly vulnerable.

Working in conditions of special vulnerability

Workers in precarious employment

Increasing numbers of workers are employed on a precarious basis, for example, on a short-term contract, day hire, casual or subcontract arrangements. Such workers are the majority of the employees in a growing number of enterprises, and some are likely to become exposed to violence because of their marginal status. Table 21 presents the findings of six large-scale studies on the distribution of occupational violence across some groups of precarious workers in Australia. In most of these studies, more than one occupational group was surveyed (exceptions were young casual workers in the fast-food industry and taxi drivers). All these studies used face-to-face interviewing of randomly selected workers, as well as a detailed questionnaire requiring both qualitative and quantitative responses.

While the level of violence appears high for all occupations included in table 21, and dramatic for occupations such as young casual workers in the fast-food industry and taxi drivers, it is difficult to make generalizations about differences in levels of risk for precariously employed workers and regular employees doing the same jobs. The empirical data show that occupational violence is higher among precariously employed workers in some industry sectors (e.g. clothing outworkers, primarily because of their limited control over their job tasks; or among outsourced building workers, where competition was so high that competing deadlines increased levels of verbal abuse). However, in other cases (childcare), employees suffered higher levels of violence. In some of the

Table 21   Occupational violence incidents experienced by workers in 13
occupational groups, Australia, 1993–98 (percentage of each sample)

Sector/occupation	Year	Total No. interviewed[1]	Verbal abuse	Threats	Physical attack	Hold-up or snatch and grab
Fast-food industry	1998					
Young casual workers		304	48.4	7.6	1.0	2.3
Clothing industry	1997/98	200				
Factory-based			4.0	1.0	1.0	
Outworkers			49.0	23.0	7.0	
Building industry[2]	1997	331				
Contractors			8.0 (17.3)	2.7 (8.0)	2.7 (2.7)	
Cabinetmakers			13.3 (16.0)	6.7 (2.7)	1.3 (2.7)	
Demolishers			35.7 (23.5)	7.1 (5.9)	7.1 (–)	
Small businesses						
(less than 5 employees)	1996/97	248				
Garage (owners/managers)			9.7	4.2	–	
Café (owners/managers)			45.7	15.7	1.4	
Newsagent (owners/managers)			62.9	11.4	1.4	
Printing shop (owners/managers)			37.1	2.9	2.9	
Outsourcing vs. employees[2]	1995	255				
Childcare			50.0 (15.0)	13.0 (2.5)	11.0 (–)	
Hospitality			57.0 (53.0)	46.0 (30.0)	11.0 (7.0)	
Transport			47.0 (13.0)	6.0 (13.0)	– (13.0)	
Building			15.0 (56.0)	– (17.0)	– (–)	
Taxi drivers	1993	100	81.0	17.0	10.0	

[1] Total sample 1,438.

[2] For the headings "Building industry" and "Outsourcing vs. employees", the first figure shown in each line is for employees in the industry; the number in brackets is the comparable percentage for outsourced workers in the same industry sub-group.

Source: Mayhew and Quinlan, 1999, pp. 183–205, especially p. 191. With kind permission of Springer Science and Business Media.

smaller groups studied, the findings did not clearly indicate differences on the basis of employment status. The authors concluded that the primary determinant of occupational violence was the risk level endemic within an industrial sector and the level of customer/worker contact. However, precarious employment status was an important secondary risk factor.[77]

Another employment feature that may mitigate the risk of workplace violence is ethnicity. As with the risks identified for precariously employed workers, immigrant workers are likely to have a reduced level of power in the labour market.

Immigrant workers and people of different ethnic origin

In the **United States,** homicide is the leading manner of traumatic workplace death for foreign-born workers.[78] This is not an exceptional situation. Very serious allegations of violence and mistreatment of immigrant workers are reported worldwide. In **Australia,** for example, research has established that Filipino women brought to the country as surrogate wives or domestic workers, or employed in bars and nightclubs, suffer much higher rates of violence than the Australian population at large.[79]

For clandestine immigrants, the risk is even higher. For these workers, abuse and maltreatment can be the rule rather than the exception, although given the nature of their employment relationships, evidence on the extent of violence at work for such workers is extremely difficult to obtain. On occasions tragic events, like the one reported in box 23, uncover the realities of the workplace violence risks encountered by these workers as they struggle to survive in a foreign environment.

Box 23　　Drownings lead to probe into people smuggling

The deaths of 19 Chinese migrants who drowned on a beach while gathering shellfish in northwest England have sparked a massive investigation of the labour agents behind the tragedy. So far, British police have nabbed five suspects who are thought to be responsible for the deaths. The suspects, three men and two women, were being questioned about any involvement they may have had in organizing the trip that led to the tragedy, said a spokesman for Lancashire Police. The nationalities of the arrested were not released. British detectives promised to do everything possible to find out who had sent the 19 low-wage workers – including 17 men and two women – to gather cockles in Morecambe Bay. The group was engulfed by the fast-rising tides of the Irish Sea on Thursday. Cockles are a small shellfish delicacy. The group is believed to have been controlled by unscrupulous profiteers, who took advantage of the immigrants' willingness to work for about a British pound a day.

The deaths have fuelled calls for laws to be tightened to stop the exploitation of migrant labourers, local media reported.

[The spokesperson] told reporters the dead workers had probably paid a lot of money to be brought to England, yet had been forced to work in appalling conditions without the proper equipment.

Source: China Daily, 2004, p.1.

Thus, there is a range of possible vulnerabilities that can be heightened for those who have limited power in the labour market. Where individual workers exhibit more than one of the labour market risk factors for workplace violence, they are likely to be even more vulnerable.

Workers in export-processing enterprises

In enterprises involved in processing and export, an especially vulnerable workforce – largely composed of unskilled young people and women on precarious jobs – is often hired. These production processes are characterized by a highly intensive production process, poor working conditions and long working hours. Abuse, sexual harassment and physical aggression can be part of this environment.[80] This is also shown by a series of studies conducted in different countries by the Global Alliance for Workers and Communities (GAWC). The Alliance was a partnership of private, public, and non-governmental organizations, established in 1999 to improve the workplace experiences and life opportunities of workers in global production and services companies (the Alliance ended its operations in 2004). A 2001 report by the Alliance on nine Nike factories in **Indonesia** indicated that:

> all nine factories have experienced or observed various forms of sexual harassment and abuse, with some factories reporting a relatively small number of such incidents, and others reporting higher levels of these activities. Verbal abuse was the most marked, with 30.2 per cent of the workers having personally experienced and 56.8 per cent having observed the problem. An average of 7.8 per cent of workers reported receiving unwelcome sexual comments, and 3.3 per cent reported being physically abused. In addition, sexual trade practices in recruitment and promotion were reported by at least two workers in each of two different factories.[81]

The report also indicated that Nike had initiated a serious investigation of these issues. A further report issued in 2003 showed a dramatic reduction in the cases of abuse and sexual harassment following the investigation and action under-taken by Nike in this area.[82] Some of these victimized workers were children.

Children

Child labour may take several forms, including separation from parents, isolation sometimes amounting to virtual imprisonment, physical cruelty, sexual abuse, or virtual serfdom or slave status. This is especially the case for children who are traded, sold as domestic servants or labourers, or forced into becoming child soldiers.

In 1999 the ILO's International Labour Conference, consisting of governments, and employers' and workers' organizations, adopted the 1999 Worst Forms of Child Labour Convention (No. 182), which focused on the elimination of the employment of children in hazardous jobs (such as deep-sea fishing), use of children in illicit activities (such as trafficking of drugs) and tasks that could harm the health, safety or morals of children. Recent ILO publications on the subject include *A future without child labour*,[83] *Combating child labour: A handbook for labour inspectors*[84] and *Child labour: Health and safety risks*.[85]

The ILO estimates that domestic work in the households of families other than the child's own is the largest single employment category worldwide of girls under the age of 16.[86] Although the numbers that this represents are not known, it is likely to run into the millions worldwide.

About 90 per cent of child domestic workers are girls, although in some countries (such as **Nepal** and **Haiti**) significant numbers of boys are also employed as domestics. The majority of children in domestic labour are aged between 12 and 17, but in many countries children routinely begin working as domestics well before 12 years old. Child domestic workers routinely suffer discrimination, a loss of freedom, identity and self-esteem and denial of schooling. They are also vulnerable to physical and verbal abuse and suffer from the effects of the work that they do and the conditions under which they do it,[87] as described in the examples in box 24.

Box 24   Abuse of domestic workers

Mention has already been made in Chapter 2 of the experience of workplace violence encountered by millions of migrant workers in countries such as Saudi Arabia, Malaysia and Indonesia. Other studies show that, in Latin America, many men who grow up in homes with domestic workers have their first sexual encounter with a domestic worker. In Lima, Peru, one study estimated the proportion at 60 per cent. Whether there is an assumption that sexual availability is an unspoken part of a domestic worker's contract varies from culture to culture.

In the view of one international NGO [non-governmental organization], the media's stereotypic portrayal of domestic workers as promiscuous is an important factor in their widespread sexual abuse in Latin America. In Fiji, eight out of ten domestic workers reported that their employers sexually abused them. In Bangladesh, girl domestic workers may be returned home or married off at puberty. A study of 71 domestics in Bangladesh found that 25 per cent of the girls interviewed (average age 11) considered that they had been sexually abused, and seven had been raped. Often families reject these "spoiled girls" because "their behaviour" has brought dishonour to the family. In these instances, domestic work typically becomes a precursor to prostitution, as the young girls have few other options available.

In one small-scale study in Calcutta, India, the majority of interviewees said they had experienced physical or psychological brutality. In the Philippines, co-worker violence is also reported, including sexual harassment from male co-workers. Quantifying the brutality endured by child domestics is difficult, as few will be bold enough to say anything about it except to a trusted confidante. Cases in which domestic workers suffer gross abuse and violence are occasionally reported in the press. NGO newsletters document a steady stream of individual cases of severe abuse perpetrated against both girl and boy domestic workers.

In South Asia, violence often takes the form of attack by a hot iron. In Sri Lanka, lawyers have spoken openly about the extreme violence used against child domestic workers, and in the Juvenile Court in Colombo cases have revealed brutality by employers towards their child domestic workers including branding, dousing in boiling water, rubbing chilli powder on the mouth, beatings and stabbings. Deaths caused by starvation, burning and forcing excessive intake of salt have also been reported.

Source: UNICEF, 1999, p. 8.

Thus child labourers in domestic service are at particular risk of workplace violence. Notably, many of these are very young.

Children working on the street are at very special risk (box 25). They are not only exposed to a hazardous social environment, but are also an easy target for all forms of violence. When involved in marginal or illegal activities, and thus coming into contact with the world of crime, the level of violence against children can be dramatic.[88]

Box 25   Abuse of street children: From trafficking to carpet weaving, hotel boys to street life

Shyam sold to employer

Shyam, 16, is from a Damai (tailor) family. He was brought to Kathmandu by his brother-in-law when he was 9 years old.

"My brother-in-law (Bhupaju) told me he would find me a good job in Kathmandu. There were also six other boys, as I now remember. We came from Lamjung to Dumre (Tanahu) and from there we came to Kathmandu. He took us to a carpet factory and told us that 'you people need to work here'. He then disappeared. Later, when we tried to run away from the factory, the supervisor told us that we had been sold to the employers. You know we had to work 16 to 18 hours there, from 6 in the morning to 11 at night. If you did not work the supervisor would beat us.

"After working six months there, I ran away with two friends from the factory and went to a hotel in Kalimati area where I worked as a hotel boy for six months. The hotel owner did not pay me, he just used to give me a little food left by the customers. I then left the hotel and came to the streets. I have been living there for the last five or six years."

/cont'd

/cont'd

Kamala tested HIV positive

Kamala, now 19, is from a Brahman family and has psychological problems. Her parents died when she was about 3 years old. She stayed with her uncle in the village till she was 9, and then came to Kathmandu and worked as a domestic child labourer for some time.

Kamala was not treated well in the house where she was working and she went on the street when she was 10 years old. When she was around 12 years of age, she was first exposed to sex and then she was frequently sexually abused by many street boys, as well as by other men. She used to stay in the street till midnight looking for clients. Sometimes they used to take her to a guest-house or to their own room. But if her clients were the street boys, they used to take her to lonely places such as temples, river banks or a narrow street for sex. She told us she prostituted herself for survival. She used to receive Rs.100-200 per act.

It is reported that she is affected by HIV/AIDS and now lives in a rehabilitation center.

Source: Adapted by Subedi, 2002.

Military and paramilitary organizations

Children are also the victims of forced labour supporting the military, in war zones, and may even be forced to join military or paramilitary groups. The most appalling forms of violence and violations of basic human rights can become the norm in this kind of situation, as shown in box 26.

A recent ILO publication *Young soldiers: Why they choose to fight* identifies and analyses the key factors relevant to young people becoming involved with the armed forces or in armed groups:

> Although war in general creates vulnerability, more specifically it puts individuals and their families at risk physically and threatens their means of survival both in terms of food and financially. The army or armed group fills this gap or promises to do so. Allied to these elements is the presence or absence of schooling, and whether the school is used physically, culturally, or psychologically as a recruiting ground. The role of schools illustrates the dual nature of some of the factors: being out of school (whether through one's own actions or by force majeure) leaves young people vulnerable to recruitment, especially if they cannot find employment or other economically viable activities. At the same time, some schools may encourage recruitment by allowing the army or the armed group access to students, presenting them as good options, or as being the fulfilment of ethnic, religious, or political imperatives. Some specific young people may be targeted, whether in or out of school, as being perceived by the potential recruiter as likely material because of age, sex, availability, aptitude, vulnerability, or for other reasons.

Box 26   Abuse of children in war zones

In dozens of countries around the world, children have become direct participants in war. Denied a childhood and often subjected to horrific violence, some 300,000 children are serving as soldiers in current armed conflicts. These young combatants participate in all aspects of contemporary warfare. They wield AK-47s and M-16s on the front lines of combat, serve as human mine detectors, participate in suicide missions, carry supplies, and act as spies, messengers or lookouts.

Physically vulnerable and easily intimidated, children typically make obedient soldiers. Many are abducted or recruited by force, and often compelled to follow orders under threat of death. Others join armed groups out of desperation. As society breaks down during conflict, leaving children no access to school, driving them from their homes, or separating them from family members, many children perceive armed groups as their best chance for survival. Others seek escape from poverty or join military forces to avenge family members who have been killed.

Child soldiers are being used in more than 30 countries around the world. Human Rights Watch has interviewed child soldiers from countries including Angola, Colombia, Lebanon, Liberia, Sierra Leone, Sudan and Uganda. In Sierra Leone, thousands of children abducted by rebel forces witnessed and participated in horrible atrocities against civilians, including beheadings, amputations, rape, and burning people alive. Children forced to take part in atrocities were often given drugs to overcome their fear or reluctance to fight.

In Colombia, tens of thousands of children have been used as soldiers by all sides to the country's ongoing bloody conflict. Government-backed paramilitaries recruit children as young as 8, while guerrilla forces use children to collect intelligence, make and deploy mines, and serve as advance troops in ambush attacks.

In southern Lebanon, boys as young as 12 years of age have been subject to forced conscription by the South Lebanon Army (SLA), an Israeli auxiliary militia. When men and boys refuse to serve, flee the region to avoid conscription, or desert the SLA forces, their entire families may be expelled from the occupied zone.

Girls are also used as soldiers in many parts of the world. In addition to combat duties, girls are subject to sexual abuse and may be taken as "wives" by rebel leaders in Angola, Sierra Leone and Uganda. In Northern Uganda, Human Rights Watch interviewed girls who had been impregnated by rebel commanders, and then forced to strap their babies on their backs and take up arms against Ugandan security forces.

Because of their immaturity and lack of experience, child soldiers suffer higher casualties than their adult counterparts. Even after the conflict is over, they may be left physically disabled or psychologically traumatized. Frequently denied an education or the opportunity to learn civilian job skills, many find it difficult to re-join peaceful society. Schooled only in war, former child soldiers are often drawn into crime or become easy prey for future recruitment.

Source: Human Rights Watch, 2004c. See also WHO, 2001, p. 235.

In a similar way, the family can be the cause of recruitment because one of its members is alienated or ill-treated or because the family (or a key member of it) is currently or traditionally involved in the armed forces or group or aligned in a way that encourages or provides approval to such involvement.

For a young person who is in trouble, at home, at school, or elsewhere, and who is seeking support, status, a sense of personal identity and role at a critical time in their own physical, emotional, and societal development, the armed forces or armed group can seem an attractive option, particularly where such involvement is condoned or encouraged by the society or culture, and/or by key influences at home, at school, or within their peer group.[89]

Yet it is not only children who are the subject of exploitation and brutality by military forces in ongoing conflicts around the globe. Increasing evidence is emerging of adult members of military and paramilitary organizations being the victims of both physical and psychological violence from within their own ranks. The real dimension of a probably long-hidden phenomenon is only now beginning to emerge.

In the **Russian Federation**, for example, some 1,200 military personnel were said to have been killed in non-combat circumstances in 2003.[90] Accidents, carelessness, bullying and suicide were cited as the main causes. The high figure continues a trend which has been occurring in the Russian military for some years. Official figures acknowledged that in 2003, 2,500 servicemen had been the victims of bullying. Of these, 16 had died. Military observers believe that the real figure may be far higher than this. The officially issued figure for suicides among servicemen has been around 300 a year over the last few years. While some of those committing suicide were officers who had become disillusioned with the hopelessness of military life, 70 per cent were conscript soldiers in their first year – the most common victims of bullying.

In **Italy** 861 cases of "nonnismo" (bullying of young conscripts) were reported in 1999. A web survey indicated that 27 per cent of those answering had suffered "nonnismo".[91]

It is not only bullying behaviours which represent a problem for the military. As box 27 demonstrates, in military and paramilitary organizations which employ both men and women as members, sexual assault and harassment can become an occupational hazard.

The fact that instances of sexual assault and harassment now seem more likely to be investigated by authorities is encouraging, and may account for the apparent rise in the number of complaints of this type recorded over recent years in a number of military and paramilitary organizations. Just how difficult it can be for a victim of this form of occupational violence to gain redress can be

Box 27   US soldiers accused of raping 100 colleagues

The Pentagon has ordered an urgent inquiry into reports that more than 100 American women deployed in Iraq and Afghanistan have been raped or sexually assaulted by fellow soldiers, it emerged yesterday. There have been 112 cases of sexual assault on women soldiers in units under central command, which oversees operations in the Middle East and central Asia over an 18-month period. Meanwhile, more than 20 women at an air force training base in Texas have told a local crisis centre they were assaulted in 2002. If only half of the cases are confirmed it will be the worst rape scandal the US military has faced in nearly a decade.

Source: Borge, 2004.

discerned from a lawsuit by a policewoman serving in London's Metropolitan Police Force, the largest law enforcement body in the **United Kingdom**.

In a case ultimately determined in the House of Lords, Britain's highest court of appeal, Mrs. Waters complained to her superiors that she had been raped and buggered in her police residential accommodation by a fellow officer. The complaint, made in 1988, was for all practical purposes ignored by her employer and Mrs. Waters was subjected to a sustained campaign of hostile treatment by her male police colleagues amounting to bullying designed to make her resign from the force. She subsequently took legal proceedings against her employer, alleging negligence in that the employer failed to exercise due care in looking after his employee.

The House of Lords, in a landmark decision reached in July 2000, ruled that an action in negligence did lie against the Commissioner of Police for the Metropolis.[92] In the course of their judgment, the Law Lords made the following observations about the bullying that occurred, and the responsibilities of an employer to handle complaints of sexual assault in a proper way:

> The principal claim raised in the action is one of negligence – the "employer" failed to exercise due care to look after his "employee". Generically many of the acts alleged can be seen as a form of bullying – the "employer" or those to whom he delegated the responsibilities for running his organization should have taken steps to stop it, to protect the "employee" from it. They failed to do so. They made unfair reports and they tried to force her to leave the police.

> If an employer knows that acts being done by employees during their employment may cause physical or mental harm to a particular fellow employee and he does nothing to supervise or prevent such acts, when it is in his power to do so, it is clearly arguable that he may be in breach of his duty to that employee. It seems to me that he may also be in breach of that duty if he can foresee that such acts may happen and if they do, that physical

or mental harm may be caused to an individual. I would accept (Evans LJ was prepared to assume without deciding) that if this sort of sexual assault is alleged (whether it happened or not) and the officer persists in making complaints about it, it is arguable that it can be foreseen that some retaliatory steps may be taken against the woman and that she may suffer harm as a result. Even if this is not necessarily foreseeable at the beginning it may become foreseeable or indeed obvious to those in charge at various levels who are carrying out the Commissioner's responsibilities that there is a risk of harm and that some protective steps should be taken.[93]

These risks of exposure to workplace bullying, sexual harassment, verbal abuse and more severe forms of violence at work may be exacerbated when all workers are under significant pressure. The most extreme form of pressure is undoubtedly deployment in zones of conflict.

Zones of conflict

The vulnerability of members of the military and other paramilitary forces to occupational violence from within the organization is equalled if not exceeded in many cases by the risks of violence encountered from external sources. Nowhere are these risks more apparent than in the growing scourge of terrorism referred to at the beginning of this book. Soldiers and police officers are frequently the deliberate targets of terrorist attacks in zones of conflict such as **Iraq, Israel, Pakistan, Afghanistan** and **Chechnya**. Journalists, aid workers and other non-combatants are also targeted by terrorists, as the following contemporary report from Iraq illustrates (box 28).

Box 28	Insurgent attacks in Iraq

Mrs Hassan, head of Care International in Iraq, was kidnapped in the capital last October. Footage of a masked man shooting her in the head was released the following month. The crime chilled the aid community and baffled security forces because no group claimed responsibility. Iraqi police said that 11 men had been arrested in a raid in Madaen, a district 22 km south of Baghdad, and five had admitted complicity in Mrs Hassan's killing .... Last Sunday an Australian engineer was taken hostage, the latest of more than 200 foreigners kidnapped since the end of the war. A tape released to al-Jazeera television showed Douglas Wood, 63, sitting on the floor between two masked men with rifles and bullet-proof vests .... In Baghdad six car bombs exploded and more than a dozen gunmen shot dead five Iraqi policemen at a checkpoint and took their weapons. In the east of the city US soldiers pulled a would-be bomber from his burning car after it failed to explode properly. He said he had been forced to carry out the attack to protect kidnapped family members, according to a US statement.

Source: Carroll and Bowcroft, 2005, p. 1.

Towards explanations

This chapter has reviewed a vast array of data providing insight into the vulnerability of particular occupational groups and work settings to workplace violence. The data suggest that the impact of workplace violence, both physical and psychological, is felt by countless millions of workers around the globe, with some occupations and settings experiencing significantly higher rates of violence because of situational factors over which they often have little control.

Chapter 4 turns its attention to a more detailed review of explanations of the causes of this violence, and the measures which have been proposed to combat workplace aggression.

Notes

[1] Upson, 2004, p. 9.

[2] Ibid.

[3] Health and Safety Executive (HSE), 2005.

[4] Ibid.

[5] Pizzino, 1994, p. 15.

[6] Hadland, 2002, p. 26.

[7] Taylor, 2002.

[8] International Confederation of Free Trade Unions (ICFTU), 1995, p. 2.

[9] Mayhew, 2000c, pp. 1–6.

[10] Richardson and Windau, 2003, pp. 673–689, especially p. 678.

[11] Duhart, 2001, p. 4.

[12] South African Institute of Race Relations, 2000, p. 4.

[13] Essenberg, 2003, p. 24.

[14] Mayhew, 2000c, p. 3. See also idem, 1999, pp. 127–139.

[15] Rail Safety and Standards Board, 2004, p. 174.

[16] Trades Union Congress, 2002, cited in Essenberg, 2003, p. 19.

[17] Rosskam, 2001, cited in Essenberg, 2003, pp. 19–20.

[18] Williams, 2000, pp. 429–435.

[19] Bowie, 2000, pp. 247–254, especially p. 250.

[20] Bor et al., 2000.

[21] European Trade Union Confederation (ETUC), 1993, p. 8.

[22] British Retail Consortium (BRC), 2003, p. 38.

[23] Idem, 2004.

[24] Pizzino, 1994, p. 6.

[25] Upson, 2004. See also Denton et al., 2000, pp. 419–427.

[26] Incomes Data Services Ltd., 1997, p. 17.

[27] Worsfold and McCann, 2000, pp. 249–255.

[28] Argrusa et al., 2002, pp. 19–31.

[29] Piñuel y Zabala, 2002, cited in Hoel and Einarsen, 2001.

[30] Ibid.

[31] Hoel and Cooper, 2000, cited in Rayner et al., 2002.

[32] Ibid., p. 5.

[33] Maticka-Tyndale et al., 2000, pp. 87–108, cited in Giga et al., 2003a.

[34] Farrugia, 2002, pp. 309–319.

[35] Taylor, 2002, p. 1.

[36] Communication Workers' Union, 2001.

[37] Hoel and Cooper, 2000, p. 5.

[38] Ibid., p. 6.

[39] Johns, 2003.

[40] Cahill and Landsbergis, 1996, pp. 731–750.

[41] Giga, Hoel and Cooper, 2003b.

[42] Institute for Security Studies, South Africa, 2003.

[43] Di Martino, 2002b. See also Mayhew and Chappell, 2003, pp. 3–43.

[44] A series of psychological risk assessment tools are being developed that aim to predict recidivist behaviour by violent offenders, sex offenders and the mentally ill, which are now widely used in correctional settings.

[45] NIOSH, 2002, p. 1.

[46] Nogareda Cuixart and Nogareda Cuixart, 1990, p. 11.

[47] Bonnesen, 1995, in Bast-Pettersen et al., 1995, p. 21.

[48] Arnetz, Arnetz and Petterson, 1994.

[49] Bergström, 1995, in Bast-Pettersen et al., 1995, p. 17.

[50] Beck et al., 1992, pp. 21–23.

[51] Menckel and Viitasara, 2002, pp. 376–385.

[52] Shaw, 2001b, cited in Verdugo and Vere, 2003, p. 14.

[53] Sharp and Smith, 1991, ibid., p. 15.

[54] Ortega and Mora-Merchan, 1999, ibid.

[55] Rigby and Slee, 1999, ibid.

[56] Lösel and Bliesener, 1999, ibid.

[57] US Departments of Education and Justice, 1999, ibid.

[58] Arnette and Wasleben, 1998, ibid.

[59] WHO, 2002b, Ch. 2, pp. 23–49. See also: WHO, 2002c.

[60] King and Peart, 1992, p. 87. For a review of the contemporary situation in Australian schools, see House of Representatives Standing Committee on Employment, Education and Training, 1994. See also Rigby, 2004.

[61] Saskatchewan Teachers' Association, 1994, p. 3.

[62] Tondreau, 2000, cited in Verdugo and Vere, 2003, p. 14.

[63] Canadian Centre for Justice Statistics, 1999, ibid.

[64] Shaw 2001a, ibid.

[65] Ibid.

[66] Shaw, 2001b, ibid.

[67] Ministère de la Jeunesse, Education et Recherche, France, 2004.

[68] Ministry of Education, Culture, Sports, Science and Technology, Japan. No date.

[69] Morita et al., 1999.

[70] Iannacone, 2003.

[71] Martine, 1994, p. 64.

[72] Hoel and Cooper, 2000, p. 2.

[73] Di Martino, 2005, p. 30.

[74] Sczesny and Stahlberg, 2000, pp. 121–136.

[75] BBC Sport, World Club 2002, "Can football violence be stopped?", 10 June 2002.

[76] Australian Sports Commission (ASC), 2002. See also Wenn, 1989.

[77] Mayhew and Quinlan, 1999.

[78] Richardson and Windau, 2003, p. 681.

[79] See Cunneen and Stubbs, 1997.

[80] Pérez and Valera, 1995, p. 31.

[81] Global Alliance for Workers and Communities (GAWC), 2001, p. 4.

[82] Idem, 2003.

[83] ILO, 2002a.

[84] ILO, 2002b.

[85] Forastieri, 2002. See also Galli, 2001.

[86] ILO, 1996b. See also Flores-Oebanda et al., 2001; Boonpala and Kane, 2001.

[87] United Nations Commission on Human Rights, 2002.

[88] O'Loughlin, 2001, p. 17. See also Black, 1993, pp. 7, 15 and 22.

[89] Brett and Specht, 2004, pp. 62–63.

[90] BBC News, 2003b.

[91] Publiweb, no date. See also Tessari, no date.

[92] House of Lords: "Opinions of the Lords of Appeal for judgement in the case Waters (A.P.) (Appellant) v. Commissioner of Police for the Metropolis (Respondent) on 27 July 2000" (see: http://www.parliament.the-stationery-office.co.uk/pa/ld199900/ldjudgmt/jd000727/waters-1.htm, accessed 4 Jan. 2006).

[93] Waters v Commissioner of Police for the Metropolis (2000) 4 All ER 934–947.

EXPLANATIONS

4

There is a strong and natural desire among most citizens to seek simple explanations and solutions to the violence which may be gripping their society and threatening "the way decent people live". As has been observed, it is often the media which provide such explanations and convey lasting impressions of the type of people responsible for "an epidemic" of violence in the workplace. Those impressions are often dominated by images of "disgruntled employees" and "angry spouses", "unhappy, desperate, often psychiatrically impaired people", venting their anger on colleagues at the workplace. Those media images, of course, also spread with amazing speed around the globe and affect public and official perceptions of violence far beyond their place of origin.

The analysis of the nature and scope of workplace violence in Chapter 2 suggests that there are cases where these media-created perceptions are both inaccurate and misleading. Despite this, they are still perceptions that can influence policy, as well as the way governments and other bodies think about and respond to the problems of violence in general, and workplace violence in particular.

Chapter 4 considers the multiple **causal** factors that may contribute to an increased risk of workplace violence, including individual, social, economic and cultural features (box 29). In particular, the discussions emphasize that

---

Box 29   Single cause, single solution?

It is tempting (or convenient) for many to regard violence as arising from a single cause, and consequently to perceive a reduction in violence as certain to arise from a single solution. For example, there are those who think that the removal of televized violence represents the answer to violent behaviour. There are others who perceive more rigorous controls on firearms as the way to eliminate violence.

The most vocal commentators on violence often reflect ideological predispositions or institutional interests. As convenient and as reassuring as it may be to crusade on behalf

/cont'd

/cont'd

of a panacea, a proper understanding of violence (and ultimately, of the means for its control) requires an understanding of the variety and complexity of contributing factors.[1]

Looking for ticking bombs

Violent crime has penetrated and gripped our society. The ticking clock of crime moves swiftly throughout the day, and a pervasive fear of violence in the workplace has become the most recent threat to the way decent people live ... It has been called an epidemic by those who study disgruntled employees and angry spouses and the violence they perpetrate on innocent employees ...

Violent crime is no longer restricted to urban centres and ghettos. Offices, factories, school playgrounds, post offices, fast-food restaurants, hospitals, shopping malls, hotels, grocery stores, banks, convenience stores, and in fact, nearly everywhere people are employed and business is carried out have become the latest sites for disgruntled, unhappy, desperate, often psychiatrically impaired people to vent their rage.[2]

[1] Reproduced with permission from the Australian Institute of Criminology, National Committee on Violence (1990), p. 60.

[2] Reproduced with permission from The McGraw-Hill Companies, from Mantell and Albrecht (1994), pp. ix–x.

simplistic explanations are inadequate – and hence simplistic solutions are inappropriate and unlikely to provide effective prevention.

Complex causes, complex solutions

Much of the current workplace violence prevention literature reflects an approach based on identifying higher-risk individuals, with the development of pre-employment tests to screen out and exclude those who might be violent; of profiles to identify those who might become violent in the existing workforce; and of measures to deal with violence when it occurs.[1] Thus a principal strategy to deal with the disgruntled, angry and possibly mentally ill people who may explode into violence at the workplace is either to deny these "ticking time-bombs" access to work sites, or to try and identify or defuse their rage before it detonates. This approach is also characterized by an emphasis on the need for "target hardening" through the use of a range of security measures to restrict entry to and movement within the workplace.[2]

Measures of this type may well assist in reducing the incidence of violence at the workplace, and in the wider community. To this extent they are measures which deserve approbation, but this praise must be restrained by the realization that they are still measures addressing limited symptoms of an extremely complex and diverse problem which defies either an easy explanation or a solution.

Box 30   The concept of violence

Violence is clearly an extremely complex phenomenon involving major ambiguity between the destruction and the creation of order. The hope that violence might prove a more precise concept at least in everyday language, because everyone knows essentially what it means, and that its analytical useful contours were only lost through its use in the social sciences, has been in vain. Public opinion polls reveal that the concept of violence is extremely diffuse, extending from physical and psychological injury, particular forms of crime and uncouth behaviour on the roads and in sports, to socio-political discrimination ...

Not only has the question what is violence remained the subject of constant debate, but also the issue of the origins of violence. There are two diametrically opposed views here, as violence is both ascribed to human nature, which is considered immutable, and also to social conditions. There is also continuous debate on appropriate strategies for dealing with violence, where the spectrum of possible answers ranges from simple repression and the threat of more severe punishment to various forms of upbringing and education.

Source: Imbusch, 2003, pp. 13–14.

Recognition and an understanding of the variety and complexity of the factors which contribute to violence must be a vital precursor of any effective violence prevention or control programme (box 30). In this chapter it is sought to provide such understanding, first through a brief review of a number of factors that have been identified as the most significant in explaining violence in general, and second by considering how these factors may interact to produce violence at work.

Violence can take many forms both in a workplace and in society at large. An argument between two employees in an enterprise that erupts into physical violence is far removed from an armed robbery of a financial institution which results in the shooting of a teller. A fight in a bar between two customers in which a manager intervenes and is injured involves very different circumstances from the predatory rape of a female employee as she travels home from her workplace. Hence any individual act of violence is likely to require a complex explanation.

Bearing in mind that the risk of violence depends on the interaction of a range of potential factors, the following have been identified as the most significant, listed in descending order of relative importance.

Violence risk factors

There is a range of possible contributing factors to violent behaviour (box 31). These potential causes may lie within individuals, within society, be ascribed to cultural norms, or be rooted in disadvantage.

- Families constitute the training ground for aggression. It is within the family that aggressive behaviours are first learned. To the extent that families fail to instil non-violent values in their children, those children will be more likely to develop a repertoire of violent behaviours as they negotiate life in society at large.

- There are correlations between aggression in children and certain characteristics in their parents, notably maternal rejection and parental use of physical punishment and threat.

- Abusive parents themselves tend to have been abused or neglected as children, but only one-third to one-fifth of abused or neglected individuals will maltreat their own children.

Cultural factors

Norms of behaviour

- In general, the orientation of a culture, or the shared beliefs within a sub-culture helps define the limits of tolerable behaviour. To the extent that a society values violence, attaches prestige to violent conduct, or defines violence as normal or legitimate or functional behaviour, the values of individuals within that society will develop accordingly.

- The use of violence to achieve ends perceived as legitimate is a principle deeply embedded in any culture. Violence on the sporting field, in the home and in school is tolerated by many people.

Economic inequality

- Violence is more common in those societies characterized by widespread poverty and inequality. Worldwide, those countries with high income inequality have the highest homicide rates.

- In most societies, both victims of violence and violent offenders are drawn from the most disadvantaged socioeconomic groups.

Cultural disintegration

- The loosening of social prohibitions against violence may flow from feelings of alienation on the part of marginal members of society. This is particularly the case with a number of young people and with a large segment of indigenous populations.

Setting

- The physical characteristics of a location and the kind of activity occurring there can communicate that violence is more or less acceptable. A dilapidated environment has the potential to invite violence; a clean, modern setting can inhibit aggressive behaviour.

Gender

- Attitudes of gender inequality are deeply embedded in many cultures and rape, domestic assault and sexual harassment can all be viewed as a violent expression of the cultural norm.

Personality factors

- The best predictor of future aggression is past aggressive behaviour; thus aggressive children tend to grow into aggressive adults.

- Two personality traits often associated with violent behaviour are lack of empathy or regard for the feelings of others, and impulsiveness, or the inability to defer gratification.

- Hostile impulses in people with unusually strong internal controls – those referred to as the over-controlled personality – can result in extreme violence.

Substance abuse

- The suggestion that "drugs cause violence" is an oversimplification. The effect of a drug on an individual's behaviour is the product of a range of drug and non-drug factors which include the pharmacological properties of the substance in question, the individual's neurological foundation, personality and temperament, his or her expectations of the drug's effects, and the social setting in which the individual is located.

- Drug use and violent behaviour may result from a common cause – the inability to control one's impulses. Beyond this, drug use may compound the impairment of impulse control in an otherwise aggressive person.

- Alcohol – a close association exists between alcohol and violence, but the relationship is complex. It is probably less a result of alcohol's pharmacological properties, but rather more a product of coexisting psychological, social and cultural factors.

- Illicit drugs – violence is infrequently associated directly with the pharmacological effects of illicit drugs. Of course, violence is frequently associated with the trafficking and distribution of these substances.

Biological factors

- Violent behaviour does not appear to be an inherited characteristic.

- Adverse perinatal experiences may indirectly result in violent behaviour.

- Autonomic nervous system dysfunction may lead to psychopathic behaviour.

- Hormones, particularly testosterone, may play a part in violent behaviour.

- Men are at least ten times more likely than women to be charged with violent offences, which indicates a real sex-based difference in behaviour, whether due to actual gender or to behavioural expectations arising from gender.

- Violence tends to be perpetrated most commonly by those aged between 15 and 30.

Mental illness

- Some forms of mental illness, notably paranoid schizophrenia, may occasionally result in violent acts, although prediction of violence in the mentally ill is regarded as extremely difficult.

/cont'd

/cont'd

Media influences

- Television viewing may be associated with subsequent aggression in some viewers. Research indicates that the relationship is bi-directional, that is, violence viewing gives rise to aggression and aggression engenders violence viewing.

- Video and film viewing may have the same effects as television viewing.

Peers and schooling

- The company of delinquent or aggressive peers may influence individuals to become aggressive.

[1] As has been noted, this list of factors associated with the risk of violence has been adapted from the NCV – a report produced well over a decade ago. Despite its "relative age", the NCV identification of these factors remains as valid today as it was in 1990. (See: www.aic.gov.au/publications/ncv.html, accessed 12 Nov. 2005.)

Source: Adapted from the Australian National Committee on Violence (1990), pp. 61–63. Reproduced with permission from the Australian Institute of Criminology and from the National Committee on Violence (NCV).

In terms of long-term strategies to tackle the general problem of violence in any society, the list in box 31 indicates that the most significant positive outcomes are likely to be achieved through a concentration on child development programmes linked to the family. It is within the family that aggressive behaviours are first learned. To the extent that families can instil non-violent values in their children, those children are more likely to negotiate life in society at large without resorting to a repertoire of violent behaviours.

From the perspective of preventing violence in the workplace, long-term strategies like these are obviously of great significance, just as are measures to deal with the range of cultural factors associated with violence. To the extent that a society values violence, attributes prestige to violent conduct, or defines violence as normal or legitimate or functional behaviour, the values of individuals within that society, and within that society's workplaces, will develop accordingly. Changing these values is clearly a formidable challenge to any society, but that challenge has been taken up in many parts of the world through broad-based programmes designed to reduce economic inequality, address problems of youth education and the marginalization of indigenous groups, and achieve gender equality.[3]

It will take time for many of the benefits of programmes in these various areas to have a widespread or macro-level impact, and to spread their influence to the workplace. Meanwhile, there are many ways in which positive micro-level change can be achieved through targeted programmes and actions within a particular society, and the workplaces of that society. Before considering these programmes and activities, however, it is necessary to examine more closely certain of the risk factors identified as being associated with violence, in order to see how they may interact to produce violence at work.

Individual behaviour and workplace violence

Workplace violence can be viewed as individual behaviour, with particular psychological roots and occurring in a specific situational context. Some writers have discussed workplace violence from this perspective. Most reports of this type specifically addressing workplace violence usually have been case-studies or accounts of personal experiences in workplace violence prevention, rather than systematic research on the interaction between personality and situational causes. Nonetheless, these reports provide useful leads.[4]

Research-based literature explaining the causes of workplace violence is very limited in its scope and disciplinary perspective, as this quotation from an authoritative American Psychological Association publication implies. Most of this literature focuses upon risk factors associated with individuals' aggressive and self-destructive behaviour, rather than upon what may be broadly termed social issues, and the link between the two. A useful framework which classifies these risk factors under these two broad headings is shown in box 32.

A summary of the British literature on workplace violence reflecting this "individual behaviour" approach concluded that the most common features seemed to be:

- **Feeling aggrieved.** A sense of being treated unfairly, whether real or imagined, could lead to violence.

- **Being forced to wait, causing irritation and frustration.** An anger-eliciting stimulus, perhaps from another person, could spark violence.

- **Perceived intrusions into private life.** Loss of self-esteem from reprimands, downsizing, layoffs and like experiences could precipitate aggression.

- **Prejudice.** Whether racial or sexual, prejudice could provoke violence against members of another group.

- **Staff attitudes.** Violence could occur if one staff member was seen as a threat to another.

- **Uncomfortable physical conditions.** These could contribute to the display of aggression.

- **Mental instability.** This may lead to aggressive behaviour.[5]

Box 32   Classification of risk factors

1.   Individual

      1.1   Psychosocial

             1.1.1   developmental factors

             1.1.2   mental illness

             1.1.3   individual histories of violence and criminal justice system involvement

      1.2   Biological

             1.2.1   genetics

             1.2.2   neurobiology and brain injury

             1.2.3   alcohol and other drugs

2.   Social

      2.1   Macro-social

             2.1.1   socioeconomic inequality

             2.1.2   access to firearms, alcohol and other drugs

             2.1.3   media influences

             2.1.4   other aspects of culture

      2.2   Micro-social

             2.2.1   gender and family violence

             2.2.2   situational factors

Source: McDonald and Brown, 1997, reproduced with permission from the Australian Institute of Criminology.

Significant efforts have been devoted by those seeking to explain violence in this way to predict also when an individual might behave in an aggressive manner. There is no doubt that certain identifiable factors do increase the likelihood that certain individuals, and population groups, will behave in such a way. These factors are to be found in both the long-term life experience of the people concerned, and in immediate, situational factors.

The fact remains that, when seeking to predict whether aggressive behaviour will occur, a distinction must be made between predicting at the level of the general population or at that of the individual. The available evidence does permit statements to be made, with some degree of accuracy and reliability, about the heightened risk of violence at work being committed by population groups who display the following key characteristics:

• a history of violent behaviour;

• being male;

• being a young adult;

- experience of difficulties in childhood, including inadequate parenting, troubled relationships within the family and low levels of school achievement;

- problems of psychotropic substance abuse, especially problematic alcohol use;

- severe mental illness, the symptoms of which are not being adequately identified or controlled through therapeutic regimes; and/or

- being in situations conducive to self-directed or interpersonal violence, including having access to firearms.[6]

Each of these factors can interact with one another. They are also cumulative in effect – the more of these factors that a population group possesses, the higher the risk is that the group may engage in violent behaviour. The dilemma remains, however, of predicting with sufficient accuracy and reliability whether a particular individual within that group may become violent. It is not possible in the current state of knowledge to predict with complete certainty that a specific person will behave in an aggressive way. Thus there is always the possibility, if prediction techniques are applied based on a list of key characteristics like those referred to above, that some individuals may be falsely identified as being at risk of committing acts of violence, and others as not being at risk.

These so-called "false positive" and "false negative" aspects of the prediction equation mean that these techniques, if considered for use in the context of the workplace, should only be applied with extreme caution and care. Enterprises and workers alike have a vested interest in ensuring that individuals who do represent a credible threat to the safety and well-being of the workplace are denied entry, or are provided with assistance to minimize the likelihood that they will behave aggressively towards either themselves or others. There is, however, a clear potential for these predictive tools to be used in a prejudicial or discriminatory fashion, in order to exclude from the workplace undesirable persons, or even groups, who are judged to fit a loosely defined category or profile.

The case of Joseph T. Wesbecker, described in box 33, continues to illustrate the lack of precision which still exists in the prediction of workplace violence, even when assisted by the application of a detailed clinical assessment tool. The present status of violence prediction efforts has been summarized in the following terms: "Violence can be predicted, meaning that within a given population we can assign different probabilities of violence to populations members based on the characteristics of these members. Nevertheless, there are significant concerns with validity, reliability and accuracy of predictions".[7]

It is suggested that a far more promising approach to an understanding of workplace violence is to be found in an interactive analysis of both individual and societal risk factors, with particular attention being given to the situational context in which certain types of work tasks are performed.

Box 33   The case of Joseph T. Wesbecker

On the morning of 14 September 1989, Joseph T. Wesbecker, an emotionally disturbed employee on long-term disability leave from the Standard Gravure Company in Louisville, Kentucky, entered the plant in downtown Louisville and killed eight co-workers and injured 12 others with a semi-automatic "assault" rifle, before taking his own life with a pistol.

The facts surrounding Wesbecker's life and the events leading up to the tragedy were examined to determine the degree of "fit" to a model for the prediction of violent behaviour proposed by Monahan.

Monahan, a leading authority in the field of dangerous and violent behaviour, has suggested that the following questions may assist in making a meaningful clinical assessment about a person's potential for violence:

- What events precipitated raising the issue of the person's potential for violence, and in what context did these events take place?

- What are the person's relevant demographic characteristics? [A suggested profile given is of a non-white male in his late teens or early twenties, occupying a low socio-economic class, with a history of alcohol or drug abuse, a relatively low IQ, relatively less formal education, and a tendency to move or change jobs frequently.]

- What is a person's history of violent behaviour?

- What is the base rate of violent behaviour among people of this person's background?

- What are the sources of stress in the person's current environment?

- What cognitive and affective factors indicate that a person may be predisposed to cope with stress in a violent manner?

- What cognitive and affective factors indicate that a person may be predisposed to cope with stress in a non-violent manner?

- How similar are the contexts in which the person has used a violent coping mechanism in the past to the contexts in which the person will likely function in the future?

- In particular, who are the likely victims of the person's violent behaviour, and how available are they?

- What means does the person possess to commit violence?

Although several of the predictors identified by Monahan demonstrated validity in the case of Joseph Wesbecker, several others did not.

Dr. Lee A. Coleman, the physician who treated Wesbecker for more than two years, met with Wesbecker just three days before the shootings. In hospital records obtained by the coroner's office, Coleman noted that Wesbecker exhibited "tangential thought" and "increased levels of agitation and anger ... I encouraged the patient to go into the hospital for stabilization but he refused".

Furthermore, Wesbecker did not fit the demographic profile of a violent person.

- He had not previously engaged in violent behaviour at work.

- He did not have a police record of domestic violence, although he had been sued for harassment on two occasions by his first wife. He was found not guilty in both cases.

- He had shown a predisposition to cope with stress in a non-violent manner through at least two years of voluntary outpatient treatment; three occasions of voluntary hospitalization; filing grievances both through his union and with the county Human Relations Commission; and by discussing work problems with a labour attorney.

Wesbecker – although he was fatherless (his father was killed when he was about a year old) – grew up with his mother and grandmother and had lived in Louisville his entire life. He was married, had children, had no criminal record, did not abuse drugs or alcohol, had several friends, held his job at Standard Gravure for 17 years, and was financially secure.

However, certain of Wesbecker's thoughts and behaviours did conform closely to elements of Monahan's model:

- There were sources of considerable stress in Wesbecker's work environment. His divorce and lawsuits concerning his first marriage also indicated significant stress in his personal life.

- Although he demonstrated a willingness to manage stress in non-violent ways, both cognitive and affective factors indicated a potential to react to stress in a violent manner: psychiatric reports of anger; bringing a revolver to work; plans to kill company executives; and a bizarre scheme to blow up the plant with explosives attached to model aeroplanes.

The Wesbecker case underscores both the difficulty in predicting violence and the challenges that occupational mental health professionals face in minimizing acts of violence in the workplace.

Sources: Adapted from Kuzmits, 1990, pp. 1014–1020, with permission; and Monahan, 1986, pp. 559–68, with permission.

Interactive model: Contextual, individual, workplace and societal risk factors

Analysis based on a combination of individual and social risk factors began with a single study that included a most valuable framework in which to consider violence at work. The study, conducted for the British Health and Safety Executive by the London-based Tavistock Institute of Human Relations,[8] recognized that a number of factors could cause or contribute to a risk of violence at work: "The problem may lie in the assailant, in that there may be something about him which makes him strike out at the employee. The employee may be partly to blame because of incompetence or because of an unsympathetic attitude, or the way the organization works may sometimes lead to misunderstanding or frustration."[9]

The Tavistock researchers brought together in a framework model the various factors they found to be relevant in explaining how an interaction between an assailant (perpetrator) and an employee (victim) produced a violent outcome in the workplace. This model, modified substantially, is displayed in figure 16.[10]

It should be emphasized that while the basic Tavistock model has been maintained in figure 16, it has to a significant degree been expanded here in order to incorporate some of the issues explored earlier in this chapter, and in Chapter 2, including the risk factors associated with the prediction of violence and the types of work task or situation recognized as having an increased vulnerability to aggressive acts. These consequences may be immediate, in the sense that they have an impact on an individual victim as well as the enterprise with which they are associated. Thus the victim may suffer both physical and psychological injury, with longer-term effects which curtail his or her ability to work, enjoy normal social interactions and affect the family environment. In extreme circumstances the victim's life may be threatened or lost. For an enterprise, the outcome of workplace violence can strike at the economic foundations of the business involved, lowering productivity, affecting worker morale, and leading to stress and the risk of further violence occurring.

As the model further indicates, the outcome of violence extends well beyond the immediate consequences displayed, and can reach out and become part of the societal and contextual risk factors that surround both the victim(s) and the enterprise(s). The flow of violence from the workplace can produce ripples on the surface of a society which is already experiencing instability and cultural disorientation, just as it can feed into the destabilizing influences of globalization and the push to rationalize work processes. These linkages are displayed diagrammatically in the arrows which lead from the outcome box in the model to the boxes headed, respectively, "societal risk factors" and "contextual risk factors", and eventually track back again into the fields of the victim and the perpetrator. It is to be noted that these linkages represent an extension to the model which appeared in the first two editions of this book.[11]

More detailed elaboration of the model is provided below under each of the principal headings shown in figure 16.

Individual risk factors

The nature and outcome of the interaction between different categories of perpetrator and victims will almost certainly differ according to the type of workplace violence, the work being performed and the work environment itself.

Figure 16 Workplace violence: An interactive model

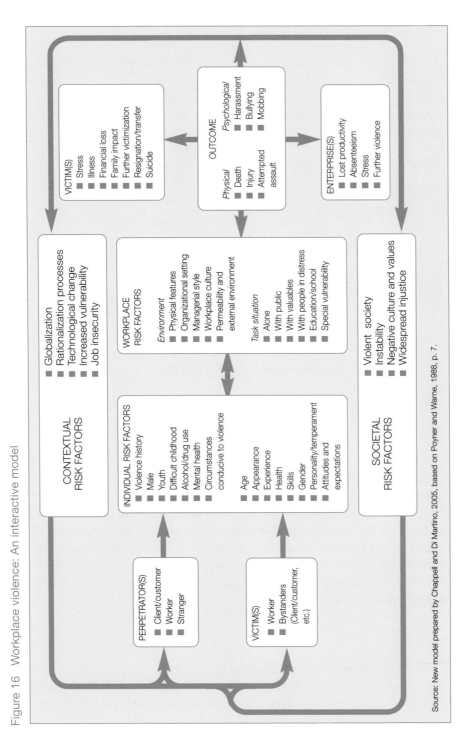

CONTEXTUAL RISK FACTORS
- Globalization
- Rationalization processes
- Technological change
- Increased vulnerability
- Job insecurity

INDIVIDUAL RISK FACTORS
- Violence history
- Male
- Youth
- Difficult childhood
- Alcohol/drug use
- Mental health
- Circumstances conducive to violence

- Age
- Appearance
- Experience
- Health
- Skills
- Gender
- Personality/temperament
- Attitudes and expectations

WORKPLACE RISK FACTORS

Environment
- Physical features
- Organizational setting
- Managerial style
- Workplace culture
- Permeability and external environment

Task situation
- Alone
- With public
- With valuables
- With people in distress
- Education/school
- Special vulnerability

VICTIM(S)
- Stress
- Illness
- Financial loss
- Family impact
- Further victimization
- Resignation/transfer
- Suicide

OUTCOME

Physical
- Death
- Injury
- Attempted assault

Psychological
- Harassment
- Bullying
- Mobbing

ENTERPRISE(S)
- Lost productivity
- Absenteeism
- Stress
- Further violence

SOCIETAL RISK FACTORS
- Violent society
- Instability
- Negative culture and values
- Widespread injustice

PERPETRATOR(S)
- Client/customer
- Worker
- Stranger

VICTIM(S)
- Worker
- Bystanders (Client/customer, etc.)

Source: New model prepared by Chappell and Di Martino, 2005, based on Poyner and Warne, 1988, p. 7.

123

Perpetrators

The assailant or perpetrator of violence is likely to fall into three principal categories – a client of the particular enterprise; a colleague or fellow worker; a relative or a stranger (box 34). There may also be variations in individual risk factors between people in distinct countries due to the influence of social or cultural differences.

Box 34   Types of perpetrator

Perpetrators of mental violence [bullying] at the workplace in Finland[1]
- 57 per cent had been intimidated by co-workers *
- 40 per cent by superiors
- 17 per cent by customers
- 5 per cent by subordinates

Perpetrators of workplace homicides in the US[2]
- 75 per cent by a stranger
- 15 per cent by a co-worker or former co-worker
- 10 per cent by a relative or other personal acquaintance

Note: *These figures overlap, although most of the persons had been intimidated only by one of these groups.

Sources: [1]Statistics Finland, *Quality of Work Life Surveys* 1997, and 2003, special elaboration for the authors, 23 Mar. 2004; and [2]Richardson and Windau, 2003, pp. 673–689, especially p. 677.

In most circumstances, the key characteristics of the perpetrator most likely to be associated with a heightened risk of violence are those which were mentioned earlier (box 32) – a history of violence; being male; being young; having a troubled childhood; substance abuse; certain forms of mental illness; and being in a situation conducive to violence.[12] The Tavistock study identified five characteristics, most of which overlap substantially with this list – personality; temporary conditions; negative/uncertain expectations; immaturity; and people with dogs.[13]

Victims

There are many attributes of a victim of workplace violence, who is in most cases likely to be an employee, which **could** be associated with the risk of violence.[14] These include appearance, health, age and experience, gender, personality and temperament, attitudes and expectations.

Appearance and first impressions are important in any job, as they can set the tone of the interaction and establish the role characteristics for an encounter. In occupations involving direct contact with members of the public, for instance, the wearing of a uniform may encourage or discourage violence. Uniforms are often worn in occupations where employees are expected to act with authority or have the respect of members of the public. Uniforms also identify staff and distinguish them from the public. It is likely that in many circumstances uniforms will discourage violence, but there are situations in which the presence of uniformed staff is resented, and which can provoke abusive or violent behaviour. In the United Kingdom, for example, an increasing number of cases of aggression against ambulance staff have been reported because of general public hostility towards people wearing a uniform like those of police officers. For this reason, ambulance staff are now beginning to wear green boiler suits rather than blue uniforms, to distinguish them from law enforcement officials.

The health of workers can also influence how they interact with clients and the public at large. Stress from a heavy workload, or mild forms of mental illness, may lead to misunderstandings or misleading behaviour which precipitate aggressive responses. The age and experience of workers are other factors that can either increase or diminish the possibility of aggression. Previous experience of handling similar difficult situations, which is obviously associated with age, should enable older workers to react more wisely than inexperienced staff.

As has been made clear earlier, a person's sex can influence aggressive behaviour in a number of ways. Men are more likely than women to respond in an aggressive way to many workplace situations, while women are also at much greater risk of certain types of victimization at work than men.

The personality and attitude of workers are also relevant in considering risks of victimization. Some staff members are often better than others in handling difficult situations – a quality which is usually associated with an individual's less tangible personality characteristics and style of behaviour. The attitude of workers, and their job expectations, can also be factors influencing aggressive behaviours. For example, staff members who are working in an enterprise which is about to be shut down, or which is experiencing massive layoffs, are less likely to be tolerant in their encounters with clients. Similarly, uncertain role definitions associated with a particular job can influence how a violent or potentially violent incident is handled. Schoolteachers expect to deal with unruly children, but bus drivers may not; police officers anticipate encounters with disturbed or dangerous people, but firefighters and other emergency service providers may not.

Overall, the ways in which victims react to aggressive behaviour appear to be important in determining whether that aggression diminishes or escalates. It seems to be essential that the victim is not seen by the aggressor to behave in some unfair or unreasonable way. Anxious or angry behaviour by the victim may also trigger violence, while controlled behaviour may help defuse tensions.

Workplace risk factors

Both the perpetrator and the victim interact at the workplace. The working environment, including its physical and organizational settings or structure and its managerial style and culture, can influence the risks of violence resulting from interactions.

The physical design features of a workplace can be a factor in either defusing or acting as a potential trigger for violence or escalation of aggressive interactions. Australian research has shown, for example, that the levels of violent and destructive behaviour in or near licensed premises (pubs, clubs, bars and like establishments) are influenced by a range of situational factors including the physical design and comfort of the premises. Overcrowded, poorly ventilated, dirty and noisy premises experience higher rates of violence than do those which exhibit good physical design features.[15]

The organizational setting appears to be equally if not more important in this respect. Poor organization may, for instance, lead to an excessive workload for a specific group of workers (while others may be relatively inactive), slow down their performance, create unjustified delays and queuing, develop negative attitudes among such workers and induce aggressive behaviour among the customers. The same effects may be induced by labyrinthine bureaucratic procedures, putting both employees and customers under serious stress.

In a broader context, the type of interpersonal relationships, managerial style, the level at which responsibilities are decentralized, and the general culture of the workplace must also be taken into consideration. A "participatory" working environment, for instance, where dialogue and communication are extensively exercised, may help defuse the risks of violence. In contrast, a "closed" authoritarian working environment where people work in isolation, with mutual suspicion and defensive attitudes towards external people, may increase the risk of violence.[16]

Along the same lines, the decentralization of services and responsibilities at a local level may help employees to become more aware of local issues and better respond to the needs of the customers, as well as to forecast difficult situations which might degenerate into violence. This localized flexibility would be quite difficult to achieve within a centralized, depersonalized organization where relationships are highly formalized. A company culture based on racial tolerance, equal opportunities and cooperation can also contribute to the establishment of a working climate where violence has little play. In contrast, if discrimination and segregation are explicitly or implicitly part of the culture of the company, this can be reflected in all behaviours and relationships, both internally and with the outside world. Two recent studies from Italy illustrate the importance of these factors.

A national study conducted in 2002 by the Department of Occupational Medicine at ISPESL (Istituto Superiore per la Prevenzione e la Sicurezza sul Lavoro) of 2,600 workers of Group ENEL in Italy revealed the key role of the organizational climate in the development of mobbing within the workplace. The majority of workers interviewed linked workplace violence with a lack of knowledge of the organizational strategies of the enterprise, and the inefficiency of the internal communication system.

As shown in figure 17, nearly 65 per cent of workers surveyed had no knowledge of organizational strategies. This lack of knowledge was compounded by an inefficient internal communication system, as shown in figure 18.

As shown in figure 18, nearly 58 per cent of those surveyed identified an inefficient communication system. Hence, if the proportions shown in figures 17 and 18 are indicative of all organizations in this area, nearly two-thirds of workers will have no knowledge of organizational strategies to deal with a workplace violence event when it unfolds, and rapid response is unlikely if communication systems are as inadequate as this survey reported.

Another survey was conducted among 300 workers in the Italian provinces of Bari and Matera in 2000. This survey highlighted the importance of company attitudes and planning to reduce or enhance the risks of workplace violence, as shown in figure 19.

The data displayed in figure 19 indicate that fully 23.5 per cent of respondents stated that the company had only superficial knowledge of the

Figure 17   Knowledge of organizational strategies of the enterprise (percentages)
"Do you have any knowledge of the organizational strategies in the enterprise?"

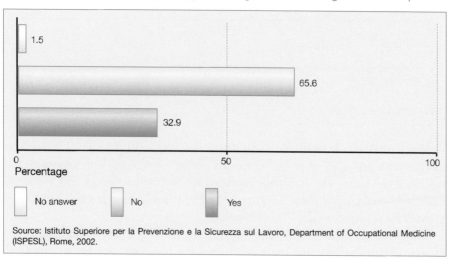

Source: Istituto Superiore per la Prevenzione e la Sicurezza sul Lavoro, Department of Occupational Medicine (ISPESL), Rome, 2002.

Figure 18   Inefficiency of the internal communications system (percentages)
            "Do you think the internal communications system is efficient?"

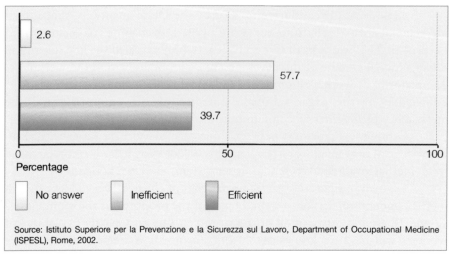

Source: Istituto Superiore per la Prevenzione e la Sicurezza sul Lavoro, Department of Occupational Medicine (ISPESL), Rome, 2002.

Figure 19   Level of company awareness of the violent situation (percentages)
            "Is the company aware of the violent situation?"

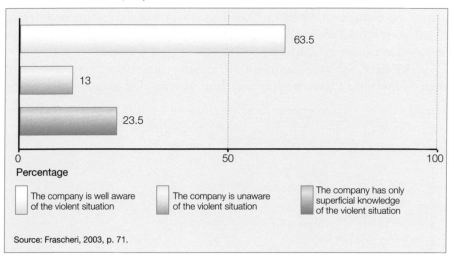

Source: Frascheri, 2003, p. 71.

violent situation. It is of concern that 63.6 per cent of the 300 workers interviewed reported that the company knew of the violent situation but tolerated the risks. The rationale provided for toleration of risk and inactivity included "own convenience". Figure 20 shows the potential for risk reduction, as cited by respondents.

The data shown in figure 20 indicate that: (a) only a very small proportion of respondents believe that there is nothing the company can do to reduce the

Figure 20   Perceived company capacity for risk reduction (percentages)
              "How do you perceive the company's capacity to address the violent situation?"

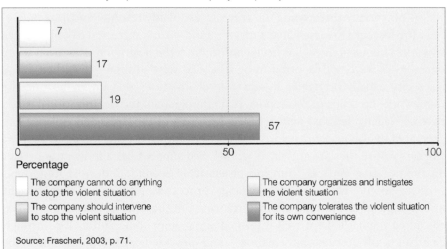

Source: Frascheri, 2003, p. 71.

risks of workplace violence; (b) somewhat surprisingly, only 17 per cent believe that the company should intervene to stop the violent situation; (c) only 19 per cent report that the company actually does organize and instigate violent events; and (d) 57 per cent believe that companies tolerate the risks of workplace violence for corporate reasons.

Each situation is a unique mixture and thus requires a distinctive analysis. That is why the prediction of specific acts of violence occurring is extremely difficult. Nonetheless, it seems possible and useful to identify, in much greater detail than has previously been attempted, a number of working situations which appear to be highly relevant both to an understanding of this type of aggression, and to the development of strategies for its prevention or control.[17]

Widespread restructuring through privatization, decentralization and rationalization is also having a profound effect on conditions of work and employment. These processes may be accompanied, although with different intensity from country to country and from situation to situation, by downsizing, layoffs, freezes or cuts in salaries, heavier workloads and faster pace of work, longer hours of effective work, less comfortable shifts and work during unsocial hours, increased contracting and subcontracting, and more temporary and precarious employment contracts. These are all recognized potential stressors and may eventually lead to a climate of violence driven by uncertainty, growing exasperation and vulnerability.

Technological innovation may act as another multiplier of stress and violence risk at work, especially when such innovation is not accompanied by adequate training and jobs are, or seem to be, at risk. The impact of all these stressors may negatively affect the commitment and motivation of the workforce concerned and jeopardize the quality of the production and services provided, as well as potentially threatening the very success of any reforms undertaken.

Job insecurity is associated with stress and with an increased risk of violence at work. This association has been confirmed in the health industry, even when stress levels were not reported to be severe or were declining.[18] Although job insecurity usually originates in macro-level situations that go far beyond the framework and scope of this report, two interpersonal and organizational issues have been identified that may defuse at least part of the stress and violence risk generated by job insecurity. First, supervisors and co-workers need to support workers whose jobs are at risk, as work-based support has a moderating effect on the negative impacts from job insecurity.[19] Second, and most important, workers should be involved in change processes, provided with sufficient information to understand planned reforms and the aims of change processes, consulted regularly, kept well informed about impending shifts (e.g. through circulation of detailed information), and provided with opportunities for feedback on temporary transitional difficulties and possible remedies.[20]

A large-scale survey conducted in Europe revealed that precariously employed workers (those hired on a casual, short-term, fixed-term contract and temporary agency basis) had poorer health-related outcomes than did those hired on permanent contracts.[21] This poorer health status persisted after adjustment for working conditions, social and environmental factors. The risk factors included a low level of control over work tasks and working time, increased pace of production, performance of lower-skilled job tasks, and insecure employment, all of which are major elements in stress building. Violence at work is also associated with real or perceived vulnerability. This and other surveys also clearly indicated that workers in precarious jobs were exposed to workplace violence to a greater extent than were those employed under permanent contracts.[22]

The interrelationship between the external environment and the working environment also appears significant in terms of predicting violence. Any prediction of the possibility of violent incidents occurring at the workplace will thus depend upon a thorough analysis of the characteristics of the perpetrator and victim in the particular situation, the specific working environment, and features from the external environment.

The permeation of external environmental, social and contextual factors

The level of "permeability" of working environments to risks from the external environment is far from homogeneous. Nevertheless, it is evident, for instance, that a bank or shop located in a very dangerous area will be more likely to be subject to robberies; that bus routes will have different levels of risks of violence depending on which part of the city they serve; and that the level of frustration and aggression of the public in an office may vary according to the level of frustration and aggression in their living environment.

Whenever violence is embedded in a society, it is also likely to be reflected in the workplace. Several studies strongly hint at direct inroads of societal problems into the workplace, with violence as one of the major issues. The examples in box 35, drawn from an ILO report on workplace violence in the health sector, reflect situations that are widespread in many countries.

In all the countries where case studies in the health sector were conducted for this international collaborative programme, there was evidence of some "cross-over" of violence from the local population into health workplaces. That is, localized population risk factors appeared to permeate workplace boundaries. However, it is not just physical violence that afflicts the victims, but many suffer emotional stress repercussions.

Box 35   Violence embedded in society

In Bulgaria violence is a normal element of life:

> Violence is all-pervasive; it is present in the life of all social strata, occupations and ethnic groups. Its psychological foundation is … found in people's dependence based on the hierarchy of power, i.e. being dependent on those above you. A society where the centre of control has always been outside the individual (such as the patriarchal, paternalist and totalitarian societies) turns out incapable to cope with violence once the external control is taken away. In the absence of any interior moral norms or, in other words, interior inhibitions, many Bulgarians turn to violence as a model to regulate family, social, interpersonal and institutional relations and society is well on the way to accepting that as a norm.

In South Africa violence in society permeates the workplace:

> The very high level of workplace violence [in the public sector] is symptomatic of a greater problem with its roots in the socio-economic realities of South Africa. It is impossible to capture the impact of management styles, the shortcomings in the management and administration of South Africa's health system, the lack of commitment to ethical conduct, the impact of societal violence on the psychosocial development of health care workers in one study.

According to the executive director of the Institute of Future Studies for Development in Thailand, that country is changing from the "land of smiles to the land of violence":

> In the past, some forms of violence, such as wife battery and the physical punishment of children, were acceptable if the perpetrators and the victims were related but unacceptable if they were strangers. Rape is a crime only if the victim is not the wife of the perpetrator. Marital rape is not an illegal act. Currently, Thai people are aware of violence and accept it as a national social problem.

Source: Di Martino, 2002b, p. 14.

Stress and violence

The relationship between stress and violence is not a straightforward and exclusive one, and concern has been expressed about the difficulties in achieving a commonly acceptable notion of stress. As the Experts who met in Geneva in October 2003 to develop an ILO code of practice entitled *Workplace violence in services sectors and measures to combat this phenomenon* indicated in their preamble: "There are some consequences of workplace violence, which may include stress, although stress is a concept which, for some, is not clearly definable."[23]

Nevertheless, the interrelationship between stress and violence is emerging as a key concern, and this potential is increasingly being given recognition in official instruments.[24] A growing number of studies are providing evidence about this inter-relationship between violence and stress.

A Finnish study on the effects of bullying on municipal employees found that 40 per cent of bullied workers felt stressed or very stressed. For example, 49 per cent had been unusually tired and 30 per cent were nervous often or constantly.[25] These reactions are all typical indicators of stress. Another recent study has identified that the emotional consequences from bullying may be more extensive than those from physical violence.[26]

The impact of emotional or "psychological" violence on psychological well-being is shown in the following.

Adverse effects of physical violence on psychological well-being

- Stress reaction and impairment of general health

- Reduced psychological well-being and greater risk of psychological problems

- Cognitive effects, e.g. concentration problems

- Reduced self-confidence

- Reduced satisfaction with work

- Fear reactions

- Post-traumatic stress

Adverse effects of psychological violence on psychological well-being

- Anxiety

- Depression

- Psychosomatic symptoms

- Aggression

- Fear and mistrust
- Cognitive effects, such as inability to concentrate and think clearly, and reduced problem-solving capacity
- Isolation and loneliness
- Deterioration of relationship
- Post-traumatic stress.[27]

Stress can also lead to frustration and anger, and thus can be an antecedent of violence at work.[28] Particular stressors have been identified as predictors of violence. In a 1997 American study covering a sample of approximately 7,000 employees of a state health agency, a relationship was found between the occurrence of on-the-job physical assaults and 11 different job stressors. Four of the 11 stressor variables examined were found to be associated with assaults on both men and women. Limited job control, high levels of responsibility for people, limited opportunities for alternative employment, and skill underutilization were all discovered to be significant predictors associated with assault for both sexes. The authors concluded that assaults may occur more frequently among highly stressed workers than those experiencing less stress.[29]

A vicious circle may thus be activated whereby the worker suffers increasing levels of both stress and violence. In addition, other forms of violence may intrude into workplaces from outside.

The "spillover" of domestic violence into workplaces

The serious impact of widespread domestic violence on the workplace is progressively being recognized, and gives cause for growing concern, as shown in box 36.

In the United States:

Nine in ten (91 per cent) corporate leaders believe that domestic violence affects both the private lives and the working lives of their employees, according to a survey conducted for Liz Claiborne, Inc., as part of the company's domestic violence awareness campaign. The survey finds that America's corporate leaders have grown more aware of domestic violence as a national problem, and as a problem that affects their employees. But despite the increase in awareness, just 12 per cent of corporate leaders say their corporations should play a major role in addressing domestic violence.[30]

According to the United Nations Development Fund for Women (UNIFEM), violence against women is rampant. One in three women and girls around the world will either be beaten, coerced into sex or otherwise

Box 36   Domestic abuse often spills over into the workplace

For battered women who are employed, a job may provide the only escape from abuse. However, a job is the one place a batterer can be certain to find his victim.[1] If she has a routine, she may have a specific time to leave for a particular place for a specified number of hours. Hence, she is reachable. The San Francisco Family Violence Prevention Fund notes that a growing number of employers recognize that personal, so-called "real life" problems such as domestic violence affect both an employee's job performance and a company's bottom line.[2]

The abused victim is not the only one who suffers the consequences of an abusive relationship. From co-workers who step in to stop an altercation to those who witness an act of violence, the confrontation affects the entire organization.[3] Abusive husbands or lovers, either in person or on the telephone, harm or harass three-quarters of employed battered women at their workplaces. In addition to having to deal with harassment on the job, employers and victims endure an increase in other problems. A study conducted in Tulsa, Oklahoma, revealed that 96 per cent of employed battered women develop other work-related problems caused by the abuse. Another study, conducted in New York and Minnesota, revealed that up to 20 per cent of these employed battered women eventually lose their jobs because of abuse-caused work problems.

[1]Levin, 1995, pp. 11–13, cited in Johnson and Gardner, 2000, pp. 197–202, especially p. 199. [2]Hudson, 1998, p. C1, cited in Johnson and Gardner, ibid. [3]*Air Conditioning Heating and Refrigeration News*, 1999.

Source: Johnson and Gardner, 2000, pp. 197–206, especially p. 199. (See also the website of the Family Violence Prevention Fund: http://endabuse.org/, accessed on 23 June 2005.)

abused in her lifetime. The UNIFEM report indicates that women are not safe from domestic and intimate violence anywhere in the world. In Cambodia 16 per cent of women were found to have been physically abused by their husbands, and 30 per cent were physically abused by partners or ex-partners in the United Kingdom, 52 per cent in the Palestinian West Bank, 21 per cent in Nicaragua, 29 per cent in Canada and 22 per cent in the United States.[31] The US Center for Disease Control and Prevention (CDC) has estimated that the costs of intimate partner violence against women in the United States alone exceed US$5.8 billion per year – US$4.1 billion for direct medical and health care services, while productivity losses account for another US$1.7 billion.[32]

Another global survey, published by the WHO in 2002, disclosed that between 10 and 69 per cent of women had been physically assaulted by an intimate male partner at some time in their lives. Over the previous 12-month period, the percentage of women who had been assaulted by a partner varied from 3 per cent or less among women in Australia, Canada and the United States; 27 per cent of ever-partnered women (that is, women who have ever had an ongoing sexual partner) in Nicaragua; 38 per cent of currently partnered women in the Republic of Korea; and 52 per cent of currently married Palestinian women in the West Bank and Gaza Strip. For many of these women, physical assault was not an isolated event but part of a continuing pattern of abusive behaviour. Physical violence in these intimate relationships was often accompanied by psychological abuse, and in up to 50 per cent of cases by sexual abuse. For example, among 613 women in Japan who had at any time been abused, 57 per cent had suffered all three types of abuse: physical, psychological and sexual.[33]

Domestic violence is chronically under-reported, but research shows that in the United Kingdom:

- one in four women will be a victim of domestic violence in their lifetime;

- on average, two women a week are killed by a current or former male partner;

- domestic violence accounts for nearly a quarter of all violent crime;

- domestic violence probably costs the country well in excess of £5 billion a year.[34]

In the United States, although the number of violent crimes by intimate partners against females declined sharply from 1993 to 2001, intimate partner violence made up 20 per cent of all non-fatal violent crime experienced by women aged 12 or older in 2001. For example, 1,247 women were killed by an intimate partner in 2000.[35]

In Latin America and the Caribbean, "anywhere between 30 and 75 per cent of adult women with partners in the region are subject to psychological abuse, and between 10 and 30 per cent suffer physical violence, the majority of studies indicate".[36]

In Eastern Europe:

domestic violence is the most widespread form of gender-based violence in all the surveyed countries. Across the region the legal systems do not properly address this issue: no specific provisions exist, nor are any restraining orders possible. There is also an insufficient understanding in society of what exactly domestic violence is and thus a failure to always recognize and name it. The lack of knowledge about the nature of domestic violence among women, and the absence of support networks in part explain why women themselves often downplay the seriousness of the abuse. There are no shelters for victims of domestic violence. It is very common for women to stay in an abusive marriage or relationship due to economic dependence on an abusive husband or male partner; at the same time, state authorities do either little or nothing to put an end to this situation. With regard to marital rape, although a few countries changed their legislation, making it an offence, in practice no cases have been decided by the courts.[37]

The final issue to be considered within the framework of the interactive model shown in figure 16 is the outcome or consequences of any violence which occurs at the workplace. At the most extreme levels of violence, as in the case of the terrorist attacks in New York and the multiple school shootings at Dunblane (both discussed in Chapter 1), this outcome can amount to death and destruction of a form normally only seen and to be coped with on a battlefield, or in a war zone. For the survivors of such violence, including those workers responding to provide emergency care and assistance as well as witnessing the events, the personal trauma and distress involved can be both extreme and long-lasting.

However, like a stone thrown into water, violence at work not only has an immediate impact on the victim, but also expands in progressively larger ripples, affecting other people directly or indirectly involved, as well as the enterprise concerned and the community. This effect explains why the cost of violence at work has often been underestimated.

Costs of violence at work

The costs of workplace violence are borne by the victim, the employing organization and society as a whole. It is only in recent times that experts have started quantifying the multiple and massive costs of such violence.[38]

Individual costs

On an individual level, the cost of personal suffering and pain resulting from violence at work is hard to quantify. Suffering and humiliation are not self-contained events. They usually lead to lack of motivation, loss of confidence, reduced self-esteem, depression, anger, anxiety and irritability. A 1993 Finnish study on psychological harassment at work indicated that 59 per cent of victims viewed the situation as "unjust", 47 per cent had thought of leaving their job, and 37 per cent suffered from depression.[39] All of these indicators are typical of stress, and stress is a very costly matter. If the causes of violence are not eliminated, or the effects of violence are not contained by adequate interventions, these symptoms are likely to develop into physical illness, psychological disorders, tobacco and alcohol and drug abuse, and so on; they can culminate in reduced employability, invalidity and even suicide.[40]

These negative consequences not only affect the person who is the focus of such violence, but often extend to people in proximity to the act, and even to people far removed or physically absent from the place where violence occurs. The effects of violence can thus pervade the entire workplace, the family of the victim and the community in which they live.

Table 22 Productivity impacts of violence at the workplace, United States, 1996

Impact	% of respondents
Decreased morale	9
Increased stress	22
Increased fear	18
Lower productivity	10
Increased absenteeism	3
Decreased worker trust	11
Increased staff turnover	3
Other	19

Source: Society for Human Resource Management (SHRM), Workplace Violence Survey 1996 (Alexandria, Virginia, SHRM, 1996). Reproduced with permission.

Organizational costs

At the level of the workplace, violence causes immediate – and often long-term – disruption to interpersonal relationships, the organization of work, productivity and the overall working environment. Employers bear the direct cost of lost work time and funding for improved security measures. Table 22 presents some aspects of the negative impact of workplace violence, which all adversely affect the performance of enterprises.

As shown in table 22, many of the costs following workplace violence are somewhat hidden. Indeed, unless the financial reporting system for an organization directly attributes costs against causes, the true expense for an organization is unlikely to ever be revealed. There are, however, further costs that are externalized to society as a whole.

Community costs

The cost of violence at work also affects the community as a whole. Health care and long-term rehabilitation costs for the reintegration of the victims of violence at work, unemployment and retraining costs for those who lost their job because of such violent events, disability and invalidity costs for those whose working capacities are impaired by violence at work, and legal and criminal justice system expenses are all part of the price paid.

An assessment of the total magnitude of the costs to the community of workplace violence also requires consideration of the indirect impact of this violence on the partners and relatives of the victim and, in a broader perspective, of its disruptive effect as a multiplier to the fear and anxiety about crime and violence in any society.

Figure 21   Combined effects of all cost elements of workplace violence

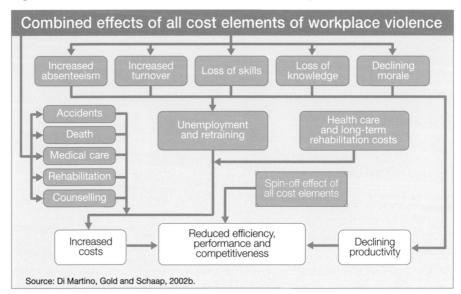

Source: Di Martino, Gold and Schaap, 2002b.

It is also important, in order to fully appreciate the overall impact of the combined effects of all cost elements, to highlight the dynamics of the inter-relationships, as shown in figure 21.

Thus, it is crucial that the full costs of workplace violence are accounted for. Concomitantly, this may provide a useful basis on which cost–benefit estimates of preventive interventions can be calculated.

Identifying the costs

Cost factors include direct, indirect and "intangible" costs.

Direct costs include workplace injuries, illnesses, disability, death, absenteeism and turnover:

* In the United Kingdom nearly half (42 per cent) of assaults at work resulted in some type of injury to the victim.[41]

* A study of bullying at two Finnish hospitals found that those who had been bullied had 26 per cent more certified sickness absence than those who were not bullied.[42]

* Data from the EU indicated a significant correlation between health-related absences and exposure to violence at work. As shown in figure 22, 35 per cent of workers exposed to physical violence were absent from

Figure 22   Absenteeism over a 12-month period, European Union, 1996 (percentages)

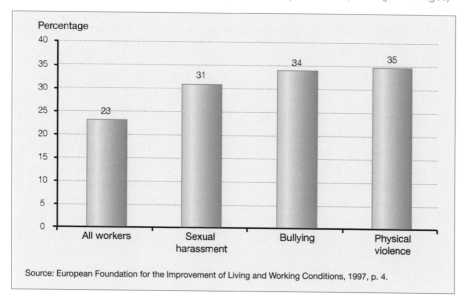

Source: European Foundation for the Improvement of Living and Working Conditions, 1997, p. 4.

work over a 12-month period, as well as 34 per cent of those exposed to bullying and 31 per cent of workers exposed to sexual harassment, compared to an average of 23 per cent among workers in general.[43]

Indirect costs include a reduction in job satisfaction, morale, commitment, efficiency, performance and productivity. For example:

- A survey of members of the Royal College of Nursing showed that nurses who were assaulted had poorer psychological well-being than those who were not assaulted. These nurses were also twice as likely to have acute psychological problems, with frequently assaulted individuals most affected.[44]

- A Swedish study of nurses reported that satisfaction with work was inversely affected by exposure to violence.[45]

- Similarly, more than half of Finnish prison employees who reported an experience of violence at work also reported reduced job satisfaction.[46]

Intangible costs include those related to the negative impact on company image, creativity, working climate, openness to innovation, knowledge-building and continuous learning. These intangible assets are essential to the competitiveness of emerging people-centred enterprises. That is, enhancement of innovation and creativity appears to be totally incompatible with the presence of stress and violence at work.

Quantifying the costs

Bearing in mind the interaction between violence and stress described earlier, a combined quantification of the relative costs is given below:

- Through detailed financial calculations based on a model by Monica Henderson, it was estimated that, overall, bullying cost Australian employers between 6 and 13 billion Australian dollars (A$) each year when both hidden and lost "opportunity costs" were included. These Australian costings were based on a conservative estimate of impact prevalence (usually the mid-point of the range of impact results). At an individual case level, they estimated that the total cost of each case of bullying for each employer was at least A$16,977.[47] Such costs can be magnified in common law cases; for example, a Queensland Supreme Court judgement awarded almost A$550,000 in damages to a plaintiff in April 1998, although this case was appealed. This case followed repeated abuse of a sales manager by her manager on a north Queensland newspaper.[48]

- In the United States the average financial cost to employers of a serious violent incident in the workplace was estimated to be US$250,000, while the more frequent, less severe incidents were estimated to cost the employer as much as US$25,000 per incident; the total cost to American employers per year for workplace violence was estimated to be US$4.2 billion.[49]

- Biddle and Hartley studied the cost of homicides in the workplace in the United States and calculated an annual cost of approximately US$970 million, including the loss of earnings of victims extrapolated to the age of 67.[50]

- Based on a typical case of workplace bullying in a British local authority, the costs to the organization were calculated (table 23).

Altogether it has been estimated that stress and violence may account for up to 30 per cent of the overall costs of workplace injuries and ill health. Based on the above figures, it has been suggested that stress/violence may account for approximately 0.5–3.5 per cent of GDP per year.[51]

Towards finding responses

Understanding the dimension of workplace violence and the way it occurs has been the subject matter of Part I of this book. Transforming the knowledge

Table 23   Estimated cost of workplace bullying in a British local authority (£)

Cost item	£
Absence	6 972
Replacement costs	7 500
Investigators' time for grievance investigation	2 110
Local management line-management time	1 847
Head office personnel	2 600
Corporate officers' time (including staff welfare)	2 100
Cost of disciplinary process (hearing/solicitor)	3 780
Witness interview costs	1 200
Total costs (minimum)	28 109

Source: Einarsen et al., 2003a.

thus acquired into action is now the challenge at stake. Part II will therefore focus on the various forms that this action either can or should take. In doing so it is perhaps wise to recall the words of Etzioni, who stated in 1971:

> Ultimately the level of violence is affected by the interaction of motivational and cognitive, "psychological", forces, societal bonds, structures and procedures, and the technologies available to the violent. Hence there is no isolated, basic treatment of violence … Only a just and cohesive society, responsive to new demands, satisfying old ones, providing a meaningful life to its members, would sharply reduce violence, and even such a society would not eliminate it.[52]

Notes

[1] A comprehensive and contemporary annotated bibliography of prevention policies, strategies and guidance material relating to occupational violence has been produced by the Australian Institute of Criminology. The bibliography, which covers the period 1989 to 2003, is to be found at http://www.aic.gov.au/research/cvp/occupational/bib.html. The issue of prevention strategies is taken up in some detail in Part II of this book.

[2] See Bush and O'Shea, 1966, cited in VandenBos and Bulatao, 1996, pp. 283–298. See also Mayhew, 2000a.

[3] The Australian NCV report provided an example of an attempt to spell out a comprehensive national strategy to prevent or control violence. The strategy encompassed recommendations affecting public sector agencies like health and welfare, education, employment and training, housing, transportation, sport and recreation, Aboriginal affairs and criminal justice. It also extended to private enterprise, including specific industries like the media and the liquor trade; to non-government bodies like religious organizations and sporting authorities; and to professional and other groups including trade unions.

Successive Australian governments have drawn either directly or indirectly upon the NCV report to give effect to many of its recommendations. Significant funding has been directed, for example, at the promotion of child development programmes. The NCV's proposals for a national gun control strategy were also influential at the time of the tragic mass shootings in April 1996 by a lone gunman at Port Arthur, Tasmania, an Australian tourist and historic site. See Chappell and Di Martino, 2000, pp. 5–6 and 79–80. See also World Health Organization, 2002b.

[4] VandenBos and Bulatao, 1996, p. 16. See also Lamnek, in Heitmeyer and Hagan (eds.), 2003, pp. 1113–1127.

[5] Hoad, 1996, pp. 64–86.

6 Adapted from McDonald and Brown, 1997, p. 2. It should be noted that much of the literature on this issue is linked to risk assessment, including the risk of re-offending by persons convicted of serious acts of violence. Useful summaries of this literature can be found in McSherry, 2004. See also Allan and Dawson, 2004.

7 Chaiken et al., in Reiss and Roth (eds.), 1993, pp. 279–280. For a more recent appraisal of the status of predictive tools see O'Gloff and Davis, 2005, pp. 301–338.

8 Poyner and Warne, 1988.

9 Ibid, p. 2. Bowie (2002, pp. 1–20) has also stressed the importance of this interactive approach in his analysis of ways of coping with workplace violence.

10 See Poyner and Warne, 1988, pp. 2–7. A revised version of the model has also appeared in HSE: "Review of workplace-related violence", prepared by the Tavistock Institute for the Health and Safety Executive, *Contract Research Report*, No. 143/1997 London.

11 Di Martino, 2003b, in Heitmeyer and Hagan (eds.), pp. 885–902.

12 McDonald and Brown, 1997, p. 2.

13 Poyner and Warne, 1988, p. 3. In the case of **personality**, the Tavistock researchers emphasized that some jobs involved contact with clients who may react more aggressively or violently, while **temporary conditions** referred to members of the public who were under the influence of alcohol or drugs, or who were suffering from some illness or stress which made their behaviour unpredictable or less controlled. **Negative/uncertain expectations** included people who anticipated an interaction which was to be difficult or frustrating, or who were uncertain about what to expect, and as a consequence were in a stressed and belligerent mood. **Immaturity** related to children or young people whose behaviour was less controlled than adults', and who in groups could be easily led or influenced to engage in aggressive behaviour. **People with dogs** reflected the phenomenon, perhaps exacerbated in the United Kingdom, of dogs biting postal workers and refuse collectors.

14 The Tavistock study equated employees with victims. There are likely to be some situations, however, where workplace violence affects non-employees. An armed robbery during business hours of a financial institution, for example, could well result in the victimization of any customers present, as well as the staff of the enterprise.

15 See Homel et al., 1992, pp. 679–697; Homel and Clark, 1994, pp. 1–46. See also Mayhew and Chappell, 2001, pp. 4–12.

16 Bowie has considered and developed this aspect of workplace violence in his review of typologies of this form of aggression. He notes that increasing attention is now being devoted to the role organizations can play in creating workplace environments that may trigger violence among staff, clients and others. See Bowie, 2002, pp. 11–14. See also Arway, 2002, pp. 41–58.

17 Grainger, 1996, p. 17.

18 Afford, 2001, p. 13.

19 V.K. Lim, 1996, pp. 171–194.

20 German Foundation for International Development, 2000, p. 51.

21 Benavides and Benach, 1999.

22 Mayhew, 2003, pp. 203–219.

23 ILO, 2004b, p. 1.

24 Di Martino and Musri, 2001.

25 Vartia, 1994, p. 29. See also idem, 2001, pp. 63–69.

26 Mayhew et al., 2004, pp. 117–134.

27 Di Martino, Hoel and Cooper, 2002, pp. 59–60.

28 Di Martino, 2002b, p. 6.

29 Hurrell et al., 1996.

30 Family Violence Prevention Fund, 2002.

31 United Nations Development Fund for Women (UNIFEM), 2003.

32 US Center for Disease Control and Prevention (CDC), 2005.

33 WHO, 2002b, p. 89.

34 Walby, 2004.

35 Rennison, 2003, p. 1.

36 Buvinic et al., 1999, p. 3.

37 United Nations Economic and Social Council, Commission on Human Rights, 2003, para 1857.

38 For a general overview of the costs of interpersonal violence see WHO, 2004, pp. 22–23.

39 Vartia, 1993, p. 21.

[40] ILO, 1992.

[41] Upson, 2004, p. 19.

[42] Kivimaki et al., 2000, pp. 656–660.

[43] European Foundation for the Improvement of Living and Working Conditions, 1997.

[44] Ball and Pike, 2000.

[45] Arnetz, Arnetz and Petterson, 1996, pp. 119–127.

[46] Vartia and Hyyti, 2000, pp. 144–48.

[47] The Henderson model costings are detailed in McCarthy and Mayhew, 2004, p. 43.

[48] Sheehan et al., 2001. See also Oberhardt, 1998, p. 1.

[49] Philbrick et al., 2003, pp. 84–90.

[50] Biddle and Hartley, 2002, p. 23.

[51] Hoel et al., 2000.

[52] Etzioni, 1971, pp. 704–741.

PART II

RESPONDING TO VIOLENCE AT WORK

LEGAL RESPONSIBILITIES AND RIGHTS   5

The legal responsibilities and rights of those involved in incidents of workplace violence can be both complex and diverse. The statutory and regulatory provisions that apply can touch upon difficult questions of criminal and civil law, occupational safety and health legislation, workers' rehabilitation and compensation statutes, and environmental and labour laws.

In earlier editions of this book it was noted that the legal regimes in place in almost all nations of the world responded to workplace violence within the broader band of protective legislation and regulation surrounding the workplace at large. Only two countries – Sweden and the Netherlands – had at the time enacted specific and comprehensive statutory measures regarding violence at work. That situation has now changed, not only at the national level but also in regional and international legal developments.

In this chapter the general nature and scope of past and contemporary legal initiatives are considered at the national level, drawing upon examples taken principally from the statute books and regulations of a number of industrialized countries which have been leaders in the field. Common-law decisions within nation States may sometimes have a profound influence on the initiation of workplace violence preventive interventions. Developments which have occurred at the international level are considered in more depth in Chapter 8.

National laws

There is a range of statutory provisions and common-law precedents that relate to workplace violence. While some of the statutory instruments apply only to certain forms of workplace violence (for example, criminal provisions are primarily applied against those who breach the criminal law), others have more generic applications, such as the "general duties of care" called up under many occupational safety and health Acts and Regulations.

Criminal law

The criminal law has long been used as a principal bulwark against the commission of acts of physical violence in all locations, including the workplace. Those who have failed to be deterred by the threat of punishment for traditional crimes of violence such as homicide, rape, robbery and assault have, if caught and convicted, been subjected to personal sanctions by the criminal justice systems involved. In most cases these systems have regarded crimes of violence as meriting some of the most severe sanctions available, ranging in many jurisdictions from the death penalty for murder to lengthy terms of imprisonment for rape and robbery. Harsher punishment has also commonly been prescribed for offences involving violence directed at certain workers while acting in the course of their duty, such as police, corrections officials or judicial officers.

In recent years, a significant change has taken place in community attitudes towards violence occurring in the context of the family, and sexual assault. Linked closely to the movements to advance women's and children's rights, behaviour which has in the past gone largely unreported and unpunished in many countries has now become a matter of widespread attention and action under criminal law and criminal justice.[1]

These developments have also had an influence and impact at the workplace, providing a fresh impetus to apply the protection of assault laws to sexual and non-sexual violence occurring in the context of employment, as well as bolstering efforts to combat such violence in the wider community. In addition, they have prompted some jurisdictions to broaden their criminal law regarding violence to encompass harassment and allied activity.

In the **United Kingdom**, for instance, 1997 legislation has made it a criminal offence to pursue a course of conduct which amounts to harassment of a person (box 37). Although not directed specifically at violence at work,

Box 37   United Kingdom: Protection from harassment legislation, 1997

Harassment: It is an offence for a person to pursue a course of conduct – involving conduct on at least two occasions – which he or she knows or ought to know amounts to harassment of another person. It is not necessary to show an *intention* on the part of the harasser to cause the victim to feel harassed: the prosecution has only to prove that the conduct occurred in circumstances where a reasonable person would have realized that this would be the effect. "Harassment" expressly includes "alarming the person or causing the person distress", and "conduct" includes speech.

It is a defence for the harasser to show that the course of conduct was pursued for the purpose of preventing or detecting crime; it was pursued under statutory authority; or, in the particular circumstances, the pursuit of the conduct was "reasonable".

A person guilty of the offence of harassment is liable on summary conviction to a term of imprisonment not exceeding six months, or a fine, or both. The court has the power to make a restraining order immediately after convicting a person of the offence.

Civil remedy: An actual or apprehended commission of the offence of harassment can be the subject of a claim in civil proceedings by the person who is or may be the victim of the course of conduct in question. An order restraining the harassment and/or damages can be sought.

Offence of putting people in fear of violence: A "higher-level" offence has been created – punishable by up to five years in prison, or an unlimited fine, or both – where a person pursues a course of conduct which he or she knows or ought to know causes another person to fear, on at least two occasions, that violence will be used against him or her. Once again, a convicting court has the power to make a restraining order (but in the case of this offence, the Act does not provide for the possibility of civil action by the victim).

The above measures apply to England and Wales only, but the legislation contains separate provisions appropriate to the law in Scotland.

Source: Based on an analysis of the Protection from Harassment Bill, in *Industrial Relations Law Bulletin* (London), No. 560, Jan. 1997, p. 4.

the legislation is of sufficient breadth to cover harassment at this and many other locations.[2] In **France**, new legislation introduced in 2002 contemplates penal provisions for cases of sexual harassment and moral harassment (see "Specific legislation against violence at work", pp. 155–159).

Employment injury legislation

This type of legislation, including social security or workers' compensation, is generally the exclusive remedy for work-related injury and disease occurring during, or arising from, employment. Whether or not injury from workplace violence is covered by specific employment injury schemes will depend on the interpretation of their particular legislative provisions. In most situations, incidents of workplace violence involving assault and bodily harm are likely to be covered, although there may be exceptions, as in the case of a quarrel between employees that is purely personal, or if the injured employee is the original aggressor.

In **Canada**, a number of regulations have amended workers' compensation provisions to make it clear that workplace violence is compensable within such schemes. For example, the Canadian province of British Columbia adopted in 1993 an Occupational Health and Safety Regulation relating to the "protection of workers from violence in the workplace". The regulation defines violence as the exercise of physical force and any threatening statement or behaviour, which gives a worker reasonable cause to believe that he or she is at risk of injury. It requires a violence risk assessment to be performed in any place of employment and, if a risk is thus identified, the development of policies, procedures and work environment arrangements to eliminate this risk. Similar provisions were adopted in the province of Saskatchewan in the Occupational Health and Safety Act 1993, and Occupational Health and Safety Regulations 1996. A number of other provinces have regulations on workers working alone with direct or indirect relevance for workplace violence.[3]

In **Italy**, mobbing is now explicitly recognized as an occupational illness entitling the worker who has been subjected to this type of treatment to an invalidity pension. In 1988 the Constitutional Court (Decision No. 179 of 18 February 1988)[4] introduced the possibility of recognizing as an occupational disease condition not included in the list of TU No. 1123[5] of 30 June 1965 – if the causal relationship between working conditions and pathological status is proved. On this basis, in Italy the National Institute for Industrial Accidents and Occupational Diseases (INAIL) has issued specific instructions[6] concerning the coverage of "psychological disturbances deriving from organizational constraints at work" and has identified relevant situations. Such situations, as shown in box 38, clearly refer to mobbing.

Box 38   List of behaviours within workplaces which may result in "psychological disturbances" covered by INAIL

- Marginalization in working activities

- Task deprivation

- No working activity assigned, forced inactivity

- No working tools provided

- Unjustified, repeated transfers

- Protracted underutilization of professional capacities

- Protracted attribution of exorbitant tasks

- Systematic and structural denial of access to information or to adequate information

- Exclusion from training and retraining initiatives

- Excessive control

Source: National Institute for Industrial Accidents and Occupational Diseases (Istituto Nazionale per l'Assicurazione contro gli Infortuni sul Lavoro), INAIL, Office Circular No. 71, 17 Dec. 2003, especially pp. 2–3.

The list of behaviours shown in box 38 has been repeatedly identified as common tactics used in bullying and mobbing.[7] Numerous researchers in various countries have expounded similar lists, although debate continues over the length of time and number of separate occurrences required to define a process as "bullying".[8] In some nation States (such as in Scandinavia), "mobbing" is a term used interchangeably with "bullying". However in the English-speaking world, the term "mobbing" is most commonly used where a group of perpetrators singles out one victim; in contrast, the term "bullying" tends to be used when a single perpetrator bullies one recipient.

Occupational health and safety legislation

In most countries, a "duty of care" is placed on employers to provide both a safe **place** and a safe **process** of work, to supervise, take appropriate measures to protect workers, minimize hazards and risks and dangerous situations, and prevent injuries. Although workplace violence is not usually directly addressed, in a growing number of countries the occupational health and safety regulatory framework is considered to impose on employers an obligation to provide a violence-free workplace.

In the **United Kingdom**, employers have a legal duty under Section 2(1) of the Health and Safety at Work Act 1974 to ensure, so far as is reasonably practicable, the health, safety and welfare at work of their employees. This duty includes the minimization of exposure to the risk of violence at work.[9]

Further, the Management of Health and Safety at Work Regulations 1992 require employers to undertake a "suitable and efficient" assessment of the risks to which employees are exposed while they are at work. If they have five or more employees, employers must record the significant findings of that assessment. The risk assessment must also identify the extent and nature of the risks, the contributing factors, the causes, and the changes necessary to eliminate or control the risk.

In **New Zealand**, the Health and Safety in Employment Act 1992 has been used as the basis for developing a guide for employers and employees on dealing with violence at work.[10] Under that law, employers have a legal duty to take all practicable steps to identify all hazards in the place of work, to determine their significance, and to eliminate, isolate or minimize the likelihood that the hazard will be a source of harm. Also relevant is the Harassment Act 1997 providing civil and criminal protection from acts of harassment in the workplace and elsewhere.[11]

In the **United States**, the Federal Government enacted the Occupational Safety and Health Act 1970, which sets uniform standards throughout the country. Responsibility for enforcement is, however, delegated to state governments.[12]

Within this general requirement, employers have an obligation to do everything that is reasonably practicable to protect the life, safety and health of employees, including removal or minimization of hazards, provision of safety devices and personal protective equipment, and the adoption of safe work practices, operations and processes in order to create a safe and healthy workplace.

The Occupational Safety and Health Administration (OSHA) guidelines play a significant role in this respect (box 39). The guidelines are not in the form of subsidiary regulations, and thus failure to implement the guidelines is not in itself a violation of the Occupational Safety and Health Act 1970. Since these guidelines are issued by OSHA (a Federal Government authority), and "identify" the hazard of workplace violence, they differ significantly from those guidelines which emanate from non-official bodies (described in Chapter 6). The OSHA guidelines can be cited in specific cases and be called up during adjudications, and have a direct bearing on court decisions. They are both detailed and comprehensive, dealing with the establishment of violence prevention programmes, management commitment to and employee involvement in such programmes, workplace risk

---

Box 39   The role of OSHA guidelines

Proponents of OSHA (and related state agency) involvement in the regulation of workplace violence envision that these agencies can improve OSH performance in a field of law in need of reform.[1] Administrative agency theorists have suggested that this strategy might be preferable even to statute or tort law reform, since relevant government agencies can promulgate comprehensive and detailed regulations.

The State of California's OSHA (CAL/OSHA) *Guidelines for safety and security of health care and community workers*, 1999 (see box 49, "Published guidelines on violence: A selection", in Chapter 6) provide a glimpse of the type of guidance that OSH agencies should be able to offer to all employers for a range of hazards and risks, including workplace violence.[2] The CAL/OSHA guidelines were developed at United States federal and state level and revised over a period of time. They were developed by individuals and organizations with expertise in preventing and mitigating violent assaults in various health-care settings, and detail preventive measures that reduce employee exposure to the hazard of workplace violence, diminish a perpetrator's ability to commit a violent act, and provide a range of administrative recommendations for employers.

The guidelines are "not a new standard or regulation": Instead "failure to implement the guidelines is not in itself a violation of the General Duty Clause of the Occupational Safety and Health Act of 1970, but employers can be cited if there is a recognized hazard of workplace violence in their establishments and they do nothing to prevent or abate it".[3]

Sources: [1] *OSHA issues draft copy of Guidelines to Protect Health Care Sector Workers*, 25 O.S.H. Rep. (BNA) No.5, p. 187 (5 July 1995) (quoting OSHA Administrator, Joseph A. Dear). [2] CAL/OSHA, 1998. [3] See also: Goldberg, 1997; Pierce, 1985, pp. 917 and 937; Calabresi, 1982, pp. 44–45. But see idem, p. 53 (arguing that in spite of the theoretical potential, agencies have been a "dismal disappointment" in legal reform).

Box 40   Finnish Occupational Safety and Health Act No. 738/2002

Section 27 – **Threat of violence**

(1) The work and working conditions in jobs entailing an evident threat of violence shall be so arranged that the threat of violence and incidents of violence are prevented as far as possible. Accordingly, appropriate safety arrangements and equipment needed for preventing or restricting violence and an opportunity to summon help shall be provided at the workplace.

(2) The employer shall draw up procedural instructions for such jobs and workplaces as referred to in subsection 1. In the instructions, controlling threatening situations must be considered in advance and practices for controlling or restricting the effects of violent incidents on the employees' safety must be presented. When necessary, the functioning of the safety arrangements and equipment must be checked.

(3) Further provisions on arrangements related to the safety and health of employees in different branches and tasks where evident threats of violence exist may be given by government decree.

Section 28 – **Harassment**

If harassment or other inappropriate treatment of an employee occurs at work and causes hazards or risks to the employee's health, the employer, after becoming aware of the matter, shall by available means take measures for remedying this situation.

Source: Unofficial translation (see: http://www.finlex.fi/pdf/saadkaan/E0020738.PDF, accessed 3 Oct. 2005).

analysis, hazard prevention and control, training and education, record-keeping and evaluation, and specific programme elements for different types of operations and facilities.

In **Finland**, in June 2002, a new Occupational Safety and Health Act was approved by Parliament and entered into force on 1 January 2003. This legislation deals with physical and psychological violence, including threats of violence and harassment (box 40).

Environmental legislation

Environmental legislation and regulation are increasingly being seen as an effective means of preventing violence at work. Measures of this type facilitate the identification of the causes of violence, the understanding of violence-related problems and the adoption of remedial strategies. By encouraging a preventive approach to violence, these measures set the scene for the development of a growing number of policies, guidelines and practices targeted at eliminating the causes of violence at work rather than merely alleviating its consequences.

In 1994, **the Netherlands** added provisions to its 1980 Working Environment Act (the Arbeidsomstandighedenwet) aimed at ensuring "safe and sound" working conditions, a high level of protection, co-determination rights for employees, and provisions that help prevent sexual intimidation, aggression and violence at work.[13] Under these provisions, aggression and violence occur when the worker is mentally or physically harassed, threatened or attacked in circumstances directly connected with the performance of his or her work.

Box 41   Monitoring the impact of anti-violence legislation in the Netherlands: The three waves

In 1995 the first evaluation of these provisions was carried out in the sectors perceived to be at major risk. The main conclusion was that most employers recognized that there were problems with aggression and (to a lesser degree) harassment, but the vast majority had not implemented serious preventive measures.

In 2000 another evaluation of the legislation (involving both employees and employers) took place, focusing on aggression, sexual harassment and bullying. Some core findings included:

- 36 per cent of workers had to deal with aggression, 10 per cent with sexual harassment, and 16 per cent with bullying;

- sick leave resulting from aggression and violence amounted to 7 per cent, sexual harassment 9 per cent, and bullying 22 per cent;

- employers in bigger companies had taken more preventive measures than had those in small and medium-sized enterprises (SMEs);

- many reported incidents had not led to significant problem solving or changes at work for the victim(s);

- in many cases incidents were not reported because of the absence of a procedure;

- however, many employers had taken measures for after-incident care and access to a trusted person for problems with harassment, bullying, conflicts, and so on;

- knowledge about workplace aggression, sexual harassment and bullying generally lagged behind in the Netherlands.

A third evaluation was undertaken in 2004 covering the entire area of "indecent behaviour at work", including all forms of aggression, violence, sexual harassment, bullying, intimidation, discrimination and conflicts at work. The extent to which particular groups of workers are involved is being assessed, including income level, precarious employment, ethnicity, sexual preference and so on.

Source: By courtesy of H. Schrama and R. van der Sluys, Ministry of Social Affairs and Employment, the Netherlands, Feb. 2004.

Also in the Netherlands, the Working Environment Act 1998 (originally passed in 1980, and amended in January 1994 as a result of the European Framework Directive 89/391/EEC on health and safety at work), in replacing the above-mentioned Act, is essentially an enabling framework which provides a basis for more detailed decrees.[14] Under Article 4(2), employers are obliged to protect employees as far as possible from sexual harassment, aggression and violence in the workplace. Under Article 5, employers are compelled to pursue a policy on sexual harassment. Sexual harassment must be included in the risk analysis and evaluation which employers are bound to carry out under the Act. Any employer who does not comply with the requirements of the Act, or associated Decrees and Regulations, can be fined by the Labour Inspectorate.[15]

The impact of these new provisions has been monitored in three waves of evaluation beginning in 1995, and continuing in 2000 and 2004 (box 41).

Along similar lines, environmental laws in **Norway** and **Sweden** highlighted the importance of a work environment designed for the people working in it; the key role of work organization and job design in reducing risks; the relevance of both physical and psychological factors at work; the need to provide each worker with meaningful job tasks and with opportunities for development, as well as for self-determination and occupational responsibility; and the need to ensure that workers are informed and involved in all matters concerning safety and health.

The linkage between the working environment and violence at work is becoming much more explicit in this type of legislation. Amendments to Norwegian environmental legislation, for example, have made clear the right of the employee "not to be subject to harassment or other improper conduct" within the work environment.[16]

Specific legislation against violence at work

In 1993, the National Board of Occupational Safety and Health in **Sweden** issued two comprehensive and innovative ordinances on workplace violence under the authority of its Work Environment Act.[17] These ordinances, which were the first of their kind in the world, cover violence and menaces in the working environment and victimization at work.[18]

These ordinances remain valuable benchmarks for other countries, with each ordinance being accompanied by practical guidance on how to implement provisions and recommendations. The emphasis is on a combination of prevention strategies that deal with violence in the context of environmental and organizational issues, rather than through containment of risk at the level of the individual. The ordinances require employers to plan and organize work in ways that remove the hazard so far as is possible, prevent the occurrence of

Box 42   Swedish Ordinance on measures for the prevention of violence and menaces in the working environment

The Ordinance of the Swedish National Board of Occupational Safety and Health containing Provisions on Measures for the Prevention of Violence and Menaces in the Working Environment (AFS 1993:2) applies to work where there may be a risk of violence or the threat of violence. At-risk jobs include those where perpetrators potentially have access to cash, goods or valuables. The Ordinance places specific responsibilities on employers. Employers are responsible for investigating the risks of, or threat of, violence, and for taking preventive action.

Workplaces and processes are to be designed to avert the risk of violence as far as is possible. There are to be special security routines for work that poses an increased risk of exposure to violence, for example, specific measures are detailed for operations involving the transport of money, securities and other valuables. If there is a risk of recurrent violence or threats of violence, employees are to receive special support and guidance. Routines need to be established for training and information provision, alarm call responses, and practical emergency exercises. The use of technical aids such as intercom telephones, hidden telephones or optical surveillance in the form of a still camera, video monitoring or observation mirrors, however, is subject to legislation governing the use of such devices. Large workplaces are expected to identify emergency personnel and implement planning for a crisis event, and to develop a special emergency plan.

Employees are to be given sufficient training, information and instruction to be able to do their work safely. Employees should be informed at the time of hiring, or before being transferred to work where job tasks are known to entail certain risks. Employees must be able to summon prompt assistance in a violent or threatening situation, and employers must ensure that alarm equipment and other necessary technical aids are provided, maintained and their use adequately explained.

There are also provisions for recording, investigating and following up on violent incidents and threats, as well as requirements to notify the Labour Inspectorate of serious injuries or incidents. Finally, employers must ensure prompt assistance and support to employees who are victimized, to alleviate both physical and mental injuries. Both medical and psychological attention is required when an employee is involved in a traumatic event.

Source: Swedish National Board of Occupational Safety and Health, *Statute Book of the Swedish National Board of Occupational Safety and Health containing Provisions on Measures against Victimization at Work Ordinance (AFS 1993:2) on Victimization at Work*, 21 Sep. Stockholm (official English translation).

violence and victimization, and ensure that violence of any form should not be tolerated in the workplace. Box 42 illustrates the key points contained in the first of these two ordinances.

In **France**, in response to increasing concern about the scope and severity of the workplace violence problem, the law on socially responsible modernization (*modernisation sociale*)[19] has introduced new provisions dealing with sexual harassment and has specifically tackled moral harassment (*harcèlement moral*) both in the Labour and Penal Codes. This new legislation had been preceded in 1999 by Debout's report to the Economic and Social Council, which revealed the extent and gravity of violence at work.[20] Court decisions had produced extensive case law on the subject,[21] culminating in two key decisions of the Supreme Court[22] establishing the full responsibility of an employer for the behaviour of those to whom authority vis-à-vis the employees had been delegated.

Following the introduction of Act 2002-73, the French Labour Code now defines moral harassment,[23] outlines employers' obligations to introduce all measures necessary to prevent such moral harassment,[24] and offers extended protection to the victim,[25] including the possibility of making recourse to an external mediator.[26] The Labour Code also accrues powers for the trade unions to intervene in cases of moral harassment in the public and private sectors. When there has been a breach of these provisions, sanctions of up to one year's imprisonment and a fine of €15,000 can be applied under the Labour Code and the Penal Code.[27]

In **Belgium**, the Act of 11 June 2002 "relating to protection from violence, moral harassment (bullying) and sexual harassment at the workplace" modifies the Act of 4 August 1996 "relating to the well-being of workers when at work", in particular Article 32, and covers a wide range of situations of workplace violence, including physical violence and verbal aggression, as well as bullying, mobbing and sexual harassment.

The law outlines employers' obligations to put into operation a series of preventive measures to reduce the risk of violence in the workplace. These include the physical organization of the working environment, establishing proper assistance and support for the victim, the availability of an adviser on prevention (*conseiller en prévention*), quick and impartial investigation of cases of workplace violence, provision of information and training, and the responsibility of the management at all levels in preventing stress.

Victims of workplace violence are offered different means of redress through the adviser on prevention, a supervisor or manager, and/or factory inspectors in the relevant jurisdiction. In order to protect the worker from reprisal, the working relationship cannot be terminated, and the working conditions cannot be modified during the recourse procedures except on grounds that are independent of the workplace violence.

The burden of proof rests with the perpetrator of the violence, since the defendant has to show that the acts and behaviours purported to be examples of workplace violence did not in fact constitute violence. Finally, workers are requested to participate actively in prevention, to abstain from any act of violence and to avoid any misuse of the means of recourse.

On 19 December 2002 the province of **Quebec, Canada**, issued an "Act to amend the Act respecting labour standards and other legislative provisions"[28] which includes provisions on psychological harassment. The Workplace Psychological Prevention Act, which came into force on 1 June 2004, defines psychological harassment as:

> ... any vexatious behaviour in the form of repeated and hostile or unwanted conduct, verbal comments, actions or gestures, that affects an employee's dignity or psychological or physical integrity and that results in a harmful work environment for the employee.

> The legislation also provides that a single serious incidence that causes a lasting harmful effect may also constitute psychological harassment.[29]

According to the Act, every employee has a right to a work environment free from psychological harassment. Employers must take reasonable action to prevent psychological harassment and, whenever they become aware of such behaviour, to put a stop to it.[30] These provisions will constitute:

> an integral part of every collective agreement. An employee covered by such an agreement must exercise the recourses provided for in the agreement, insofar as any such recourse is available to employees under the agreement. At any time before the case is taken under advisement, a joint application may be made by the parties to such an agreement to the Minister for the appointment of a person to act as a mediator.[31]

In **Argentina** new legislation specifically addressing workplace violence (*violencia laboral*) has been recently introduced by the city of Buenos Aires,[32] the province of Buenos Aires,[33] and the province of Tucuman.[34]

The legislation of the province of **Buenos Aires**, which appears in many respects to be the most comprehensive of the three, provides a detailed definition of workplace violence including:

- physical abuse or any other behaviour that is aimed directly or indirectly at causing physical harm to workers;

- psychological and social abuse of workers, continuous and repeated hostility, psychological harassment, scorn and criticism;

- harassment in the workplace, persistent and repeated actions to make the worker uncomfortable through words, acts, specific behaviours, gestures and written messages, when making an attempt against the person, the dignity or the physical or psychological integrity of the individual, endangering his or her job or degrading the working environment;

- differences in wages, when wage disparity exists between men and women who carry out the same functions working for the same employer.

The new law also establishes that "if the prohibition defined in Article 1 of this law is not respected, it can generate corrective sanctions, including an official warning or suspension up to 60 continuous days, unless because of its dimension and seriousness, or because of the grade of the officer, it can cause unemployment, exoneration or it can be considered as a serious offence, according to the disciplinary regime that is being applied".[35]

In **Poland** the Labour Code[36] has been amended to include a definition of mobbing, obligations of the employer to counteract mobbing, and procedures for examination of employees' claims in a situation of alleged mobbing. Mobbing means actions or behaviours directed against a worker and involving persistent and long-term harassment, intimidation, humiliation, denigration of his or her vocational usefulness, isolation or his/her elimination from a working team.[37]

The employer is obliged not only to refrain from mobbing, but should also prevent victimization of individuals by other workers, for example line managers or colleagues. If mobbing results in a work-related injury or illness, compensation for the damage may be claimed. If a worker terminates an employment contract because of this inappropriate behaviour, he or she has the right to claim compensation from the employer for the damages to an amount not lower than the fixed minimum wage/salary (as specified under separate regulations). A declaration of termination of the employment contract by the worker must be made in writing, stating the reasons.[38]

Special legislation

The continuing trend towards enactment of specific legislation and regulations on violence at work has been accompanied by identification of higher-risk occupations and particular risk factors associated with special types of violence. Some examples of these developments follow, described under separate headings.

Sexual harassment

The legislative framework covering sexual harassment is rapidly changing. Equal opportunity, labour and employment, and criminal laws may all be applied separately or in combination to deal with this behaviour. Common-law decisions also influence preventive action. However, in many countries there is still no law concerning sexual harassment as a legally distinct and prohibited activity.

When equal opportunity law is used to deal with sexual harassment, it is generally equated with a type of discriminatory employment practice. Labour laws, tort and criminal laws frequently address the issue in terms of an abuse

Box 43   Enactment of EU Directive 2002/73/EC

Austria: Federal Act to amend the equality of treatment Act No. 44, 1998.

Belgium: Loi du 11 juin 2002 relative à la protection contre la violence et le harcèlement moral ou sexuel au travail. [Act of 11 June 2002 relating to protection against violence and moral or sexual harassment at work.]

Denmark: Gender Equality (Consolidation) Act No. 553 of 2 July 2002.

Finland: Act on equality between men and women, as amended by law 206/1995 of 17 February 1995.

France: Loi 2002-73 du 17 Janvier 2002 sur la modernisation sociale. [Act No. 2002-73 of 17 January 2002 making provision for social modernization.]

Germany: Gesetz zum Schutz der Beschäftigten von sexueller Belästung am Arbeitsplatz, 24 June 1994. [Law relating to protection of employees against harassment at work.]

Greece: Law 1414.30.01.84 on equality.

Ireland: Employment Equality Act No. 21 of 1998; Unfair Dismissals Act, 1977.

Italy: Law 125/91 on equal opportunities and positive action.

Luxembourg: Loi sur le harcèlement sexuel du 27 mai 2000. [Law on sexual harassment of 27 May 2000.]

Netherlands: Working Conditions Act, 1998.

Portugal: Ley No. 61/91 por la quel se garantiza la proteccion adecuada de las mujeres victimas de violencia. [Act No. 61/91 relating to guarantees of adequate protection to women who are victims of violence.]

Spain: Workers' Statute, 10 March 1980. Ley orgánico No. 11/1999 de modificación del código penal; ley orgánico No. 10/1995 del código penal. [Organic Law No. 11/1999 relating to modification of the penal code: organic Law No. 10/1995 of the penal code.]

Sweden: Equal Opportunities Act, 1991.

United Kingdom: Sex Discrimination Act 1975.

Source: European Commission: *Sexual harassment at the workplace in the European Union* (Luxembourg, Office for Official Publications of the European Community, 1998); ILO: *Sexual harassment – An ILO survey of company practices* (Geneva, 1999), with updating.

of power, or an unacceptable affront to the dignity and privacy of the individual victimized. The question of legal liability for sexual harassment is not always clear – it can fall on the employer, the harasser alone, or both.

Where specialized institutions exist to deal with complaints of sexual harassment, the worker has an avenue outside the workplace to pursue a case. This may result in resolution of the issue through conciliation, or in an enforcement action against the employer or alleged harasser, or both. Remedies for sexual harassment can include payment of damages, and court orders against employers or harassers to stop the harassment complained of. Employers may also be ordered to repair the damage caused by the harassment, including reinstatement of the complainant or transfer of the harasser, and be required to implement a policy to prevent future sexual harassment. In terms of internal sanctions, employers can discipline harassers, including ordering their dismissal, depending upon the seriousness of the offence.

In a growing number of countries, however, these issues have now been addressed by specific initiatives relating to sexual harassment. In the European Union, and in most industrialized countries, including Australia, Canada, Japan and the United States, sexual harassment measures are now well developed, either by statute or case law.

In the **European Union** Directive 2002/73/EC on equal treatment for men and women[39] was to be implemented in the Member States from 2005, affecting existing national legislation relevant to sexual harassment,[40] as shown in box 43 (see also Chapter 8, pp. 283–284).

There has also been a significant increase in legislative attention to sexual harassment in developing countries and countries in transition. Thus Argentina, Bangladesh, Belize, Costa Rica, Croatia, Dominican Republic, Fiji, Guyana, Honduras, Israel, the Republic of Korea, Lesotho, Mauritius, Namibia, Panama, Paraguay, the Philippines, Romania, South Africa, Sri Lanka, Thailand, the United Republic of Tanzania, Uruguay and Venezuela have each adopted specific legislation declaring sexual harassment to be a prohibited activity, or general legislation covering sexual discrimination under which protection from sexual harassment can be provided. Other countries have prohibited sexual harassment only at the state or provincial level or for specific sectors. Some of this legislation is particularly advanced, as illustrated by measures adopted in the Philippines as early as 1995 (box 44).

Box 44   Philippines Anti-Sexual Harassment Act of 1995 (excerpts)

Section 2. Declaration of policy

The State shall value the dignity of every individual, enhance the development of its human resources, guarantee full respect for human employees and applicants for employment, students or those undergoing training, instruction or education. Towards this end, all forms of sexual harassment in the employment, education or training environment are hereby declared unlawful.

/cont'd

/cont'd

Work, education or training-related sexual harassment is committed by an employer, employee, manager, supervisor, agent of the employer, teacher, instructor, professor, coach, trainer, or any other person who, having authority, influence or moral ascendancy over another in a work or training or education environment, demands, requests or otherwise requires any sexual favour from the other.

In a work-related or employment environment, sexual harassment is committed when:

- the sexual favour is made as a condition in the hiring or in the employment, re-employment or continued employment of said individual, or in granting said individual favourable compensation, terms, conditions, promotions, or privileges; or the refusal to grant the sexual favour results in limiting, segregating or classifying the employee which in any way would discriminate, deprive or diminish employment opportunities or otherwise adversely affect said employee;

- the above acts would impair the employee's rights or privileges under existing labour laws; or

- the above acts would result in an intimidating, hostile, or offensive environment for the employee.

Section 4 b. Duty of the employer

It shall be the duty of the employer to prevent or deter the commission of acts of sexual harassment and to provide the procedures for the resolution, settlement or prosecution of acts of sexual harassment. Towards this end, the employer shall promulgate appropriate rules and regulations in consultation with and jointly approved by the employees, through their duly designated representatives, prescribing the procedure for the investigation of sexual harassment cases and the administrative sanctions therefor. The employer shall also create a committee on decorum and investigation of cases on sexual harassment. The committee shall conduct meetings, as the case may be, with officers and employees, to increase understanding and prevent incidents of sexual harassment. It shall also conduct the investigation of alleged cases constituting sexual harassment.

Section 5. Liability of the employer

The employer shall be liable for damages arising from the acts of sexual harassment committed in the employment, education or training environment if the employer, or head of office, is informed of such acts by the offended party and no immediate action is taken thereon.

Section 6. Independent action for damages

Nothing in this Act shall preclude the victim of sexual harassment from instituting a separate and independent action for damages and other affirmative relief.

Section 7. Penalties

Any person who violates the provisions of this Act shall, upon conviction, be penalized by imprisonment of not less than one month nor more than six months, or a fine or both, such fine and imprisonment at the discretion of the court.

Source: Anti-Sexual Harassment Act No. 7877, 14 February 1995, in *Official Gazette* (Manila), Vol. 91, No. 15, 10 Apr. 1995, pp. 2144–2146.

Thus, some countries have been proactive in initiating a robust legislative framework to deal with sexual harassment. However, much remains to be done. Another form of workplace violence that appears to be increasingly reported over time is known as "air rage".

Air rage

In **Japan** a new revised Aviation Law came into force on 15 January 2004, and was intended to secure the safe operation of aircraft by banning "air rage" or acts that cause public nuisance aboard aircraft. The law prohibits acts by passengers that violate the safe operation of the aircraft (such as using mobile phones aboard), that disrupt order in the aircraft, or that interfere with the work of flight attendants. The captain of an aircraft can issue a restraining order to the person concerned, and anyone that does not comply is subject to a fine of up to 500,000 Japanese yen.[41] Similar – and often more stringent – provisions are being implemented in most industrialized countries, including provisions within criminal codes for those who threaten (or even make jokes about threats to) aircraft security.

While air rage is predominantly carried out in a public place with multiple observers, other forms of workplace violence (including sexual harassment) often occur one-to-one out of the sight of onlookers and potential witnesses. As a result, workers who work alone are often at increased risk of exposure to a range of forms of workplace violence.

Working alone

In **Canada**, the provinces have responsibility for much regulation, including for occupational safety and health, and as a result there is a lack of uniformity. However, the cooperative inter-governmental harmonization project was initiated in 1992 to improve harmonization of standards and procedures.[42] The Canadian Labour Code addresses a particular risk factor for violence created by the organization of work, that of working alone. It provides that:

> It remains the responsibility of the employer to ensure the safety and health of every employee at work. Through discussion with the safety and health committees, the affected worker(s), and examination of the work site, many different alternatives may be found to be available to ensure that the solitary worker would not be placed in a situation of undue risk, by virtue of their solitude.[43]

In **Australia**, there is also a federal system of government with some legislative variations between states. While there is a move to greater harmonization over time, it remains the case that one jurisdiction generally tends to take the lead on each specific issue. For example, the Western

Australian OSH authority was the first to develop subsidiary legislation enhancing protection against workplace violence,[44] although this was subsequently enhanced in the state of Victoria.[45] The WorkSafe Western Australia Commission also initiated the first Guidance note on working alone, pursuant to section 14 of the Occupational Safety and Health Act 1984.[46]

Collective agreements

Legislation on violence at work is sometimes anticipated or supplemented by collective agreements dealing with this issue. Such agreements, which can be regional, national or industry-sector specific, often allow greater flexibility and immediacy of response to workplace violence threats than is possible under statutory or regulatory frameworks.

Regional agreements

In the **European Union**, for example, a path-breaking agreement on combating crime and violence in commerce was signed in 1995 by EUROFIET, the European Branch of the International Federation of Commercial, Clerical, Professional and Technical Employees, and its counterpart EuroCommerce. In this statement, EUROFIET and EuroCommerce emphasized that crime and violence were a safety and health problem. The statement stressed the necessity for close cooperation between the social partners and public authorities at European and national levels in order to tackle these problems effectively. In particular, the following measures should be promoted:

- national and local public authorities urged to pay attention to the risk of workplace violence;
- emphasis placed on the obligations of employers to protect the safety and health of their employees;
- tripartite cooperation encouraged;
- guidelines introduced to help employers and employees prevent violent incidents;
- adequate training provided to employees to enable them to deal with workplace violence and be aware of their rights and obligations;
- specific information guides provided;
- effective procedures implemented for the handling of cash and valuables, and for dealing with suspected shoplifters and robbers;
- risks identified;

- recording and reporting of violent workplace incidents improved;
- proper after-care support programmes developed; and
- social dialogue pursued at the European level.[47]

In May 2004, the European social partners reached a European framework agreement on work-related stress (box 45). Although the agreement does not deal specifically with violence, harassment and post-traumatic stress, it is likely to have a significant bearing given the close and important relationship between stress and workplace violence, as discussed in the previous chapters.

Box 45   European social partners reach framework agreement on stress at work

On 27 May 2004, following nine months of intense negotiations, the European Trade Union Confederation (ETUC), the Union of Industrial and Employers' Confederation of Europe/European Association of Craft, Small and Medium-sized Enterprises (UNICE/UEAPME) and the European Centre of Enterprises with Public Participation and of Enterprises of General Economic Interest (CEEP) reached a European framework agreement on work-related stress. The agreement:

- acknowledges that stress can potentially affect any workplace and any worker, but that not all workplaces or workers are necessarily affected;

- recognizes that stress is not a disease and that pressure can be positive;

- gives a nuanced description of work-related stress, taking account of differences in individual reactions to stress;

- proposes a method to identify whether there are problems of work-related stress and defines ways of preventing, eliminating or reducing them, which

  - takes full account of the multi-faceted character of stress;

  - encompasses both health and safety and organizational aspects of stress;

  - leaves full latitude for decisions to be taken at company level and recognizes that the responsibility for determining the appropriate measures rests with the employer.

With regard to its implementation, the proposed agreement:

- contains a commitment of the members of the signatory parties to implement the agreement;

- leaves the choice of the tools and procedures of implementation to the members of the signatory parties in accordance with national practices;

- includes a procedure for reporting on the actions taken to implement the agreement;

- foresees a possibility to review the agreement after five years if one of the signatory parties requests it.

Source: Adapted from T. Weber, Social Affairs Committee Rapporteur, CEEP, *Monthly Newsletter*, Issue 1, June 2004. (See: http://www.ceep.org/en/themes/SocialAffairs/SACNewsletterJune2004.doc, accessed 25 Oct. 2005.)

In addition to European-wide guidance, a number of organizations within EU Member States have introduced additional measures to reduce stress and the risks of workplace violence, as well as related issues. Some of these are briefly reviewed below.

National agreements

In **Norway** the basic agreement of 1994 between the Norwegian Confederation of Trade Unions (LO) and the Confederation of Norwegian Business and Industry (NHO) established the express right of workers to refuse to work with persons who have exhibited improper conduct:

> Employees have the right to refuse to work with, or under the management of, persons who have shown such improper conduct that, according to the norms of working or social life generally, it ought to justify their dismissal. Discussions between employers and shop stewards should be held immediately if such situations arise. If they fail to reach agreement, there shall not be any stoppage or other forms of industrial action.[48]

In **Denmark** a central agreement on the psychological working environment was signed in 2001 by the Danish Working Environment Authority, the Central Organisation of Industrial Employees in Denmark and the Danish Federation of Unions (LO). Under the new agreement, bullying and harassment are to be dealt with by employers and employees within companies, using local agreements to tackle these issues.[49]

Industry sector agreements

Model agreements on work-related violence have also been developed by industry-specific groups. For example, in the **United Kingdom** UNISON was one of the first to develop a Model Agreement on Tackling Violence in the National Health Service.[50] The development and implementation of policies to tackle violence need to be negotiated between management and trade union representatives, involve safety representatives and committees, and be agreed at all stages. Essential components in such industry-sector agreements include the provision of information, opportunities for additional union-approved training for safety representatives, adequate resources to investigate violent events, and measures for reviewing the effectiveness of anti-violence policies by safety committees.

Along similar lines, the Manufacturing Science and Finance union (MSF) in the United Kingdom has published the *Guide to prevention of violence at work*,[51] which stresses that a successful strategy in this area can be achieved only if employees are fully involved in its development. For example, the employer must consult fully with safety representatives over the violence-prevention strategy, and the planning and organization of any training provided.

The model agreement in box 46 is proposed by the MSF to make operational an effective violence prevention strategy.

Box 46   Model agreement on violence at work

The agreement on violence at work between ABC [...] (employer) and MSF explains procedures to deal with violence. It is part of the Health and Safety Policy and will be regularly reviewed and updated as appropriate. The next review date will be [...]

1.   Definition of violence

The working definition of violence will be:

Any incident in which an employee is abused, threatened or assaulted by a member of the public in circumstances arising from his or her employment. This includes verbal abuse and threats (with or without a weapon), rude gestures, innuendos, sexual and racial harassment, discrimination because of a person's disability or sexuality as well as physical assault, whether or not it results in injury. Physical assault includes being shoved or pushed as well as hit, punched, etc. When in a vehicle, it can also include another driver behaving in a threatening manner. Members of the public include patients, clients and co-workers.

2.   ABC (employer)

(i.)   recognizes the potential for violence arising from employment and undertakes to do all that is reasonably practicable to eliminate and/or reduce the risk of violence to employees;

(ii.)   will develop a policy on the prevention of violence in consultation with the Health and Safety Committee and with union Safety Representatives and will develop local strategies and guidelines to all staff, based on this policy;

(iii.)   affirms that employees are instructed not to take risks on behalf of the employer to protect the employer's property, etc., and affirms that the procedures for serious and imminent danger under Regulation 7 of the Management of Health and Safety at Work Regulations 1992 cover violence at work;

(iv.)   undertakes to assess the potential for violence arising from the work, to identify any group of employees especially at risk, to take all practical steps to eliminate/reduce the risks, including the provision of training, work environment, information about potentially violent clients/customers (and those who may be with them) and information about the area/location in which the work is to be carried out;

(v.)   requires full reporting of all incidents of violence, including abuse and near misses, and provides a reporting system;

(vi.)   will investigate all incidents and report to the Health and Safety Committee;

/cont'd

/cont'd

(vii)   will provide support and aftercare, including counselling and professional help where appropriate, to those who have experienced violence;

(viii.) will agree to move the perpetrator of the violence where this is possible (recognizing that in many cases this may not be possible);

(ix.)   will agree to a change of duties/location/redeployment for a person who is unable to undertake their former duties as a result of experiencing violence, without prejudice to future prospect or any detriment;

(x.)   will in consultation with union Safety Representatives provide full training to employees who may be at risk from violence, enable them to recognize violent or potentially violent situations, and to provide retraining and training updates where appropriate;

(xi.)   will take seriously and investigate report(s) from employees about the potential for violence, and will take preventive measures to reduce the risk;

(xii)   will regularly monitor and review the prevention of violence policy, in consultation with the Health and Safety Committee; and

(xiii.) will identify the person responsible for the implementation of the prevention of violence policy.

Source: Manufacturing, Science and Finance union (MSF), 1993, p. 9 and pp. 24–25.

Corporate agreements

In **Germany** an agreement has been in operation at Volkswagen since 1996, aimed at establishing an enterprise culture based on partnership, the development of a positive working climate and enhancement of economic success of the company.

This agreement indicates that any forms of racial or gender discrimination, sexual harassment or mobbing are violations of the dignity of the worker. It provides for extensive means to combat these workplace problems and involves management, the works council, those responsible for women's issues, the personnel office, and health and safety officers – all of whom must immediately intervene when situations of sexual harassment and mobbing are brought to their attention. The measures to be taken against a perpetrator are progressive and escalate to dismissal in the worst cases. Positive action is also envisaged by way of training, seminars, circulation of information, and sensitization campaigns.

This first agreement has inspired many other agreements with trade unions and has been actively promoted, with sample documents being provided as policy models. For the private sector, IG Metall has published ten sample agreements on the Internet, all following the same structure but adjusted to the special characteristics of each enterprise.

One model of a policy statement in **Germany** is based on the collective agreement at FRAPORT AG, the Frankfurt Airport company, Frankfurt/ Main, which took effect in January 2001. This policy document is a rare example where monitoring and evaluation aspects are integrated in the agreement and not subjected to a separate procedural agreement (see Chapter 7).[52]

In **Italy**, company agreements have also been concluded that specifically address workplace violence, such as those at ATM/Satti in Turin (see Chapter 7),[53] and the Ministry of Cultural Works and Activities and ASL (Local Health Agency) of Catanzaro. These agreements provide essentially for the constitution of anti-mobbing committees (called "climate committees" in the ATM/Satti Agreement) and for the periodic evaluation of the risks of mobbing in the ASL case.

The role of the courts

Within the context of these legislative and allied developments, the courts play a major role. Court decisions often anticipate interpretations and legal solutions that will later be incorporated in national legislation; provide clarification as to the extent and limits of the protection granted to victims of workplace violence; and greatly contribute to defining the responsibilities of employers, particularly in those countries that have not introduced new specific workplace violence legislation (box 47).

Box 47   Postman harassed: Post Office to blame

Yesterday the Brussels criminal court handed out suspended prison sentences of up to 22 months to the four colleagues and direct superior of David Van Gysel, a young postman from Wezembeek-Oppem, who committed suicide by throwing himself under a train on 17 October 2000. Handing down the sentence, the court took the view that there was a direct connection between the young man's death and the harassment he had suffered on the part of his colleagues. The court also fined the enterprise La Poste, as a legal person, around 238,000 euros. This judgment set a precedent in that this was the first time an enterprise had been found guilty on such grounds. Didier Putzeys, the lawyer defending La Poste, immediately announced that the enterprise would appeal the judgment, because it had not taken account of the principle whereby a corporation cannot be held responsible if the perpetrators of the violation have been identified. The parents of David Van Gysel said they were satisfied. According to their lawyer, they could now begin to come to terms with the loss of their son.

Source: Hermine Bokhurst, *Le Soir*, 21 Jan. 2004.

Employers' responsibilities

Negligent hiring

In the **United States**, at least 28 state jurisdictions now recognize the tort of negligent hiring that holds an employer to a duty of reasonable care in selecting employees, thus precluding the hiring of persons who may present dangers to other workers and the public.[54] Employers may be found negligent, for example, for failing to conduct a proper background investigation, such as checking references and contacting former employers, which would have shown that a job applicant had a propensity for violence.[55]

American courts have in certain circumstances recognized as a valid cause for action an employer's negligent training of its employees that results in injury to a third person. An employer may also be liable in the case of retaining an employee who has demonstrated a propensity for violent behaviour. In other decisions, American courts have recognized vicarious liability for an employer who should have taken reasonable care in supervising an employee who threatens others with violent behaviour.[56]

Breach of confidence

In **Australia**, a 1996 court case (Burazin v Blacktown City Guardian Pty. Ltd.) proposed enlargement of the scope of the employment contract which would include an implicit obligation on the employer to ensure that the contract "will not, without reasonable cause, conduct itself in a manner likely to damage or destroy the relationship of confidence and trust between the parties as employer and employee".[57]

Elaborating, the judge indicated that "[as] the very purpose of the implied term is to protect the employee from oppression, harassment and loss of job satisfaction, it is difficult to see why it should not be regarded as a term designed 'to provide peace of mind or freedom from distress' ".[58]

This case is seen as offering important new opportunities in the use of civil remedies against all types of violence at work.[59]

Pre-employment screening

As employers in general attempt to prevent workplace violence and meet obligations to provide a safe workplace, they often seek to identify and "weed out" potential problem employees. Various methods may be employed, such as questionnaires and interviews, background checks, polygraph tests, alcohol and drug tests, psychological or personality tests, and honesty tests. In doing so, however, consideration must also be given to privacy rights, which can limit the method chosen or the way it is implemented. Employers who do not exercise due care in finding out about a person who may have a history of violence could be liable for negligent hiring or failure to provide a safe workplace. On the other hand, employers face restrictions when seeking information that could be considered an invasion of a person's privacy or be discriminatory. Thus, in many situations, it will be necessary to balance the duty to protect employees from a violent individual, and to provide a safe working place, with an individual's right to privacy.

In the **United States**, psychological tests and other background checks to exclude "unstable" or unfit employees may lead to disability discrimination liable under the Americans with Disabilities Act or the Rehabilitation Act of 1973 (box 48). Employers may also be considered liable for racial discrimination under Title VII or equivalent state laws if their screening practices have a disproportionate impact on a particular group. For example, inquiries into arrest records during background screening have been held to violate Title VII of the Civil Rights Act because of their negative impact on minorities.[60]

Box 48   Caught between violence and Americans with Disabilities Act compliance

Companies face a Catch-22 when an employee with a psychiatric disorder poses a risk of violence: they must comply with the Americans with Disabilities Act (ADA) while also maintaining a safe workplace, according to *Fair employment practices*, published by the Bureau of National Affairs, Washington, DC.

The dilemma: employers may be considered liable for discrimination if they dismiss workers who have mental disabilities. Under the ADA, employers cannot discriminate against such employees unless they pose a "direct threat" to someone's health and safety that cannot be solved with a reasonable accommodation. But if the company does not dismiss the worker, because the actual or threatened misconduct does not amount to a direct threat, co-workers or other injured parties may charge the employer with negligence.

Strong policies against workplace violence are one safeguard, says *Fair employment practices*. For example, employees who violate such policies may not be fit for duty, even if the violation is due to a disability. That's the tack taken by Wells-Fargo. The bank's workplace violence policy calls for the immediate dismissal of employees who engage in bodily harm, physical intimidation or threats of violence.

Employers also can protect themselves and their workers by asking a professional to evaluate an employee who exhibits disruptive behaviour. If a suit is later brought under the ADA, a court will see that the employer made an effort to comply with the law and protect its workers, says the newsletter.

Source: Reprinted by permission of the publisher, from HR Focus, New York, American Management Association, Mar. 1996, p. 19.

There are a range of other scenarios where common-law decisions have had a profound impact on organizational policies. A few core precedent cases are listed below.

Outsourcing of hiring

In 1998, a Massachusetts jury made the largest negligent hiring award ever, US$26.5 million, to the estate of a cerebral palsy victim murdered by a health-care worker. In this case, a local health-care providing company was hired to give daily nursing care. The firm then outsourced the hire of a nurse to another local firm. The estate sued both local firms and proved at the trial that neither firm had conducted a background check on the employee–killer, who had in fact never attended nursing school and had six felony convictions. The firm that outsourced the job argued that it should not be held liable for the torts of its independent contractor. The jury found for the plaintiff, noting that the first firm gave its independent contractor several guidelines, but did not require that employees be screened.[61]

In **Australia**, the relationships between principal, contractor and host employer are not explicitly addressed under occupational safety and health statutes in all the different jurisdictions. However, both prosecutions under statute law and tort cases now provide guidance in that there are numerous cases where both the host employer and the leasing firm have been convicted and fined.[62]

Constructive dismissals

In the **United Kingdom** there is no specific legislation on workplace violence, but several general Acts have relevance in this area. Among the most significant are the Health and Safety at Work Act 1974, the Management of Health and Safety at Work Regulations 1999 and the Protection from Harassment Act, No. 40, March 1997. The Employment Rights Act 1996 provides that employees may not be unfairly dismissed. Of particular relevance to bullying is the concept of "constructive dismissal". An employee is constructively dismissed when he or she voluntarily leaves the employment because the employer has fundamentally breached an express or implied term of the employment contract. Subjecting an employee to bullying could be a form of breach of an implied contractual term. Some court decisions appear to confirm this, although the jurisprudence has not been consolidated. For example, in Abbey National PLC v Robinson (2000 – WL1741415 (EAT)), an Employment Appeal Tribunal upheld a finding of constructive dismissal where the worker's manager "had been bullying and harassing her in the workplace to a degree she found insufferable".[63]

Illicit behaviour

In **Germany**, during 2001, the Thüringen Higher Labour Court (Landesarbeitsgericht Thüringen) issued two important decisions on mobbing. In the first case,[64] the Tribunal stated that mobbing had not only affected the personal dignity of the bank employee concerned, but also the health and safety of the victim to the extent that it had penal relevance. The Tribunal confirmed a previous decision against the illicit "humiliation" (*Degradierung*) of the worker concerned and threatened a fine of DM50,000 if the mobbing did not stop. In the second case,[65] the judge confirmed the dismissal of a bullying manager of a supermarket as legitimate since he had insulted and "broken" a worker to the point of attempting suicide.

Burden of proof

In **Italy**, a decision of the Supreme Court of Cassation (Supreme Corte di Cassazione)[66] established that the employer has to prove that all necessary measures to protect the psychological and physical health of workers have been introduced. It is up to the workers to give evidence of the injury suffered and the occupational nature of such conditions.

In **Spain**, a decision of the Social Court of Madrid (Juzgado de lo Social de Madrid)[67] established that, in the case of mobbing, the victim has to produce evidence of the alleged facts, but not direct proof that these constitute mobbing. Thus while tort law has still not been consolidated, the pattern of court decisions across countries is clear. As a result, common-law decisions support the general trend within statutes and organizational policies to prohibit all forms of workplace violence.

From intervention to action

This chapter has now traversed a wide range of legislative and regulatory interventions taken over recent years to deal with violence in the workplace. It should be emphasized, however, that while encouraging and comprehensive advances have been made on the broad legislative and regulatory front across numerous countries, responses to workplace violence remain fragmented within and between many national jurisdictions. Access to remedies can often be difficult, and the pursuit of statutory remedies after an incident of violence can draw plaintiffs into costly, indeterminate and stressful litigation.

McCarthy and Mayhew (2004), in a recent international review of legislative and regulatory responses to workplace violence, have suggested the following recommendations to improve statutory endeavours in this area:

- A web of statutory constraints oriented to "best-practice" international standards is desirable, since lowest common denominator guides are unlikely to be effective in preventing the multiplicity of forms of workplace bullying/violence.

- An international database to record workplace bullying/violence events could be established to inform the development of statutory initiatives. For example, programmes such as the United Nations Surveys on Crime Trends and Operations of the Criminal Justice System ... and the International Crime Victimisation Survey ... could be extended to record occupational violence and bullying.[68]

- The development of subsidiary legislation in respect of bullying/violence within OSH statutes could be undertaken to provide more stringent compliance standards.

- Enhanced training and resourcing of OSH inspectors to identify breaches of OSH duty of care and powers to issue provisional improvement notices in respect of workplace bullying/violence would further early preventive efforts.

- Both victims and alleged perpetrators should be entitled to natural justice. Complainants should also be protected from risks of defamation through procedural arrangements.

- Where possible, no-blame conflict mediation and transformative approaches should be applied, with provision for developmental options for both perpetrators and recipients, together with escalating sanctions for proven serial offenders. Difficulties in defining and evidencing less overt forms of workplace bullying/violence and its normalization in work cultures justify this approach.

- In adjudicating complaints about workplace bullying/violence, the focus should be on the perpetrator's behaviour. The physical or psychological inadequacies of the recipient should not excuse perpetrator behaviours or work practices that are unlawful or unreasonable. Furthermore, unreasonable work practices that contribute to conflicts need consideration in adjudication of responsibility.

- Regulatory obligations for emergency services and environmental design should be aligned with the anti-workplace bullying/violence policies.

- Responses by emergency services (ambulance and fire), police SWAT (special weapons and tactics) teams, and health authorities (testing for toxic chemicals, decontamination, and treatment of infectious diseases) should also be consistent.

- The cost of insurance protection premiums can be aligned to the quality of preventive strategies implemented to safeguard against workplace bullying/violence.

- Ombudsmen should be empowered to address complaints that are unable to be resolved within organizations, to provide pathways for mediation that do not impose unreasonable costs and distress on recipients.

- The protection of whistle-blowers needs to be strengthened within legal statutes to safeguard against the use of bullying/violence to enable corruption to persist.[69]

The review in this chapter has concentrated deliberately upon broad trends and developments, without examining how specific governments, enterprises, trade unions and other bodies have sought to give practical meaning and direction to these legislative and regulatory dictates. A review at this more specifically focused level is now pursued in the following chapters.

Notes

[1] For example, Article 19 of the United Nations Convention on the Rights of the Child provides that:

"1. States Parties shall take all appropriate legislative, administrative, social and educational measures to protect the child from all forms of physical or mental violence, injury or abuse, neglect or negligent treatment, maltreatment or exploitation, including sexual abuse, while in the care of parent(s), legal guardian(s) or any other person who has the care of the child.

2. Such protective measures should, as appropriate, include effective procedures for the establishment of social programmes to provide necessary support for the child and for those who have the care of the child, as well as for other forms of prevention and for identification, reporting, referral, investigation, treatment, and follow-up of instances of child maltreatment described heretofore, and, as appropriate, for judicial involvement." This Convention was adopted by the United Nations General Assembly on 20 November 1989.

[2] Protection from Harassment Act No. 40, 21 March 1997.

[3] See Canadian Centre for Occupational Health and Safety (CCOHS), 2005b.

[4] Corte Costituzionale: "Assicurazione obbligatoria centro gli infortuno sul lavoro e malattie professionali – Indennizzabilità delle malattie", 1988 (see: http://normativo.inail.it/bdninternet/docs/cost17988.htm, accessed 15 Nov. 2005).

[5] Consolidated text of regulations concerning the insurance against work accidents and occupational diseases, approved with presidential decree of 30 June 1965, No. 1124.

[6] Istituto Nazionale per l'Assicurazione contro gli Infortuni sul Lavoro (INAIL), Italy, Office Circular No. 71, 17 Dec. 2003, especially pp. 2–3.

[7] See, for example, CCOHS, 2005a.

[8] Einarsen et al., 2003. See also Leymann, 1990, and McCarthy and Mayhew, 2004.

[9] This comprises the Health and Safety Commission and the Health and Safety Executive approach to tackling violence and psychological violence at work in the United Kingdom (see: http://www.hse.gov.uk/violence/hschse.pdf, accessed 15 Nov. 2005).

[10] Department of Labour, Occupational Safety and Health Service, Government of New Zealand, 1995.

[11] The following legislation is relevant: Health and Safety in Employment Act 1992: Act No. 96, 27 October 1992 as amended in 1993, 1998, 2002 and 2004; Harassment Act 1997: An Act to provide criminal and civil remedies in respect of harassment, No. 92, 1 December 1997 (see: http://www.legislation.co.nz, accessed 15 Nov. 2005).

[12] Johnstone, 1997, p. 305.

[13] Article 3, part 2 of the Working Environment Act, 8 November 1980, in *Staatsblad*, No. 664, 1980 as amended up to Act dated 21 February 1996, in *Staatsblad*, No. 133, 1996.

[14] See detailed analysis of this legislation in the Netherlands in Popma et al., 2002, pp. 177–209.

[15] Arbeidsomstandighedenwet (Working Conditions Act) 1998, in *Staatsblad*, No. 184, 1999, 18 March 1999 (see: http://www.bbzfnv.nl/arbowet1998.html, accessed 20 Nov. 2005).

[16] Arbeidslivets lover (Act relating to workers' protection and the working environment) as subsequently amended, last by Act No. 66 of 2 July 2004, Section 12. Workplace arrangements. 1. General requirements (see: http://www.arbeidstilsynet.no/regelverk/lover/pdf/7529.pdf, accessed 20 Dec. 2005).

[17] Svensk författningssamling (Work Environment Act 31), Act No. 1160, 19 December 1977, as amended up to Act No. 1239, 30 November 1995. (Svensk författningssamling, No. 1239, 1995) [LS 1977–Swe. 4].

[18] Swedish National Board of Occupational Safety and Health: Ordinance (AFS 1993:2) on Violence and Menaces in the Working Environment, 14 January 1993 and Ordinance (AFS 1993:17) on Victimization at Work, 21 September 1993.

[19] Act of 2002-73, 17 January 2002.

[20] Debout, 1999.

[21] Cassation criminelle, 12 June 1992 and 30 April 1996; Chambre sociale de la Cour d'appel de Riom, 22 Febuary 2000; Court d'appel de Versailles, 20 March 2000.

[22] Cassation sociale, 15 March 2000, No. 97-45.91; Cassation sociale, 10 May 2001, No. 99-400.59

[23] Article L 122-49, para. 1.

[24] Article L 122-51.

[25] Ibid.

[26] Article L 122-54.

[27] Article L 152-1-1 of the Labour Code and Article 222-32-2 of the Penal Code.

[28] C-452, Workplace Psychological Prevention Act, 1 June 2004 (see http://www.gouv.qc.ca/en/lois/normes/harcelement.asp, accessed 24 Oct. 2005).

[29] Ibid., sect. 81.8.

[30] Ibid., sect. 81.19.

[31] Ibid., sect. 81.20.

[32] Law No. 1.225 of the Autonomous City of Buenos Aires, 5 January 2004.

[33] Law No. 13.168 of the Province of Buenos Aires, published in *Boletín Oficial*, 25 Feb. 2004.

[34] Law No. 7232, Violencia laboral en el empleo público de Tucumán (Workplace violence in public employment of Tucumán), 23 September 2002.

[35] Law No. 1.225 of the Autonomous City of Buenos Aires, op. cit.

[36] Act of 26 June 1974, Labour Code as at 1 January 2004, in *Gazeta Prawna*, 13–15 Feb. 2004.

[37] As discussed earlier in this chapter, the terms "mobbing" and "bullying" overlap, with some variations in interpretation in different cultures. In the English-speaking world, the term "mobbing" is most commonly used where a group of perpetrators singles out one victim. However, particularly in Scandinavia, the term "mobbing" often applies to scenarios where there is a single perpetrator.

[38] Poland, Labour Code, Article 94(3), paras. 1, 3, 4 and 5.

[39] Directive 2002/73/EC on the implementation of the principle of equal treatment for men and women, as regards access to employment, vocational training and promotion, and working conditions, 23 September 2002.

[40] Ibid., paras. 8 and 9.

[41] Ministry of Land, Infrastructure and Transport, Japan, 2004.

[42] Johnstone, 1997, p. 305.

[43] Canadian Labour Code, 1966, as amended up to 23 June 1993 (Revised Statutes of Canada, ch. 42, 1993).

[44] WorkSafe Western Australia, 1999a.

[45] WorkSafe Victoria, 2003.

[46] WorkSafe Western Australia, 1999b.

[47] EuroCommerce and EUROFIET statement on combating violence in commerce, March 1995.

[48] LO–NHO Basic Agreement, 1994, para. 10.1.

[49] European Industrial Relations Observatory (EIRO); European Foundation for the Improvement of Living and Working Conditions, 2005.

[50] UNISON, 1992, p. 7.

[51] MSF, 1993.

[52] IG Metall: FRAPORT AG, 2001.

[53] The texts of the ATM/Satti agreement are included in Di Martino and De Santis, 2003.

[54] Sinclair-Bernadino, no date.

[55] Some recent and somewhat disturbing examples of failures to check the background of employees come from the following media report: "A routine police inquiry disclosed that a private guarding company was employing an individual using a false name. It turned out that not only had he escaped from prison, but was a convicted murderer. The company had employed the man without any background checks. Police investigating a theft suspected a private security guard, and conducted a full check on all 26 employees at his company. Eleven were found to have previous convictions for a total of 74 crimes, including rape, threats to kill, illegally possessing guns, burglary and assault. The firm's directors were not aware of their staff's criminal backgrounds. The managing director of one company gave a reference to support an employee's application for a shotgun certificate. The director said he had known the man for a year, he had a "sociable nature and a good and even temperament", and was "an honest and very reliable person who can be trusted". Police inquiries showed he had 15 convictions for dishonesty and violence, and one for the manslaughter of his wife while attempting to carry out an illegal abortion. A man with previous convictions for theft, deception and stealing cars was released from prison after serving time for driving while disqualified. He then set up his own security company, installing intruder alarms, security lighting and CCTV. A private security guard working at a court was found stealing money from a judge's handbag in his own Chambers" (*The Guardian*, 16 July 1997).

[56] Littler et al., 1994, p. 11.

[57] Burazin v Blacktown City Guardian Pty. Ltd., 142 ALR 144.

[58] Ibid, 142 ALR 154.

[59] Barron, 1998.

[60] National Clearinghouse for Legal Services, 1994.

[61] Anderson, 1998, pp. 89–102.

[62] For example, WorkCover Authority of NSW (Inspector Ankucic v Drake Personnel Ltd (1997) 89IR374.

[63] Yamada, 2003, p. 402.

[64] Az: 5 Sa 403/2000.

[65] Az: 5 Sa102/2000.

[66] No. 5491 of 2 May 2000.

[67] Sentencia JS-Madrid 1803/2002.

[68] Barkley and Tavares, 2002.

[69] McCarthy and Mayhew, 2004, pp. 214–215.

TACKLING WORKPLACE VIOLENCE 6

The vast majority of workers do not expect to be a victim of workplace violence. Yet, as we have seen in preceding chapters, every year millions of workers around the globe experience violent incidents while on the job.

The ILO believes that every worker deserves to work in a safe and secure environment where violence is not tolerated, and where respect, equal treatment and productive working relationships are encouraged. This vision is not an unattainable dream. Research and experience demonstrate that steps can and should be taken to prevent the occurrence of workplace violence within organizations. In a separate publication the ILO has already presented these steps and examined how organizations in many parts of the world are approaching this important occupational safety and health issue.[1]

This chapter focuses upon the control cycle of violence at work, while Chapters 7 and 8 provide more detailed examples of programmes implemented in a range of settings to combat the risk of violent events.

Guides and publications on workplace violence prevention

Guidelines on workplace violence have proliferated in recent years. The list provided in box 49 includes a selection of general guidelines, and some directed to occupations/situations at special risk, particular types of violence, and specific audiences.

Based on these guidelines, an extremely valuable body of knowledge can now be applied to the development of strategies to deal with workplace violence. Despite different approaches and methods being used, the guidelines listed in box 49 reveal common themes:

- Preventive action is possible and necessary.

- Work organization and the working environment hold significant keys to the causes and solutions to the problem.

Box 49   Published guidelines on violence: A selection

Guidelines for occupations/situations at special risk

AFL-CIO (American Federation of State, County and Municipal Employees): *Preventing workplace violence* (Washington, DC, 1998).
(See: http://www.igc.org/afscme/health/violtc.htm, accessed 30 Nov. 2005.)

CAL/OSHA (California, Department of Industrial Relations): *Guidelines for security and safety of health care and community service workers* (San Francisco, 1998).
(See: www.dir.ca.gov/DOSH/dosh_publications/hcworker.html, accessed 30 Sep. 1999.)

Danish Food and Allied Workers' Union: *Have you talked with your colleague today?* (on bullying) (Copenhagen, 2001).

Danish Labour Inspectorate: *Risk of violence in connection with work performance* (Copenhagen, Oct. 1997).

Danish Union of Commercial and Clerical Employees: *Dialogue creates understanding* (on bullying) (Copenhagen, 2002).

Department of Transport, United Kingdom: *Protecting bus crews – A practical guide* (London, 1995).

HSAC (Health Services Advisory Committee): *Violence and aggression to staff in health services* (London, 1997).

HSC (Health and Safety Commission): *Violence in the education sector* (London, 1997).

HSE (Health and Safety Executive): *Prevention of violence to staff in banks and building societies* (London, 1993).

—: *Preventing violence to retail staff* (London, 1995).

IATA (International Air Transport Association): *Guidelines for handling disruptive/unruly passengers* (Geneva, 1999).

ILO (International Labour Office): *Workplace violence in services sectors and measures to combat this phenomenon*, ILO code of practice (Geneva, 2003).

—/ICN (International Council of Nurses)/WHO (World Health Organization)/PSI (Public Services International): *Framework guidelines for addressing workplace violence in the health sector*, Joint Programme on Workplace Violence in the Health Sector (Geneva, 2002), pp. 19–20.

Long Island Coalition for Workplace Violence Awareness and Prevention: *Workplace violence awareness and prevention: An information and instructional package for use by employers and employees* (New York, Long Island, 1996).
(See: www.osha-sle.gov/workplace_violence/wrkplaceViolence.intro.html, accessed 1 Mar. 2001.)

MSF (Manufacturing, Science, Finance Union): *Working alone: Guidance for MSF members and safety representatives* (London, 1994).

NHS (National Health Service), United Kingdom: *We don't have to take this: Resource pack*, NHS Zero Tolerance Zone (London, 2000).

—: *Withholding treatment from violent and abusive patients in NHS trusts: We don't have to take this - Resource guide*, NHS Zero Tolerance Zone (London, 2001).

Occupational Safety and Health Service, New Zealand: *Guidelines for the safety of staff from the threat of armed robbery* (Wellington, 1995).

OSHA (Occupational Safety and Health Authority), United States Department of Labor: *Recommendations for workplace violence prevention programs in late-night retail establishments* (Washington, DC, 1998).

—: *Guidelines for preventing workplace violence for health care and social service workers* (Washington, DC, 2004).

RCN (Royal College of Nursing): *Challenging harassment and bullying: Guidance for RCN representatives, stewards and officers* (London, 2000).

—: *Dealing with harassment and bullying at work: A guide for RCN members* (London, 2000).

—: *Bullying and harassment at work: A good practice guide for RNC negotiators and health care managers* (London, 2002).

—: *Dealing with bullying and harassment: A guide for nursing students* (London, 2002).

Suzy Lamplugh Trust: *Personal safety for social workers* (London, 1994).

—: *Personal safety for health-care workers* (London, 1995).

—: *Personal safety for schools* (London, 1996).

—: *Personal safety in other people's homes* (London, 1998).

Swanton, B.; Webber, D: *Protecting counter and interviewing staff from client aggression* (Canberra, Australian Institute of Criminology, 1990).

TUC (Trades Union Congress): *Protect us from harm: Preventing violence at work*, report by Julia Gallagher (London, TUC Health and Safety Unit, 1999).

UNISON: *Working alone in safety – Controlling the risks of solitary work* (London, 1993).

United States, Departments of Education and Justice: *A guide to safe schools* (Washington, DC, 1998).
/cont'd

/cont'd

Victorian WorkCover Authority (VWA): *Prevention of bullying and violence at work: Guidance note* (Melbourne, 2003).[1]

WorkCover Authority of New South Wales: *Armed hold-ups and cash handling: A guide to protecting people and profits from armed hold-ups* (Sydney, 1994).

—: *Violence in the workplace* (Sydney, 2002).

WorkCover Corporation of South Australia: *Guidelines for aged care facilities* (Adelaide, 1996).

Workplace Health and Safety Queensland: *Guide to personal security in the retail industry* (Brisbane, Department of Industrial Relations, 2004).

WorkSafe Western Australia: *Code of practice: Workplace violence* (Perth, 1999).

—, Department of Consumer and Employment Protection: *Guidance note on working alone* (Perth, 1999).

Guidelines for special types of violence

Commission of the European Communities: *How to combat sexual harassment: A guide to implementing the European Commission code of practice* (Brussels, 1993).

Danish Labour Inspectorate: *Bullying and sexual harassment* (Copenhagen, 2002).

Department of Employment, United Kingdom: *Sexual harassment in the workplace: A guide for employers* (London, 1992).

Equal Opportunities Commission, United Kingdom: *Sexual harassment at work: Consider the cost* (London, 1994).

European Council: *Good practice guide to mitigate the effects and eradicate violence against women* (Brussels, 2002).

ICN (International Council of Nurses): *Guidelines on coping with violence in the workplace* (Geneva, 1999). (See: www.icn.ch, accessed 15 Nov. 2000.)

Irish Department of Enterprise, Trade and Development: *Procedures for addressing bullying in the workplace* (Dublin, 2002).

Irish Equality Authority: *Code of practice on sexual harassment and harassment at work* (Dublin, 2002).

—: *Code of practice – Prevention of workplace bullying* (Dublin, 2002).

—: *Guidelines on the prevention of workplace bullying* (Dublin, 2002).

Malaysia Ministry of Human Resources: *Code of practice on the prevention and eradication of sexual harassment at the workplace* (Kuala Lumpur, 1999).

Manufacturing, Science, Finance Union (MSF): *Bullying at work: Confronting the problem* (London, 1994).

South Africa, Department of Labour: *Code of good practices on the handling of sexual harassment cases* (appended to the Labour Relations Act 66 of 1995).

TUC (Trades Union Congress): *Guidelines: Sexual harassment at work* (London, 1992).

—: *Racial harassment at work: A guide and workplace programme for trade unionists* (London, 1993).

UNISON: *Bullying at work: Guidance for safety representatives and members on bullying at work and how to prevent it* (London, 1996).

—: *Bullying at work: Guidelines for UNISON branches, stewards and safety representatives* (London, 1996).

United Nations: *UN action against terrorism* (Geneva, 2004). (See: www.un.org/terrorism, accessed 30 Nov. 2005.)

Working Women's Centre: *Stop violence against women at work* (Adelaide, 1994).

Guidelines for special audiences

Center for Occupational and Environmental Health, University of California: *Violence on the job: A guidebook for labor and management* (Berkeley, California, 1997).

HSE (Health and Safety Executive): *Violence at work: A guide for employers* (London, 1997).

Occupational Safety and Health Service, New Zealand: *A guide for employers and employees on dealing with violence at work* (Wellington, 1995).

PERSEREC (Defence Personnel Security Research Center): *Guidance for employers* (Washington, DC, 1995).

Suzy Lamplugh Trust: *Violence and aggression at work: Reducing the risks. Guidance for employers* (London, 1994).

—: *Personal safety at work: Guidance for all employees* (London, 1994).

UNISON: *Violence at work. A guide to risk prevention for UNISON branches, stewards and safety representatives* (London, 1997).

United States Office of Personnel Management: *Dealing with workplace violence: A guide for agency planners* (Washington, DC, 1997).

Workers' Compensation Board of British Columbia, Canada: *Take care - How to develop and implement a workplace violence programme - A guide for small business* (Vancouver, 1995).

[1] This and the other VWA's publications were based on and refer to the Occupational Health and Safety Act 1985. The VWA is currently updating these publications to ensure currency and consistency with the new Occupational Health and Safety Act 2004.

- The participation of workers and their representatives is crucial both in identifying the problem and in implementing solutions.

- The interpersonal skills of management and workers alike cannot be underrated.

- There cannot be one blueprint for action, but rather the uniqueness of each workplace situation must be considered.

- Continued review of policies and programmes is needed to keep up with changing situations.

Organizational commitment to preventing and minimizing risk

The correct and preferable response to the risk of workplace violence is seen increasingly to be an essential part of **work organization** and **human resource management**. It is also clear that government, trade unions, workers, occupational safety and health professionals, the mental health and public health communities, and security professionals have important roles to play in developing, promoting and implementing strategies to prevent workplace violence, and dealing with its consequences when it does occur.

Of necessity, the appropriate control strategies vary according to the type of workplace violence and for different perpetrator groups. Box 50 lists strategies relevant to prevention and minimization of impact for the **bullying** form of workplace violence.

Box 50   The organizational model of managing workplace bullying

- Stage 1: Assessment of personal, organizational, and societal vulnerability to inform risk management

- Stage 2: Promotion of constructive coping, zero tolerance policies and regulatory obligations

- Stage 3: Resolution of informal/formal complaints/grievances in ways that reduce absenteeism and workers' compensation

- Stage 4: Constraining the escalation of risk/severity to the point legal claims are launched and the victim is forced out of the workplace

- Stage 5: Managing the transition from workers' compensation to rehabilitation and return to work with positive relationships and ongoing attention to post-traumatic stress disorder (PTSD) symptoms

- Stage 6: Moving on from legal action, suicidal ideation and revenge seeking, to learning, re-affirmation, reconciliation and constructive re-engagement with work and life.

Source: McCarthy and Mayhew, 2004, p. 191.

Box 51   The control cycle of violence at work

As with other OHS hazards, a hierarchy of control approach where the elimination of risk is prioritised is likely to be the most effective in reducing occupational violence. Strategies higher up the OHS hierarchy of control have been proven to be effective in diminishing the risk of occupational violence in other industry sectors. Higher order controls that focus on elimination of risk are also essential in health care. Most important among these strategies is CPTED.[1] Thus, an essential first step in risk management is close examination of building designs, fittings, furnishings, and access restrictions.

Any comprehensive violence prevention strategy also requires organisational and administrative elements to help control the risks ... Hence a second core step in risk management is unequivocal CEO commitment to a zero tolerance policy which is clearly stated and enforced across visitor, staff and client/patient categories. Other essential strategies include a risk identification process that incorporates regular violence vulnerability audits, encouragement of formal reporting of threats and events, flagging of higher-risk perpetrators' files, identification of particular diagnoses that are higher-risk (including symptoms, diagnoses and behaviours), and widespread implementation of interventions tailored to site-specific risk factors.

That is, comprehensive occupational violence prevention strategies are multi-faceted, require organisation-wide implementation of risk management principles ...

[1] Crime Prevention Through Environmental Design (CPTED) is a common strategy applied in criminological interventions to prevent crimes such as hold-ups in retail businesses.

Sources: Mayhew, 2005a, pp. 121–153, especially pp. 147–8.

The prevention and minimization strategies vary somewhat when the perpetrators are based outside the organization, for example clients or customers. The guidelines developed in this area emphasize the importance of a **systematic approach** to workplace violence prevention, involving several steps and the application of a "control cycle". Certain steps have been identified (box 51).

On the basis of the above principles, and recognizing the fundamental role of prevention and the need for a systematic approach in dealing with workplace violence, new models for the management of workplace violence need to be proposed.

Models of prevention at the organizational level

One new model, prepared by Di Martino, takes into account previous efforts by other authors.[2] This model identifies the sequence of actions needed for effective management of the risk of workplace violence and organizes them into three main areas of intervention:

*   primary prevention – approaches that aim to prevent violence before it occurs, largely centred on organizational issues;

- secondary prevention – approaches that focus on the more immediate responses to violence, such as emergency services, medical treatment and debriefing;

- tertiary prevention – approaches that focus on long-term care in the wake of violence, such as rehabilitation and reintegration, and attempts to lessen trauma or reduce the long-term disability associated with violent events.[3]

Within this holistic strategy, prevention at the structural level is emphasized. The model also highlights the importance of post-incident emergency support for individuals victimized, and rehabilitation and reintegration, as well as periodical and comprehensive evaluation of policies and measures to combat workplace violence. The various mechanisms whereby this evaluation can be conducted are set out in figure 23.

As shown in figure 23, the reduction of risks is complex and requires reliable data on the full range of forms of workplace violence. It has been suggested that a targeted response to violence at work can be provided according to the type of "hazardous agent" involved.

Figure 23   The Di Martino model for the management of violence at work

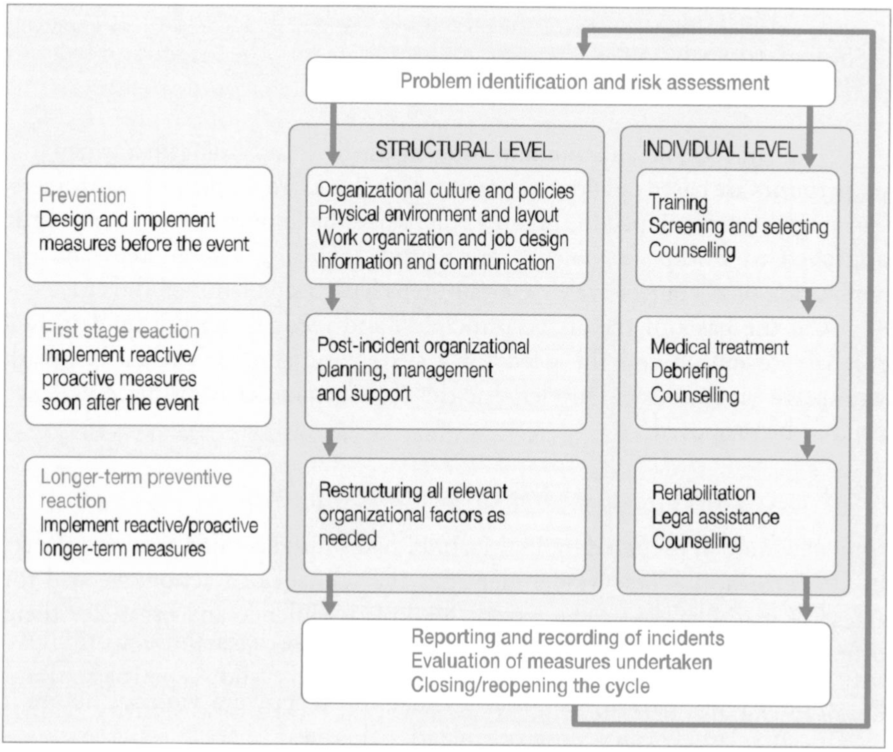

Types of perpetrators of workplace violence

One typology focused on perpetrator characteristics has been incorporated into official guidelines in the state of California,[4] and identifies three main types of "hazardous agent":

Type I – Criminal intruder: In this form of workplace violence, the perpetrator is "external" to the organization and usually enters the work site to commit a robbery or other criminal act.

Type II – Dissatisfied client: In this form of workplace violence, the perpetrator is either a client, recipient or patient of a service provided by the affected workplace or the victim (or wishes to become one).

Type III – Scorned employee: With this form of workplace violence, the perpetrator has an employment-related involvement with the workplace. He or she may be a current or former employee, supervisor or manager who victimizes another worker at the site, for example through bullying, initiation rites or physical violence.

Of crucial importance, the most appropriate prevention strategy varies according to which type of "hazardous agent" category the perpetrator belongs to.[5] Thus, the "hazardous agent" adds a further dimension to the interactive model of violence at work that was expounded in Chapter 4, figure 16. More detailed analysis of each of these three basic types of perpetrators of workplace violence is provided below.

External intruder (or Type 1) workplace violence

To many people, **Type 1** workplace violence appears to be part of society's "crime" problem, and not a workplace safety and health problem at all. According to this view, the workplace is an "innocent bystander" and the solution to the problem is societal, not occupational. The ultimate solution to Type 1 events may indeed involve societal changes, but until such changes occur, it is still the employer's legal responsibility under the OSH legislative framework (as detailed in Chapter 5) to provide a safe place and a safe process of work for their employees.

For example, the employers of employees known to be at risk of Type 1 events and who may handle cash late at night (such as those working in taxicabs, liquor outlets, convenience stores, grocery shops, petrol stations, hotels or motels open late at night and jewellery stores, or as security guards) are required to implement workplace security to reduce the hazard of exposure

---

Box 52   Retail establishments: Administrative and work practice controls

- Integrate violence prevention activities into daily procedures, such as checking lighting, locks and security cameras, to help maintain worksite readiness.

- Keep a minimal amount of cash in each register (e.g. US$50 or less), especially during evening and late-night hours of operation. In some businesses, transactions with large bills (over US$20) can be prohibited. In situations where this is not practical because of frequent transactions in excess of US$20, cash levels should be as low as is practical. Employees should not carry business receipts on their person unless it is absolutely necessary.

- Adopt proper emergency procedures for employees to use in case of a robbery or security breach.

- Establish systems of communication in the event of emergencies. Employees should have access to working telephones in each work area, and emergency telephone numbers should be posted by the phones.

- Adopt procedures for the correct use of physical barriers, such as enclosures and pass-through windows.

- Increase staffing levels at night at stores with a history of robbery or assaults and located in high-crime areas. It is important that clerks be clearly visible to patrons.

- Lock doors used for deliveries and disposal of garbage when not in use. Also, do not unlock delivery doors until the delivery person identifies himself or herself. Take care not to block emergency exits – doors must open from the inside without a key to allow persons to exit in case of fire or other emergency.

- Establish rules to ensure that employees can walk to garbage areas and outdoor freezers or refrigerators without increasing their risk of assault. The key is for employees to have good visibility, thereby eliminating potential hiding places for assailants near these areas. In some locations, taking trash out or going to outside freezers during daylight may be safer than doing so at night.

- Keep doors locked before business officially opens and after closing time. Establish procedures to assure the security of employees who open and close the business, when staffing levels may be low. In addition, the day's business receipts may be a prime robbery target at store closing.

- Limit or restrict areas of customer access, reduce the hours of operation, or close portions of the store to limit risk.

- Adopt safety procedures and policies for off-site work, such as deliveries.

Administrative controls are effective only if they are followed and used properly. Regular monitoring helps ensure that employees continue to use proper work practices. Giving periodic, constructive feedback to employees helps to ensure that they understand these procedures and their importance.

Source: OSHA, 1998, pp. 7–8, as adapted and published in Rogers and Chappell, 2003, p. 59.

---

to workplace violence, satisfy regulatory requirements and maintain an effective injury and illness prevention programme.

The first step in establishing and implementing an effective workplace security component is strong management commitment. The cornerstone of an effective workplace security plan is appropriate reduction of the risk wherever possible for all employees, supervisors and managers. Some of these steps for retail businesses are detailed in box 52.

Employers with employees at risk of workplace violence must also educate them about the risk factors associated with the various types of workplace violence, and provide appropriate training in crime awareness, assault and rape prevention and defusing hostile situations. Also, employers must instruct their employees about what steps to take during an emergency incident. Somewhat different risk-reduction steps apply to the prevention of workplace violence emanating from clients or customers of the organization.

Client or customer perpetrators of workplace violence (or Type 2)

Employers concerned with **Type 2** events need to be aware that the control of physical access through workplace design is an important preventive measure. Steps may include controlling access into and out of the workplace, and restriction of freedom of movement within the workplace, in addition to placing barriers between clients and service providers. Escape routes can also be a critical component of workplace design.

Employers at risk of Type 2 events must also be attentive to communication problems and provide their employees with instruction in how to effectively defuse hostile situations involving their clients, patients, customers, passengers and members of the general public to whom they must provide services. In certain situations, the installation of alarm systems or "panic buttons" may be an appropriate back-up measure. Establishing a "buddy" system to be used in specified emergency situations is often also advisable. The presence of security personnel should also be considered in higher-risk scenarios, where appropriate.

Some measures to combat Type 2 events in the airline industry are shown in box 53.

"Internal" perpetrators of workplace violence (or Type 3)

Type 3 events are more closely tied to employer–employee relations than are Type 1 or 2 events (described above). The design of effective workplace violence policies and procedures, and their careful implementation and

Disruptive/unruly behaviour in the airline industry is first of all a safety issue. It also puts great mental strain on the passengers and employees involved. Prevention of (escalated) disruptive behaviour should therefore be the focus of an airline's approach. Dealing firmly and legally with disruptive behaviour may serve as a deterrent, but an airline cannot rely on its effect. In many disruptive incidents, passengers behave irrationally and will not calculate the consequences of their behaviour.

The study of disruptive behaviour shows that often a series of events builds up to the disruptive behaviour and early signs of potential disruptive behaviour can be observed.

The focus of company policy should be first on prevention by acting on these early signs, rather than dealing exclusively with the escalated incident.

Research further indicates that many incidents (and those which tend to be particularly violent) are related to excessive alcohol consumption, as well as to nicotine withdrawal symptoms of smokers. The service on board provided by the crew must take a responsible approach with regard to the serving of alcohol and should provide alternatives (such as nicotine gum) for smokers.

Measures to maximize prevention of incidents

Internally within the carrier by:

* providing staff with a clear written policy on how to deal with disruptive behaviour, especially in its early stages;

* ensuring a smooth operation: defusing the frustration that occurs over long waiting times, the flight being overbooked, lack of information, technical deficiencies, etc.;

* providing training for frontline staff. This includes instructing both ground staff and crew (flight deck and cabin) to learn how to recognize the early signs of potentially disruptive behaviour (e.g. drinking heavily); ensuring that those who come in contact with customers have acquired the necessary verbal skills and that they understand the importance of informing other operational areas of the situation to enable them to deal with the passenger effectively (not simply "passing" the passenger onwards without identifying that the passenger is showing early warning signs of potentially problematic behaviour);

* maintaining accurate and updated reports and statistics of incidents that do occur so as to continually monitor the types of incidents and identify potential training needs, etc.

Externally by communicating with passengers:

* prior to boarding, especially when groups are travelling together;

* by having dedicated information cards placed in seat pockets;

* through information on the flight ticket/e-receipt.

Source: International Air Transport Association (IATA), 1999, pp. 9–10, as adapted and published in Rogers and Chappell, 2003, p. 62.

enforcement, are likely to be effective in preventing and/or minimizing Type 3 events.

Some mental health professionals believe that verbally assaultive behaviour by an employee or by a supervisor, including belligerent, intimidating and threatening behaviour, is an early warning sign of an individual's propensity to commit a physical assault, and that monitoring of such behaviour is also a part of effective prevention (box 54).

Employers at risk of a Type 3 event need to establish and implement procedures to respond to workplace security hazards when they are identified, and to provide training as necessary to their employees, supervisors and managers in order to satisfy the regulatory requirement of establishing, implementing and maintaining an effective violence prevention strategy.

Box 54   Violence among co-workers and managers

Violence among co-workers and managers can take many forms. For example, an individual worker may threaten other workers or his or her supervisor, a manager may harass workers, or a group of workers may act disrespectfully to their supervisors and each other, or behave in other inappropriate, potentially violent ways. To further complicate matters, the causes of this type of violence can be numerous, difficult to identify, and not always easy to resolve.

Some of the same factors associated with violence committed by patients, clients or intruders may also contribute to violence among co-workers and managers. Such factors include a lack of security, workplace layouts that trap employees behind furniture, inadequate escape routes and a lack of training.

But for conflicts occurring among employees or their managers, other factors may play a role. These may be caused by the workplace itself or stem from outside the workplace, such as personal problems that employees bring to work. Both workplace and non-workplace factors ought to be considered as potential causes of violent behaviour.

Workplace risk factors

Violence among workers and managers may be linked to the work climate and job stress. Signs of a troubled or at-risk work environment that could lead to worker-on-worker violence include:

- chronic labour–management disputes;

- frequent grievances filed by employees (or a marked reduction in the number of grievances if employees don't believe the system works);

- an extraordinary number of workers' compensation claims (especially for psychological illness or mental stress);

/cont'd

/cont'd

- understaffing or excessive demands for overtime;

- a high number of "stressed-out" workers;

- limited flexibility in how workers perform their jobs;

- pending or rumoured lay-offs or "downsizing";

- significant changes in job responsibilities or workload;

- an authoritarian management style.

If the workplace creates the potential for violence, the union should urge management to correct the problems identified. By addressing problems in the work environment, the union and management may prevent employees from becoming threatening or violent.

Source: AFSCME, 1998, Ch. 5, as adapted and published in Rogers and Chappell, 2003, p. 67.

To effectively prevent Type 3 events from occurring, employers need to establish a clear anti-violence zero tolerance policy that includes all forms of inappropriate behaviour, including initiation rites, bullying, harassment, threatening behaviours and assault. This policy needs to be applied consistently and fairly to all employees, supervisors and managers. Employers also need to provide appropriate supervisory and employee training in workplace violence prevention. Enforcement of expected behavioural standards, irrespective of the perpetrator's position in the hierarchy, is essential. Clearly, effective prevention of exposure to the hazard of workplace violence is the preferred option whenever possible, as much suffering can be averted by means of preventive measures, efficient routines and proper care of a person who has been subjected to violence or menaces.[6]

Preventive strategies and measures

As was seen in Chapter 5, to an ever-increasing degree governments, employers and workers now view incidents of workplace violence as potentially preventable, rather than as random acts by criminals. Attention is consequently focusing on the elimination of the causes of violence, rather than the treatment of its effects, and on the positive implications, in terms of cost-efficiency and long-standing results, of preventive strategies.

The prevention of violence in the workplace is of critical importance if employers want to continue the national trend towards increased productivity. Deming, the late founder of the quality improvement movement, exhorted managers to "drive out fear".[7] One source of fear that Deming did not anticipate was the fear of violence in the workplace. Yet it appears that the aftermath of violent episodes are associated with substantial drops in productivity as workers are traumatized, distracted by fear, and spend time seeking reassurance and social support. Thus, the prevention of violence is in the best interest of productivity and profitability. It is also in the best interest of management because, as Losey, chief executive officer of the Society for Human Resource Management (SHRM), noted,[8] the firing manager and the human resources manager are the most likely targets of retribution by an employee going through the process of termination. Executives have also been the targets of kidnappers and terrorists. The motivation for prevention should be clear.

Administrative means to reduce the risks of workplace violence

Common elements of preventive strategies and plans to combat violence usually include the involvement of all those concerned – "the best way to tackle violence is for the employer and the employees to work together to decide what to do".[9] The development of a human-centred workplace culture requires a clear statement of intent from a CEO that a workplace will be violence free (box 55).

Box 55   A human-centred workplace culture

Priority should be given to the development of a human-centred workplace culture based on safety and dignity, non-discrimination, tolerance, equal opportunity and cooperation. This requires actively promoting the development of socialization processes, new participative management styles and the establishment of a new type of organization where:

- social dialogue and communication are extensively utilized;

- the organization and staff share a common vision and goals;

- the manager is committed to combating workplace violence;

- services and responsibilities are decentralized so that managers, supervisors and workers become more aware of local issues and are better able to respond to the needs of the patients;

- the organization encourages problem-sharing and group problem-solving;

- the organization provides an environment where the efforts of the staff are recognized, feedback given and opportunities created for personal and professional development;

- there is a strong and supportive social environment.

Source: ILO/ICN/WHO/PSI, 2002, p. 17.

The commitment of a CEO to a violence-free workplace will usually be accompanied by the establishment of a written policy, as in the case of the Violence-Free Campus Policy at Sonoma State University, California (see Chapter 7, "Best practices", p. 224). Increasingly, zero tolerance policies also accompany the setting up of workplace violence preventive strategies (box 56).

Box 56   Zero tolerance policies

The Zero Tolerance campaign, launched in 1999 in the United Kingdom, aimed to underline to the public that violence against National Health Service (NHS) staff is unacceptable and that the Government was determined to stamp it out. Hard-hitting posters were produced, showing the types of weapons used on NHS staff in attacks, including bottles, syringes and Stanley knives.

Under Zero Tolerance, NHS trusts are expected to have systems in place to record all incidents of violence against staff and have published strategies for reducing such incidents. A national target was established – to reduce incidents of violence against NHS staff by 30 per cent by 2003.

Health minister John Denham emphasized the need for employers to carry out risk assessments for violence, just as they should in other areas of health and safety. He said: "This new Zero Tolerance campaign will show how NHS employers can assess the risks to staff, and develop strategies to tackle violence."

Since the launch of Zero Tolerance, the Department of Health has issued guidelines on withholding treatment from violent and abusive patients as a last resort. NHS trusts have been encouraged to work with police and the Crown Prosecution Service to prosecute individuals who assault staff, and the courts have been encouraged to impose heavier sentences for those committing violence against workers. Some new money has been made available for fitting central locking systems in ambulances, buying personal alarms, and installing closed-circuit television (CCTV) and swipe card systems.

Unions have generally welcomed the initiative. Nigel Bryson, until recently director of health and environment at the GMB general union, says: "Zero Tolerance has raised awareness of the issue in the NHS and placed direct responsibilities on managers to address violence and meet targets to reduce violence." He said it "has also been bold in dealing with persistent perpetrators of violence. We would like to see a similar national campaign introduced across all at risk workplaces".

Health union UNISON has also welcomed the campaign, but is more cautious. It says Zero Tolerance has highlighted the issue of violence in the NHS, and some personal protective measures such as alarms and CCTV have been introduced. But in some trusts managers have focused too much on dealing with perpetrators of violence after the event rather than preventing it in the first place.

Source: "Can zero tolerance deliver?" in *Labour Research*, May 2003, p. 13.

Experts emphasize the importance of a response which includes the largest possible number of different preventive interventions. Because exposure to the hazard of workplace violence varies across jobs, different preventive measures need to be implemented in various ways according to risk factors in specific situations.

Pre-employment testing and screening of potential employees

Selection tools such as written tests, interviews, performance tests, psychological profiles and other prediction devices are commonly recommended. Selection and screening may have an important bearing in terms of violence prevention although, as noted in Chapter 4, the various predictive tools should be used and interpreted with care and caution. Nevertheless, the use of such tools may help in identifying those individuals who are more tailored to certain jobs, less likely to get stressed, frustrated or angered because of task stressors, and consequently less prone to violent workplace responses. Alternatively, selection may be used to screen out the "bad apples" – those whose profile suggests they have a greater propensity to violence which may constitute a risk to the workplace. Some suggestions for pre-employment screening appear in box 57.

The effectiveness of pre-employment screening has, however, been questioned, as have the limits that should be imposed on such practices. In particular, psychological, alcohol, drug and genetic testing are contentious issues, and are likely to be scrutinized closely by a range of interested groups, including trade unions.

Box 57   Screening

Use a job application form that includes an appropriate waiver and release (permitting the employer to verify the information reported on the application). Prior to hiring any applicant, check references and inquire about any prior incidents of violence. In addition, conduct thorough background checks and use drug screening to the extent practicable.

Also evaluate the need for screening contract personnel who work at your facility. Vendors and service organizations whose personnel make frequent visits or spend long periods of time working at your facility should certify that those individuals meet or exceed your firm's safety and security requirements. Conversely, contractors who assign personnel to work at other organizations' facilities should also consider the host firm's safety and security policies and practices.

Source: PERSEREC, 1995.

Psychological testing may certainly help to clarify the personality of the applicant and appropriateness to the job tasks to be undertaken. However, while it is generally accepted that these tests might be employed, there are questions regarding their reliability and validity. Legal regulations covering principles of privacy and equal opportunity employment often place major restrictions on psychological testing in a significant number of countries. These legal limitations frequently impose, on the one hand, an obligation on the employer to collect information that is relevant only to a given employment decision and, on the other hand, an obligation not to request information unjustifiably invasive of the privacy of an individual.[10]

One of the most controversial issues in screening is the use of **alcohol and drug tests**. Workers' and employers' organizations often have divergent opinions in this respect. The National Association of Manufacturers in the United States,[11] for example, expressed the opinion that while drug testing should be done in a fair and equitable manner, with due concern for the employee's privacy, it nonetheless opposes any legislation that would prohibit employers from testing applicants and employees for substance abuse, believing that a company's testing policy should be left to the company itself.

On the other hand, unions that have addressed the issue, such as the AFL-CIO and the Canadian Labour Congress, have generally been opposed to it. They argue that many of the tests that companies use to screen workers for drugs and alcohol are open to serious abuse by employers; are inaccurate and unreliable; cannot determine whether an employee is unable to perform job functions because of drug use; do not by themselves establish that the employee has a pattern of abuse; and can constitute an invasion of workers' rights and privacy.[12]

Despite its controversial nature, the use of alcohol and drug testing appears to be sharply increasing in some countries, as examples from the United Kingdom and the United States in box 58 indicate.

Similar concerns have been expressed about **genetic screening**, with recommendations made to limit this during staff selection. In Switzerland, the Union of Swiss Trade Unions (USS) has argued that genetic tests, if applied to workers, could give a new and dangerous basis to medical tests which are already applied in the hiring process; genetic characteristics could be called defects and considered to be a sickness; and the persons concerned excluded from work and social benefits.[13]

The USS has argued that such tests would give an employer the possibility to use a "highly problematic selection process to identify and eliminate workers with a risk". The union has taken the position that no genetic analysis should be carried out for employment or insurance purposes,

Box 58   Drug testing boom at work

On current trends within two years it will be almost impossible for recreational drug users to get a job with larger companies. Drug testing at work is probably the single most effective weapon we have against adult substance abuse. It is a proven, low-cost strategy which identifies those needing help, reduces demand, cuts accidents and sick leave, improves attendance and increases productivity.

Yet drug testing is (or rather was) highly controversial: it penalizes users with positive drug tests that can bear little or no relation to work performance, encourages knee-jerk dismissal and discrimination at interview. It costs money, invades privacy and smacks of authoritarianism.

Despite all this, almost overnight it has become fashionable to talk of testing millions of people at work for both alcohol and drugs. Just over six months ago the idea seemed so extreme that the [United Kingdom] government cut it out of the White Paper altogether – with small concessions for prisons and roadside.

In a dramatic policy shift, drugs czar [name deleted] and government Ministers have started encouraging drug testing by employers. They are following a quiet revolution, largely unreported because firms have been scared of drug tests by bad publicity.

The government's own Forensic Science Agency alone carried out over a million workplace drug tests last year, with a rush of interest from transport, construction, manufacturing and financial services industries. Last month the International Petroleum Exchange joined London Transport and many others in random drug testing.

This stampede to test follows spectacular drug testing success in America when many had declared the mega-war against drugs all but lost. The drugs industry accounts for 8 per cent of all international trade according to the United Nations. Education, customs, police, crop destruction and prison sentences have failed to deliver so drug testing has become highly attractive, even at the cost of civil liberties.

80 per cent of all large companies already spend over £200 million a year testing for drugs at work, affecting 40 per cent of the US workforce. By 2005 up to 80 per cent of all workers will be covered by drug tests.

Source: P. Dixon, "Drug testing boom at work", in *Future-2004*, p. 1 (see: http://www.globalchange.com/drugtest.htm, accessed 23 June 2005).

maintaining that "genetic information does not belong to employers, company doctors and social insurance bodies. Each individual should decide whether he or she believes it is appropriate that a genetic analysis be carried out by a physician of his or her own choice".[14]

In Germany, an investigative commission issued recommendations in 1988 on the subject of the risks and opportunities of gene technology. The commission's recommendations included the following:

- restricting the right to ask questions on genetic traits, as well as preventing doctors and medical institutions that have carried out genetic tests not required by law from furnishing such information to employers;

- excluding genetic screening which would permit a diagnosis of whether an individual might be predisposed to developing a disease, unless expressly allowed by legislation;

- specifying in law that co-determination between workers' representatives and employers is required for genetic diagnosis within the framework of medical examinations provided for by law;

- ensuring that only scientifically approved tests are used;

- requesting professional associations to state in their accident-prevention regulations the methods to be used in such tests and the conclusions which can be drawn; and

- requiring that workers be informed of the nature of such tests and that written consent by the worker and the medical practitioner be obtained.[15]

Against this background the Council of Europe Convention for the Protection of Human Rights and Dignity of the Human Being with Regard to the Application of Biology and Medicine bans all forms of discrimination on the grounds of a person's genetic make-up and only allows for tests to be carried out for medical purposes:

Article 12 – Predictive genetic tests

Tests which are predictive of genetic diseases or which serve either to identify the subject as a carrier of a gene responsible for a disease or to detect a genetic predisposition or susceptibility to a disease may be performed only for health purposes or for scientific research linked to health purposes, and subject to appropriate genetic counselling.[16]

In line with this Convention, several countries have taken the step of outlawing access to genetic tests at work. Australia, Austria, Denmark, France, the Netherlands and Norway have passed laws that either severely limit or forbid the use of a person's genetic information for anything other than medical or scientific purposes. The United Kingdom currently has a moratorium on gene testing at work. In Germany, a controversial Bill is under consideration that would allow limited genetic testing for workers in jobs such as construction or public transport, for symptoms of colour blindness among other things. In 2003 the United States Senate voted with an overwhelming majority to approve legislation that would prohibit companies from using genetic test results to make employment decisions, deny health coverage or raise insurance premiums. Employers could, however, require testing to monitor potential ill-effects from workplace exposure to hazardous substances.[17]

Thus far in this chapter, prevention strategies based on individual characteristics have been detailed. The discussion now turns to the role of on-the-job training provided by employers as part of a comprehensive workplace violence prevention strategy.

Training

Regular and updated training is one essential part of an overall comprehensive violence-prevention strategy. Training may involve any or all of the following:

- instilling interpersonal and communication skills which defuse a potentially threatening situation;

- developing competence in particular functions to be performed;

- improving workers' ability to identify potentially violent situations and people;

- preparing a "core group" of mature and especially competent staff who can take responsibility for more complicated interactions; and

- planning emergency scenarios and the use of procedures and equipment.

Guidelines for specific occupations may also include the development of special skills required to prevent or cope with violence under different circumstances. For counter staff and interviewing officers, for instance, improved interpersonal relations skills are a vital element in reducing aggression. Employees should also have knowledge of the nature of client aggression, the motivations of aggressors, cues to impending aggression, how to conduct interviews properly, adherence to prescribed procedures, and how to respond to emotional clients. Specific advice should be given on when and how contact with a client should be ended to protect the employee from violence.[18]

Special training of employees who have responsibility for public safety is crucial. This is often the case at airports and other public transport facilities.

Inadequate training of employees can contribute to disasters involving members of the public. One such at-risk group of workers is bus drivers, as detailed in box 59.

Box 59   Bus drivers become social actors: Experience from Montpellier, France
          (excerpts)

Recent events have put problems of violence in urban transport high on the public
agenda. Whether they like it or not, drivers are active participants in social questions, and
new ideas and experiments are emphasizing their new-found role.

"If people would recognize the social and human dimension of drivers' work, we would
get better results in terms of preventing conflict on public transport." (Y.B.). This has led
to an experimental project by the Montpellier City Bus Company (SMTU). "Instead of
trying to change society, we've simply tried to teach drivers to become quality social
actors. In Montpellier, that has brought about a spectacular decline in the number of
attacks taking place on our bus network – from 71 to five in three years." L.G., a training
officer with SMTU since 1978, also believes in this approach: "A driver meets about 700
to 1,000 people per day. His or her main job is driving, but there's also a social
component to the work. It can be minimal, but it is always there, and therefore requires
some training; not to make them social workers, but to help them face the day-to-day
problems they encounter."

Source: *L'Observation des Nouveaux Risques Sociaux*, 1998, p. 6.

Thus, training helps workers deal with exposure to aggressive clients.
Training also assists workers to improve their understanding of how to
communicate clearly with their clients and customers about a range of issues.

Information and communication

Circulation of information, open communication and guidance can greatly
reduce the risk of violence at work by defusing tension and frustration among
workers. This need for good communication and information provision
applies to the prevention of all forms of workplace violence, including that
between workers on a site:

> Violence at the two plants of Wainwright Industries in the US "is just
> nonexistent", says David Robbins, the company's vice president and a co-
> owner with his two brothers-in-law. "Knock on wood, it's just never been a
> problem. I attribute that in no small part to our very, very open
> communications. Employees may still get frustrated sometimes", he says,
> "but there is always an avenue to talk it out".[19]

Circulation of information is of particular importance in removing the
taboo of silence which often surrounds cases of sexual harassment, mobbing
and bullying. Information sessions, personnel meetings, office meetings,
group discussions and problem-solving groups can all prove very effective in
this respect (box 60).[20]

Box 60   Information and communication

Among the staff and working units

Circulation of information and open communication can greatly reduce the risk of workplace violence by defusing tension and frustration among workers. They are of particular importance in removing the taboo of silence which often surrounds cases of sexual harassment, mobbing and bullying.

The following should be promoted:

- information sessions;
- personnel meetings;
- office meetings;
- group discussions;
- team working;
- group training.

With the patients and the public

The provision of timely information to patients, and their friends and relatives, is crucial in lessening the risk of assault and verbal abuse. This is particularly the case in situations involving distress and long waiting periods, as often occurs in accident and emergency departments. In particular:

- protocols or codes of conduct, explaining the obligations as well as the rights of patients, relatives and friends, should be compiled, distributed, displayed and applied;
- sanctions in response to violence against personnel should be made known:

For workers at special risk

Information on the risks involved in specific situations and effective communication channels should be provided to workers at special risk, such as community and home-care workers or ambulance staff. This includes:

- providing protocols for informing staff that a colleague is away from base, where he or she has gone, and the approximate or expected time of return. Procedures for reacting to failed protocols should also be in place;
- providing emergency codes so that staff can request help without having to explain the situation and, therefore, without alerting an assailant;
- providing information on the possible risks involved in future contacts and their location;
- maintaining links with the local police to acquire up-to-date information on problem locations or known violent patients;
- providing alarm systems as indicated … under "workplace design".

Source: ILO/ICN/WHO/PSI, 2002, pp. 19–20.

Effective communication can also do much to prevent violence during contact with clients and the public. For example, the provision of information to patients, their friends and relatives is crucial in lessening the risk of assault within hospitals. This is particularly the case in situations involving distress and long waiting periods, as often occurs in accident and emergency departments. Even the usually well-balanced individual may be apprehensive and anxious about unfamiliar surroundings and procedures. In such situations, people are less worried when they have sufficient information to reduce uncertainty. Many staff, having become accustomed to the hospital environment, fail to appreciate how disconcerting it is to patients who are experiencing that environment for the first time, often when in a state of distress or apprehension.[21]

It is also recommended that staff be informed in the most effective means possible to cope with aggression, by providing guidelines and staff development programmes devoted specifically to violence at work. Assistance from supervisors and co-workers should be available if a client or member of the public becomes aggressive or physically violent. Mutual support among staff members is an essential component and should be emphasized.[22]

Thus far, individual and organizational strategies to reduce the risk of workplace violence have been discussed. At a more fundamental level, exposure to the hazard of workplace violence can be reduced through redesign of the physical workplace and its surroundings.

Workplace violence prevention through physical and environment layout

A core component of any comprehensive workplace violence prevention strategy is the designing-out of risk. In the context of reducing possible violence and aggression in the workplace, design issues include the physical structure, layout, fittings, temperature control, access limitations, and risk-specific interventions.

General factors to be considered at the design stage include control of entrances, protective barriers, security screens, ventilation and thermal controls, and noise level. The comfort and size of waiting-rooms is also of importance, including seating (crucial where lengthy waiting periods occur), colour, lighting, and toilet facilities. Other considerations include employment of security guards in higher-risk settings, surveillance cameras and effective alarm systems to alert co-workers when urgent help is needed.[23]

Additional measures will need to be taken in higher-risk situations. For example, in cash-handling businesses it is suggested that the bulk cash-handling areas be situated as far as possible from the entrance and exits.[24] In educational institutions, however, it is suggested that the reception area be located close to the premises' main entrance.[25]

Special protection is needed by **people working alone**, as previous assessments have indicated these workers are generally at increased risk.[26] The risk factors can vary by geographical location, if particular high-risk scenarios are encountered, if members of the public are constantly in contact with workers, and at particular times of the day or night. One such higher-risk occupation is work in transport services, such as bus drivers (box 61).

However, the acceptability and perceived effectiveness of certain measures can differ. While in British studies screens around bus drivers reduced assaults on them, in France enclosing the seat in this way has not always been perceived to be effective, nor has it been received positively by passengers. In Australia, the New South Wales State Transit experimented with partitions at night, but discarded them in favour of emergency buttons and hidden microphones linked to the bus office, which were found to be of greater deterrent value. Radios can also be connected to police sources or street supervisors. However, the potential for radios, silent alarms, flashing lights and cameras to prevent assault depends upon the drivers' ability to reach the particular apparatus, and the speed of the response by police.

Box 61   Protecting bus drivers against attacks

Installing appropriate equipment can help to protect staff and passengers from attack, as well as to improve services and the company's public image.

Here are four examples:

1. Two-way radios. Fitting such radios to vehicles enables staff to communicate rapidly with the control point and from there with the police. Staff find the radios helpful. They give greater confidence and may well act as a deterrent against assaults. Radios can also be used for tracking a vehicle's progress, giving the added benefit of improved service quality and reliability. Where radios are installed, staff must be properly trained to use them.

2. Protective screens for drivers. Some versions are fixed, while others can be closed by the driver.

3. Alarm systems. These have proved to be of value. There are two main types: those fitted to the vehicle, which sound a siren or flash the lights; and pocket-sized, personal alarms which can be carried by the individual staff member.

4. Video cameras, CCTV, etc. Video cameras and closed circuit TV can help identify assailants and vandals. They also act as a deterrent. Dummy cameras can also be fitted. Ensure that the equipment is visible, and fit warning notices to enhance the deterrent effect.

Source: Department of Transport, United Kingdom, 1995, p. 8. Crown copyright, reproduced with the permission of the Department of the Environment, Transport and the Regions.

Other elements of bus design and special procedures have proved effective. For example, exit doors in the centre can reduce assaults which occur when passengers disembark; fare systems where drivers have a minimal amount of money reduce the risk of theft-related assault; fare systems based on zones and pass systems reduce a common source of violence – disputes over fares; having the number of buses geared to the volume of passengers reduces frustration over lengthy waits; and training drivers can help them defuse potentially aggressive interactions.[27] Other features in the design of work processes may also reduce the risks of workplace violence.

Work organization and job design

Work organization and job content are key considerations in the development of preventive strategies against workplace violence. Engineering out the organizational risk factors at the source usually proves much more effective and less costly than increasing the coping capacity through intervention at the individual level: "Unsolved, persistent organizational problems cause powerful and negative mental strain in working groups. The group's stress tolerance diminishes and this can cause a 'scapegoat' mentality and trigger acts of rejection against individual employees". [28]

Employers and supervisors can ensure that staffing levels are appropriate, that tasks are assigned according to experience and competence, and are clearly defined, that working hours are not excessive and that shifts are adequate to the particular situation. These and other job design measures are effective means to reduce tension and avoid aggression between workers in their contact with the public (box 62).

Changing work practices to limit dissatisfaction from clients is also extremely important. The most influential factors for reducing client aggression are speedy and efficient service, which can be stimulated by various strategies such as rotating staff for particularly demanding jobs, rostering more staff at peak periods, designing how staff move between different working areas, tailoring client flow systems to suit needs and resources, and keeping waiting times to a minimum.

Organizational solutions can also be applied to reduce the risks of exposure to criminal attack. Such solutions may include changing the job or system of work to give less face-to-face contact with the public, thus limiting the opportunity for violent and threatening behaviour. The improvement of cash-handling procedures and the introduction of automatic ticket dispensers/collectors and cash machines can also assist. However, it is important that these measures do not exacerbate the risks because staff are less visible.

Box 62   Job design and working time

Job design

Job design is an essential factor in respect of violence at the workplace. An efficient design should ensure that:

- tasks performed are identifiable as whole units of a job rather than fragments;

- jobs make a significant contribution to the total operations of the organization which can be understood by the worker;

- jobs provide an appropriate degree of autonomy;

- jobs are not excessively repetitive and monotonous;

- sufficient feedback on task performance and opportunities for the development of staff skills are provided;

- jobs are enriched with a wider variety of tasks;

- job planning is improved;

- work overload should be avoided;

- pace of work is not excessive;

- access to support workers or team members is facilitated;

- time is available for dialogue, sharing information and problem solving.

Working time

To prevent or diffuse workplace violence, working-time management should avoid excessive work pressure by:

- arranging, as far as possible, working time in consultation with the workers concerned;

- avoiding too long hours of work;

- avoiding a massive recourse to work overtime;

- providing adequate rest periods;

- creating autonomous or semi-autonomous teams dealing with their own working-time arrangements;

- keeping working-time schedules regular and predictable;

- keeping, as far as possible, consecutive night shifts to a minimum.

Source: ILO/ICN/WHO/PSI, 2002, p. 21

In the end, comprehensive violence-prevention strategies always include multiple components (box 63). Comprehensive prevention strategies also involve the full range of employees, including casual and off-site workers.

Try to balance the risks to your employees against any possible side-effects to the public. An atmosphere that suggests employees are worried about violence can sometimes increase its likelihood.

Here are measures that have worked for some organizations:

- Changing the job to less face-to-face contact with the public, for example, introducing automatic ticket dispensers/collectors and cash machines (care should be taken that such measures do not increase the risks of violence to members of the public because there are no visible staff).

- Staff who have to wear a company "uniform", e.g. bank or building society staff, are encouraged not to wear it (or at least to cover it up) when travelling to and from work.

- In one housing department, it was found that protective screens made it difficult for staff and the public to speak to each other (deaf people, for instance, can find screens a real problem). This caused tension on both sides. Management and trade unions agreed a package of measures, including taking screens down, providing more comfortable waiting areas and better information on waiting lists. These measures reduced tension and violent incidents.

- Using cheques, credit cards or tokens instead of cash can make robbery less attractive. For example, some milk delivery staff now operate a token system.

- Checking the credentials of "clients" and, if possible, the place and arrangements for meetings away from the office. This is standard practice now for some estate agents.

- Making sure that staff can get home safely. The threat of violence does not stop when work has ended. The Health and Safety at Work Act requires employers to protect employees only while they are at work, but some employers will take further steps where necessary. For example, if your staff work late, try and arrange for them to be able to drive to work and park their cars in a safe area. Many publicans [pub managers] arrange transport to take their staff home.

- Training your employees, either to give them more knowledge and confidence in their particular jobs, or to enable them to deal with aggression generally, by spotting the early signs and avoiding or coping with it.

- Changing the layout of public waiting areas. Better seating, decor, lighting and more regular information about delays have helped to stop tension building up in some hospital waiting-rooms, housing departments and benefit offices.

- Using wider counters and raising the height of the floor on the staff side of the counter to give staff more protection. Some pubs have done this.

- Installing video cameras or alarm buttons. On buses, cameras have protected staff *and* reduced vandalism and graffiti.

- Putting protection screens around staff areas, as in some banks, social security offices and bus drivers' cabs.

- Using "coded" security locks on doors to keep the public out of staff areas.

Source: Suzy Lamplugh Trust, 1994b, pp. 6–7. © The Suzy Lamplugh Trust, 2005 (see: http://www.suzylamplugh. org/home/index.shtml, accessed 25 Oct. 2005).

Hence, a combination of different measures is usually recommended. Since every working situation is unique, so is the mix of measures that is most appropriate to site-specific risks. It is also important that control of threatened incidents be considered during workplace violence planning processes.

Dealing with violent incidents

While prevention is by far the best way to deal with the threat of violence at work, every effort should be made to tackle the causes of violence rather than its effects. It is also important that workers are prepared and procedures are established to defuse difficult situations and to avoid violent confrontation.

Defusing aggression

Even in the most difficult circumstances, there is often some room for manoeuvre before aggression escalates into an assault. Control of a situation may not be easy, but many guidelines recommend ways to minimize the risk of a violent incident. Personal attitudes and behaviour are extremely important, as shown in box 64.

Box 64   Advice on defusing aggression

Fear is information. It tells you something is threatening you. So if you feel your hair prickling at the back of your neck, stop and assess the situation. It may be a natural reaction to change, or fear of the unknown – or it might be something more. So when you are frightened, ask yourself:

- Is this person's anger/hostility directed at me, the organization, or themselves? Is it a form of distress?

- Am I in danger? If you think you are, leave and get help immediately.

- Am I the best person to deal with the threat? If you find a particular situation difficult, perhaps someone else could handle it more effectively. This is a positive step, not a cop-out [means of escape].

Never underestimate a threat, but do not respond aggressively. This will increase the chance of confrontation:

- Stay calm, speak gently, slowly and clearly.

- Do not be enticed into an argument.

- Do not hide behind your authority, status or jargon.

- Tell the person who you are, ask their name and discuss what you want him, or her, to do.

/cont'd

/cont'd

- Try to defuse the situation by talking things through as reasonable adults, while remembering your first duty is to yourself.

- Avoid an aggressive stance. Crossed arms, hands on hips, a wagging finger or a raised arm will challenge and confront.

- Keep your distance and try to avoid looking down on your aggressor.

- Never put a hand on someone who is angry.

A person on the brink of physical aggression has three choices: to attack, to retreat or to compromise. You need to guide them towards the second or third. Encourage them to move, to walk, to go to see a colleague. Offer a compromise such as talking through the problem. Or divert their aggression into actions like banging on a table or tearing up paper.

If violence is imminent, avoid dangerous locations such as the top of staircases, restricted spaces, or places where there is equipment which could be used as a weapon. Keep your eye on potential escape routes. Keep yourself between the aggressor and the door and, if possible, behind a barrier such as a desk.

Never turn your back, be prepared to move very quickly if necessary, and never remain alone with an actively violent person. To leave, move backwards gradually.

If you manage to calm the situation, re-establish contact cautiously.

Source: Suzy Lamplugh Trust, 1994a, p. 3. ©The Suzy Lamplugh Trust, 2005.

General advice of this nature has been more finely tuned and adapted for occupations at special risk. Box 65 offers recommendations for teachers, for example.

Box 65   Teachers dealing with aggression

- Avoid confrontation in front of an audience, particularly groups of pupils. The fewer people that are involved in an incident, the easier it is for the aggressor to back down without losing face.

- Ask another, preferably senior, member of staff to help talk things through with the visitor.

- Stay calm, speaking slowly, so as not to be drawn into heated argument.

- Avoid aggressive body language such as hand on hips, wagging fingers, looking down on the aggressor.

Source: Health and Safety Commission, United Kingdom, 1990, p. 5. Crown copyright.

Immediate action after violent incidents

Post-incident action is also important. Post-incident processes vary according to the type of workplace violence and the severity of the event.

Depending on the nature and gravity of the violence, police intervention may be required, especially in the case of major incidents. Guidelines often provide special recommendations relating to such incidents, particularly robberies involving violence or threats (box 66).

Box 66   Reporting incidents to the police

Notifying the police

The police must be notified as soon as it is safe to do so, before any other action is taken. The police will require to be told:

- the type of crime – armed robbery, etc.;

- the identity of the caller;

- the exact location of the crime for easy identification, not just the street number;

- whether anyone has been injured;

- description of events;

- the number of offenders, whether any are still present and, if they have left, the direction of escape;

- a brief description of offenders and any vehicles used; and

- whether firearms or other weapons have been seen or used.

If possible, the telephone line with the police should be left open until the police arrive, in order to maintain contact and enable instructions and information to be passed without delay.

Awaiting the police

While waiting for the police to arrive, the following basic measures need to be followed:

- If required, first aid should be rendered to any victims, and confirmation given that professional help is on the way.

- Shut and lock the outside doors, and post a member of staff there to allow urgent access to the emergency services when the police arrive.

- Preserve the scene and the evidence. As far as possible, avoid touching anywhere the robbers may have left fingerprints, footmarks or other evidence.

- Discourage witnesses from leaving before the police have arrived and spoken to them, or take their names and addresses and give them to the police.

/cont'd

/cont'd

- Ensure that those present do not discuss the events prior to being interviewed by the police. Written descriptions of the offender(s), such as height, build, clothing, footwear, speech, mannerisms, name(s) used, jewellery worn, other distinguishing features such as tattoos, description of weapon(s), vehicle(s) used and registration number(s) should be separately recorded by each witness.

On arrival at the scene of the incident

When the police arrive:

- Help them as much as possible.

- They will need to interview all witnesses, including staff as appropriate. They will, however, ensure that private details of staff are not released to defence counsel, the media or through the court process. Police should be asked to ensure that the amount stolen is not released to the media.

- Make an inventory of stolen money or property, and give it to the police as soon as possible.

- Discuss and agree arrangements for liaison with the media.

Staff should be told that in order to preserve the scene, the police may ask to conduct all interviews at a police station or in a place away from the premises that have been robbed.

Source: With the permission of the Department of Labour, Occupational Safety and Health Service, New Zealand, 1995, p. 15.

While police will normally lay charges against an aggressor where an offence is evident, this does not always happen. In situations like this, a victim may wish to institute personal proceedings against the aggressor. In those cases where criminal proceedings are instituted, staff will need particular care and support. Many will not have any experience of the criminal justice system, and will be worried about dealing with the police and giving evidence. It is recommended that help and advice be provided at the initial response stage, and that this support be continued throughout the police investigation and court hearing processes. Issues to consider will include additional support for staff called as witnesses or involved in identification parades as such tasks can often reawaken bad memories of the incident itself.

Post-incident management

The first error many organizations make is failing to plan and prepare for traumatic incident management. Another common error is a failure to take appropriate post-event action because staff problems are not overtly evident or observable.

Planning

Numerous sources emphasize the need for preparation of plans for handling situations after a violent incident. A plan which details the organization's incident response – and how these events are to be managed – can help to bring the confusion and uncertainty of such episodes under control quickly. Post-incident planning can consider a variety of levels of response, as indicated in box 67.

Box 67   Post-incident planning

Where incidents cannot be prevented, preparation focuses on lessening their impact – minimizing the duration and severity of any event and increasing the employee's capacity to cope.

The degree and duration of employees' trauma will in part depend upon how well the incident, and staff, are managed at the time and thereafter. A plan which details the organization's incident response – how these events are to be managed – can help to bring the confusion and uncertainty of such episodes under control quickly.

Matters which need to be considered include the following:

- Providing information and support to families of the people involved.

- Providing information to the media. Ill-informed media reports can add to trauma. Who will brief the media and when?

- Management should communicate directly with each person involved in an incident to express the organization's gratitude for the person's efforts. The manager's role is to take an interest, not to counsel. While some managers are hesitant about dealing with people who are emotional, it is better to say something, particularly to those who are most distressed, rather than to ignore these employees.

- Necessary investigatory procedures following an incident need to be fully explained to those involved. People otherwise commonly fear being "dumped" by the employer and/or being made a scapegoat.

- Providing direct support such as help with completing necessary forms or transport home.

Policy development

The organization's policy should detail the entitlements and support available to employees who are victims of trauma. A clear policy of support and action may help to alleviate trauma and mitigate grievances.

The policy can outline how support will be provided in terms of providing paid leave, dealing with medical expenses, other losses incurred by the employer for transfer or alteration of duties, specialist trauma counselling services, legal representation, pursuing charges or seeking compensation against offenders.

/cont'd

/cont'd

Policy and procedures should be interpreted into safety, personnel and operations manuals. Regular policy and procedures review is needed, as the type and extent of problems change over time.

Source: Commercial Clearing House (CCH), 2004b, Ch. 65, sections 52–436 to 52-462, pp. 62, 423-62, 444.

Victims of violence can experience a wide range of disturbing reactions such as anxiety, feelings of vulnerability and helplessness, disturbed sleep, difficulty in concentrating, increased fear, irritability, obsessive thoughts and images, feelings of shame, anger, frustration, guilt, changes in beliefs and values, and a desire to retaliate. Experts emphasize the necessity of psychological help for victims of violence, to deal with the distressing and often disabling after-effects of a violent incident, as well as to prevent severe psychological problems from developing later. The quicker the response, the more effective and less costly it will be.

Management support

Management should provide immediate and continuing support to all those affected by workplace stress following violence. In particular, management should:

- deal with the immediate aftermath of violence;

- minimize the impact of workplace violence by facilitating or advising on provision of leave, assisting with costs and addressing legal issues;

- provide information and support to the families of those affected;

- initiate a timely internal investigation;

- follow up the case for as long as is deemed necessary.

Medical and psychological treatment

Appropriate medical and psychological treatment should be made available to all workers (including those working unsocial hours), and its existence should be made known to all those affected by workplace violence. In the case of enterprises that have access to medical services, the employer should refer those who appear to have violence- or stress-related problems to the support services, as appropriate, if this is within the competence of the professionals engaged. When companies do not have such services or the caseload exceeds the competence of in-house professionals, the employer should refer workers to appropriate treatment outside the enterprise.

Debriefing

The term "debriefing" refers to post-incident services which may involve one-to-one or group meetings and discussions. These may be run by professional staff and involve all or some of the people concerned in the incident. The aim is to give the victims of violence an opportunity to vent their feelings and to share the traumatic experience with others, as illustrated in box 68.

Box 68   Chain of care and support policy – "Time to talk"

British Rail safety directive

What is the purpose of the safety directive?

To ensure that every member of staff who has been involved in a distressing incident is looked after properly. After such an incident, it will be normal procedure for staff to be offered the services of a trained debriefer to talk about what has happened.

Who is the debriefer?

A member of staff who has been trained to support people after a distressing incident. Anything you say to a debriefer is confidential. Debriefers do not pass reports to management unless you want further help. In this case, the manager will make the necessary arrangements with the Occupational Health Service.

What is a distressing incident?

It is difficult to give a complete list – some people are distressed by events which leave others unaffected – but it would include accidents, suicides, near misses, vandalism, robbery, assault. Staff affected may have been directly or indirectly involved.

Why do we need a safety directive?

Railway workers have very high demands placed upon them. Incidents that can be everyday occurrences on the railway bring sights and experiences which most people would not encounter in a lifetime. A distressed reaction can be normal, and managers must make sure staff are supported, so that they can continue to work safely and effectively.

What good is talking?

Going over a distressing incident can help to put it in perspective. After a trespasser fatality, for example, many people ask themselves – is there anything I could have done? Why did it happen to me? Will it happen again? They may start to think about death and dying. A debriefer will understand that these feelings can be quite normal and, for most people, such feelings will lessen over time.

Isn't it better just to forget it?

If a member of staff has been upset by a distressing incident, they cannot just forget it. Everyone reacts differently. There is evidence that bringing a problem out "into the open" straight away can help prevent problems later on.

/cont'd

The widely used critical incident stress management debriefing (CISD) process includes seven phases, as shown in figure 24. A CISD process involves a general introduction, followed by establishing the facts of an event; discussion of how the violent event progressed and impacted on the worker; his or her feelings about the event; the worker's reactions; strategies adopted to deal with the impact; and evaluation of the mechanisms whereby the workers are best able to re-enter the workplaces and continue to do their jobs.

Depending on the gravity of the violence, it is recommended that the managers responsible for the area or people affected by it, as well as those with special information or relevant expertise on violence, be present. External consultants may also be involved in debriefing activities.

Although CISD may help victims of violence, concern has been expressed that an unreasonable expectation of its usefulness may be developing among field practitioners.[29] Nevertheless, there remain many critics and universal support for critical incident debriefing remains elusive. Similar reservations are associated with the use of post-incident counselling.

Counselling

It is also recommended generally that trauma-crisis counselling be incorporated as an option into post-incident responses. Counselling should be made available by the employer to all those affected by workplace violence, as required, in consultation with workers' representatives. Appropriate and promptly rendered post-incident counselling may reduce acute psychological trauma and general stress levels among victims and witnesses. In addition, such counselling educates staff about workplace violence and positively influences workplace and organizational cultural norms, thus reducing trauma associated with future incidents. Post-incident counselling can include:

- counselling when workplace violence or stress is manifest, to help employees to cope with these problems;

- helping individuals recognize aggressive impulses in their present behaviour or reactions, and how to change their conduct and attitude; and/or

- peer counselling provided by co-workers, where appropriate.

Figure 24   Seven phases of critical incident stress debriefing

Introduction
Set scene: introduce facilitators, group, purpose and ground rules

Fact phase
Each participant, in turn, tells role, participation in event, what happened as they saw it and factual information (not too much detail)

Thought phase
Each participant, in turn, tells their first thought about the incident

Feeling phase
Each participant tells what feelings were generated by the event; this may take time and is not likely to be in turn

Reaction phase
Each participant shares what reactions they have experienced since the event; immediate, within the first day or two, and now

Strategy phase
Education of the group in normal critical stress reactions, sharing their strategies for dealing with reactions and demonstrating how experience can help in the future

Re-entry phase
Summary of the event, reasons and strategies; opportunity for participants to clear up any misunderstandings and confirm understandings

Source: Mitchell, 1983, pp. 36-39, and Mitchell and Everly Jr, 2001, cited in McNally, 2004.

Certified employee assistance professionals, psychologists, psychiatrists, clinical nurse specialists or social workers could provide this counselling, or the employer can refer staff victims to an outside specialist. In addition, an employee counselling service, peer counselling or support groups may be established. In any case, counsellors must be well trained, as well as having a good understanding of the issues and consequences of assaults and other aggressive, violent or bullying behaviours.

Some victims, especially in the case of major violent incidents, may need **long-term support**. Depending on the specific situation, such support will include extended professional counselling to help such victims come to terms with the long-term effects of the incidents and enable them to return to work.

While maintenance of confidentiality is essential for all forms of counselling, it is most important that the organization collate records about the type, pattern and incidence of all forms of workplace violence. Good record keeping is very important because preventive strategies can be targeted to higher-risk sites and scenarios.

Recording and reporting

The importance of recording and reporting workplace violence is emphasized by all experts (box 69). It is recommended that recording and reporting extends to **all i**ncidents, including both minor and potential incidents where no actual **physical** harm has resulted. Apparently trivial events should not

---

Box 69   Recording and reporting incidents

Using reporting systems to assist hazard identification

It is important for organizations to match their reporting requirements to the features and culture of the workplace.

For example, employees working with clients with some psychological conditions may be regularly exposed to physical and verbal abuse. However, if this behaviour is consistent with the assessed conditions of the clients, employees may regard it as being "part of the job" and not report such behaviour until it becomes extreme. In these circumstances, employers should consult with health and safety representatives and employees about using established reporting systems to identify all occupational violence hazards.

As an example, incidents could be recorded on relevant patient case management forms. Employee concerns and the effectiveness of current prevention measures should be regularly monitored.

For high-frequency situations, variations to traditional reporting systems can include:

- incident sampling [i.e. taking a detailed sample of incidents at regular intervals];

- regular review of existing patient/client treatment documentation.

Why hazard and incident reporting is important

The reporting of conditions likely to give rise to occupational violence, or actual incidents, has a number of benefits for employers.

Employers are able to:

- identify accurately the nature and extent of occupational violence;

- act quickly on issues being reported to "nip them in the bud";

- assess whether measures are making a difference;

- ensure employees involved in an incident receive prompt assistance through employee assistance or debriefing programs.

Source: Victorian WorkCover Authority, 2003, pp. 20–21. The Victorian WorkCover Authority website (www.workcover.vic.gov.au) should be consulted for more information and future updates on the references used.

---

be neglected, since they may become relevant later, assisting in detecting persistent patterns of behaviour or identifying an escalation in aggression.

Employers, in particular, are encouraged to devise a system that allows all workers to readily record and report violent incidents. Some incidents may be wrongly considered to be not worthwhile recording:

> Employers may be reluctant to record workplace homicides, and some non-fatal assaults, because they often represent criminal law violations. However, the employer's recording of an injury or illness does not necessarily imply that the employer or employee was at fault, or that the injury or illness is compensable under workers' compensation or other systems, or that a violation of a Title 8 Safety Order or, more important, a Penal Code section, has occurred.[30]

It is also recommended that all employees should know how and where to report violent acts or threats of violence, without fear of reprisal or criticism. Employees should also be encouraged to report on conditions where they are subjected to excessive or unnecessary risk of violence; and to make suggestions for reducing the risk of violence or improving negative working conditions.

In addition to collation of records about workplace violence events, employers have a range of other data sources. These include insurance claims, prosecutions under OSH Acts, and common-law actions. If workers, supervisors or managers have legal cases pending following a workplace violence event, it may be necessary to provide access to legal support services.

Legal assistance

Post-incident support may also include legal assistance to facilitate the often complex and lengthy compensation procedures. Workers' organizations, professional organizations and, where appropriate, colleagues should be involved in providing representation and legal aid. This support may include:

* assistance and support with police procedures;

* consultation with sources of legal advice in relation to options available in specific cases;

* attending meetings, investigations and hearings;

* access for union and shop stewards to training on legal issues relating to workplace violence;

* representation for union members from an ethnic or other minority community group by a steward from a similar background, if that is requested.

Thus, comprehensive support following a violent event may involve a range of functional areas of the organization. If a severe injury or disability resulted from the workplace violent event, rehabilitation services may be involved for a greater or lesser period of time until the worker regains his or her functional abilities or reaches optimal recovery point.

Rehabilitation

Long-term rehabilitation and help in relocation of employment may also be required. Rehabilitation should be made available, and its existence made known to all those affected by workplace violence and its stress consequences. The employer, in collaboration with workers' representatives, should provide support to workers during the entire period of rehabilitation and allow all necessary time to recover. Whenever possible and convenient, workers should be encouraged to return to work, avoiding high task demands with too much stress at first. Special working arrangements may need to be made initially to facilitate reintegration. Finally, as the sources of threat change over time, the post-incident support plan and strategies must be adjusted.

Monitoring and evaluation

Finally, there is a need to regularly review and check the effectiveness of anti-violence measures after they have been introduced. This review and monitoring process is essential and will be strongly emphasized in any comprehensive policy and strategy. Components can include the following:

- Monitoring the results of changes that have been introduced, using a system where employees can provide regular feedback, to check how well they are working and to make more modifications as necessary.

- Careful monitoring of the situation not only allows the effects of each change to be assessed, but it also ensures that any remaining problems or changes in the nature of the problem can be identified.

- It may be appropriate to hold joint management–employee meetings to discuss the measures put in place.

- If the measures work well, keep them up. If violence is still a problem, try something else. Go back through steps two and three and identify other preventive measures that could work.

- Review the management plan on a regular basis.[31]

Guidelines generally provide special recommendations for monitoring and evaluation in specific industry sectors, such as banking. In principle, the higher the risk of violence at work, the more stringent the preventive measures to be adopted, and the more frequent and intense the monitoring and

Box 70   Modelling and evaluation of anti-violence measures

While acknowledging that some groups of employees (such as women, young workers and those in precarious employment) are, on the whole, more vulnerable to violence than their counterparts, the report distances itself from simplistic explanations of violence, which tend to focus on personality characteristics and profiles of offenders as well as of victims. By contrast, it is argued that only a holistic model, integrating individual, situational, organizational and societal or socio-economic factors, can reflect the complexity of the phenomena under investigation. Such a model must also capture the dynamics of the processes involved, where action and reaction are often tightly interwoven and where outcomes may not always be fully predicted. Still, it is unlikely that a single model or framework will fully account for all types of violence, physical and physiological. Thus, in order to fully explain harassment on the grounds of gender, race and sexuality, one may have to draw on more ideologically anchored theories and models.

High levels of physical violence appear to be closely associated with particular situational factors, many of which are associated with the type of work undertaken, and thus cannot be easily removed. In contrast, many of the organizational factors identified as antecedents of violence and harassment may be under the control of the organization and thus susceptible to influence and change ... must take up the challenge to make a concerted effort to intervene.

Source: Di Martino, Hoel and Cooper, 2003, p. 87.

evaluation of such measures. A "plan-›do-›check" cycle should therefore be activated whereby evaluation is the final stage of a cycle of anti-violence measures (box 70).

Having considered the various stages in the control cycle of workplace violence, the discussions now turn to consider some specific examples of programmes which have applied this approach in a range of workplace settings.

Notes

[1] See Rogers and Chappell, 2003.

[2] See Isolatus, 2002, pp. 13–15; and Rogers and Chappell, 2003, pp. 15–17.

[3] Rogers and Chappell, 2003, pp. 15–17.

[4] CAL/OSHA, 1995, pp. 2–3. See also idem, 1998. Quotations given below are reproduced with permission from the Department of Industrial Relations, Division of Occupational Safety and Health, State of California.

[5] See also Commercial Clearing House (CCH), 2004b, Ch. 65, sections 52-000 to 52-090, pp. 61, 501–61, 622.

[6] Swedish National Board of Occupational Safety and Health, AFS 1993:2, 14 Jan. 1993, p. 9.

[7] Cited in Bush and O'Shea, 1996, p. 295.

[8] Ibid.

[9] Health and Safety Executive (HSE), 1991, p. 4.

[10] ILO, 1993b, pp. 81–82.

[11] Ibid., 1987, p. 5.

[12] Ibid.

[13] ILO, 1993b, p. 62.

[14] Ibid.

[15] Ibid., p. 63.

[16] Council of Europe: Convention on Human Rights and Biomedicine, Oviedo, Spain, 4 April 1997.

[17] ETUC, 2004. See also ibid., 2003.

[18] Swanton and Webber, 1990, p. 41.

[19] Nation's Business, Feb. 1995, p. 22.

[20] Beermann and Meschkutat, 1995, pp. 31 and 38.

[21] Health Services Advisory Committee, 1997, p. 8.

[22] Swanton and Webber, 1990, p. 35.

[23] Ibid., pp. 11–38. See also Mayhew and Chappell, 2001.

[24] Department of Labour, Government of New Zealand, 1995, p. 9.

[25] Health and Safety Commission, United Kingdom, 1990, p. 4.

[26] Health and Safety Executive, United Kingdom, 2003.

[27] Easteal and Wilson, 1991, p. 39.

[28] Swedish National Board of Occupational Safety and Health, AFS 1993, 21 Sep. 1993, p. 5.

[29] Hiley-Young and Gerrity, 1994.

[30] CAL/OSHA, 1998, p. 15.

[31] Department of Labour, Occupational Safety and Health Service, New Zealand, 1995, p. 15.

BEST PRACTICES

7

With a growing awareness of the need to tackle the issue of workplace violence, many initiatives have been launched that assist with prevention, both in the public and private sectors. The initiatives described in this chapter have been drawn from a number of countries, and from a variety of enterprises and organizations. Collectively, they represent examples of what can be achieved with imagination and effort to prevent or diminish the damaging and costly impact of workplace violence. Individually, they indicate how important it is to identify and design programmes which reflect the particular needs and nuances of a specific workplace. While there is no model template for preventing and responding to workplace violence, much can be learned by examining these examples of "best practice" in the field.

Prevention frameworks in organizations and multinational enterprises

Preliminary to any specific interventions made to tackle workplace violence, best practice suggests that the stage must be set for specific interventions within particular given settings. Employers and workers must demonstrate, through declarations of intent and policy, their commitment to the values and principles which underpin a safe, secure and violence-free workplace. The following declarations and related action programmes are drawn from a multinational enterprise; a state-based health service; a university campus; a local government authority; a trade union; a national government; a private airport corporation; and a public transport company.

A multinational enterprise

Toshiba is a multinational enterprise with detailed performance expectations specified for a range of behavioural standards to be maintained by all members of the workforce. The Toshiba Group Standard of Conduct states:

> Directors and Employees shall:

> accept and accommodate different values, and respect the character and personality of each individual, observe the right to privacy and human rights of each individual, avoid any discriminatory actions based on race, religion, sex, national origin, physical disability or age and avoid physical abuse, sexual harassment or violation of the human rights of others.[1]

A public health authority

In one state of Australia, a public health service established a task force to examine the range of policy options, assess the incidence of different forms of violence, identify the risk factors and develop interventions. One of the many outcomes from this task force was the publication of detailed policy documents,[2] including *Zero Tolerance: Response to Violence*. Some pertinent extracts from the online policy framework are provided in box 71.

Box 71   NSW Health response to violence

NSW [New South Wales] Health staff have the right to work in a violence free workplace. Patients and others have the right to visit, or receive health care, in a therapeutic environment free from risks to their personal safety.

All Health Services must have in place a violence prevention program that focuses on the elimination of violent behaviour. Where the risks cannot be eliminated, they must be reduced to the lowest possible level using control strategies developed in consultation with employees.

In addition, NSW Health, as a result of a key recommendation from the NSW Health Taskforce on the Prevention and Management of Violence in the Health Workplace, has adopted a zero tolerance response to all forms of violence by any person towards any other person on health service premises, or towards any NSW Health staff working in the community.

The zero tolerance response means that in all violent incidents, appropriate action will be taken to protect staff, patients and visitors from the effects of such behaviour.

Health Services must ensure that managers and staff are appropriately trained and equipped to enable them to respond promptly, consistently and appropriately to effectively manage violent incidents if they do occur, and as far as possible, to prevent their recurrence.

Managers must know and exercise their responsibilities in relation to preventing and managing violence, and encourage and support appropriate staff responses consistent with this document when they are confronted with violence.

Staff must comply with local violence prevention policies and strategies, report all violent incidents, know their options when confronted with violence, exercise them consistently and know that they will be appropriately supported in doing so.

Health Services will work towards establishing and maintaining a culture of zero tolerance to violence, as well as work systems and environments that enable, facilitate and support the zero tolerance response.

This document provides advice on violence risk management and the zero tolerance response, and its implementation should be given priority.

...

Creating a zero tolerance culture

In order for the zero tolerance response to be successful, every Chief Executive Officer (CEO), manager and staff member needs to recognize and acknowledge that violence is unacceptable and that NSW Health is committed to addressing this issue.

However, the message cannot be delivered in isolation, and the operational success of the zero tolerance response is based on the principles that staff:

* know how to report a violent incident and are encouraged and supported in doing so;

* have access to training, work environments, equipment and procedures to enable them to respond confidently in violent situations;

* know that their response will be supported by management;

* know that management will respond appropriately after an incident.

Management commitment, particularly that of the CEO and senior management, is vital to the success of creating a zero tolerance culture. Without the visible support of the CEO, it is likely that such an approach will meet with only limited success. The CEO and senior managers should therefore take a visible and active interest and role in establishing a zero tolerance culture and, most importantly, leading by example.

Source: NSW Health, 2003, pp. 7–8.

The range of outcomes from this task force established benchmarks for other public health authorities in different states of Australia. Many of these other jurisdictions are now using the NSW Health principles and publications as the basis for similar zero tolerance and other preventive programmes. However, it is not only workers in public health authorities who are facing a rising tide of violence from their clients and customers.

A university

The education sector is also at risk, including workers in secondary schools, technical training colleges and universities. The perpetrators may be students,

Box 72   Workplace violence risk reduction in a university

Sonoma State University is committed to creating and maintaining a campus environment for all members of the university community that is free from violence.

Civility, understanding, and mutual respect toward all members of the university community are intrinsic to excellence in teaching and learning, to safety in the workplace, and to maintenance of a culture and environment that serves the needs of all campus constituents.

Sonoma State University will not tolerate violence and threats of violence on campus or at campus-sponsored events by members of the university community against other persons or property.

For the purposes of this policy, violence and threats of violence include, but are not limited to:

- any act that is physically assaultive; or

- any threat, behaviour or action which is interpreted by a reasonable person to carry the potential:

- to harm or endanger the safety of others;

- to result in an act of aggression; or

- to destroy or damage property.

Any member of the university community who commits a violent act or threatens to commit a violent act toward other persons or property on campus or at campus sponsored events shall be subject to disciplinary action, according to established procedures, up to and including dismissal from employment or expulsion from the university, exclusive of any civil and/or criminal penalties that may be pursued, as appropriate.

It is the responsibility of every administrator, faculty member, staff member, and student to take any threat or violent act seriously, and to report acts of violence or threats of violence to the appropriate authorities.

Source: Sonoma State University, 1998.

co-workers or members of the public who come onto the site and engage in workplace violence or deliberately damage property. Box 72 contains a statement committing a university to a violence-free campus.

The perpetrators of these acts of violence are frequently the students – or clients – receiving an education. However, the perpetrators are sometimes employees who are acting out aggression against other workers within the same organization, or employees who are aggressive to clients or customers.

A local government authority

Local government authorities in a number of geographical areas are now detailing the standards of behaviour expected from all staff members. In addition to managers, supervisors and workers, the behavioural standards can be applied to all contractors and providers of services. A zero tolerance policy in a local government authority is shown in box 73.

Box 73   A zero tolerance policy of a local government authority

The City of El Centro [California] has adopted this zero tolerance policy for workplace violence because it recognizes that workplace violence is a growing problem nationally that needs to be addressed by all employers. Consistent with this policy, acts or threats of physical violence, including intimidation, harassment, and/or coercion which involve or affect the City of El Centro or which occur on City property, will not be tolerated.

Application of prohibition

The City of El Centro's prohibition against threats and acts of violence applies to all persons involved in the City's operation, including but not limited to City personnel, contract and temporary workers, and anyone else on City of El Centro property. Violations of this policy by any individual on City property, or by an individual acting off of City property when his/her actions affect the public interest of the City's business interests, will be followed by legal action, as appropriate. Violation by an employee of any provision of the policy may lead to disciplinary action (up to and including termination, as provided in the City Personnel Rules and Regulations or Memoranda of Understanding). This policy and any sanctions related thereto are to be deemed supplemental to the City's Personnel Rules and Regulations, and Memoranda of Understanding provisions related thereto, and applicable state and federal laws.

Employee obligations

Each employee of the City and every person on City of El Centro property is encouraged to report incidents of threats or acts of physical violence of which he/she is aware.

In cases where the reporting individual is not a City employee, the report should be made to the City of El Centro Police Department.

In cases where the reporting individual is a City employee, the report should be made to the reporting individual's immediate supervisor, a management-level supervisory employee if the immediate supervisor is not available, or to the City's Personnel Division. Each supervising employee shall promptly refer any such incident to the appropriate management-level supervisor, who shall take corrective action in accordance with the City's Personnel Rules and Regulations and any applicable Memoranda of Understanding. Concurrently with the initiation of any investigation leading to a proposed disciplinary action, the management level supervisor shall report the incidents of threats or acts of physical violence to the El Centro Police Department, which shall make a follow-up report to the City's Personnel Division.

/cont'd

/cont'd

Nothing in this policy alters any other reporting obligations established in City policies or in state, federal or other applicable law.

Training

The City will provide opportunities for employees to be trained in the risk factors associated with workplace violence, and proper handling of emergency situations in order to minimize the risks of violent incidents occurring in the workplace.

Dissemination of policy

All employees will be given copies of this policy. All new employees will be given a copy of this part of this policy as part of their orientation by the Personnel Division.

Source: El Centro, letter from Douglas G. Detling, 8 May 1996.

The risk of workplace violence in the City of El Centro has also been evaluated since the Zero Tolerance Policy was introduced. It is clear that while **enforcement** of the principle is occurring, supportive training does not always occur. Hence, as with most workplace violence policies and strategies, regular review and evaluation results in fine-tuning:

> The Zero Tolerance Policy for workplace violence is still in effect for the City of El Centro. Between 1996 and to-date, I am aware of three incidents that were related to workplace violence between employees. Disciplinary action, up to termination [was carried out] on two of the three cases with one being overturned. Also, two of these cases were within the last year. Due to the two recent cases and that our Personnel Division has not conducted training in this area for many years, our Safety Committee is recommending mandatory training for all employees to comply with the regulations and to eliminate all workplace violence.[3]

A trade union

In 1998, the Spanish Trade Union Confederation of Workers' Commissions (Confederación Sindical de Comisiones Obreras or CC.OO) initiated a research project on sexual harassment at work, funded by the Daphne Programme, an EU initiative to combat violence towards women, young people and children. This project aimed to gain a better understanding of dimensions, patterns and risk factors for workplace violence.

The project – called the Pandora Project – was coordinated by the women's secretariat of CC.OO in cooperation with the Spanish Woman's Institute (Instituto de la Mujer), and partner trade unions in Sweden and Ireland. The project recognized the importance of basing its findings on women's everyday experiences and problems. A survey was conceptualized and carried out in parallel in three countries: Spain, Sweden and Ireland. Several focus group discussions were organized to examine women's and men's perceptions of their work, their relationship with co-workers and their experiences of sexual harassment. The participants represented a cross-sectional sample of employees in different hierarchical positions and professional groups, with different functions.

The survey results for Spain showed that 18.4 per cent of female workers had experienced sexual harassment, compared with 8.8 per cent of male workers.[4] Official figures probably did not represent the real size of the problem since many women did not report incidents and/or chose avoidance or escape mechanisms to deal with sexual harassment. Blaming the victim was found to be a usual consequence of complaints. "The project found harassment to be linked to the sort of tasks women perform, and to coincide with discrimination and lack of appreciation."[5]

The project concluded that sexual harassment is deeply rooted in workplace culture, including behaviour codes and promotion systems, and that legislation alone would not solve the problem. Two approaches were recommended as preventive measures:

- enhanced efforts in the promotion of equal rights for women and men and the redistribution of working hours;

- increased awareness among female staff at all levels, through information campaigns, meetings and discussions.

The project report also urged that:

- both trade unions and companies should do more to prevent harassment, by promoting collective bargaining, and adopting internal procedures for reporting incidents;

- building support structures for women workers among colleagues and union representatives should be the first priority;

- work inspectors need training in how to handle problems relating to gender, especially those who deal with small businesses;

- labour law (rather than penal law) should only be used as a last resort.[6]

Since awareness raising and information were found to be priority needs, the Pandora Project initiated a press conference and a publicity campaign. In the follow-up, a guide to sexual harassment was published for use by management, workers and trade unions. Furthermore, a Europe-wide network was established to combat sexual harassment, with inevitable links with national governments.

National government level

Violence and stress at work are, arguably, major threats to society and to enterprises in Malaysia. Government bodies, trade unions, employers' organizations, non-governmental organizations and the media are reporting increasing numbers of people affected through stress and violence-related situations at work. According to a study on cases of violence at the workplace compiled by the Royal Malaysian Police between 1997 and May 2001, there were 11,851 rape and molestation cases at the workplace (6,082 rape cases and 5,769 molestation events) during this period. Previously these issues were looked at only from the criminal viewpoint. However, increasing attention by the media and the lessons learned from the experiences of other countries have made this a priority occupational safety and health problem.

The Government of Malaysia, through the Department of Occupational Safety and Health (DOSH), has taken steps to address these risks. In particular, the issues of stress and violence at work were one of the areas given priority under the joint collaborative project named "Occupational Safety and Health Institutional Capacity Building" and involving DOSH and the United Nations Development Programme (UNDP).

One of the components of the project was to increase the knowledge of DOSH officers about stress and violence at work. Under the aegis of this component, a senior officer from Malaysia was sent to attend a fellowship programme in Europe, and a senior officer from ILO Headquarters in Geneva was attached to DOSH as a consultant for one month in October 2001. One of the outcomes from this project was a document entitled *Guidance for the prevention of stress and violence at the workplace*.[7]

Di Martino and Musri also prepared a training manual on the prevention of stress and violence at the workplace.[8] A pilot course based on this training manual was conducted at DOSH in October 2001. As part of a collaborative project involving DOSH, NIOSH, the Science University of Malaysia and the ILO, two workshops focused on the management of emerging risks at work, using a methodology called "SOLVE" (stress, violence, tobacco, alcohol, drugs, HIV/AIDS – see Chapter 8, pp. 271–272 for more information on SOLVE). These workshops aimed to provide the participants with the knowledge and skills necessary to enable them to integrate the above issues into a comprehensive corporate policy, and to follow this up with a programme of action to alleviate the problems.

With globalization and increasing industrialization, it is envisaged that the incidence of workplace violence in Malaysia will increase in the future. To mitigate the impact on businesses, a policy framework for the integration of stress and violence at work into the DOSH work programme has been developed and is under consideration for further action in this area.

A private airport corporation

The Frankfurt Airport company in Frankfurt/Main in Germany developed the FRAPORT AG agreement, which took effect in January 2001.[9] This agreement is based on a corporate culture characterized by partnership-based conduct at work, and aims to combat a climate of hate and violence at work, prevent discrimination, and promote equal opportunity for all employees. The principle of non-discrimination applies to all employees; covers all forms of discrimination on the grounds of colour, nationality, ethnicity, religion, age and gender; and includes careless and intentional degradation, humiliation, harassment and assault. Management and works councils together are responsible for the implementation of the policy and the related programmes, with the written policy communicated to all staff.

Under the FRAPORT AG agreement, victims have the right to file a complaint. Several contact people and offices are responsible, including superiors, works councils, youth representatives, women's advancement coordinator or the personnel referent. The role of these people is to advise and support those involved, to investigate and record the incident, to inform bodies and recommend measures. They are required to take responsibility immediately, or within one week after the incident is known. Further, submission of a complaint must not lead to disadvantages for the victim and confidentiality has to be ensured.

Measures taken in the event of discrimination or other unwanted conduct include both informal and formal sanctions. Informal sanctions may consist of verbal warnings, cautions or lectures. Formal sanctions apply according to work legislation, or may include reassignment, written warning or dismissal.

Equal opportunity is promoted through training of personnel and organizational measures that take into account the diversity of employees. Examples include language courses for foreign workers and/or courses for their German colleagues to assist with a better understanding of the needs and culture of foreign workers. Training programmes for supervisors and election of moderators are noted.

The FRAPORT AG agreement is one of the rare policy documents where monitoring and evaluation are integrated in the agreement and not subject to a separate procedure. A report on partnership-based conduct is presented to the works council annually, involving the women's advancement coordinator, among others. The employer recommends improvement measures to be taken on the basis of situational analysis in consultation with the works council. The results of the report, recommendations and new measures are then communicated to the staff through assemblies or internal publication media.

Such comprehensive policy documents are becoming commonplace in a number of larger organizations in several countries. Both private enterprise and public sector organizations are increasingly looking towards "best practice" examples to emulate.

A public transport organization

There have been a series of reports about workplace violence directed to employees of public transport authorities.[10] While the risks are not homogeneous across all forms of public transport, they appear to exist in most if not all countries, including in Europe:

> In an effort to reduce the continuous increase in vandalism and aggression in the Brussels public transport system, the operator has decided to introduce a series of preventive measures, including:
>
> – immediate reinforcement of the surveillance services (general surveillance, dog brigade) as well as the introduction [of] groups of two or three agents on each vehicle;
>
> – the introduction of an aggression management programme including prevention, employee training and care and support for victims;
>
> – installation of video cameras and silent alarms;
>
> – sale of tickets outside the vehicles or on board with credit cards;
>
> – selective preventive action; and
>
> – improved collaboration with police agencies.[11]

That is, "best practice" workplace violence prevention in the public transport sector is multifactorial and fine-tuned to the specific risk factors identified in particular modes of transport. The interventions need also to vary according to site-specific risks, for example, additional measures may need to be implemented at higher-risk times, such as on Friday or Saturday nights.

Guidelines to prevent harassment and bullying

Policies need to be underpinned by collective agreement and internal work culture support to ensure a fair and informed approach, and to cover difficulties in reporting and investigation of complaints. There are a number of essential steps which have been identified by the European Agency for Safety and Health and Work.

The formulation of a policy with clear guidelines for positive social interactions includes:

- ethical commitment from employer and employees to foster an environment free from bullying;

- outlining which kinds of actions are acceptable and which are not;

- stating the consequences of breaking the organizational standards and values, and the sanctions involved;

- indicating where and how victims can get help;

- commitment to ensure "reprisal-free" complaining;

- explaining procedure for making a complaint;

- clarifying the role of manager, supervisor, contact/support colleague, trade union representatives;

- details of counselling and support services available for victim and perpetrator; and

- maintaining confidentiality.[12]

It is important to set out procedures and actions to be taken with regard to complex issues such as harassment and bullying in a clear and comprehensive policy that is developed and introduced with the participation of employees and their representatives. However, a policy will not be effective unless it is actively implemented, and its effectiveness monitored and reviewed.

Primary preventive interventions

Many of the examples identified above illustrate good practice policy statements. These policies also need to be implemented effectively in a practical way on the shop floor. Practical preventive measures are focused on reduction or elimination of the risk of workplace violence and may include environmental measures, work procedures and interventions integrating the community.

The working environment

The following prevention strategy example is taken from Amsterdam, the Netherlands.[13] Measures were implemented by the Social Services Department to address the risk of client-initiated violence using the technique of "crime prevention through environmental design" (CPTED). It is known from studies in criminology sciences that a well-designed, pleasant, well-maintained environment is likely to reduce aggression. In contrast, poorly designed features in the physical environment of a workplace may trigger aggression or exacerbate stressful situations.

Preventive measures implemented in the Amsterdam example started with careful location of offices to ensure easy access for the public and through provision of sufficient car parking spaces. The ambience of the interior of the building and offices was created with improved client-friendliness: signs to direct the way, a clear waiting-number system and provision of facilities, such as automatic coffee machine and telephone. The waiting zones also offered special space for children to play, and entertainment for clients, including a television and reading materials. The colours selected also enhanced an atmosphere of calm. For the safety of employees, special attention was given to fixtures, including special office furniture that improved the safety of staff, and incorporated ergonomic principles while maintaining a client-friendly atmosphere.

Two particular office features were incorporated into the Social Services Department in cooperation with a design consultancy: counters and conversation rooms. Counters were designed to be broad enough so that an employee could not be touched by a client and were also high enough so that nobody could jump over them. On the client side of counters, each interviewing space was separated from the neighbouring place through use of noise-absorbing materials. Thus even when two clients stood side by side at the counter, privacy was maintained. If needed, there is the potential to place safety glass between the employee and the client.

In conversation rooms, the desk size is dedicated to safety, being broad and high and sufficiently heavy to preclude throwing. A second exit is installed wherever possible, allowing for the employee to escape without any impediments, if necessary.

Security measures installed include alarms at counters, as well as CCTV (closed-circuit television/video system), and monitors which can be fixed to the counters or walls. Clients are informed of the CCTV monitoring via posters – which may have a deterrent effect. Security personnel may be employed to support staff (temporarily at high-risk times of the year or permanently in high-risk areas), which also has a deterrent effect.

The results of the strategy are generally positive and result in reduced work stress and improved working environment for employees, as well as improved service delivery for clients. A change in working culture has also been implemented through the creation of an open communication atmosphere where violent incidents are discussed, and incorporating a shift away from a victim-blaming culture. One of the crucial success factors has been keeping the policy and strategies visible and dynamic. However, one identified failure is that many superiors still underestimate the seriousness of the problem. Nevertheless, cost–benefit analysis indicates that direct costs for the violence prevention strategy were €275,000 per year, compared with indirect violence-related costs (such as sickness leave) estimated at €900,000 per year.

Appropriate strategies for the prevention of aggression between members of the same workforce in one worksite are quite different. One particular problem that may arise is aggression based on ethnicity or racial differences.

Respect for diversity and prevention of discrimination and harassment

One enterprise introduced a strategy addressing all forms of internal violence and harassment through primary interventions, with emphasis on sexual harassment and discrimination. GIANT is a bicycle manufacturer, which relocated production for the European market from Taiwan, China, to the Netherlands in 1996.[14] Its strategy is an integral part of the overall personnel management policy. Because the staff of GIANT consist of 22 different nationalities, the need for managing their diversity positively became clear.

The emphasis of the policy is prevention of all forms of inappropriate behaviour and promotion of a culture of respect for the diversity of all persons. A zero tolerance statement regarding violence and harassment is clearly communicated to every staff member from the outset. Major efforts are made to maintain a good working atmosphere, with the main preventive instruments being:

- Workshops: Several are organized every year, discussing such subjects as job satisfaction and quality. Workshops are obligatory for every employee, being organized within working time and lasting for a couple of hours each. As a result of the workshops, all rules and regulations concerning conduct and communication at work have been developed with the involvement of all staff members.

- Meetings: These are organized every two weeks, giving staff the opportunity to talk about their feelings and problems in general.

- Communication: Every new worker receives a folder with introductory information, including the code of conduct and zero tolerance statement. Other channels to communicate the message to staff are blackboards and an internal newsletter.

- Leadership: All supervisors are informed of the strategy and trained on management of violence and harassment.

Grievance procedures are also in place. Victims can report to their direct supervisor, an external workers' representative or the internal social worker. The personnel manager has responsibility for all measures to be taken. The procedures include mediation, official investigation, sanctions, and victim support via the internal social worker.

The policy has been developed and implemented through middle managers, who, because they have to deal with a range of discrimination, harassment and other forms of workplace violence during their daily work, are supportive. Workers have been involved in formulating the norms and values described in the policy and strategies described above, and the policy is sustained through ongoing participatory communication, and an annual evaluation discussion in the workshops. Another positive result is a good working atmosphere. The costs of implementing the workshops, meetings and communication strategies are included in the personnel budget. However, these costs are estimated to be fully paid back in terms of overall benefits to the organization.

Policies and strategies that enhance respect for diversity and promote positive behavioural standards can also be implemented in organizations that deal frequently with members of the public. For example, public transport organizations frequently have passengers from a range of socio-economic and ethnic backgrounds, some of whom adopt very aggressive postures when dealing with employees.

Community-based interventions focused on potential perpetrators

The Bremen Tram Company is a public transport organization in a northern German medium-sized city. This company implemented a range of comprehensive strategies to address the problem of "internal" aggression from other employees, as well as "external" violence from patrons, including prevention, intervention and rehabilitation measures. In one unusual initiative the company assisted with developing leisure facilities for the young perpetrators:

> In one area of the town known as a "hot spot" or problematic social environment, conflicts emerged between young people and the staff of the tram company. The lack of leisure facilities for young people in the area led to a situation where one of the company's terminal stations was being used as a meeting point for the bored youth. The situation escalated, with vandalism, threats against clients and assaults towards staff. Police intervention was increasingly necessary, with a major intervention likely if damages and threats did not stop.

At this stage, a voluntary multicultural project team, founded in 1996 by employees to address conflicts with the youth under the slogan "Communication instead of Confrontation", initiated cooperation with all parties concerned to solve the problem. They developed a community-based action at the terminal station, involving young people and other citizens of the area, as well as community services such as the Social Services and police. Together, they built a meeting point for the youth, with a shelter from the weather, organized get-togethers, meetings and discussions.

The outcome of this initiative has been very positive, with the main effects observed being the parties getting to know each other and thus creating a better mutual understanding of the day-to-day problems of all those involved and a willingness to look for solutions in cases of conflict.

Results for the company include:

- improvement of the working environment at the terminal station, with staff feeling safer;

- increased client satisfaction; and

- 30 per cent reduction in damages due to vandalism, accounting for €300,000 per year.[15]

This comprehensive initiative involved close liaison between the organization, both perpetrators and "victims" of the aggression, as well as local community members. Other workplace violence preventive strategies have involved partnerships between organizations, the workforce at risk, the local community and the police service.

Community involvement and partnership with police

Emergency departments are known to be at extreme risk of violence and harassment against staff. In one of the NHS Trust's hospitals in the United Kingdom, the levels of abuse were increasing so much that they were becoming part of daily work and the effects on employees, who described themselves as becoming "punch drunk", were significant.[16] Only the most serious incidents were reported.

Initial measures included the introduction of security cameras and protection screens for staff. However, this did not show sufficient results in reducing violent incidents, and the physical and verbal abuse continued. Subsequently, a partnership with the local police was initiated.

In the beginning, a police presence in the emergency department was agreed for Friday and Saturday nights, as well as for all nights over the

Christmas and New Year periods. These times had been identified as those when staff were particularly at risk. The police presence was very successful not only in reducing the incidents of violence and harassment, but also in improving staff morale.

Encouraged by these positive effects, a next step was to relocate a police base in the hospital area itself, right beside the emergency department. Accommodation and car parking facilities are provided by the hospital, while the police cover all other expenses. This intervention has resulted in great mutual benefit, achieved at low cost. Police are present now between 8.00 a.m and 2.00 a.m every day, which has had a deterrent effect on violence and harassment against staff. In addition, hospital employees feel reassured and greatly appreciate the police presence, leading to improved relationships between hospital and police, and a better understanding of each other's procedures.

Thus far in the chapter, a series of interventions that may prevent or minimize exposure to the hazard of workplace violence have been described. However, no matter how exemplary the development and implementation of workplace violence prevention policies and strategies, some violent events may still occur. Hence one aspect that must always be considered during planning processes is post-event action and support.

Secondary interventions

Secondary intervention measures include planning for appropriate responses in the event of a violent incident and effective reporting procedures. The examples presented below provide guidance for employees on appropriate action in higher-risk situations, and a description of one instrument that may be used for reporting violent incidents.

Workplace violence at a hospital in the Netherlands

In 2001, 300 incidents were recorded at the Westfries Gasthuis hospital in Hoorn, the Netherlands. As a result, feelings of insecurity among the staff were growing.

A "Safe Care" plan was developed, a plan of action presented at a meeting, and a forum discussion held with the project leader, representatives of the police, the Public Prosecutor's Office and the executive board.[17] A working party composed of various members of staff from at-risk departments was formed. A survey showed that most incidents occurred in reception/switchboard, accident and emergency, and psychiatry departments at the weekend, in the evening and at night.

The working party drew up a risk inventory and, using colours, the higher-risk areas were mapped on the hospital floor plans. This risk map with colour coding was used as a basis for discussion about how improvements could be made:

- Red: high risk of aggression and violence area, and the area may contain valuable goods attractive to criminals.

- Yellow: some risk of aggression and violence, and area contains goods which are attractive but not valuable.

- Green: low risk of aggression and no valuables on site.

Each member of staff carries an alarm which can be activated immediately if there is any form of threat. Security staff then arrive on the scene within minutes, assess the seriousness of the situation, and attempt to bring the situation under control. If that is not possible, the police can be called.

Violent events are categorized and recorded under a "card system" which breaks down the types of aggression into three main categories:

- Verbal aggression: swearing, threatening behaviour, non-serious threats, sexual intimidation.

- Serious threats: serious threatening, pestering, following, threatening families, threatening with an object, attempting to injure, attempting to strike or kick a person, discriminatory remarks.

- Physical violence: assault, including sexual assault, smashing furniture, throwing objects, preventing individuals from leaving the room, pushing, pulling, spitting, biting or scratching, striking, kicking or head-butting, inflicting injury.

In **verbal aggression events**, the doctor/nurse attempts to calm the patient/visitor and then records the incident. If this is unsuccessful, assistance is sought by means of an alarm button and the incident is subsequently recorded.

In **serious threat events**, the alarm button is pressed immediately; security staff intervene, record the incident, issue the threatening individual with a "yellow card", and subsequently report the incident to the police.

In **physical violence events**, the alarm button is pressed immediately; security staff intervene; the incident is recorded; the threatening individual is given a "red card"; security staff report the incident to the police; and the perpetrator is brought before the assistant public prosecutor. The assistant public prosecutor then makes a decision on the matter and either a settlement is reached or a summons is issued. Because of an agreement with the Public Prosecutor's Office, the perpetrator may be banned from entering the hospital other than for emergency or psychiatric care, and is handed a letter to that effect.

Figure 25   Caring in safety at work

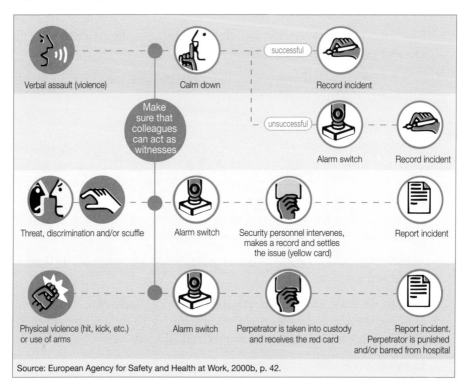

Source: European Agency for Safety and Health at Work, 2000b, p. 42.

Since this "Safe Care" policy and strategies were implemented, physical violence at the Westfries Gasthuis hospital has fallen by 30 per cent and verbal aggression by 27 per cent. Subsequently, after a pilot of several months with this programme, a decision was made to extend the "Safe Care" programme to 24 hospitals. The policy and programme flow-chart is depicted in figure 25.

The case study of workplace violence secondary prevention initiatives implemented at Westfries Gasthuis hospital in the Netherlands clearly operates well in the fixed environment of a hospital or clinic. The risk factors are, however, somewhat different for those health-care workers who perform their job tasks in the community in less well-controlled environments.

Workplace violence incidents in less well-controlled environments

Ambulance officers are at additional risk of workplace violence because they work in less well-controlled environments, may have to wait some time for additional emergency back-up to arrive, and frequently go about their tasks in emotionally charged scenarios, such as following a motor vehicle crash. One component of the British NHS Zero Tolerance campaign has focused on the heightened vulnerability of ambulance personnel to the risk of workplace violence, and specific risk-minimization strategies have been developed, for example:

Vehicle signs – all A&E [Accident and Emergency] and PTS [Patient Transport Service] vehicles carry the following warning notice situated in a clearly visible place, endorsed by the Chief Executive: "Our staff provide a vital service to the public and have the right to go about their duties without fear of attack or abuse. London Ambulance Service will fully support the Crown Prosecution Service and the Police in the prosecution of those who assault its staff."

Technology – the importance of maintaining contact with colleagues, whether a crewmate or Control, cannot be overstated. This is particularly so when operational crews are away from their vehicle. Staff are required to carry and use allocated hand portable radios at all times. The Trust is committed to ongoing review of technology systems and procedures to improve both operational response and staff safety.

Personal protective garments – the Trust recognizes that considerable research is being undertaken by manufacturers … It continues to support the provision and use of protective clothing such as body armour in controlled operations under the guidance of police officers …

Prosecution of assailants and working with the police – managers support staff through any court proceedings ….[18]

One specific example is the Lincolnshire Ambulance and Health Transport Service NHS Trust, which provides A&E and non-emergency patient transport services (PTS) to a largely rural population, spread over approximately 3,400 square miles. This is the largest area covered by a single ambulance service in England. In addition to residents, the Trust provides services for a substantial transient population. With responsibility for three main urban areas and several seaside resorts, the increase in activity, especially during the summer months, is significant. To meet its responsibilities, the Trust currently operates 16 ambulance stations and four operational bases. In addition, there is a headquarters incorporating a central control complex and a separate training centre.

The Trust has detailed procedures and guidelines to implement in the event of an incident occurring. These procedures cover reporting systems, support to staff and the prosecution of assailants.

Reporting of all workplace violence incidents

The reporting of incidents ensures that: all violent events can be investigated; safety measures can be reviewed and modified to improve future protection for staff; there is a secure basis for any legal redress or prosecution following the event; and police are given the opportunity to investigate and apprehend the perpetrators. In the United Kingdom NHS, staff are required to complete both a "violence to staff" report and an "untoward incident" form, which are transferred to a central database. Senior managers are required to note follow-up actions taken and any aftercare such as hospital treatment, staff debriefing or counselling. The NHS has emphasized reporting requirements, for example:

> Establish robust, uncomplicated reporting systems to encourage your staff to record details of all incidents of violence. This means systems that are easy to use and not too time consuming. As a minimum, the following information should be recorded in the event of a violent incident:
>
> • details of the individuals involved;
>
> • the cause of the incident and when/where it happened;
>
> • any injury(ies) suffered by the victim and any resulting absence; and
>
> • the action taken by managers to prevent the incident occurring again.[19]

The Trust also has clear formal procedures for staff and line managers, which specify required key actions and communications together with responsibility. Flow charts list the steps to be taken when reporting a violent incident (the procedures for operational staff to follow are shown in figure 26).

In 2002, for the first time, an annual risk register of "untoward" incidents was compiled for the health and safety committee on one NHS Trust.[20] This committee was responsible for analysing the data, identifying patterns and trends, and developing an appropriate response strategy. For example, the risk register was used to identify highest-risk ambulance stations, allowing targeted risk assessments to be carried out, and for liaison with station managers to improve levels of staff safety in the environment.

When a violent incident does occur, a senior manager debriefs the individual involved, investigates what happened and assesses the need for post-incident support. Outcomes can include informal follow-up by line managers, or detailed specialist assistance from the personnel manager or from occupational health services. Managers involved in post-incident care should routinely offer these services, although they may also be accessed directly by the individual concerned. Following more serious workplace violence events, the duty officer advises a senior member of staff (at director level) about the incident and the aftercare provided for the individual.

Figure 26   Violent incident reporting procedures for operational staff at the
Lincolnshire Ambulance and Health Transport Service NHS Trust

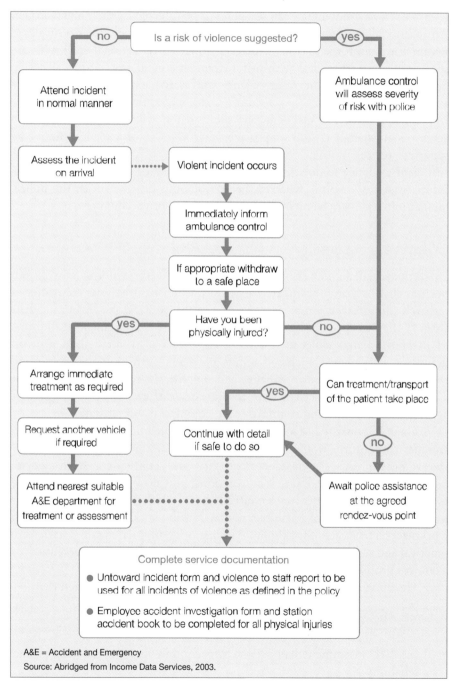

A&E = Accident and Emergency

Source: Abridged from Income Data Services, 2003.

The occupational health and safety department is a "one-stop shop" for all related issues, including confidential stress counselling. Help lines are always open and individuals can self-refer or be referred by their line manager. An additional source of help and support is provided by volunteer counsellors within the workforce – from managers down to operational staff who are specifically trained to deal with major, traumatic incidents but can also help facilitate discussions in cases where staff have experienced violent or aggressive behaviour.

Finally, the NHS makes it very clear that it will not tolerate violence against staff members and emphasizes that all acts of violence should be reported to the police. The police will charge offenders when there is sufficient evidence to do so, but if criminal proceedings are not initiated, the NHS Trust may explore what further actions can be taken with the police. Similar initiatives are being implemented in many other countries.

Objective measurement of violence against staff

In response to an increasing number of violent incidents against health personnel, a research team at Sweden's Karolinska Institute conducted a research and intervention project. As part of this project, the violent incident form (VIF) was developed as a practical tool for the measurement of all forms of patient-initiated violence towards staff.[21] The instrument used a broad definition of violence, included minor incidents such as verbal abuse and threats, and was initiated to enhance and simplify the recording of all violent events. Additional objectives were to increase staff awareness of triggers of aggressive behaviours and to improve the coping skills of all staff.

The VIF consisted of a checklist of 20 items in a multiple-choice format, summarizing information on the incident, including time and place, details of the aggressor, the circumstances, activity and consequences, immediate responses, the victim's injuries or reactions, and details of the victim. The evaluation of the VIF involved a controlled, prospective study over a one-year period whereby the tool was integrated into daily work routines at 47 health workplaces in Greater Stockholm. The majority of participating staff were practical and registered nurses who were allocated to either an intervention or a control group.

The main results of the evaluation of the intervention indicated that:

- the intervention group reported an increased awareness of higher-risk situations for workplace violence; and

- the VIF instrument had satisfactory content in terms of validity and reliability;

- while staff at the intervention sites reported 50 per cent more violence than the control group, this may have resulted from an enhanced capacity for registration and recording of violent events.[22]

However, the study was not able to identify whether increased awareness and better violence management skills would result in a decrease in the number of violent incidents, within the one-year time frame of the research project. As a practical result of the project, several work sites continued to use the VIF instrument, having incorporated it into their workplace routines. Following such violent incidents, a range of supports may be called upon to assist the victim to deal with the aftermath.

Tertiary interventions

Once a violent incident has occurred, the treatment of the victim should be a priority. Other post-event supports needed may include: follow-up, complaint and grievance procedures; counselling; and any rehabilitative procedures aimed at establishing a normal working life for the victim and all those involved. Where support services are not available, it may be possible with modern technologies to provide electronic and telephone access.

Phone counselling

The Japanese National Network in Solidarity sponsored a successful three-day phone counselling service for abused foreign women in Japan over the period 18–21 September 2002.[23] Known as the "Domestic Violence Hotline", the counselling service was offered in different languages including English, Korean, Chinese, Filipino, Thai, Spanish, Portuguese and Russian.

It was believed that the language barrier has prevented many victims of domestic violence in Japan from coming forward. Some of these include migrant workers with expired work visas who are abused by their partners, but who fear that reporting incidents of abuse could lead to their deportation. One problem is that while Japan has a law against domestic violence, there are no punitive measures against it. The law does not recognize domestic violence as a crime, and only mandates national and local authorities to implement measures to prevent it from happening and to provide protection to victims.

The phone counselling, which took place in 13 locations in Japan, encouraged a number of abused women to come forward because it promised anonymity and privacy. Counsellors said some abuse stemmed from discrimination based on race, especially for those who worked in Japan as entertainers or domestic helpers.

The "best practice" examples provided in this chapter have so far focused on particular solutions adopted in specific organizations, including private enterprise, government authorities and at national level. A recurring theme in those policies and strategies that have been evaluated as successful is that they are multifactorial and comprehensive.

Comprehensive approaches

Comprehensive responses to the risk of workplace violence address, in an organized way, the complex causes of violence and include a wide range of coordinated prevention measures. Such multifaceted responses are rare. The following best practices are therefore exceptional and deserve special attention to orient future, much-needed, comprehensive action in this area.

Victim Empowerment Programme, South Africa

Violence in society and in the workplace has been, and is still, a crucial problem in South Africa. Addressing widespread violence across this country involves a major community and governmental effort. One of the major strategies adopted in South Africa was the setting up of a centre of excellence to tackle the problem at its roots, as detailed in box 74.

Box 74   Centre for the Study of Violence and Reconciliation (CSVR) in South Africa: Victim Empowerment Programme

The primary objectives of the CSVR's Victim Empowerment Programme are:

- Helping South Africans to better understand the effects of the past on the present.

- Developing ways to prevent violence and combat its effects, as well as to overcome intolerance.

- Building a human rights culture in South Africa.

- Facilitating the process of human development through rebuilding the social fabric and the origins of civil society.

- The management and facilitation of reconstruction and development initiatives, so as to ensure that these do not lead to increased social conflict.

- The transformation and democratization of state institutions inherited from the past.

- Developing and transferring skills necessary to build sustainable reconciliation and democracy in South Africa.

Treatment

The following treatment is given at CSVR: trauma counselling; debriefing and long-term therapy; training in trauma awareness; management treatment to front-line workers and communities; and psychiatric and psychometric assessment.

Training

The training activities target caregivers, refugees/asylum seekers, ex-combatants, health professionals, and the social and educational services.

Research

Research is conducted into the issues of violence, PTSD [Post-Traumatic Stress Disorder], treatment methods and needs of vulnerable groups, i.e. refugees, women and children, ex-combatants and victims of human rights abuses. The Victim Empowerment Programme has one full-time research psychologist.

Documentation

Case histories and courses of treatment are documented in a patient file. A new computerized client tracking system was implemented in 2003. It was developed by us and our partners in the South African Trauma Network, Themba Lesizwe. All client details are catered for with this system. It will, however, not replace the paper system.

Prevention

Prevention activities include the training of border police and primary health care workers (i.e. trauma and refugee issues); work with young offenders in prison; manuals on trauma work with children; and seminars and work with the media.

Information and advocacy

Information and advocacy activities include work in all areas of the media; governmental lobbying; participation in international forums; and contributions to various articles, conference papers and culturally specific magazines.

Networking

The CSVR Victim Empowerment Programme belongs to the Southern African Trauma Network. Our clinic serves as an internship site for Wits University community psychology interns. Social work students from the University Social Work Department spend between three and 12 months in the clinic and are supervised by our staff. Our clinic has a relationship with Johannesburg Child Welfare, whereby we will see and assess some of their child abuse cases. Our clinic also has a contract with the South Eastern Africa UNICEF desk to service their staff throughout the region in the face of traumatic exposure or incidents.

Funding

Funding is received from the European Union (through Themba Lesizwe) and the UNVFVT [United Nations Voluntary Fund for the Victims of Torture].

/cont'd

/cont'd

Staff

Staff comprises four social workers, six psychologists, two psychiatric nurses, one (sessional) psychiatrist and one research psychologist.

Future plans

Future plans include include developing a victim empowerment programme and a human resource structure whereby we can combine the social worker and psychologist roles into one trauma professional role to address a disparity in remuneration.

Source: Centre for the Study of Violence and Reconciliation (CSVR): *Victim Empowerment Programme* 2005.

The CSVR clearly provides a benchmark that should be applauded. Other individual organizations also provide comprehensive advice on prevention and management of violence at work.

Reduction of community violence on public transport and buses

Bus drivers and conductors potentially face difficult customers every day, with many incidents arising out of fare evasion, changes in fares, scheduling and dealing with customers under the influence of alcohol.[24] Some companies are taking a very proactive and practical approach to tackling the issue of violence through changes in vehicle design, the provision of training and guidance, and working in partnership with the police.

Situational crime prevention techniques have been widely used in recent years to combat crime problems, including the problems of violence on public transport. These techniques comprise opportunity-reducing measures that involve the management, design or manipulation of the immediate environment so as to increase the effort and risks of crime and reduce the rewards as perceived by a wide range of offenders. A considerable body of evidence now exists supporting the effectiveness of a range of situational techniques in the reduction of crime including aggression on public transport. One advantage of this type of crime prevention approach in the prevention of violence on public transport is that it has been successful in reducing not just opportunities for violence but also in providing effective situational techniques to combat fear, incivility, graffiti and vandalism.

A variety of community crime prevention strategies, aimed at changing the social conditions that are believed to sustain crime in communities, have also been aimed at reducing violence on public transport including reducing community fear of crime, neighbourhood incivilities, graffiti, vandalism, social disorder and delinquency.[25]

London Central and London General Buses have also implemented detailed workplace violence risk reduction measures (box 75). Their comprehensive policy and strategies have a number of facets.

Box 75   London Central and London General Buses

Training and guidance

All new recruits receive comprehensive training. The initial induction process includes basic training in areas such as garage procedures, health and safety issues, dealing with public enquiries and incident and accident reporting procedures. A new standard in bus operating practices has been recently introduced by London Buses and is currently being rolled out across the contracted bus companies. It was developed following consultation with a wide range of bus operators, training providers and trade union representatives, and is designed to improve the quality and consistency of training across all London operators.

The new qualification builds on training procedures already in place at London Central and London General. Previously the training was comprehensive but only took place at the start of the job. The BTEC [a national diploma] promotes continuous learning through refresher training and ongoing assessment. For example, after three months "on the job", staff now attend a further session on customer care, focusing on disability awareness including dealing with mental illness, which, in itself, can be a source of conflict. Staff are actively encouraged to share and discuss their experiences at work and to learn from them.

All staff are also given a leaflet on "dealing with difficult situations". It is designed to be a comprehensive yet quick reference guide for staff, featuring illustrative cartoons.

Using CCTV

London Central and London General were two of the first companies to equip their buses with CCTV cameras on the most problematic routes. Not only has this helped to protect passengers, drivers and conductors, but it also provides key evidence in the event of an incident and acts as a deterrent to likely offenders. This example of good practice was quickly adopted by London Buses and there is now a contractual requirement for all buses, both new and existing, to be fitted with CCTV.

Assault screens

Drivers of Routemasters sit in a cab separated from the saloon of the bus. To protect drivers of the rest of the fleet, assault screens have been fitted. While creating a barrier between the drivers and their customers and, in consequence, not universally popular, the duty of care to staff has overridden those concerns. London Central and London General are continually looking at further improvements on the design of the screens to minimize opportunities for assaults and attempted robberies to occur.

New cash-free "bendy" buses

London General is one of the first operating companies under contract to introduce new "bendy" and cashless bus services in London. Although this initiative from London Buses is not specifically aimed at reducing violent incidents on staff, it is anticipated that it will

/cont'd

/cont'd

nonetheless have a positive effect. Since the driver has no cash on board, it should help to combat the number of actual and attempted robberies.

Publicity

London Buses is proactively campaigning to minimize aggressive or violent incidents against staff. As well as an ongoing initiative to install CCTV on all buses and making the public aware of them, every bus displays posters inside stating that attacks on staff will not be tolerated and that prosecution is likely.

Dealing with actual incidents

Conductors are trained, wherever possible, to walk away from a potentially violent or aggressive situation. However, if an incident does occur, the driver is alerted as quickly as possible. Drivers are instructed not to leave their cab unless absolutely necessary as the cab gives them protection and control of the bus and they are within easy reach of the emergency radio and vehicle alarm button. After road traffic incidents, drivers are also advised not to lean out of the cab window as they may be assaulted or dragged from the vehicle. All cabs are fitted with radios and following an incident which requires the attendance of an emergency service, the "code red" radio procedure is activated. Calls go straight through to a central communications unit "CentreComm", manned in partnership by London Buses and TOCD, the dedicated transport policing service that is then responsible for contacting the appropriate emergency service.

Reporting forms

There are various reporting forms that staff must complete after an incident of violence or aggression. The recording of incidents is usually cross-referenced to CCTV footage, to improve the quality of evidence and thereby increasing the chances of successful prosecution against offenders.

Staff support

Every member of staff who experiences and reports a violent or aggressive incident has a debrief with a senior member of the garage, usually the general manager, operational manager or the accident and prevention manager. The senior managers are trained to acknowledge the seriousness of the incident and staff are given the opportunity to talk about it, including what happened, how they felt, what triggered the incident and so on.

Senior staff are also trained to spot indications of deeper problems which may need to be addressed. If the manager deems it necessary, the individual may be referred back to the training centre for further help and guidance. This would involve a full day with a qualified trainer, looking in detail at the incident, why it happened, what could have been done to prevent it, and discussing techniques on how to prevent it from happening again.

If staff feel they need further help and support, they or their line manager can request independent counselling support arranged at company expense through the personnel team. There is an agreement in place for "assault pay" to ensure there is no loss of earnings following an incident. Depending on how long the individual is off work and the severity of the incident, the garage manager has discretion to continue this payment or transfer the member of staff to the sick pay scheme.

Legal support

Depending on the severity of the incident and the quality of the evidence available, the police may take further action. However, in cases where the police state that they do not intend to pursue a prosecution, the member of staff can decide to ask the company to follow up the matter on their behalf. In such circumstances, the case is passed onto the Revenue and Protection Service section of London Buses, which takes over the investigation and may help individuals to prosecute assailants through the courts.

Monitoring

Each garage logs all incidents of assault on a summary sheet, including key details such as whether the member of staff is a driver or conductor, the bus route involved and the location and time of the incident. This allows analysis for common patterns or types, frequency and location of incidents.

Details of incidents also get fed electronically to London Buses which collates data from all bus operators in the capital. It is able to identify patterns across London and works closely with the Metropolitan Police on targeted operations and initiatives.

Source: Income Data Services Ltd., 2003.

The above case studies indicate that the risks for workers in large organizations in both fixed and mobile working environments can be reduced significantly. Nonetheless, for those who work alone and/or in isolated sites, additional protective measures need to be taken.

Risk reduction for lone workers

In the United Kingdom, the Health and Safety Laboratory (HSL) (the research arm of the Health and Safety Executive) approached over 400 organizations of various sizes and across a range of different occupational sectors in England, Wales and Scotland. Detailed questionnaires were sent and interviews were conducted by HSL staff with members of the selected organizations between October 2002 and February 2003.

Organizations were asked to list the most successful ways of managing and preventing violence to their lone working staff. The findings from this survey are summarized in box 76.

This survey again highlighted the need to enhance the level of workplace violence prevention for lone workers who are perceived to have a heightened vulnerability. Another vulnerability that may emerge over time is complacency.

Box 76   Risk reduction for lone workers in the United Kingdom

Training and information

The provision of training and information was predominant.

- Risk assessments. Conducting a risk assessment of the tasks of the lone worker was seen as essential. Employers need to find out if there is a problem, decide what action to take, take action, and review the action.

- Training. Some sort of personal safety or violence prevention training was provided by all organizations. Training was provided in-house or by an external organization, and could be formal or informal. The key training messages conveyed were:

  - Do not go into a situation if you feel at risk.

  - Use conflict resolution or defusing techniques. These include being aware of non-verbal communication; how to behave in a non-confrontational way; the importance of good customer care; being polite; and listening to clients.

  - Be aware of surroundings. Keep your wits about you at all times and be aware of the situation you are in. Be aware of your own actions and how others may perceive you.

  - If you feel threatened, make your excuses and leave. Make sure you can leave the premises quickly if you need to.

Communication

Good communication and sharing of information between employees, and with external organizations and professional bodies where appropriate, was seen as essential. This included:

- Liaison with police. The police have helped some of the participating organizations, providing advice on personal safety and related issues; helping with specific visits or incidents; and also providing local knowledge of the area.

- Letting staff know where lone workers are. The use of work diaries and information boards to show the location of lone workers during the day was seen as essential by some of the participating organizations.

- Sharing experiences and concerns. This happened between employees within an organization and between other relevant organizations. Organizations have found the following practices helpful:

  - Use an early warning or flagging system. This alerts colleagues about potentially violent clients, or problem areas.

  - Talk about specific concerns and incidents. Organizations believed that relevant and practical solutions can be more easily found when problems and ideas are shared.

  - Report all incidents. This helps management to evaluate and monitor the true scale and nature of violence and abuse incidents and so help to develop an effective policy to deal with the problem.

- Company policy, guidance, leaflets and posters. All staff should be made aware of the company policy on work-related violence.

- Management support. In many organizations violence prevention measures have the full commitment and support of senior management. Managers felt that it was important that all staff should know this.

Work equipment and environment

Work equipment:

- Use of mobile phones or other communication device. Mobile phones were very popular. Lone workers use them to call for help if needed and to let others know where and how they are.

- Personal alarms. These were also popular and helped staff feel more confident about their safety.

Work environment

The environment in which lone working is carried out will determine how and whether it can be modified or designed to help prevent incidents of violence. The following measures were the most common:

- Panic alarm in building. This alerts other colleagues who work nearby or the security room.

- CCTV. Some organizations had CCTV installed in areas where lone workers operate.

Job design

- Doubling-up. Some organizations send two people to carry out a job if there is thought to be a possible risk of violence or if the employee has particular concerns.

- Self-risk assessments. The lone worker is encouraged to regularly assess the situation they are in and the risks to which they are exposed.

- Recruitment and selection. Some organizations apply strict recruitment criteria to ensure that only those who are highly suited to lone working are selected for the job.

- Withdrawal of service/sanctions/prosecution. As a last resort, organizations can withdraw their service, implement sanctions, or threaten prosecution if their lone workers experience violence or abuse.

Factors which reduce the effectiveness of measures

The main difficulty with many of the measures described in these case studies was reliance on individual action. Some measures rely on the individual to do something, for example, to tell someone where they are or to activate an alarm or system, etc. This means that human error or neglect to do so can make even the best system ineffective. Companies commented that other factors can also reduce the effectiveness of measures, including:

- lack of attendance at training courses due to pressures of work;

- not carrying a personal alarm within easy reach or knowing how to use it; and

/cont'd

/cont'd

- not always being able to avoid potentially violent situations because it goes against a person's "natural instincts". For example, in a robbery situation, a member of staff might find it difficult to hand over expensive equipment/money without resistance.

Some organizations had tried and then abandoned measures which were found to be less successful, or had decided at the outset against introducing particular measures. Some examples were teaching staff in self-defence techniques, the wearing of formal security-style uniforms, and use of "hot lines" to the police.

Source : HSE, 2003 (excerpts).

That is, while "best-practice" preventive steps may have been implemented, and may well have achieved excellent results, the level of effectiveness may diminish over time. Hence sustainability of "best-practice" interventions is of core importance.

Sustainability

Sustainability of any project is a key element of success. Many initiatives, even those looking promising in a first phase, are confronted with difficulties at later stages in their development and may be terminated. For those which continue in the long term, evaluation of the project is a rare event.

At the European Week for Safety and Health at Work held in Bilbao in November 2001, 20 award-winning examples of good practice on prevention of violence and stress at work were presented. These represent a unique body of information gathered at the same time and analysed according to common criteria.

In January 2004 a questionnaire was sent to all award-winning project leaders asking them about any follow-up to their projects. The responses obtained from two of these projects (others have already been referred to earlier in this chapter) are presented below.

Task Force on the Prevention of Workplace Bullying, Ireland

In 1999, the Minister for Labour, Trade and Consumer Affairs in Ireland established a task force on the prevention of workplace bullying. It was coordinated by the Health and Safety Authority, with participating representatives from different government departments, agencies and bodies dealing with workplace welfare and equality issues. The main objectives of the Task Force were to identify the size of the problem of workplace bullying and the sectors most at risk. Based on this information, practical prevention programmes would be developed and a coordinated response from state agencies produced.

As a first step, an independent national survey was commissioned to obtain as much information as possible, through a participatory approach involving the public. Besides the survey, a national advertising campaign was undertaken and the public were invited to make submissions to the Task Force on the subject of workplace bullying.

In total, 256 submissions were received from a variety of sources, representing a broad body of views and information from individuals, groups and organizations. The submissions were analysed by a psychologist. More than half the responses were received from victims of bullying and the findings show that the majority of the victims suffered from severe health effects, such as physical and emotional symptoms, which had often resulted in sick leave or quitting their job. The submissions from the public further provided information on the forms of bullying behaviour and the sectors of risk.

Additionally, suggestions on how to address the problem were included, indicating that proper procedures in the workplace were needed, as well as staff training and special anti-bullying policies. The submissions received, together with the survey findings and a review of existing research, were carefully considered by the Task Force for the formulation of recommendations. The Task Force recommended the following definition of workplace bullying:

> Workplace bullying is repeated inappropriate behaviour, direct or indirect, whether verbal, physical or otherwise, conducted by one or more persons against another or others, at the place of work and/or in the course of employment, which could reasonably be regarded as undermining the individual's right to dignity at work.
>
> An isolated incident of the behaviour described in this definition may be an affront to dignity at work but as a one off incident is not considered to be bullying.[26]

This definition is now widely accepted as a benchmark "best-practice" classification which is increasingly being called up in official documents around the world.

The Irish Health and Safety Authority (HAS) and the Task Force also developed a *Code of practice detailing procedures for addressing bullying in the workplace*,[27] which identifies the types of behaviour that constitute bullying, and details a range of precautionary measures that employers may take to implement an effective anti-bullying policy, investigation procedures and training needs. Also appended to the code of practice are extracts from the Safety, Health and Welfare at Work Act 1989. Further, the Irish Government has enacted a code of practice directed at stamping out sexual harassment and other forms of harassment at work, given effect under the Employment Equality Act 1998.[28]

The HAS was one of the organizations reviewed in 2004, following the Bilbao meeting. The responses to the questionnaire by a representative from HAS are summarized in box 77.

Box 77   Questionnaire: Health and Safety Authority, Ireland

Q. Is the initiative you presented at the conference in Bilbao in 2002 still on?
A. Yes

Q. Is it monitored?
A. Yes

Q. How has it developed since?
A. The programme has gone on to result in a code of practice on prevention of bullying and a dedicated unit to handle complaints and assistance to all concerned. However, some callers see it as a counselling line, which it is not; others see it as a way to take on the bully, which it is not; others see our role as enforcement, but we cannot realistically take criminal cases against organizations where bullying is the "safety" issue as it doesn't lend itself to the evidence-based approach required in criminal law cases. We are hoping to initiate a talk-shop meeting where others will liaise with us in the industrial relations area and come up with some other route for this workplace relations issue.

Q. Which are the main results obtained?
A. (a) We have a higher profile as dealing with the issue has brought us to a greater media attention.
   (b) Many employees feel better having spoken to an outside agency.
   (c) Many employees feel our intervention and very presence helped process their case.
   (d) Some employers feel more confident with our assistance and advice.

Q. Is it going to continue in time?
A. Yes, but it will hopefully be modified at a policy level, maybe through legislation or regulation and through interdepartmental alterations concerning the state agency responsible.

Q. What is your global assessment?
A. The workings of the system weren't checked out properly before being put in place, the system is not robust, nor is the service workable as far as enforcement is concerned. So there should be another state agency with a bigger remit, as criminal law is not the right arena for this issue. However, as there was nothing in place prior to our initiative, what we do is an improvement and does help in certain cases. Globally, it does raise the issue and recognize it as a very important workplace relations concern, with serious health effects among Irish workers.

Source: By courtesy of P. Murray, Dublin, Health and Safety Authority, 20 Feb. 2004.

Prevention plan for violence in an urban public transport company, Amiens, France

This urban public transport system operated over 16 routes, transported 14,500,000 people in 2001, and employed 335 staff. Staff who were in contact with the customers were experiencing workplace violence, predominantly verbal and physical attacks on employees, but also material damage such as broken windows. This violence caused deterioration in working conditions and a state of permanent strain for the staff concerned, resulting in strikes, illness, absenteeism and recourse to tranquillizers for some. The implementation of a prevention plan,[29] included:

- human and material resources detailed in the company agreement of 4 March 1999: "Agreement on the safety of staff and vehicles of SEMTA, the Amiens Urban Public Transport Company";

- assistance following an attack or serious incident involving the company's employees, including legal support and counselling;

- involvement of the company with the Amiens suburban authority. The company joined the watchdog committee, in which different partners participated, including the City of Amiens and its metropolitan authority, national and municipal police, judicial authorities, sponsors of social initiatives, education authorities, a psychotherapist and others;

- close collaboration with elected staff representatives and the members of the Committee for Health and Safety and Working Conditions. A quarterly statistical review is prepared detailing reports of attacks on staff and material damage, and a public presentation is made of any new prevention and safety interventions;

- communication with all the company employees has been improved through messages on the radio, network broadcasts and information put up on noticeboards. A report of each incident is also sent to the relevant public authorities.

Other preventive measures included:

- strengthening of inspection teams by assigning assistants to ticket inspectors;

- gradual installation of CCTV cameras on all buses;

- tight control over areas prone to stone-throwing. The safety coordinator and intervention officers familiarize themselves with these higher-risk districts, go out to meet people and associations there who participated in Anti-Aggression Week activities;

- greater involvement of the judicial authorities in speeding up cases and easing all stages of the judicial proceedings following the systematic filing of a complaint.

Costs and benefits

The costs include:

- human resources: including 18 intervention officers throughout the network, a prevention officer with outreach responsibilities in schools, external trainers for stress management and problem situations, and a psychotherapist who is responsible for psychological monitoring;

- rapid intervention resources: e.g. radiotelephony, locating vehicles using GPS [Global Positioning System] location-tracking technology, the installation of CCTV cameras in buses, and the fitting of protective cabins for drivers, separating them from the public, and protective coatings on the side windows of buses for driver–conductors.

The benefits included:

- Since 2002 the preventive measures adopted began to show positive results, both in terms of the number of attacks observed and the frequency of broken windows, including:

  - an 18-month absence of days lost through industrial action because of violence;

  - enhanced cooperation between the social partners who are now involved in signing collective agreements, including on flexible and reduced working time;

  - one individual indicator is the perception that employee concerns are taken into consideration.

Public transport is a priority sector for reducing violence at work. This initiative illustrates how effective partnerships can help reduce the risks, and implement innovative outreach activities. It is noteworthy that the social partners and workers were actively involved in the identification of solutions, which subsequently had wider benefits beyond improved safety and directly led to improvements in industrial relations.

The public transport authority in Amiens, France, was also one of the organizations reviewed in 2004, following the Bilbao meeting. The responses to the questionnaire by a representative from this urban public transport system authority are summarized in box 78.

The discussions now turn to the potential implementation of global action against workplace violence. Chapter 8 evaluates some global initiatives.

Box 78   Questionnaire: Amiens public transport authority

Q. Is the initiative you presented at the conference in Bilbao in 2002 still ongoing?

A. Yes.

Q. Is it monitored?

A. Yes.

Q. How has it developed since?

A. In the event of aggression, the following measures have been taken:

   – individual treatment for the victim, consisting of legal support and psychological counselling;

   – complete openness in relation to all the staff;

   – special protection for the victimized driver over a limited period, including temporary re-routing of the bus line;

   – if the driver has to take leave on medical grounds as a result of the aggression, he or she is given personalized support on returning to work, as in the case of any extended absence due to sickness or accident.

Over a three-year period, more than 200 drivers received training in how to deal with aggression-related risks and behavioural patterns, conducted by a psychiatrist and a psychologist trained to teach stress management. This helps drivers to react professionally rather than emotionally in case of conflict.

Q. What results has this achieved?

A. – a sharp drop in the number of aggressions and smashed windows (from over 180 incidents in 2001 to less than 100 in 2003);

   – a fall in the number of days of sick leave resulting from aggression, from more than 1,500 in 2001 to less than 500 in 2003 (the figure for 2003 includes 365 sick days taken by a single employee as a result of an attack sustained in October 2002).

Q. Is this progress likely to continue?

A. The following initiatives are scheduled:

   – signing of a new safety agreement to boost safety measures;

   – improved organization of prevention/assistance;

   – continuation of the training programme on conflict prevention and management; extending it to all services that come into contact with passengers;

   – introduction of a new training course designed to improve the quality of service and comfort on buses;

   – replacement of the fleet of buses with new ones adapted to people with reduced mobility.

/cont'd

/cont'd

Q. What is your overall assessment?

A. We believe that the two prizes received for the above measures - the European Prize (awarded at Bilbao) and the "Social Initiative Trophy" (awarded at Lyons by VEOLIA) – reflect the recognition of our ongoing efforts, which we will continue to build upon in line with our corporate culture. From the very outset, this was sharply focused on dealing with insecurity. The focus can now begin to shift to the quality of passenger services.

Source: By courtesy of Dominique Glacet, Responsable des Ressources Humaines SEMTA, Société d'Economie Mixte des Transports Amiénois [Amiens Urban Transport Company], 18 Mar. 2004.

Notes

[1] Toshiba Group CSR, no date, Ch. 2.

[2] New South Wales Health, 2003.

[3] Information from Teri Brownlee, Risk Manager, 5 Mar. 2004.

[4] European Commission, Justice and Home Affairs, 1998.

[5] Ibid, p. 2.

[6] Ibid.

[7] Ministry of Human Resources, Malaysia, 2001.

[8] Musri and Daud, 2002 (excerpts).

[9] IG Metall; FRAPORT AG, 2001.

[10] See, for example, Easteal and Wilson, 1991. See also Bowie, 2000, pp. 247–254.

[11] Essenberg, 2003, p. 32.

[12] European Agency for Safety and Health and Work, 2002a, p. 2.

[13] TNO Arbeid, 2002.

[14] Ibid., pp. 36–38.

[15] Nowak, et al. 2002, unpublished material cited in Di Martino, Hoel and Cooper, 2003, pp. 80–81.

[16] Department of Health, United Kingdom, 2000.

[17] European Agency for Safety and Health at Work, 2002b, p. 42.

[18] National Health Service (NHS), 2000a.

[19] NHS, 2000b, p. 6.

[20] Income Data Services, 2003.

[21] Arnetz, 1998a, pp. 17–28. See also Arnetz, Arnetz and Soderman, 1998, pp. 107–114.

[22] Arnetz and Arnetz, 2002, pp. 668–676, especially p. 674.

[23] We! (A weekly newsletter from Isis International Manila), 2002.

[24] Essenberg, 2003.

[25] Ibid., p. 30.

[26] Health and Safety Authority, Ireland, 2001, p. viii.

[27] Idem, 2002.

[28] Irish Equality Authority, 2002.

[29] European Agency for Safety and Health at Work, 2002b, p. 54.

ACTION AGAINST WORKPLACE VIOLENCE BY INTERNATIONAL AGENCIES

8

Action at the international level to combat workplace violence has included a number of new and important initiatives. These initiatives form the principal subject matter of this chapter, which looks initially at violence at work in the context of human rights. Attention is then turned to the efforts made by various international bodies, including the United Nations (UN), to deal with this form of violence. The findings obtained from a small survey of a number of international agencies about their own internal policies regarding violence at work form part of this analysis, as does a consideration of the regional activities of the European Union.

Protection of human rights and violence at work

The **Universal Declaration of Human Rights**, adopted by the UN General Assembly on 10 December 1949, proscribes discrimination of any kind;[1] asserts the right of everyone to life, liberty and security of their person;[2] and provides that no one should be subject to torture or to cruel, inhuman or degrading treatment or punishment.[3] These fundamental rights were restated and further elaborated by the **International Covenant on Civil and Political Rights** and the **International Covenant on Economic, Social and Cultural Rights**, both of which were adopted by the UN General Assembly on 16 December 1966. This last instrument, in particular, expressly required the States which were parties to the Covenant to recognize the right of everyone to the enjoyment of "safe and healthy working conditions".[4]

Protection of women workers and violence at work

However, it was not until the adoption by the UN General Assembly on 18 December 1979 of the **Convention on the Elimination of All Forms of**

Discrimination against Women that the issue of violence at work was addressed in a specific way. Article 1 of the Convention states:

> For the purposes of the present Convention, the term "discrimination against women" shall mean any distinction, exclusion or restriction made on the basis of sex which has the effect or purpose of impairing or nullifying the recognition, enjoyment or exercise by women, irrespective of their marital status, on a basis of equality of men and women, of human rights and fundamental freedoms in the political, economic, social, cultural, civil or any other field.

Article 11 of the Convention requires ratifying States to "take all appropriate measures to eliminate discrimination against women in the field of employment". It was against this general background that in January 1992, the **Committee on the Elimination of Discrimination against Women (CEDAW)**, set up under the Convention, adopted General Recommendation No. 19 on violence against women. The Recommendation, in particular, addressed the problem of sexual harassment providing, for the first time, a clear definition of this behaviour and listing actions to be taken against this form of violence by States:

- (Para.) 17. Equality in employment can be seriously impaired when women are subjected to gender-specific violence, such as sexual harassment in the workplace.

- (Para.) 18. Sexual harassment includes such unwelcome sexually determined behaviour as physical contact and advances, sexually coloured remarks, showing pornography and sexual demands, whether by words or actions. Such conduct can be humiliating and may constitute a health and safety problem; it is discriminatory when the woman has reasonable grounds to believe that her objection would disadvantage her in connection with her employment, including recruitment or promotion, or when it creates a hostile working environment.

- (Para.) 24. In light of these comments, the Committee on the Elimination of Discrimination against Women recommends that:

    (j) States parties should include in their reports information on sexual harassment, and on measures to protect women from sexual harassment ... in the workplace;

    (t) States parties should take all legal and other measures that are necessary to provide effective protection of women against gender-based violence, including, inter alia:

(i) Effective legal measures, including penal sanctions, civil remedies and compensatory provisions to protect women against all kinds of violence, including ... sexual harassment in the workplace;

(ii) Preventive measures, including public information and education programmes to change attitudes concerning the roles and status of men and women.[5]

In June 1993, the World Conference on Human Rights held in Vienna, Austria, stressed the importance of working towards the elimination of violence against women in public and private life. One outcome of the Conference was the appointment of a Special UN Rapporteur on Violence Against Women. The Rapporteur, who examined the causes and consequences of violence against women, and recommended ways and means to eliminate them, now reports on an annual basis to the UN Commission on Human Rights.

In December 1993, the General Assembly adopted a landmark resolution on gender violence called the **Declaration on the Elimination of Violence against Women**. This Declaration defines what constitutes an act of violence against women, and calls on governments and the international community to take specific measures to prevent such acts. Violence against women is defined as "any act of gender-based violence that results in, or is likely to result in, physical, sexual or psychological harm or suffering to women, including threats of such acts, coercion or arbitrary deprivation of liberty, whether occurring in public or in private life".[6]

The Declaration also lists abuses that are encompassed by the term "violence against women":

(a) Physical, sexual and psychological violence occurring in the family, including battering, sexual abuse of female children, dowry-related violence, marital rape, female genital mutilation and other traditional practices harmful to women, non-spousal violence and violence related to exploitation;

(b) Physical, sexual and psychological violence occurring within the general community, including rape, sexual abuse, sexual harassment and intimidation at work, in educational institutions and elsewhere, trafficking in women and forced prostitution;

(c) Physical, sexual and psychological violence perpetrated or condoned by the State, wherever it occurs.[7]

In September 1995, at the Fourth World Conference on Women held in Beijing, this definition was confirmed and action to be undertaken to combat violence against women was further specified (box 79).

Box 79   Fourth World Conference on Women, Beijing, 1995: Call for action to combat violence against women at work

Actions to be taken by Governments:

"Enact and/or reinforce penal, civil, labour and administrative sanctions in domestic legislation to punish and redress the wrongs done to women and girls who are subjected to any form of violence, whether in the home, the workplace, the community or society;" (para. 124.c)

Actions by Governments, NGOs, educational institutions, enterprises, etc.:

"Recognize the vulnerability to violence and other forms of abuse of women migrants, including women migrant workers, whose legal status in the host countries depends on employers who may exploit their situation;" (para. 125.c).

Actions by Governments, employers, trade unions, etc.:

"Develop programmes and procedures to eliminate sexual harassment and other forms of violence against women in all educational institutions, workplaces and elsewhere;" (para. 126.a)

"Take special measures to eliminate violence against women, particularly those in vulnerable situations, such as young women, refugee, displaced and internally displaced women, women with disabilities and women migrant workers, including enforcing any existing legislation and developing, as appropriate, new legislation for women migrant workers in both sending and receiving countries;" (para. 126.d)

Actions by Governments, the private sector, NGOs, trade unions and the UN:

"Enact and enforce laws against sexual and other forms of harassment in all workplaces." (para. 180.c)

Source: United Nations, 1995, pp. 54, 56 and 82.

Twenty years after the adoption of the Convention on the Elimination of All Forms of Discrimination against Women, another UN instrument made it possible for individual women or groups of women to submit claims directly to the Committee on the Elimination of Discrimination against Women in cases, inter alia, of violence at the workplace.

On 12 March 1999 the 43rd session of the Commission on the Status of Women adopted an **Optional Protocol to the Convention on the Elimination of All Forms of Discrimination against Women**, at the recommendation of its Working Group.[8] The Protocol contains two procedures: a communications procedure allowing individual women, or groups of women, to submit claims of violations of rights to the Committee on the Elimination of Discrimination against Women; and an inquiry

---

Box 80   Sexual harassment at work

The mere prohibition of sexual harassment is not adequate to assist victims of violence. It is imperative that institutions, whether public or private, educational or industrial, have internal procedures that ensure redress in cases of sexual harassment. The Canadian Federal Labour Code serves as a model in this regard. It requires employers to issue a sexual harassment policy that condemns sexual harassment, indicates that disciplinary measures will be taken against transgressors, provides for procedures to deal with instances of harassment and informs employees of their rights.

Most private companies have been slow to respond to victims' needs since the company's first priority generally is seeking to avoid negative publicity. In some companies, informal mechanisms to address employees' complaints have been institutionalized. Internal mechanisms, if not implemented or enforced vigorously, may, however, serve to privatize the violation and impede the victim's recourse. Often such mechanisms are designed to resolve conflicts through mediation rather than to address the victim's needs and hold the perpetrator accountable. Such practices add pressure to the victim in deciding whether or not to pursue a claim against the harasser. With little or no institutional support for reporting, the victim's concerns about her own job status may encourage silence. In this connection, some jurisdictions render the employer vicariously liable for sex discrimination if he or she does not take adequate preventive measures.

Source: United Nations, Commission on Human Rights, 1999. See also Optional Protocol to the Convention on the Elimination of All Forms of Discrimination against Women (note 8).

---

procedure enabling the Committee to initiate inquiries into situations of grave or systematic violations of women's rights. In either case States must be party to the Protocol. It was adopted by the General Assembly on 6 October 1999 and entered into force on 22 December 2000, following the ratification of the tenth State party to the Convention.

Against this background, reports to the Commission on Human Rights by the Special Rapporteur on Violence Against Women have highlighted sexual harassment. The Special Rapporteur's 1997 report contained a detailed analysis (box 80).

Reports to the Commission on Human Rights by the Special Rapporteur on Violence Against Women have also paid particular attention to violence against women migrant workers. The Special Rapporteur's 1997 report also contained a detailed analysis of this issue (box 81).

A closely related issue, violence against women in the family, is addressed in the 1999 Special Rapporteur's report. The links between violence at work and in the family, and their cumulative impact on victims, are emerging as a key to understanding the dramatic magnitude of overall violence against women. States and enterprises are beginning to realize the importance of the problem.

In 2003 the Special Rapporteur produced a major survey on international, regional and national developments in the area of violence against women

Box 81   Women migrant workers

In astonishingly large numbers, women are migrating great distances across international boundaries to engage in poorly remunerated labour that isolates them in a subordinate position in a private realm, exposing them to acute risks of physical or psychological violence and to expropriation of their economic gain.[1]

The largely unregulated informal sector is the site of numerous violations of women's human rights. More than 2,000 cases of ill-treatment and abuse of migrant domestic workers in the United Kingdom have been documented. The abuses have included confiscation of passports, enforced change of contract, withholding of wages, deprivation of food and malnourishment, lack of access to medical and health services, imprisonment in the home of the employer, prohibition on engaging in social contacts, the interception of letters from home, and physical and sexual violence ...

In Latin America and the Caribbean, domestic labour migration has an extensive history plagued by reports of violence and abuse. In Asunción, there are roughly 15,200 domestic workers between the ages of five and 18 who have migrated from rural areas and work for free. Many of the girls receive education and accommodation in lieu of a salary. Such domestic arrangements increase their vulnerability to exploitation and violence ...

Similar conditions and consequences are reported among Colombia's *floristerias* [female workers in the flower export industry] who are also exposed to pesticides. In Guatemala, internal women migrants either work as domestic labourers or work in *maquilas* [garment assembly factories]. In order to encourage foreign investors, *maquilas* are exempt from regulations guaranteeing workers' rights; women are subject to sexual violence and harassment, forced overtime, intimidation and generally poor working conditions.

In Morocco, young rural girls are placed with wealthy urban families as domestic servants. Despite promises of education and a better standard of living, the girls are often subjected to inhumane working conditions and forced to live in a state of indentured servitude. This situation is exacerbated in cases of "adoptive servitude", in which wealthy families adopt orphan girls for the explicit purpose of providing labour and there are widespread reports of physical abuse of the girls. Conditions in Asian countries with migrant domestic worker populations, including Japan, Malaysia, Cambodia and Singapore and in Hong Kong (China), are often characterized by such abuse.

In countries of the Persian Gulf, the estimated 1.2 million domestic workers constitute 20 per cent of the estimated 6 million migrants on whom these countries rely heavily. Sri Lanka, Indonesia, India, and the Philippines are the primary sending countries to the Gulf region. The often violent and inhumane conditions in countries such as Saudi Arabia and Kuwait have been widely documented.[2]

Sources: [1]Fitzpatrick, United Nations, 1999, p. 9, cited ibid.

[2]United Nations, Commission on Human Rights, 1997.

See also: UNIFEM, 2003 and the ILO Worst Forms of Child Labour Convention, 1999 (No. 182); and Chapter 3 of this book.

from 1994 to 2003.[9] The findings from this survey confirm the widespread persistence of all forms of violence against women, from domestic violence to societal violence, from sexual violence to violence on women workers.

Thus working women are at risk of violence from a number of sources. However, both migrant women and men may be at some risk because of their poor labour market bargaining power.

Protection of migrant workers and violence at work

The protection of migrant workers is the specific object of another UN instrument, the **International Convention on the Protection of the Rights of all Migrant Workers and Members of their Families**, adopted by the General Assembly in 1990. The Convention extends the protection of fundamental human rights to all migrant workers and their families, irrespective of whether they are legal or illegal residents of the host country. Legally resident migrants are ensured, in addition, equality of treatment with nationals of the host country in a number of legal, political, economic, social and cultural areas. In particular, Article 7 explicitly provides that non-discrimination with respect to rights shall exist "without any distinction of any kind, such as sex, race, colour, language, religion or conviction, political or other opinion, national, ethnic or social origin, nationality, age, economic position, property, marital status, birth or other status".

Article 16.2 of the Convention specifically grants to migrant workers and members of their families "effective protection by the State **against violence, physical injury, threats and intimidation**, whether by public officials or by private individuals, groups or institutions".

Since its adoption, this UN Convention has been ratified or acceded to by 21 States, most of them being nations which primarily send migrants abroad. It entered into force in July 2003.

Violence at work in the context of racial discrimination

A third UN instrument which is relevant to violence at work is the **International Convention on the Elimination of All Forms of Racial Discrimination**. Adopted in 1965, this Convention calls on States to condemn racial discrimination, to pursue by all appropriate means and without delay a policy of eliminating racial discrimination in all its forms, and to promote understanding among all races. The Convention prohibits, in particular, all forms of racial discrimination in respect of "the rights to work, to free choice of employment, **to just and favourable working conditions**, to protection against unemployment, to equal pay for equal work, to just and favourable remuneration".[10]

In addition to the UN bodies operating in the area of human rights, a number of UN agencies and other international bodies are becoming increasingly active in the fight against violence at work. Depending on the nature of the agency or body, violence at work is tackled as a labour, occupational health and safety, or criminal justice issue.

The ILO and protection against violence at work

Concerns expressed about violence at work, and calls for action voiced by public authorities, enterprises and workers, are now being transformed into specific initiatives. Guidelines have been issued by governments, trade unions, special study groups, workplace violence experts and employers' groups which address many aspects of the problem. A growing number of enterprises are also introducing violence prevention programmes which include participation by workers and their representatives in their development and implementation. Workplace violence is being targeted by laws and regulations with greater frequency, and new collective agreements are being signed by the social partners. As a result, the search for ways of ensuring a violence-free workplace is becoming a major policy issue and a concern for the ILO: "The primary goal of the ILO today is to promote opportunities for women and men to obtain decent and productive work, in conditions of freedom, equity, security and human dignity."[11]

This concern is part of the ILO's long-standing and continuing commitment, expressed through a series of fundamental Conventions, to worker protection, dignity at work, and safe and productive work environments. Particularly relevant to violence at work are the Freedom of Association and Protection of the Right to Organise Convention, 1948 (No. 87), the Abolition of Forced Labour Convention, 1956 (No. 105), the Discrimination (Employment and Occupation) Convention, 1958 (No.111), and the Conventions on the prohibition of child labour, notably the Worst Forms of Child Labour Convention, 1999 (No. 182).

Convention No.111 defines discrimination as "any distinction, exclusion or preference made on the basis of race, colour, sex, religion, political opinion, national extraction or social origin, which has the effect of nullifying or impairing equality of opportunity or treatment in employment or occupation".[12]

Action against sexual harassment

In examining ILO member States' reports on Convention No. 111 over the years, the ILO Committee of Experts on the Application of Conventions and Recommendations[13] has expressed its view that sexual harassment is a form of sex discrimination and should be addressed within the requirements of the Convention. The Committee noted that sexual harassment undermines equality at work by calling into question integrity, dignity and the well-being of workers. Sexual harassment also damages an enterprise by weakening the bases upon which work relationships are built and impairing productivity.[14]

In view of the gravity and serious repercussions of this practice the Committee, in its 2003 General Survey of Convention No. 111, "urged governments to take appropriate measures to prohibit sexual harassment in employment and occupation".[15] Over the years, the Committee has had the opportunity to review various national legislative and policy approaches, judicial decisions and collective agreements on this subject, which revealed similar approaches, definitions and procedures. Definitions contain the following key elements:

> (1) (*quid pro quo*): any physical, verbal or non-verbal conduct of a sexual nature and other conduct based on sex affecting the dignity of women and men, which is unwelcome, unreasonable, and offensive to the recipient; and a person's rejection of, or submission to, such conduct is used explicitly or implicitly as a basis for a decision which affects that person's job; or (2) (*hostile work environment*): conduct that creates an intimidating, hostile or humiliating working environment for the recipient.[16]

Action to combat violence against children in workplaces

The ILO, through promotion of its international labour standards and the projects of its International Programme on the Elimination of Child Labour (IPEC), is tackling child labour in all its forms worldwide. It pays attention to situations where violence is most likely to affect children: hazardous work, sexual exploitation and trafficking of children. All too often, children are found working, when and where they should not: at too young an age, for too long, in hazardous conditions. In those working situations they are exposed to and become victims of violence, aggravating the injustice done to them in the first place by denying them education.

The UN Secretary-General has appointed an Independent Expert, Paulo Sérgio Pinheiro, to lead a global study, "Violence against children". The study, rooted in children's human rights to protection from all forms of violence, aims to promote action to prevent and eliminate violence against children at international, regional, national and local levels. It is a UN-led collaboration, mandated by the General Assembly[17] to draw together existing research and relevant information about the forms, causes and impact of violence which affect children and young people (up to the age of 18 years). A major report will be published in 2006 and recommendations presented to the General Assembly.

The ILO, as a key partner in the study, is leading the process of distilling the key issues related to violence against working children. Children are frequent victims of maltreatment through physical and psychological violence or abuse by supervisors, co-workers and outsiders in places where they work – in factories, fields, mines, private homes and other settings. Such violence is always harmful to the child but also compounds the exploitative practices of child labour – one more reason why children should not be put to work in contravention of international labour standards. Because of their vulnerability, children are more likely to be subjected to violence and suffer grave, sometimes lifelong consequences. Adolescents who have reached the minimum working age but who may be inexperienced or insecure in their jobs are also more vulnerable to workplace violence than adult workers.

The study features a chapter on the 250 million child labourers, too many of whom are affected or threatened by different types of violence. It seeks to focus attention on this situation and calls for expanded networks to take action to withdraw children from such situations and get them into school instead; to prevent violence from occurring; and to engage the commitment and the know-how of all those who can help: governments, employers and trade unions, as well as community leadership.

Action against workplace stress

The ILO has been long involved in the area of **occupational stress**, which may be closely related to violence at work. Between 1995 and 1997 a series of five anti-stress manuals was produced to provide practical guidance on how the principles of risk auditing and stress prevention could be translated into practice in specific industry sectors.[18] More recently, the **Work Programme of the European Social Partners 2003–2005** initiated a "Stress at Work" seminar with the aim of subsequently negotiating a voluntary agreement.[19]

The work of the ILO in this area has shown that stress prevention makes much more sense from an economic and health point of view than a series of reactive treatments for afflicted individual workers. It has also been established that a cycle of stress auditing – identifying stress risk factors and then changing the workplace or work process to reduce the sources of stress, and auditing again to confirm that these were the right modifications, and so on – is the best approach to stress risk management.

The interrelationship between stress and workplace violence in the health sector

In 2003 the interrelationship between violence at work and occupational stress was the object of a special study within the context of a Joint Programme on Workplace Violence in the Health Sector by the ILO, the ICN, the WHO and

PSI. This programme was initiated to identify the risks, and then develop sound policies and practical approaches for minimizing violence in the health sector.

In practically all cases of workplace violence, including minor acts, distress is generated in the victims with long-lasting, deleterious effects on their health.[20] The study identified negative stress as one cause of violence. The more negative stress generated the greater the likelihood of violence, up to the most extreme forms such as burnout, suicide and homicide. The connection is not, however, an automatic one. The vast majority of people under severe negative stress – which happens to everyone at times – do not become perpetrators of violence. It is usually the combination of stress with a number of additional factors, such as alcohol abuse, that triggers violence at the workplace. That is, while the relationship whereby stress results in violence is usually mediated, the relationship between violence and stress is direct and straightforward.

As a result of the ILO/ICN/WHO/PSI joint programme, a series of issue papers and country case studies on workplace violence in the health sector, conducted in Brazil, Bulgaria, Lebanon, Portugal, South Africa, Thailand and Australia, were published in 2002.[21] In addition, a synthesis report, *Workplace violence in the health sector*, brought together the findings from the country-specific case studies.[22] Several thematic studies were also produced.[23] Another outcome from the joint programme was *Framework guidelines for addressing violence in the health sector*.[24]

The ILO/ICN/WHO/PSI collaborative programme identified that while workplace violence affects practically all industries and all categories of workers, the health sector is at major risk. As seen in Chapter 3, violence in this sector may constitute almost a quarter of all workplace violence events. Under the strain of reforms, growing assertiveness and demands from clients/ patients, increasing work productivity pressures and stress, social instability and the deterioration of personal interrelationships, workplace violence is rapidly spreading in this sector. Some of the country-specific case studies indicated that domestic and street violence were increasingly spilling over into health institutions. The negative consequences of such widespread violence impacted heavily on the delivery of health-care services, potentially leading to deterioration of the quality of care provided and the decision by some health workers to leave the health-care professions. Widespread resignations of health-care professionals can result in a reduction in health services available to the general population, and an increase in health costs. In developing countries particularly, equal access to primary health care is threatened if health workers, already a scarce resource, abandon their profession because of the threat of violence.

In response to these problems, the *Framework guidelines*[25] provide definitions of workplace violence, guidance on general rights and responsibilities, best approaches to managing the risk of workplace violence, risk assessment and recognition, workplace interventions, monitoring and evaluation.

A *Companion education and training kit for practitioners* to accompany the *Framework guidelines* is also in preparation. The companion kit is intended to be a practical, user-friendly tool which complements the policy approach of the guidelines and fosters social dialogue among interested parties. The two documents will create a package that will encourage proper dissemination and use of the guidelines. ILO constituents, as well as other actors in health services, will thus have easy access to the concepts and be provided with readily available risk management guidance.

The ILO code of practice on workplace violence

Further guidance was provided by a Meeting of Experts held in Geneva in October 2003 which led to the development and adoption of the 2004 ILO code of practice *Workplace violence in services sectors and measures to combat this phenomenon*.[26] Prior to the development of the code, in 2003 the ILO's Sectoral Activities Programme commissioned a series of working papers that examined the extent and severity of workplace violence in various service industry sectors, including the postal sector,[27] the performing arts and journalism,[28] the transport sector,[29] the services sector (with implications for the education sector),[30] financial services,[31] and hotels, catering and tourism.[32]

These working papers showed that violence at work affects millions of workers in the services industry sectors around the world, and has become a threat to quality of service, productivity and decent work in a variety of industries. The harmful impact of workplace violence is felt in both industrialized and developing countries, across a far-reaching range of occupations and work settings, and in the public and private sectors. Violence can impair the quality of services provided, disrupt efficient and effective workplaces, blight interpersonal relationships and trust among colleagues, and make the workplace bleak, unwelcoming and sometimes dangerous. It was reported that in the services industry sectors, the problem of workplace violence may be greater than in primary or secondary industries, because of the direct contact between workers and their customers or the general public.

The ILO code of practice on workplace violence in services sectors focuses on the prevention of workplace violence and mitigation of its direct adverse consequences, including stress repercussions. The primary emphasis for governments, employers, workers and their representatives in dealing with the hazard of workplace violence is to pursue a proactive preventive approach taking into consideration the occupational safety and health management systems approach. Guiding principles detailed in the code of practice include:

- A healthy and safe work environment, in accordance with the provisions of the Occupational Safety and Health Convention, 1981 (No. 155), facilitates optimal physical and mental health in relation to work, and can help to prevent workplace violence.

- Social dialogue between employers, workers and their representatives, and with government, where appropriate, is a key element in the successful implementation of anti-violence policies and programmes. Such dialogue is enshrined in the ILO Declaration on Fundamental Principles and Rights at Work and its Follow-up, 1998.

- Policy or action against workplace violence should also be directed at promoting decent work and mutual respect, and combating discrimination at the workplace, in accordance with the Discrimination (Employment and Occupation) Convention, 1958 (No. 111).

- Promoting gender equality could help to reduce workplace violence.[33]

The ILO code of practice identifies the policies and strategies required for an effective fight against violence at work, together with the roles and responsibilities of governments, employers' and workers' organizations, and the public, customers and clients. Guidance is also provided on training, communication and information provision, and recording and notification of violent events, as well as on the planning and implementation of interventions. The code lays the foundations for risk assessment through the processes of risk identification, recognition of warning signs, assessment, implementation of prevention strategies, reduction of incidence, and management and coping strategies to address these problems. It concludes by emphasizing the monitoring and review of workplace violence prevention policies and of organizational learning on issues related to violence.

The code is intended to serve as a basic reference tool for stimulating the development of similar instruments at the regional, national, industry sector, enterprise, organization and workplace levels, and to be specifically targeted at and adapted to different cultures, situations and needs. Although it is focused specifically at the services industry sectors, many of the suggestions contained in it could also be applied, with appropriate modifications, to manufacturing and other industries.

Initiatives on multiple hazards linked with workplace violence

Intensive action has also been undertaken by the ILO at the interface between violence, stress, tobacco, drug and alcohol abuse, and HIV/AIDS, which are closely linked. In 2002 a specific response was provided by the ILO with a new training package – known as SOLVE (Stress, Tobacco, Alcohol and drugs, HIV/AIDS and Violence: Addressing Psychological Problems at work).[34] SOLVE is designed to offer an integrated workplace response to these interlinked problems that often manifest themselves together at a worksite. The package also introduces an innovative approach whereby workers' health, safety and well-being become integral parts of the economic sustainability and organizational development of enterprises. By directly linking health and safety issues with managerial and developmental issues, the project offers the tools for immediate, self-sustained policy and action at the workplace to reduce and eliminate the above problems.

Within the general framework of SOLVE, three practical tools produced in 2002 were targeted at recognizing, dealing with and preventing sexual harassment at the workplace.[35] Finally, in 2003 an issue of *Labour Education*, the periodical of the ILO Bureau for Workers' Activities, was entirely devoted to violence at work.[36] Other UN agencies have also been active in minimizing workplace violence.

The World Health Organization and protection against violence at work

In 1996 the WHO, at its 49th World Health Assembly, adopted a resolution which recognized the serious immediate and long-term implications of violence on the health, psychological and social development of individuals, families, communities and countries. This resolution declared violence to be a leading worldwide public health problem.[37] As requested in the resolution, a plan of action for progress towards a science-based public health approach to violence prevention was presented to, and approved by, the WHO Executive Board in January 1997. The plan highlighted the dramatic dimensions and consequences of violence, including violence at work, and indicated priorities and means of action to deal with the problem (box 82).

Box 82   WHO plan of action against violence (excerpts)

Introduction

1.   The burden of ill-health caused by violence is staggering. Violence undermines the social and economic conditions of communities. The atmosphere generated by frequent and severe personal or organized violence discourages investment, destabilizes national labour and industry, discourages tourism, and contributes to the emigration of skilled citizens. Violence in the home, on the street, and in the classroom disrupts education and the provision of basic services; it inhibits the delivery of curative and preventive health care. As an expression of power, it increases gender-based and social inequity. For various reasons the attitude of the health sector to violence has been until now ambivalent, insufficiently committed to

preventing it and resorting to ad hoc solutions. Without a new public health vision to tackle the growing problem of violence, the cost to society can only increase.

2.   While there is no universally accepted typology of violence, the groupings commonly used are:

- Self-inflicted violence, for which suicide represents the fatal outcome. Other types include attempts to commit suicide and non-lethal self-mutilation.

- Interpersonal violence occurs in many forms and can best be classified by the victim-offender relationship: domestic violence (family and intimate partners), violence among acquaintances, and violence involving strangers. It may also be specified according to the age or sex of the victim (child abuse, or rape). Social institutions may be the setting for violence: bullying, harassment or criminally linked violence may be found in schools, the workplace, the commercial sector, and the military.

- Organized violence is violent behaviour of social or political groups motivated by specific political, economic or social objectives. Racial or religious conflicts are other forms of violence occurring among groups. Armed conflict and war are the extreme form of organized violence.

[...]

5.   The consequences of violence extend far beyond physical injury: violence has profound psychological implications for its victims, perpetrators and witnesses, as well as close sur-viving relations and friends. For others, such as women and children who live under the daily threat of violence from partners or parents, the quality of life is drastically affected.

The WHO integrated plan of action on violence and health

6.   This plan is the first step in consolidating the activities of several WHO programmes con-cerning violence, and in building a coherent WHO public health approach to violence and health. During the first three years, the first objective and the highest priority will be better to define the problem.

Objective 1. To describe the problem (first priority) [...]

Objective 2. To understand the problem: conduct risk-factor identification and research: to promote research and increase information on determinants and consequences of violence through all appropriate technical programmes of the Organization. [...]

Objective 3. Identification and evaluation of interventions: to determine measures and programmes aimed at preventing violence and mitigating its effects, and to assess their effectiveness. [...]

Objective 4. Programme implementation and dissemination: to strengthen the capacity, primarily of the health system but also of all concerned parties on the basis of the evaluation of existing activities, in order to implement coherent programmes.

Source: WHO, Executive Board, 1997, pp. 1–4.

In 2002, the WHO launched the first *World Report on Violence and Health*.[38] The report is directed at raising awareness about the problem of violence globally and making the case that violence is preventable. Following the launch of the *World Report*, a Global Campaign for Violence Prevention was launched. The objectives of the Campaign are to raise awareness about the problem of violence, highlight the crucial role that public health can play in addressing its causes and consequences, and encourage action at every level of society. The Campaign serves as the main platform for implementing the recommendations of the *World Report*.

An array of other activities is being conducted in the context of the Global Campaign. More than 30 governments have organized national launches or policy discussions of the *World Report*. Resolutions endorsing the report and calling for its implementation have been passed in a number of policy fora such as the World Health Assembly, the Commission on Human Rights, the African Union, and so on.[39]

Action against workplace violence by other United Nations agencies

To obtain more direct and up-to-date information about current internal policies, practices and actions regarding violence at work among international agencies, a small survey was conducted by the ILO on this subject.[40] A short questionnaire was distributed in December 2003 to the main organizations within the UN system. Thirteen of these bodies, listed in box 83, responded to the questionnaire, including several employing large numbers of international civil servants.

Box 83   Violence at work: Organizations responding to the ILO survey

Economic Commission for Latin America and the Caribbean

Economic and Social Commission for Western Asia

Food and Agriculture Organization

International Maritime Organization

International Monetary Fund

United Nations Educational, Scientific and Cultural Organization

United Nations Industrial Development Organization

United Nations Office at Vienna/United Nations Office on Drug and Crime

United Nations University

World Food Programme

World Intellectual Property Organization

World Meteorological Organization

World Trade Organization

The questionnaire included the following questions:

Question 1:   Is violence at work a concern in your Organization?

Question 2:   If "yes" under which form? ❏ physical attacks; ❏ sexual harassment; ❏ bullying/mobbing; ❏ verbal aggression; ❏ threats; ❏ other?

Question 3:   Do you have any of the following anti-violence initiatives? (planned or implemented) ❏ policies; ❏ employees' assistance programmes; ❏ codes of practice; ❏ guidelines?

Question 4:   Do you have any statistics available on the extent of violence at work in your Organization?

The results of this survey, conducted among organizations within the United Nations System, are summarized in figures 27–29. Figure 27 shows responses to the question "Is violence at work a concern in your organization?"

As seen in figure 27, violence at work was of concern to almost half (45 per cent) of the responding organizations, although to different degrees

Figure 27   ILO survey on workplace violence: Response to question "Is violence at work a concern in your organization?"

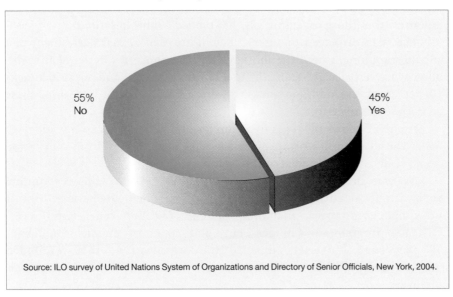

55%
No

45%
Yes

Source: ILO survey of United Nations System of Organizations and Directory of Senior Officials, New York, 2004.

Figure 28   ILO survey on workplace violence: Response to question "Type of concern"

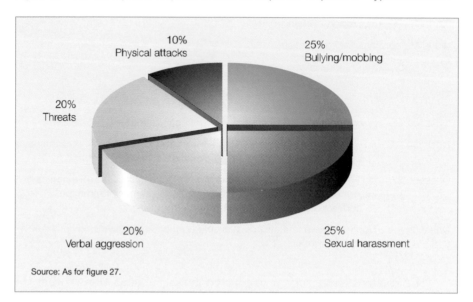

Source: As for figure 27.

between organizations and even within the same organization, depending on the type of violence and the geographical location of the workplace.

In figure 28, the particular type of workplace violence causing concern is separated into five distinct categories: bullying/mobbing, sexual harassment, verbal aggression, threats and physical attacks. Readers should note that this distribution between different forms of workplace violence is based on responses from those organizations that replied to this question.

The data displayed in figure 28 indicate that sexual harassment and bullying/mobbing caused the most widespread concern (25 per cent each), followed by verbal aggression/threats (20 per cent each) and physical attacks (10 per cent). As multiple answers were allowed to this question, these categories may overlap.

Figure 29 shows the types of action taken by the organizations surveyed. Again, the distribution of action taken reflects responses from only those organizations that responded to this question.

As can be seen from figure 29, almost all of the responding organizations stated that they had planned or implemented some form of anti-violence initiative, including policies (39 per cent), employees' assistance programmes (26 per cent) and codes of practices/guidelines (35 per cent). However, none of the organizations that responded had statistics available on the extent of violence at work among their employees.

Figure 29   ILO survey on workplace violence: Response to question "Action taken"

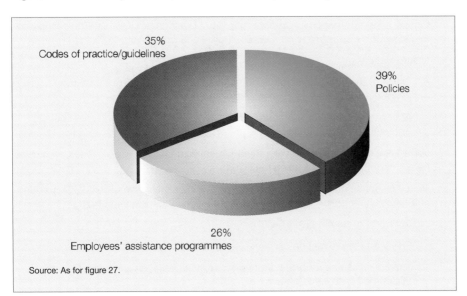

35%
Codes of practice/guidelines

39%
Policies

26%
Employees' assistance programmes

Source: As for figure 27.

Overall, evidence suggests that action in the area of workplace violence has greatly increased in recent years. Most international agencies and organizations are now equipped with instruments which give special consideration to the new forms of violence at work. Box 84 provides a selection of these.

Box 84   Combating violence within international organizations: Specific new action

- Asian Development Bank (ADB): *Prevention of sexual harassment, A guide to staff.*

- European Commission: *Memorandum by Mr. Kinnock to the Commission on Psychological Harassment Policy at the European Commission*, Oct. 2003.

- Food and Agriculture Organization of the United Nations (FAO): *Policy on prevention of harassment*, administrative circular No. 2003/17 of 26 June 2003.

- International Labour Organization (ILO): *Collective agreement on conflict prevention and resolution between the International Labour Office and the ILO Staff Union, 2004*, circulars 6/648 and 649.

- International Maritime Organisation: *Right to work in a harassment free environment*, Interoffice memorandum, 14 May 2003.

- International Monetary Fund (IMF)

  – *Code of conduct*, 1998 (to be revised)

  – *Discrimination Policy*, 2003.

/cont'd

/cont'd

- Organisation for Economic Co-operation and Development (OECD): *Preventing and dealing with harassment at the OECD – Policy and guidelines*, C (2002)141.

- United Nations

  - Office of the Ombudsman – appointment and terms of reference of the Ombudsman, Secretary-General's Bulletin, 15 Oct. 2002.

  - Special measures for protection from sexual exploitation and sexual abuse, Secretariat, 9 Oct. 2003.

- United Nations Industrial Development Organization (UNIDO): *Guidelines on sexual harassment* (available but being reviewed.)

- United Nations Educational, Scientific and Cultural Organization (UNESCO): Existing anti-harassment policy is currently being redesigned to include mobbing.

- World Food Programme (WFP)

  - *Policy on the prevention of harassment*, HR99/002, 19 Feb. 1999.

  - *Special measures for protection from sexual exploitation and sexual abuse*, ED2004/001, 22 Jan. 2004.

- World Intellectual Property Organization (WIPO): *Harassment at work*. The Office of the Mediator, Office instruction No. 20/2003.

- World Meteorological Organisation (WMO): *Prevention and resolution of harassment*, Service Note No. 26/2003.

- World Trade Organization (WTO): *Procedures for dealing with staff members' complaints and grievances*, Administrative memorandum No. 941, 2002.

Thus, a range of UN agencies have initiated action to reduce the risk of workplace violence in recent years. Many countries are also now equipped with regulatory instruments (as discussed earlier). The EU has promulgated some of the most influential instruments to protect the health and safety of workers, including from workplace violence.

Action against workplace violence by the European Union

The issue of violence at work has long been on the agenda of the EU, with occupational health and safety mentioned in the Treaty of Rome of 1957.

EU Framework Directive 89/391/EEC

On 12 July 1989, the EU Framework Directive 89/391/EEC on the Introduction of Measures to Encourage Improvements in the Safety and

Health of Workers at Work comprehensively expressed a commitment to occupational safety and health (OSH). The Directive emphasized a framework of duties for employers to improve OSH performance, provided for participative rights for workers, and allowed for flexibility to reduce risks in rapidly changing work environments.[41] Article 6 of the Directive, reproduced in box 85, is often referred to as a provision that can be directly applied to cases of workplace violence.

Box 85 European Directive on the Safety and Health of Workers at Work, 1989: General Obligations on Employers

1. Within the context of his responsibilities, the employer shall take the measures necessary for the safety and health protection of workers, including prevention of occupational risks and provision of information and training, as well as provision of the necessary organization and means. The employer shall be alert to the need to adjust these measures to take account of changing circumstances and aim to improve existing situations,

2. The employer shall implement the measures referred to [above] ... on the basis of the following general principles of prevention:

    (a) avoiding risks;

    (b) evaluating the risks which cannot be avoided;

    (c) combating the risks at source;

    (d) adapting the work to the individual, especially as regards the design of work places, the choice of work equipment and the choice of working and production methods, with a view, in particular, to alleviating monotonous work and work at a predetermined work-rate, and to reducing their effect on health;

    (e) adapting to technical progress;

    (f) replacing the dangerous by the non-dangerous or the less dangerous;

    (g) developing a coherent overall prevention policy which covers technology, organization of work, working conditions, social relationships and the influence of factors related to the working environment;

    (h) giving collective protective measures priority over individual protective measures;

    (i) giving appropriate instructions to the workers.

3. [...] The employer shall, taking into account the nature of the activities of the enterprise and/or establishment:

    (a) evaluate the risks to the safety and health of workers, inter alia in the choice of work equipment, the chemical substances of preparations used, and the fitting-out of work places.

/cont'd

/cont'd

Subsequent to this evaluation and as necessary, the preventive measures and the working and production methods implemented by the employer must:

- assure an improvement in the level of protection afforded to workers with regard to safety and health;

- be integrated into all the activities of the undertaking and/or establishment and at all hierarchical levels;

(b) where he entrusts tasks to a worker, take into consideration the worker's capabilities as regards health and safety;

(c) ensure that the planning and introduction of new technologies are the subject of consultation with the workers and/or their representatives, as regards the consequences of the choice of equipment, the working conditions and the working environment for the safety and health of workers;

(d) take appropriate steps to ensure that only workers who have receive adequate instructions may have access to areas where there is serious and specific danger.

Source: European Parliament, 1989.

Directive 89/391/EEC has been of enormous importance for improvement of the regulatory framework for OSH. The EU has also commissioned many other reports and initiatives.

Other EU initiatives to combat workplace violence

In 1997, the European Commission issued a document entitled *Guidance on the prevention of violence at work* (first published in 1996). This publication includes a review of the scientific literature in this area, a survey to identify the prevalence of violence at work as well as existing guidelines, and draft guidance plans for implementation at the level of the EU. The survey findings remain relevant generally and are summarized in box 86.

Box 86   Survey on violence at work in the EU

The findings from the questionnaire suggested the following situation:

- There is a considerable difference in awareness of the issue of violence in the context of health and safety between countries.

- The legislative position, with the exception of the Netherlands, is that violence at work is generally covered by both framework type health and safety legislation and by the civil and criminal codes.

- Research into the issue of violence appears to be a relatively recent phenomenon where it occurs. Research seems to be concentrated in the more developed countries in Europe.

- The implementation of legislation was generally reported to take place, both within the general implementation of the requirements of health and safety legislation, and to some extent, using the criminal and civil codes.

- Significant barriers to the implementation in many countries include lack of awareness, difficulties in implementing legislation in SMEs, and limited resources for enforcement of legislation.

The overall impression from the data supplied by the respondents to the survey is that there is limited awareness of the issue of violence at work in many countries, but that legislative provisions appear to exist in general terms and are generally implemented. However, there are grounds for questioning this impression.

Firstly, a major finding from reviewing the literature is that the extent of the problem is usually underestimated. In the absence of specific and comprehensive research on the prevalence and extent of workplace violence, it is difficult to believe that the problem is being adequately dealt with.

Secondly, the existence of guidelines to deal with violence is not uniform across the EU. In their absence, it is unlikely that consistent and comprehensive management of the issue actually takes place.

Thirdly, the situation with regard to the implementation of legislation must be questioned. While the respondents to the survey generally reported good levels of implementation, the precise nature of implementation is, at best, unclear. While there is no doubt that the appropriate agencies dealing with health and safety carry out their duties with regard to the range of health and safety issues, they do so only in the context of the resources provided to them. In practice, this often means that they have limited resources available to them for enforcement, and that SMEs in particular tend not to be subject to high levels of enforcement. Furthermore, in the context of limited awareness of the problem, the extent of actual management activity within enterprises must be questioned.

For these reasons, it is likely that the operation of legislation in the area is somewhat less than optimal.

A final issue of concern is that despite the apparently positive situation in many countries, some countries reported low levels of concern and activity with regard to violence at work. Without wishing to single out specific countries, it is evident both by some of the comments made, and by the absence of response from some countries, that there is considerable room for improvement in the management of this issue at all levels.

Source: Wynne et al., 1997, pp. 28–29.

In providing further guidance to combat violence at work, the document stresses the need for organizations to address the following issues:

- a definition of violence and abuse;

- recording procedures for violent incidents;

- analysis of data on violent incidents;

- the need for a balanced approach involving preventive, protective, treatment and security measures;

- the need for sensitive and early treatment of victims of violence;

- the need to facilitate organizational learning about the issues of violence.[42]

This review also stressed the need for a risk assessment cycle, as shown in table 24.

In recent years, EU action in this area has further intensified, with important new initiatives in the field. Violence at work is now a topical and priority issue.

Table 24   Risk assessment cycle

Phase of the cycle	Activities
1. Assess the scope of the problem	– Find out if there is a problem – Accept the existence of the problem – Define violence
2. Assess the problem	– Develop, implement and improve recording systems – Identify hazards – Identify risks – Analyse and classify all events
3. Design interventions	– Identify potential interventions (preventive, protective, treatment, security, training) – Select interventions collaboratively – Develop company policy
4. Implement interventions	– Implement measures in a visible way
5. Monitor interventions	– Monitor the interventions including process, uptake and outcomes – Modify interventions on the basis of evaluation data – Publicize findings from the monitoring activity

Source: Wynne et al., 1997, p. 44.

EU Directives on harassment and sexual harassment

Article 13 of the Treaty of Rome 1957, amended in 1999 by the Treaty of Amsterdam, enables the Council to take appropriate action to combat discrimination based on sex, racial or ethnic origin, religion or belief, disability, age or sexual orientation. Two directives have been adopted, one in 2000 and another in 2002, addressing harassment and sexual harassment, respectively:

• Council Directive 2000/43/EC of June 2000 implements the principle of equal treatment between persons irrespective of racial or ethnic origin;[43] and

• Council Directive 2002/73/EC of September 2002 amending Council Directive 76/207/EEC, implements the principle of equal treatment for men and women as regards access to employment, vocational training and promotion, and working conditions.[44]

These directives include new definitions of racial and sexual harassment applicable across Europe; provide directions on the effective enforcement of the law and sanctions; and make clear the responsibility of EU Member States to designate a body or bodies to promote the work of the directives.

While the first directive applies to all situations of racial harassment, the second refers specifically to sexual harassment at work. Directive 2002/73/EC introduced the concepts of harassment related to sex and sexual harassment, stating that they are forms of discrimination in violation of the equal treatment principle. This is an area where the EU bodies have concentrated their efforts for many years. As long ago as 1992, a code of practice on *Measures to combat sexual harassment* was issued by the European Commission. In 2001, the European Parliament stressed the need for interventions tackling harassment in the workplace, particularly bullying and sexual harassment, to be made a priority:

> Calls on the Member States, with a view to counteracting bullying and sexual harassment at work, to review and, if appropriate, to supplement their existing legislation and to review and standardise the definition of bullying ...

> Urges the Commission to consider a clarification or extension of the scope of the framework directive on health and safety at work or, alternatively, the drafting of a new framework directive as a legal instrument to combat bullying and as a means of ensuring respect for the worker's human dignity, privacy and integrity; emphasises in this connection the importance of systematic work on health and safety and of preventive action;[45]

Currently, only a few countries within the EU have specific sexual harassment laws, while in the majority of countries protection is granted under equal employment opportunity laws as well as labour, tort and criminal laws.

Extensive jurisprudence and the provisions of collective agreements supplement these.

The above-mentioned directives are only the beginning of more intense legislative intervention. Various EU bodies have reiterated the need for further action in the area of workplace violence, including regulatory action.

In its Communication "Adapting to change in work and society: A new Community strategy on health and safety 2002–2006", the Commission stressed the need to adapt the legal framework to cover the emerging psycho-social risks:

> The increase in psycho-social problems and illnesses is posing a new challenge to health and safety at work and is compromising moves to improve well-being at work. The various forms of psychological harassment and violence at work likewise pose a special problem nowadays, requiring legislative action. Any such action will be able to build on the acquis of recently adopted directives rooted in Article 13 of the EC Treaty, which defines what is meant by harassment, and make provision for redress ... The Commission will examine the appropriateness and the scope of a Community instrument on psychological harassment and violence at work.[46]

Along similar lines, the European Commission's Advisory Committee on Safety, Hygiene and Health Protection at Work calls for the issuing by the Commission of guidelines in this area:

> The Commission should therefore draft guidelines based on the definition of the phenomenon in all its various forms and on its inclusion among the risk factors that employers are obliged to assess under the terms of the Framework Directive. A model for the assessment of the specific risk as part of the overall assessment would therefore be useful.[47]

The Commission's action has been complemented by that of the EU specialized agency competent in this area.

Other European agencies

In 2001 the European Foundation for the Improvement of Living and Working Conditions, Dublin, published the results of its Third Survey on Working Conditions in Europe. The results confirmed the amplitude and complexity of the problem of workplace violence.[48] In 2003 the Foundation issued a report on violence and harassment in the workplace.[49] The report identifies the different forms and patterns of violence and harassment in the workplace in the EU and describes the recent upsurge in activity and initiatives with respect to violence and harassment within the legal arena, with new legislation addressing these problems enacted or in the pipeline in a number of countries. The European Foundation reports also present evidence of adverse effects on individuals, organizations and society, and assess the potential financial costs. Finally, the reports analyse the factors that may contribute to, and cause, physical and psychological violence, and review a variety of good practice prevention and management strategies for violence and harassment at work.

In 2005 the European Foundation published a report on evidence of work-related stress, based on the 2000 European Working Conditions survey.[50] This study identified that workers are reporting an increasing level of work-related stress – which is now the second most common occupational safety and health problem across the EU. This report identifies differences between the EU Member States, provides evidence on the probable causes of work-related stress, describes an evaluation of preventive interventions, and gives examples of best practices.

In 2002 the European Agency for Safety and Health at Work devoted its "European Week" to stress and other psycho-social risks, including violence and bullying at work. Box 87 provides an overview of EU initiatives relevant to workplace violence.

Box 87   EU action on violence at work, 2000–04

Communication from the Commission: "Adapting to change in work and society: a new Community strategy on health and safety at work 2002-2006", Brussels, 11 Mar. 2002, COM (2002) 118 final.
(See:http://www.europa.eu.int/comm/employment_social/news2002/mar/new_strategy _en.pdf, accessed 6 Dec. 2005.)

"Council Directive 2000/43/EC of 29 June 2000 implementing the principle of equal treatment between persons irrespective of racial or ethnic origin", in *Official Journal of the European Communities*, No. L180, 19 July 2000, pp. 22–26.
(See: http://www.europa.eu.int/infonet/library/m/200043ce/en.htm, accessed 6 Dec. 2005.)

"Council Directive 2000/78/EC of 27 November 2000 establishing a general framework for equal treatment in employment and occupation", in *Official Journal of the European Communities*, No. L303/16, 2 Dec. 2000, pp. 16–22.
(See: http://www.europa.eu.int/comm/employment_social/news2001/jul/dir200078_en.html, accessed 6 Dec. 2005.)

"Council Resolution of 3 June 2002 on a new Community strategy on health and safety at work (2002-2006)", in *Official Journal of the European Communities*, No. C.161/1, 5 July 2002, pp. 1–4.
(See: http://europa.eu.int/eur-lex/pri/en/oj/dat/2002/c_161/c_16120020705en00010004.pdf, accessed 22 Sept. 2005.)

/cont'd

/cont'd

"Directive 2002/73/EC of the European Parliament and of the Council of 23 September 2002 amending Council Directive 76/207/EEC on the implementation of the principle of equal treatment for men and women as regards access to employment, vocational training and promotion, and working conditions", in *Official Journal of the European Communities*, No. L269, 5 Oct. 2002, pp. 15–20.
(See: http://www.ei-ie.org/payequity/EN/docs/EU%20Documents/2002%2073. pdf, accessed 6 Dec. 2005.)

European Parliament, Directorate General for Research: *Bullying at work*, Social Affairs Series SOCI 108 EN, working paper, Luxembourg, August 2001.
(See: http://www4.europarl.eu.int/workingpapers/soci/pdf/108_en.pdf, accessed 22 Sept. 2005.)

European Parliament: "Resolution on harassment at the workplace" (2001/2339(INI)), A5-0283/2001, session doc.
(See: http://www3.europarl.eu.int/omk/omnsapir.so/pv2?PRG =TITRE&APP=PV2& LANGUE=EN&TYPEF=TITRE&YEAR=01&Find=harassment&FILE=BIBLIO&PLAGE=1, accessed 22 Sept. 2005.)

European Parliament: *Work Programme of the European Social Partners 2003–2005*, Brussels, 28 Nov. 2003, including "Stress at Work: seminar in view to negotiate a voluntary agreement", p. 2.
(See: http://europa.eu.int/comm/employment_social/news/2002/dec/prog_de_travail_comm_en.pdf, accessed 22 Sept. 2005.)

"Report on harassment at the workplace (2001/2339(INI))", Committee on Employment and Social Affairs, Rapporteur: Jan Andersson, 16 July 2001. FINAL A5-0283/2001.
(See: http://www.europa.eu.int/eur_lex/accessible/en/archive/2002/ce07720020328en.html, accessed 6 Dec. 2005.)

Spanish Presidency: "Good practice guide to mitigate the effects and eradicate violence against women", Instituto de la Mujer and Complutense University of Madrid, Brussels, 2002.

The evidence presented in this chapter shows that international agencies have initiated numerous policy documents and strategies over the past decade to counteract workplace violence. Nevertheless, much work remains to be done to reduce the exposure of workers to this increasingly common workplace threat. The following – and final – chapter draws together the evidence and discussions presented throughout this book.

Notes

1 Article 2.

2 Article 3.

3 Article 5.

4 Article 7(b).

5 United Nations, 1992, pp. 1–6.

6 United Nations, 1993a, Article 1.

7 Ibid., Article 2.

8 United Nations, Division for the Advancement of Women, 2000.

9 United Nations, Commission on Human Rights, 2003.

10 Article 5(e)i.

11 ILO, 1999b, p. 3.

12 Article 1, 1(a).

13 ILO, 2003a, p. 463. For updated information on ILO action in the areas of sexual harassment see McCann, 2005.

14 Haspels et al., 2001. See also: ILO, 2001a, 2001b; and Reinhart, ILO, 1999.

15 ILO, 2003a, p. 463.

16 Ibid.

17 United Nations, General Assembly Resolution A/RES/57/190, adopted December 2002.

18 ILO: *Occupational stress and stress prevention in air traffic control*, CONDI/T/WP.6/1995; *Stress prevention in the offshore oil and gas exploration and production industry*, CONDI/T/WP.1/1996; *Bus drivers: Occupational stress and stress prevention*, CONDI/T/WP.2/1996; *Work-related stress in nursing: Controlling the risk to health*, CONDI/T/WP.4/1996; *Stress prevention for blue-collar workers in assembly-line production*, CONDI/T/WP.1/1997 (all published in Geneva, 1995–97).

19 ETUC/UNICE/UEAPME/CEEP, 2002, p. 2.

20 Di Martino, 2003a.

21 Lebanon: Deeb, 2002; Portugal: Ferrinho et al., 2002; Brazil: Palácios et al., 2002; Thailand: Sripichyakan et al., 2002; South Africa: Steinman, 2002; Bulgaria: Tomev et al., 2002; and extracts from an Australian case study were also included: Mayhew and Chappell, 2002.

22 Di Martino, 2002b.

23 Cooper and Swanson, 2002; Richards 2002; Wiskow 2002.

24 ILO/ICN/WHO/PSI, 2002.

25 Ibid.

26 ILO, 2004b.

27 Giga, Hoel and Cooper, 2003b.

28 Idem, 2003a.

29 Essenberg, 2003.

30 Verdugo and Vere, 2003.

31 Giga and Hoel, 2003.

32 Hoel and Einarsen, 2001.

33 ILO, 2004b, pp. 6–7.

34 See Di Martino, Gold and Schaap, 2002b.

35 Idem, 2002a.

36 ILO, Bureau for Workers' Activities, 2003b.

37 WHO, 1996.

38 Idem, 2002b.

39 Ibid.

40 United Nations, 2003.

41 A detailed evaluation of the impact of Framework Directive 89/391/EEC in different European Member States can be found in Walters, 2002.

42 Wynne et al., 1997, p. 43.

[43] European Parliament, 2000a, Article 2(3).

[44] Ibid., 2002a, para. 10.

[45] Ibid., 2001b, para. x.

[46] European Commission, 2002, 118 final, 3.3.1, paras. 2 and 4, pp. 12–13.

[47] European Commission, Advisory Committee on Safety, Hygiene and Health Protection at Work, 2001, doc. 1564/2/01.

[48] European Foundation for the Improvement of Living and Working Conditions, 2001.

[49] Di Martino, Hoel and Cooper, 2003. (See summary at www.eurofound.ie/publications/ef0330.htm, accessed 11 Oct. 2005.)

[50] European Foundation for the Improvement of Living and Working Conditions, 2005.

PART III

FUTURE ACTION

BEYOND VIOLENCE: LESSONS

9

Traditionally, the workplace has been viewed as a quite benign environment where, despite certain levels of robust confrontation and dialogue, people usually manage to resolve their dilemmas in a peaceful and constructive way. Forward-looking employers recognize that the health and well-being of their enterprise are consistent with, if not dependent upon, the health and well-being of their employees. Further, a healthy and happy workforce is generally assumed to be more productive. Thus employer investment in the identification and control of the risk factors for workplace violence can be profitable.[1]

From a hidden to a disclosed issue

Despite employers' recognition of the negative consequences of violent events in the workplace, and the increasing endorsement by them of a zero tolerance policy towards violence, unwanted and unwarranted aggression can and does emerge in workplaces which may transform sites into hostile and hazardous settings. The intrusion of gross acts of violence into a workplace is most obvious in the cases of terrorism directed at worksites, as described in Chapter 1 of this book. However, most violent events do not involve multiple victims or attract media attention. Nevertheless, workplace violence is an issue around the world.

This book has described the mounting evidence from around the globe which suggests that violence at work is now an issue transcending the boundaries of a particular country, work setting or occupational group. No country, worksite or industry sector can realistically claim to be entirely free of workplace violence, although some nations, like some workplaces and occupations, are undoubtedly at higher risk than others.[2]

Exposure to the hazard of workplace violence is not homogeneous across all jobs. Those job tasks that require frequent contact with clients, customers and members of the public are at higher risk: protective services (police, etc.), but also those employed in health care and education. Another risk factor for workplace violence is the presence of cash or valuable goods on a site. Easy access to these goods may increase the risk of "external" or instrumental workplace violence from desperate perpetrators. The incidence and severity rates of workplace violence also vary across countries as labour market conditions and risk factors vary, such as variable access to firearms.

It is increasingly recognized that violence at work is not limited to a specified workplace, like an office, factory or retail establishment. Workplace violence may also occur during commuting, and in non-traditional workplaces such as home-based offices, satellite centres and mobile locations, which are being used increasingly as a result of the spread of new information technologies and new forms of work organization. The overlap between domestic violence and workplace violence is also becoming apparent.

The damaging impact of repeated acts of psychological aggression

The evidence also shows that a new profile of violence at work is emerging, which gives equal emphasis to physical and psychological aggression. The available data indicate that the cumulation of repeated negative and inappropriate interpersonal interactions can have a very serious impact on victims. Thus, aggressive behaviours that on a "one-off" basis may appear to be relatively minor can have a very serious cumulative effect.[3] These behaviours may include sustained verbal abuse, sexual harassment, bullying and/or mobbing.

The increased recognition of the importance of psychological violence has been accompanied by a decline in attention to physical assaults. This change in focus may reflect a change in the incidence patterns of different types of violence over recent years in several countries.

However, statistics presented in Chapter 2 of this book showed the persistence of physical violence in both the developing and the industrialized world. Thus reduced attention to physical violence appears premature and full recognition should still be given to all forms of workplace violence.

The gender dimension of violence at work

Both men and women are victims of violence at work. However, gender-based patterns of exposure to the hazard of workplace violence are significantly influenced by the sexual division of labour: men are concentrated in some types of jobs and women in others. For example, male workers may be disproportionately concentrated among those working evening shifts in small retail outlets, and may therefore be more frequently subjected to hold-up related violence. Conversely, women may be disproportionately concentrated among health-care workers exposed to aggression from clients/patients.[4]

As a result of this gendered difference in labour market exposure to the hazard of workplace violence, there are real differences between the incidence rates for male and female workers.[5] Where male and female workers do the same job tasks under similar conditions these variations are minimal, although men appear to experience slightly higher levels of physical violence and women are marginally more frequently victimized through verbal abuse and sexual assaults. These gender-based variations in levels of exposure to risk are also apparent across countries. Additional explanations for gender-based differences include that men may be more likely to meet aggression with aggression, while women may be better at defusing, coping with and avoiding aggressive incidents.

The global impact of violence on women, both inside and outside the workplace, is dramatic. Women are concentrated in many of the higher-risk occupations, particularly as teachers, social workers, nurses and health-care workers, as well as bank and shop workers.[6] It has also been shown that women are more vulnerable to violence from co-workers, due to their inferior position in the labour market with concomitant reduced bargaining power. The continued segregation of women in low-paid and low-status jobs, while men predominate in better-paid, higher-status jobs and supervisory positions, contributes to gender-based differences in exposure to particular forms of workplace violence, such as bullying.[7] It is, however, important to consider that, while women may experience increased levels of victimization, this fact does not justify a generalized statement such as "all men are perpetrators, all women are victims". In fact, although often to a lesser extent, women are also perpetrators.

The special impact of violence on vulnerable workers

Another common finding is that younger workers are more vulnerable to violence than more experienced staff members. There are a range of contributing factors, including relative inexperience in dealing with potentially violent situations, concentration in job tasks with greater exposure to members of the public, increased vulnerability to bullying and initiation rites perpetrated by more senior employees, diminished knowledge and awareness of employee rights, and a reduced willingness to speak out about inappropriate behaviours.[8] For example, previous experience with aggressive clients may enable employees to react more appropriately and behave with more self-confidence compared with inexperienced staff. This may in turn reduce aggression and the likelihood of overt violence.

The evidence presented in this book indicates that vulnerability lies at the root of a great deal of violence at work. Under the pressure of technological change, globalization and drastic reform, a growing number of workers enter employment on a precarious basis. Precariously employed workers include those who are hired on a casual, short-term contract, subcontract or day-hire basis. There is a growing body of evidence indicating that precariously employed workers are concentrated in jobs with increased levels of exposure to the hazard of workplace violence.[9] Women, children, immigrant workers, unskilled labourers and those with disabilities, among others, suffer an increased amount of workplace violence because of their vulnerabilities. When, as it is often the case, multiple vulnerabilities converge in the same person, the impact of a range of disadvantages – including violence both inside and outside the workplace – can be devastating.

The global dimension of violence at work

Violence in the workplace is to be found in both developing and industrialized countries, although as the chapters in this book indicate, information from developing countries about violent events is frequently limited, episodic and ill-defined. For long a "forgotten" issue, workplace violence in developing countries is increasingly emerging as a priority area of concern.[10] While the evidence is still limited and scattered – and often anecdotal – a picture is appearing that reveals the importance of the phenomenon in both developing and industrialized countries.

What we witness, particularly in developing countries, is most probably only the tip of the iceberg. Situations of workplace violence are frequently hidden by other critical problems that may divert attention away from this specific one, while significant under-reporting seems to be the norm rather than the exception.

Different perceptions and cultural backgrounds can also contribute to diverse understandings and evaluations of the various situations. Behaviours that would not be condoned in one country may be accepted or tolerated in another one. Such differences in approach may eventually lead to distorted representations of the reality whereby countries with better awareness of the problem are statistically "penalized" vis-à-vis countries with more limited attention to the phenomenon of workplace violence.

Different sensitivities in diverse contexts and cultures also contribute to variations in the reporting of violence at work, so that comparative data have to be used and interpreted with great caution. However, despite the fact that concepts and definitions are loaded with cultural significance, and that violent events may be perceived in different ways in developing countries compared with industrialized ones, it would appear that a general, common understanding of workplace violence is emerging.

The need to encourage reporting

This book has stressed that the real magnitude of workplace violence is only now being widely disclosed, as is its potential to harm the individual, the workplace and the community. Nevertheless, a large proportion of violent events remain unreported. Many employees, and in particular women and precariously employed workers, may remain silent about their victimization through fear of job loss and other reprisals. Reporting behaviours may also be influenced by different cultural sensitivities to violence, and the contexts in which violent events occur. In recent times, for instance, an enhanced awareness that sexual harassment, bullying and mobbing are completely unacceptable behaviours has resulted in higher rates of reporting of such incidents by victims.[11]

Despite the broad patterns of risk outlined in this book, violence at work remains a relatively unexplored area, with a knowledge base which is often incomplete, imprecise or contradictory. Entire sectors, like mining and agriculture, have received minimal consideration, while certain occupations have been the object of sustained attention. The situation prevailing in entire countries can remain virtually unknown, and comparative analysis is often very limited in both its scope and outcome. Precise definitions and descriptions of the different forms of violence at work still remain in a state of flux, and the causes of much workplace violence remain matters of conjecture.

The deficiencies which have been identified in the unequivocal information available on workplace violence point to a pressing need for further and better systems of data collection and analysis. The issues which seem to require specific attention include:

* enhancement of the capacities of most data collection systems to obtain information on all forms of violence at work;

* expansion of data gathering across countries, industry sectors, occupations, and types of violence that have received insufficient attention to date;

* promotion of comparative analyses on the nature and extent of violence at work, including at the international level;

* development of commonly accepted definitions for the different forms of violence, and particularly for new and emerging types of workplace violence such as bullying or mobbing;

- development of targeted research in areas of particular concern, such as occupations at special risk, vulnerable categories of workers, violence against women, young workers and children, and the cost of violence;

- comprehensive analysis of violence at work in specific sectors of industry, services or trade, including the causes of this violence and the remedies experimented with; and

- expansion of networking about violence at work among researchers and research centres.

From a restricted to a public issue

As this book has emphasized, the level of public awareness and concern about the issue of violence at work has been heightened by media reporting of dramatic events. Immediate information on what is known about major incidents of violence at work is almost invariably obtained through "the media lens". Thus media attention, while sometimes inaccurate and misleading, has done much to sensitize both the community and governments to the damaging consequences of workplace violence.

There is also a growing awareness that violence at work is not merely an episodic, individual problem but a structural, strategic problem rooted in wider social, economic, organizational and cultural factors; that violence at work is detrimental to the functionality of the workplace; and that any action taken against such violence is an integral part of the organizational development of a sound enterprise. Violence at work is seen increasingly to be a major problem that has to be tackled, and tackled now.

Growing awareness of the need to tackle the problem of violence at work

Workers, trade unions, employers, public bodies and experts across a broad international spectrum are now expressing common concern about the issue of violence at work. This concern is being matched by calls for action to prevent such violence and, when it occurs, to deal with it in a way which alleviates the enormous social, economic and other costs to the victims, their families, employers and the community at large.

In responding to the problem of workplace violence, it is now recognized to an increasing degree that violence can no longer be accepted as a normal part of any job, even where it would seem to be an occupational hazard, such as in law enforcement. Similar to the way in which risk management strategies have been adopted to reduce exposure to other hazards in manufacturing, strategies need to be put in place to minimize the possibility of assault, harassment and abuse to employees in all other industry sectors.

There is also a growing recognition that, in confronting violence, it is important to think comprehensively. This means that instead of searching for the single solution good for any and all problems and situations, the full range of causes which generate violence should be analysed and a variety of intervention strategies applied. Recognition and understanding of the variety and complexity of the factors which contribute to violence must be a vital precursor of any effective workplace violence prevention or control programme.

Recognition that violence at work is a varied and complex problem

In terms of long-term strategies to tackle the general problem of violence in any society, the most significant positive outcomes are likely to be achieved through a concentration on child development programmes linked to the family. It is within the family that aggressive behaviours are first learned. To the extent that families can instil non-violent values in their children, those children are more likely to negotiate life in society at large without resorting to a repertoire of violent behaviours. Meanwhile, there are many ways by which positive micro-level change can be achieved through targeted programmes and actions within a particular society, and the workplaces of that society.

Significant effort has been devoted to prediction of when an individual might behave in an aggressive manner. There is no doubt that certain identifiable factors do increase the likelihood that certain individuals, and population groups, will behave in such a way. These factors are to be found in both the long-term life experience of the people concerned, and in immediate, situational factors.

Nevertheless, the fact remains that – when seeking to predict whether aggressive behaviour will occur – a distinction must be made between predicting at the level of the general population, or at that of the individual. The available evidence does permit statements to be made with some degree of accuracy and reliability about the heightened risk of violence being committed by different population groups. The dilemma remains, however, of predicting with sufficient accuracy and reliability that a particular individual within that group may become violent. It is not possible in the current state of knowledge to predict with complete certainty that a specific person will behave in an aggressive way. The situational conditions under which the perpetrator and the victim interact also play an important role.

Interactions between individuals, work environments and the external environment are the key generators of violence

A far more promising approach to an understanding of workplace violence is to be found in an interactive analysis of individual, community and environmental risk factors, with particular attention being given to the situational context in which certain types of work tasks are performed. Because the perpetrator and the victim interact at the workplace, working environment factors can influence the risks of violence resulting from this interaction.

The physical design features of a workplace can be an important factor in either defusing or acting as a potential trigger for violence.[12] The discussions in Chapter 6 of this book identified that significant reduction in risk can be achieved through implementation of the principles of "crime prevention through environmental design" (CPTED). CPTED essentially focuses on the design of a worksite, the placement of windows and doors, selection of particular furniture and fittings, appropriate colour and ambience, and attention to restrictions on access and egress to particular parts of working areas.[13]

The interrelationship between the external environment and the working environment also appears significant in terms of predicting violence. Although the "permeability" of the working environment to the external environment is far from automatic, it is evident that violence in the external environment or community can find its way into the working environment and vice versa. Thus in geographical areas where community-level violence is higher, the increased risks can "cross over" into work environments, as was clearly identified in the South African country case study of violence in health care, described in Chapter 8 of this book.[14]

In a broader context, the type of interpersonal relationships, managerial style, the level at which responsibilities are decentralized, and the general culture of the workplace must also be taken into consideration. Thus the organizational setting appears to be equally important as individual and work environment features.

The difficulty of predicting where or when violence will occur

Any prediction of the possibility of violent incidents occurring at a workplace will thus depend upon a thorough analysis of the characteristics of the working environment, the external environment, and those of the perpetrator and victim in the particular situation. Each situation is unique and thus requires a unique analysis. That is why predicting the occurrence of specific acts of violence is extremely difficult. Nevertheless, it seems possible and useful to identify a number of working situations which appear to be at higher risk – and hence are relevant to the development of strategies for workplace violence prevention or control.

These "situations at risk" include jobs requiring working alone, work with the public, working with valuables, dealing with people in distress, education and health sector jobs, and working in conditions of special vulnerability.[15] These higher-risk jobs were described in depth in early chapters of this book.

The importance of identifying situations at special risk, while recognizing that each one is unique

There is a substantial body of evidence that workplace violence is more common for those who work in small shops, chemist and liquor shops and petrol stations;[16] working alone outside normal hours; employed as a journalist, and especially as an investigative reporter or in unsettled conditions;[17] and work as a taxi driver or sex worker. Among those working with members of the public, bus, train and subway workers appear at special risk,[18] as are flight attendants, shop workers in the retail sector and workers providing social services. Hotel, catering and restaurant staff are another group at risk.

Working with valuables, including handling cash, is a major area of risk. Violence associated with such activity is reported to be a particular problem in the postal service and in financial institutions, as well as for people employed in the private security industry. Health-care workers employed in emergency care units, psychiatric hospitals, old-age care units and drug abuse rehabilitation centres are also among those at highest risk.[19]

A worrying escalation of violence is also reported in schools across a number of countries, including in juvenile detention centres and technical colleges.[20] However, much research remains to be done on violence in the education sector.

Evidence also suggests that a disproportionate share of violent incidents is experienced by vulnerable categories such as migrant workers, workers in free trade zones, those who are precariously employed, and certain categories of rural workers. These violent incidents result in enormous costs for the individuals victimized, employers and society at large.

Recognition of the socio-economic consequences of violence at work

The cost of violence at work has often been underestimated. It is only in recent times that experts have started qualifying and quantifying the multiple and massive costs of such violence.[21] It is increasingly recognized that these costs include:

- those borne by the individual, including personal suffering, pain, injuries, illnesses, permanent and short-term disability, loss of human rights and dignity at work, and even death;

- those borne by the employer, including absenteeism, turnover, intangible costs following negative impact on company image, reduced creativity, negative working climate, decreased openness to innovation, and a decline in knowledge-building and continuous learning. These intangible assets are essential to the competitiveness of new people-centred enterprises where creativity is totally incompatible with the presence of violence at work. Further, bullying behaviours can smother overt signs of impending trouble and deflect early intervention. For example, in an organization where bullying or mobbing is tolerated, individuals who are aware of defects and deficiencies may refrain from bringing them to the attention of their superiors because of fear of reprisal and retribution.[22] The consequences of allowing such a culture to prevail may be fatal to the long-term health of an enterprise, as has been illustrated by a number of corporate failures of large multinational corporations in recent years;

- those borne by society at large include: drains on the social support system; health-care treatments; criminal justice system investigations, prosecutions and imprisonment; and a decreased sense of security among the wider population.

The fight against violence at work thus becomes an essential element of the economic success of enterprises and of sound economic development of communities and countries. Awareness of these negative consequences following workplace violence is increasing. This book suggests that full costings of the negative consequences of workplace violence need to include the entire socio-economic consequences following workplace violence: individual, enterprise and societal.

The need to involve all interested parties in understanding and shaping the response to violence

Despite significant progress in understanding the causes of violence at work, and situations where such violence is most likely to occur, this book shows that analyses and discussions in this area have been largely confined to experts and specialists. The other interested parties, particularly employers and workers, have entered the arena and voiced their concern but have not yet been widely involved in a fully participatory way. Participation by these

Box 88	From an issue for discussion to an issue for action

- Information on violence at work is widely circulated among all interested parties.

- Concrete opportunities are offered to interested parties so that they may be informed about workplace violence, such as through workshops, seminars, conferences, etc.

- Awareness campaigns are launched to sensitize responsible bodies, enterprises, workers and the general public to the risk of workplace violence.

- Easy access to specialized data banks on workplace violence is provided to public officials, employers and workers' representatives, who are then encouraged to establish integrated networks (including electronic networks) among themselves on this issue.

- Individual workers become actively involved in the identification of risk factors for violence at their workplace.

- Access to the media is facilitated for interested parties, including the victims of violence.

- Encouragement is provided for the production of joint statements, policies and strategy documents by the interested parties.

interested parties in assessing and responding to the problem of violence at work is an essential prerequisite for the development of realistic priorities, strategies and policies. Open discussion and extended engagement by all those concerned would seem to be a matter for priority action. Box 88 lists the prerequisites to achieve this goal.

The importance of a preventive, systematic and targeted approach to violence at work

The approach chosen for dealing with the problem of violence at work is of paramount importance. Most attention is now focused on proactive approaches which utilize the potential of people within the workplace itself to control the risk factors for workplace violence, with emphasis on the key role of preventive rather than reactive strategies.

The importance of a systematic approach to violence at work has also been stressed. This involves the application of a "control cycle" based usually on the sequence: hazard identification; risk assessment; design and implementation of control strategies; evaluation of the interventions and reassessment of the risks; and so on. It is also recommended that a targeted response be provided according to the type of "hazardous agent" involved, the occupation and situation, and the form of violence anticipated. The regulatory framework is a major underpinning bulwark.

The emergence of specific legislation on violence at work

In responding to violence at work, new legislation, guidelines, policies and practices are being developed and introduced. Legislative responsibilities and rights were discussed at length in Chapter 5 of this book. The scope of existing criminal, civil and common law, social security, occupational safety and health, labour and environmental legislation is being extended progressively and adapted to deal with the issue of workplace violence.

As a reflection of the growing awareness of the importance of responding directly to the risk of violence at work, legislation that strengthens existing controls and sanctions is being supplemented increasingly by legislation that addresses this behaviour in specific terms. Violence at work is emerging as a separate legal issue within national legislation, regulations and legislative interventions in various countries. An enhanced regulatory framework appears to be more effective at tackling the problem of workplace violence in a targeted way and in addressing new forms of violence, particularly psychological aggression. International law is also progressively addressing the problem of workplace violence.

This trend has been accompanied by legislation and regulations relating to specific risk factors for violence, occupations at special risk and particular forms of violence. It has been advanced by a growing number of collective and "model" agreements paving the way for, or supplementing, legislative and regulatory provisions.

The key role of guidelines in shaping an effective response to workplace violence

An important body of guidelines on violence is emerging from governments, trade unions, special study groups, workplace violence experts, and employers' groups. Many of these were detailed in Chapters 6 and 7 of this book. Despite different approaches and methods used, such guidelines reveal common themes: preventive action is possible and necessary; work organization and the working environment hold significant keys to the causes of and solutions to the problem; the participation of workers and their representatives is crucial both in identifying the problem and in implementing solutions; the interpersonal skills of management and workers alike cannot be underrated; there cannot be one blueprint for action, but rather the uniqueness of each workplace situation must be considered; and continued review of policies and programmes is needed to keep up with changing situations.

Attention is increasingly focused on the positive implications of preventive strategies. Experts emphasize the importance of comprehensive preventive planning, including: worksite and fittings design; selection and training of workers; information and communication; quality of the work environment; work organization and job design; and CEO commitment to zero tolerance in shaping effective preventive responses to violence at work.[23]

The importance of both immediate intervention and long-term assistance to victims of violence

While prevention is by far the best way to deal with workplace violence, and every effort should be made to tackle the causes of violence rather than its effects, it is important that workers be prepared and procedures established to defuse difficult situations and avoid violent confrontation. Even in the most difficult circumstances, there is often some room for manoeuvre before violence is released. Control of these situations is not easy, but is frequently possible, and many guidelines now recommend ways for minimizing the risk of violent incidents at the early stages of aggressive interactions.

Victims of violence can experience a wide range of disturbing reactions such as anxiety, feelings of vulnerability and helplessness, disturbed sleep, difficulty in concentrating, increased fear, irritability, obsessive thoughts and images, feelings of shame, anger, frustration, guilt, changes in beliefs and values, and a desire to retaliate. Experts emphasize the necessity of support and help for victims of violence, to deal with the distressing and often disabling after-effects of a violent incident and to prevent severe psychological problems from developing later. The quicker the response, the more effective and the less costly it will be.

Early intervention and prevention measures lead to more permanent results, and eventually pay for themselves

Tackling violence at work by preventive strategies and early intervention is becoming recognized as the most effective way to contain and defuse such behaviour. These principles are progressively being incorporated in strategic responses to violence at work. However – despite the lessons to be learned from forward-looking legislation, innovative guidelines and leading enterprises introducing successful anti-violence programmes based on these principles – their application is far from universal. Reactive responses remain prevalent.

Reactive responses concentrate on the effects of violence, rather than on its causes, with consequent waste in terms of the cost-effectiveness of the action undertaken. In too many situations the potential of the workplace itself to defuse violence is underexploited. In too many cases the risk of workplace violence is a forgotten issue, and little or no action is taken to prevent it. The lessons on prevention spelt out in this book need to be transformed into widespread practice.

To achieve the goal of widespread preventive action against workplace violence, the following initiatives might be envisaged:

- dissemination of information about positive examples of innovative legislation, guidance and practice in this area, to act as multipliers for other anti-violence initiatives;

- encouragement of anti-violence programmes, particularly at enterprise level, specifically addressed to combating violence at work;

- assistance to government departments, and employers' and workers' organizations, to develop effective policies against violence at work;

- assistance with the elaboration of training programmes for managers, workers and government officers dealing with or exposed to violence at work;

- elaboration of procedures to enhance the reporting of violent incidents; and

- assistance with the coordination of a range of anti-violence initiatives into organized strategies and plans.

Focusing international action

Rejection of the use of violence as a means of resolving inter- or intra-state conflicts, or disputes between individual groups, has been at the centre of a long-lasting international campaign. A growing body of conventions, recommendations, resolutions, and guidelines have addressed this problem, targeting different forms of violence including violence in the family, in the community, by the State or at work. Depending on the nature of the international body or agency involved, including the UN, violence at work has been tackled as human rights, labour, occupational health and safety, or criminal justice issues.

For many years the ILO's concern and action in areas closely related to workplace violence has resulted in a series of studies and publications, in particular on occupational stress, and drug and alcohol abuse at the workplace. One specific form of violence – sexual harassment – has, for a long time, been high on the action agenda of the ILO.

The ILO as a unique forum for combating violence at work

The ILO has the distinction of being the first international body to adopt an instrument containing an express protection against sexual harassment. The Indigenous and Tribal Peoples Convention, 1989 (No. 169), states that governments shall adopt special measures to ensure that the people concerned "enjoy equal opportunities and equal treatment in employment for men and women, and protection from sexual harassment".[24]

Building on this action, several ILO programmes of work since 1998 have targeted violence at work as a key issue within the fundamental scope of safeguarding the dignity and equality of workers. In 2002 a first response was provided by the ILO with a new training package – SOLVE. This package was designed to offer an integrated workplace response to the problems of drugs and alcohol, violence, stress, tobacco and HIV/AIDS, issues that often manifest themselves together at the workplace. In 2002, framework guidelines for addressing violence in the health sector were produced in collaboration with WHO, ICN and PSI.[25] In October 2003 a Meeting of Experts was held in Geneva leading to the adoption of a code of practice on workplace violence in services sectors and measures to combat this phenomenon.[26]

These actions undertaken – and new initiatives from the ILO in this area – have a firm basis in the spirit and mandate provided to the Organization by the ILO Constitution and the Declaration of Philadelphia. While the Preamble to the Constitution calls for all nations to "adopt humane conditions of labour", the Declaration affirms the fundamental principles on which the organization is based and, in particular, that " labour is not a commodity..." and that "all human beings, irrespective of race, creed or sex, have the right to pursue both their material well-being and their spiritual development in conditions of freedom and dignity, of economic security and equal opportunity...". Furthermore, as stated by the Director-General of the ILO in his Report to the 85th Session of the International Labour Conference in 1997, the role of the ILO in this area goes beyond the simple protection of fundamental rights: "There are many other rights which, without being termed 'fundamental' (meaning that their implementation is considered a priority), are nevertheless of fundamental – one might even say vital – importance for workers; for an example, one has to look no further than certain occupational safety and health standards, without which there could be a heavy loss of human lives."[27]

The right to a violence-free working environment would appear to fall into the category of "vital" rights as defined above. Thus, the ILO constitutes a unique forum for dealing effectively with violence at work. Its tripartite composition must add greatly to its effectiveness in this area, since dialogue and interaction among the constituent parties are an essential prerequisite to the formulation of policies and the launching of initiatives on violence at work.

Without doubt, the action of the ILO is critical in shaping an effective response to the challenge of violence at work. Indeed that challenge is one in which the ILO is already fully engaged, as the preparation of this third edition of *Violence at work* demonstrates. It is a challenge in which the ILO stands shoulder to shoulder with other international bodies, like the WHO, which have expressed their long-term commitment to tackling the growing problem of violence.

The broad lessons which should guide future action have been documented. The path to further progress now lies clearly in the direction of applying these lessons to the task of minimizing or eliminating the heavy toll that violence inflicts on so many of the world's workplaces. The slogan is clear: **Let us repudiate violence and remove it from the workplace now!**

Notes

[1] Prevention strategies are detailed in Rogers and Chappell, 2003.

[2] O'Neil, 2001, PhD Dissertation, funded by US Department of Justice.

[3] Mayhew et al., 2004, pp. 117–134.

[4] Santana and Fisher, 2002, pp. 90–113.

[5] Mayhew, 2002a, pp. 21–40.

[6] Upson, 2004.

[7] Health and Safety Authority, Ireland, 2001, p. 26.

[8] Mayhew, 2004, pp. 75–94.

[9] Mayhew and Quinlan, 1999, pp. 183–205.

[10] See, for example, Human Rights Watch, 2004a. See also idem, 2004b.

[11] National Committee on Violence (NCV), Australia, 1990.

[12] Swanton and Webber, 1990.

[13] Gill, 1998. See also Mayhew, 2000b.

[14] Steinman, 2002.

[15] Upson, 2004.

[16] Taylor, 2002.

[17] International Federation of Journalists, 2003a, 2003b.

[18] Easteal and Wilson, 1991.

[19] Di Martino, 2002b.

[20] Mayhew and McCarthy, 2004, pp. 511–521.

[21] Hoel, Sparks and Cooper, 2000.

[22] McCarthy and Mayhew, 2004, especially pp. 38–58.

[23] Rogers and Chappell, ILO, 2003. See also Mayhew and Chappell, 2003, pp. 3–43.

[24] Article 20, para. 3(d).

[25] ILO; ICN; WHO; PSI, 2002.

[26] ILO, 2004b.

[27] ILO, 1997a, p. 20.

BIBLIOGRAPHY

ABC Radio Australia. 2002. "Japan executes man who killed eight schoolchildren", 14 Sep.; online news service downloaded 15 June 2005 (see also: *People's Daily Online*: english.people.com.cn/, accessed 16 June 2005).

Afford, C. 2001. *Privatization of health care in Central and Eastern Europe*. Geneva, ILO.

Air Conditioning, Heating and Refrigeration News (Troy, Michigan), 1999.

Allan, A.; Dawson, D. 2004. "Assessment of the risk of reoffending by indigenous male violent and sexual offenders", in *Trends and Issues in Crime and Criminal Justice* (Canberra, Australian Institute of Criminology), No. 280, July.

American Federation of State, County and Municipal Employees (AFSCME); American Federation of Labor and Congress of Industrial Organizations (AFL-CIO). 1998. *Preventing workplace violence*. Washington, DC (see: afscme.org/health/violtc.htm, accessed 2 Jan. 2006).

Anderson, T. 1998. "Judicial decisions", in *Security Management*, Vol. 42, pp. 89–102.

Anti-Slavery. 2002. "The relationship between child domestic servitude and the exploitation of children", Submission to the United Nations Commission on Human Rights, Sub-Commission on the Promotion and Protection of Human Rights, Working Group on Contemporary Forms of Slavery, 27th Session, 27–31 May (see: antislavery.org/archive/submission/submission2002-childlabour.htm, accessed 7 Nov. 2005).

Argrusa, J.; Coats, W.; Tanner, J.; Leong, J. 2002. "Hong Kong and New Orleans: A comparative study of perceptions of restaurant employees on sexual harassment", in *International Journal of Hospitality and Tourism Administration*, Vol. 3, No. 3, pp. 19–31.

Arnette, J.; Wasleben, M. 1998. *Combating fear and restoring safety in school*. Washington, DC, US Department of Justice; bulletin cited in Verdugo and Vere, 2003, p. 15.

Arnetz, J. 1998a. "The violent incident form (VIF): A practical instrument for the registration of violence incidents in the health care workplace", in *Work and Stress*, Vol. 12, No. 1, pp. 17–28.

—. 1998b. *Violence towards health care personnel: Prevalence, risk factors, prevention and relation to quality of care*. Stockholm, Department of Public Health Science, Division of Psychosocial Factors and Health, Karolinska Institutet.

—; Arnetz, B. 2002. "Implementation and evaluation of a practical intervention programme for dealing with violence towards health care workers", in *Journal of Advanced Nursing*, Vol. 313, No. 3, Mar., pp. 668–676.

—; —; Petterson, I. 1994. *Violence, sexual and psychological harassment toward nurses: Occupational and lifestyle factors*. Stockholm, National Institute for Psychosocial Factors and Health.

—; —; —. 1996. "Violence in the nursing profession: Occupational and lifestyle risk factors in Swedish nurses", in *Work and Stress*, Vol. 10, No. 2, pp. 119–127.

—; —; Soderman, E. 1998. "Violence toward health care workers: Prevalence and incidence of a large regional hospital in Sweden", in *AAOHN Journal*, Vol. 48, No. 3, Mar., pp. 107–114.

Aromaa, K. 1993. "Survey results in victimization to violence at work", in *OECD Panel Group on Women, Work and Health: National report*. Helsinki, Institute of Occupational Health, Ministry of Social Affairs and Health.

Arway, A.G. 2002. "Causal factors of violence in the workplace: A human resource professional's perspective", in M. Grill, B. Fisher and V. Bowie (eds.): *Violence at work – Causes, patterns and prevention*. Cullompton, Devon, Willan Publishing, pp. 41–58.

Asian Development Bank. 2005. *Prevention of sexual harassment: A guide for staff*. Manila.

Asian Migrant Centre (AMC). 2000. *Baseline study on racial and gender discrimination towards Filipino, Indonesian and Thai domestic helpers in Hong Kong*. Hong Kong, China. Cited in Haspels et al., 2001, p. 59.

Australian Federal Police. No date. *When the roof became stars: The Australian Federal Police investigation into the Bali bombings*. Canberra, Australian Federal Police Museum.

Australian Institute of Criminology. No date. *Occupational violence: Annotated bibliography of prevention policies, strategies and guidance materials, 1989–2003* (see: aic.gov.au/research/cvp/occupational/bib.html, accessed 22 June 2005).

Australian Sports Commission (ASC). 2002. *Harassment of Officials Survey*. Canberra (see: ais.org.au/info/topics/violence.asp, accessed 8 Nov. 2005).

Ball, J.; Pike G. 2000. *Bullying, harassment and assault: Preliminary findings from the Royal College of Nursing Working Well 2000 Survey*. London.

Barkley, G.; Tavares, C. 2002. *United Nations Surveys on Crime Trends and Operations of the Criminal Victimisation Survey*. Geneva, United Nations.

—; —. 2003. *International Comparisons of Criminal Justice Statistics*, Issue 12/03, 24 Oct.

Barron, O. 1998. *Bullies, media and the law,* Paper presented at the Bullying at Work 1998 Research Update Conference, Staffordshire University, United Kingdom, 1 July. Carlton, Victoria, Australia, Job Watch Inc., Oct.

Bast-Petterson, E.; Bach, E.; Lindstrom, K.; Toomings, A.; Kiviranta, J. (eds). 1995. *Research on violence, threats and bullying as health risks among health care personnel,* Proceedings of the workshop for Nordic Researchers, Reykjavik, 14–16 Aug.

BBC News. 2001. "Record violence among Japan's teachers", by S. Moushavi, 27 Dec. (see: news.bbc.co.uk/1/hi/world/asia-pacific/1730161.stm, accessed 5 Jan. 2006).

—. 2003a. "Attacks spark bus driver crisis", Sep. (see: newsvote.bbc.co.uk/mpapps /pagetools/print/news.bbc.co.uk/1/hi/england/3147870.stm, accessed 18 Jan. 2005).

—. 2003b. "Death rate in Russian Army", by S. Dalziel, 13 Sep. (see: news.bbc.co.uk /2/hi/europe/3106368.stm, accessed 28 Sep. 2005).

—. 2004. "Patient jailed for NHS violence", Aug. (see: news.bbc.co.uk/1/hi/Scotland/ 3535606.stm, accessed 16 Aug. 2005).

BBC Sport, World Cup 2002. "Can football violence be stopped?", 10 June (see: news.bbc.co.uk/sport3/worldcup2002/hi/sports_talk/newsid_2035000/2035888.stm).

Beck, C.; Robinson, C.; Baldwin, B. 1992. "Improving documentation of aggressive behaviour in nursing home residents", in *Journal of Gerontological Nursing* (Thorofare, New Jersey), Vol. 18, No. 2, pp. 21–23.

Beermann, B.; Meschkutat B., 1995. *Psychosocial factors at the workplace: Taking account of stress and harassment.* Dortmund, Federal Institute for Occupational Safety and Health.

Benavides, F.; Benach, J. 1999. *Precarious employment and health-related outcomes in the European Union.* Barcelona, University Pompeu Fabra, Jan.

Bergström, A.-M. 1995. "Threats and violence against health-care personnel", in Bast-Petterson et al., 1995.

Biddle, E.; Hartley, D. 2002. "The cost of workplace homicides in the USA, 1990–1997", in *Injury Prevention and Control,* Sixth World Conference, pp. 421–422. Montreal, Les Presses de l'Université de Montreal.

Black, M. 1993. *Report on the Innocenti Global Seminar on Street and Working Children.* Florence, UNICEF/ICDC, pp. 7–22.

Bokhorst, H. 2004. *Le Soir* (Belgium), Oct.

Bonnesen, B. 1995. "Violence and threats in psychiatric hospitals", in Bast-Pettersen et al. (eds.), 1995.

Boonpala, P.; Kane, J. 2001. *Trafficking of children: The problem and responses worldwide.* ILO/IPEC.

Bor, R.; Russell, M.; Parker, J.; Papadopoulos, L. 2000. "Managing disruptive passengers: A survey of the world airlines" (London, Guildhall University); see also *International Civil Aviation Journal*, Mar./Apr. (see: www.aic.gov.au/research, accessed 2 Jan. 2006).

Borge, J., 2004. *The Guardian* (Manchester), 27 Feb.

Borzycki, M. 2003. "Bank robbery in Australia", in *Trends and Issues in Crime and Criminal Justice*, No. 253. Canberra, Australian Institute of Criminology (see: aic.gov.au/publications/tandi2/tandi253.pdf, accessed 4 Nov. 2005).

Bowie, V. 2000. "Planes, trains and prostitutes: Dealing with potential workplace violence encountered by Olympic support services", in *Journal of Occupational Health and Safety – Australia and New Zealand*, Vol. 16, No. 3, pp. 247–254.

—. 2002. "Defining violence at work: A new typology", in M. Gill, B. Fisher and V. Bowie (eds.): *Violence at work – Causes, patterns and prevention*. Cullompton, Devon, Willan Publishing, pp. 1–20.

—; Fisher, B.; Cooper, C. Forthcoming. *Workplace violence: An international perspective*. Cullompton, Devon, Willan Publishing.

Brett, R.; Specht, I. 2004. *Young soldiers: Why they choose to fight*. Geneva and New York, ILO/Lynne Rienner.

British Crime Survey (BCS); British Health and Safety Executive (HSE). 2005. *Violence at work: Reporting of Injuries, Disease and Dangerous Occurrences Regulations (RIDDOR)*. London, HSE Statistics (see: hse.gov.uk/statistics/index.htm, accessed 2 Jan. 2006).

British Retail Consortium (BRC). 2002. *10th Annual Retail Crime Survey*, London.

—. 2003. *11th Annual Retail Crime Survey*. London.

—. 2004. *12th Annual Retail Crime Survey*. London (see: brc.org.uk/publications. reports.htm, accessed 2 Jan. 2006).

Budd, T. 2001. *Violence at work: New findings from the 2000 British Crime Survey*. London, HSE and Home Office, July.

Bukowska, S.; Schnepf, E. 2001. *Mentoring Project: Centre for Counselling on Sexual Harassment and Mobbing*. Vienna, University of Vienna (see: univie.ac.at/women/engl/index.htm, accessed 2 Jan. 2006).

Bush, D.F.; O'Shea, P.G. 1996. "Workplace violence: Comparative use of prevention practices and policies", in VandenBos and Bulatao (eds.), 1996, pp. 283–298.

Buvinic, M.; Morrison, A.; Shifter, M. 1999. *Violence in Latin America and the Caribbean: A framework for action*, Technical Study. Washington, DC, Inter-American Development Bank, Sustainable Development Department (see: iadb.org/sds/doc/1073eng.pdf, accessed 22 June 2005).

Cahill, J.; Landsbergis, P. 1996. "Job strain among Post Office mailhandlers", in *International Journal of Health Services*, Vol. 26, No. 4, pp. 731–750.

Calabresi, G. 1982. *A common law for the age of Statutes.* Cambridge, Mass., Harvard University Press.

California, Department of Industrial Relations, Division of Occupational Safety and Health (DOSH), CAL/OSHA. 1994. *Guidelines for workplace security.* San Francisco.

—. 1995. *Injury and Illness Prevention Model Program for Workplace Security.* State of California, Aug. (see: dir.ca.gov/DOSH/dosh_publications/iipsecurity.html, accessed 30 Sep. 1999).

—. 1998. *Guidelines for security and safety of health care and community service workers.* San Francisco (see: dir.ca.gov/DOSH/dosh_publications/hcworker.html, accessed 30 Sep. 1999).

Canadian Centre for Justice Statistics. 1999. *Youth violent crime.* Ottawa, Juristat, Vol. 19, No. 13, cited in Verdugo and Vere, 2003, p. 14.

Canadian Centre for Occupational Health and Safety (CCOHS). 2005a. "What is workplace bullying?" (see: ccohs.ca/oshanswers/psychosocial/bullying.htm, accessed 8 Sep. 2005).

—. 2005b. "What is workplace violence?" (see: ccohs.ca/oshanswers/psychosocial/violence.htm, accessed 9 Sep. 2005).

Carroll, R.; Bowcroft, O. 2005. "Hassan killer suspect held in Iraq raid", in *Guardian Weekly*, Vol. 172, No. 20, 6–12 May, p. 1.

CBS News Online. 2005. "Indepth: Iraq: Foreign hostages in Iraq", 15 May (see: cbc.ca/news/background/iraq/hostages.html, accessed 27 Sep. 2005).

Center for Occupational and Environmental Health, University of California. 1997. *Violence on the job: A guidebook for labor and management.* Berkeley, California.

Centre for the Study of Violence and Reconciliation. 2005. *A world without torture. Victim Empowerment Programme (CSVR).* Johannesburg (see: irct.org/usr/irct/home. nsf/unid/JREW-5MSCSM, accessed 16 Sep. 2005).

Chaiken, J., et al. 1993. "Predicting violent behaviour and classifying violent offenders", in A. Reiss and J. Roth (eds.): *Understanding and preventing violence*, Vol. 4, pp. 279–280. Washington, DC, National Academy Press.

Chappell, D.; Di Martino, V. 2000. *Violence at work*, 2nd edition. Geneva, ILO.

China Daily. 2004. "Drownings lead to probe into people smuggling", by Wang Zin. 10 Feb. (see: china.org.en/english/doc/2004-02/09/content, accessed 19 Jan. 2005).

Clark, J. 1994. "The prediction and prevention of violence in pubs and clubs", in *Crime Prevention Studies* (New York), Vol. 3, pp. 1–46.

CNN.com/US. 2003. "Seven die in Chicago Warehouse Shooting", 28 Aug. (see: cnn.com/2003/US/Midwest/08/27/chicago.shooting/, accessed 27 Sep. 2005).

Commercial Clearing House (CCH). 1991. *Managing violence and traumatic incidences at work.* North Ryde, New South Wales.

—. 2004a. *Managing trauma at work,* 17 Feb., Ch. 65. North Ryde, New South Wales.

—. 2004b. *Managing workplace bullying,* 17 Feb., Ch. 65, sections 50-000 to 52-090, pp. 61, 501–61, 622. North Ryde, New South Wales.

Communication Workers' Union (CWU). 2001. *Stress survey.* London, May (see: www.tuc.org.uk, accessed 2 Jan. 2006).

Confederación Sindical de Comisiones Obreras (CO.OO), Spain. 2000. *El alcance del acoso sexual en el trabajo en España.* Madrid, Instituto Valencia de la Dona.

Cooper, C.; Swanson, N. 2002. *Workplace violence in the health sector: State of the art,* ILO/ICN/WHO/PSI Joint Programme on Workplace Violence in the Health Sector. Geneva.

Council of Europe. 1997. "Convention for the Protection of Human Rights and Dignity of the Human Being with Regard to the Application of Biology and Medicine (Convention on Human Rights and Biomedicine)". Oviedo, Spain, 4 Apr.

Cullen, W. D. 1996. *The Public Inquiry into the Shootings at Dunblane Primary School on 13 March 1996.* CM. 3386. Edinburgh, Scottish Office.

Cunneen, C.; Stubbs, J. 1997. *Gender, "race" and international relational violence against Filipino women in Australia.* Sydney, Institute of Criminology, Monograph Series No. 9.

Danish Food and Allied Workers' Union. 2001. *Have you talked to your colleague today?* (on bullying). Copenhagen.

Danish Labour Inspectorate. 1997. *Risk of violence in connection with work performance.* Copenhagen, Oct.

—. 2002. *Bullying and sexual harassment.* Copenhagen.

Danish Union of Commercial and Clerical Employees. 2002. *Dialogue creates understanding.* Copenhagen.

Debout, M. 1999. *Travail, violences et l'environnement,* rapport au Conseil économique et sociale. Paris.

Deeb, M. 2002. *Workplace violence in the health sector – Lebanon country case study,* ILO/ICN/WHO/PSI Joint Programme on Workplace Violence in the Health Sector. Geneva.

Delawareonline. No date. "The News Journal" (see: delawareonline.com/newsjournal/local(2001/09/11terrortimeline400.html, accessed 27 Sep. 2005).

Denton, M.; Zeytinoglu, I.; Webb, S. 2000. "Work related violence and the OHS of some health care workers", in *Journal of Occupational Health and Safety – Australia and New Zealand*, Vol. 16, No. 5, pp. 419–427.

Department of Employment, United Kingdom. 1992. *Sexual harassment in the workplace: A guide for employers*. London.

Department of Health, United Kingdom. 2000. *NHS Zero Tolerance Zone*, Resource Sheet 4. London.

Department of Labour, Occupational Safety and Health Service, Government of New Zealand. 1995. *Guidelines for employers and employees on dealing with violence at work*. Wellington.

Department of Occupational Health and Safety (DOSH), Ministry of Human Resources of Malaysia. No date. *Guidance for the prevention of stress and violence at the workplace*. Kuala Lumpur, Government of Malaysia (see: ilo.org/public/english/protection/safework/papers/Malaysia/guide.pdf, accessed 1 Dec. 2005).

Department of Transport, United Kingdom. 1995. *Protecting bus crews: A practical guide*. London. Reproduced with the permission of the Department of the Environment, Transport and the Regions.

Detling, D. *El Centro*. 1996.

Développement Ressources Humaines Canada (DHRC). 2000. *Travailler en sécurité pour un avenir en santé. Analyse des statistiques: Accidents et mortalités survenus au Canada*.

Di Martino, V. 2001. "The high road to teleworking". Geneva, ILO; unpublished (see: ilo.org/safework/telework/index.htm, accessed 27 Sep. 2005).

—. 2002a. "Workplace violence, definitions and understanding", unpublished working paper for the ILO Ombudsperson's Office. Geneva, ILO.

—. 2002b. *Workplace violence in the health sector. Country case studies: Brazil, Bulgaria, Lebanon, Portugal, South Africa, Thailand and an additional Australian study*, ILO/ICN/WHO/PSI Joint Programme on Workplace Violence in the Health Sector, synthesis report. Geneva (see: ilo.org/public/english/dialogue/sector/papers/health/violence-ccs.pdf, accessed 22 June 2005).

—. 2003a. *Workplace violence in the health sector: Relationship between work stress and workplace violence in the health sector*. Geneva, ILO (see: ilo.org/public/english/dialogue/sector/papers/health/stress-violence.pdf, accessed 5 Dec. 2005).

—. 2003b. "Work related violence", in Heitmeyer and Hagans (eds.), 2003, pp. 885–902.

—. 2005. *Telework in Latin America and the Caribbean*. Montevideo, International Development Research Centre, ILO Regional Office for Latin America and the Caribbean.

—; De Santis, R. 2003. *Mobbing.* Troina, Sicily, Città Aperta ed.

—; Di Cola, G.; Schenk, R. 2003. *YSP – An action-oriented training package to address addiction, violence, HIV/AIDS, child labour and social exclusion among young people through sport and labour opportunities.* Geneva, ILO/International Olympic Committee (IOC).

—; Gold, D.; Schaap, A. 2002a. *Micro Solve on sexual harassment.* Geneva, ILO.

—; —; —. 2002b. *SOLVE Training Package – Managing emerging health problems at work – Stress, violence, tobacco, alcohol, drugs, HIV/AIDS.* Geneva, ILO.

—; Hoel, H.; Cooper, C. 2002. *Violence and harassment in the workplace.* Dublin, European Foundation for the Improvement of Working and Living Conditions.

—; —; —. 2003. *Preventing violence and harassment in the workplace.* Dublin, European Foundation for the Improvement of Living and Working Conditions (see summary at: eurofound.eu.int.publications/htmlfiles/ef0330.htm, accessed 11 Oct. 2005).

—; Musri, M. 2001. *Guidance for the prevention of stress and violence at the workplace.* Kuala Lumpur, Malaysia Ministry of Human Resources, Department of Occupational Safety and Health (see: ilo.org/public/english/protection/safework/papers/malaysia/guide.pdf, accessed 14 Nov. 2005).

Dixon, P. No date. "Drug testing boom at work", in *Future-2004*, p. 1 (see: globalchange.com/drugtest.htm, accessed 23 June 2005).

Donne & Qualità della Vita. No date. "In ufficio. Quando esplode l'atra metà del mobbing", by C. Dino (see: dweb.repubblica.it/archivio_d/2002/09/21/attualita/attualita/135mob318135.html, accessed 2 Dec. 2005).

Duhart, D. 2001. *Violence in the workplace, 1993–99,* National Crime Victimization Survey. US Department of Justice, Bureau of Justice Statistics Special Report, NCJ 190076, 8 Dec. (see: ojp.usdoj.gov/bjs/pub/pdf/vw99.pdf, accessed 17 Oct. 2005).

Easteal, W.; Wilson, P. 1991. *Preventing crime on transport: Rail, buses, taxis, planes.* Canberra, Australian Institute of Criminology.

Effah-Chukwuma, J.; Osarenren, N. 2001. *Beyond boundaries: Violence against women in Nigeria.* Lagos, Project Alert on Violence Against Women.

Einarsen, S.; Hoel, H.; Zapf, D.; Cooper, C. (eds.). 2003a. *Bullying and emotional abuse in the workplace: International perspectives in research and practice.* London/New York, Taylor and Francis.

—; —; —; —. 2003b. "The concept of bullying at work: The European tradition", in Einarsen et al. (eds.), 2003a, pp. 3–30.

—; Mikkelsen, E. 2003. "Individual effects of exposure to bullying at work", in Einarsen et al., 2003a, pp. 127–144.

Equal Employment Opportunity Commission (EEOC), State Fair Employment Practices Agencies (FEPA), United States. No date. "Sexual harassment charges EEOC and FEPAs combined: FY 1992-FY 2002" (see: eeoc.gov/stats/harass.html, accessed 2 Jan. 2006).

Equal Opportunities Commission, United Kingdom. 1994. *Consider the cost.* London.

Essenberg, B. 2003. *Violence and stress at work in the transport sector,* ILO Sectoral Activities Programme, Working Paper No. 205. Geneva, ILO.

Etzioni, A. 1971. "Violence", in R. Merton and R. Nisber (eds.): *Contemporary social problems.* New York, Harcourt Brace Jovanich, pp. 704–741.

European Agency for Safety and Health at Work. 2002a. *Facts: Bullying at work*, No. 23. Bilbao (see: agency.osha.eu.int, accessed 1 Dec. 2005).

—. 2002b. *Prevention of psychosocial risks and stress at work in practice.* Bilbao, European Week for Safety and Health at Work, Nov.

European Centre of Enterprises with Public Participation and of Enterprises of General Economic Interest (CEEP); Weber, T. 2004. *European Framework Agreement on Work Related Stress.* Brussels.

European Commission. 1992. "Measures to combat sexual harassment", in *Official Journal of the European Communities* (Luxembourg), 24 Feb.

—. 1993. *How to combat sexual harassment: A guide to implementing the European Commission code of practice.* Brussels.

—. 1998. *Sexual harassment at the workplace in the European Union.* Luxembourg, Office for Official Publications of the European Communities.

—. 2001. *Report on harassment in the workplace* (2001/2339 (INI)). Luxembourg, Office for Official Publications of the European Communities, 16 July.

—. 2002. "Adapting to change in work and society: A new Community strategy on health and safety at work 2002–2006", Communication from the Commission, 11 Mar. Brussels.

—. 2003. "Memorandum by Mr. Kinnock to the Commission on Psychological Harassment Policy at the European Commission", Oct.

—, Advisory Committee on Safety, Hygiene and Health Protection at Work. 2001. "Opinion on Violence at the Workplace", adopted on 29 Nov., doc. 1564/2/01. Brussels.

—, Justice and Home Affairs. 1998. *The Daphne Programme: An end to sexual harassment at work* (see: europa.eu.int/comm/justice_home/project/daphne/ilustratives_cases_en/case_6_en.htm1998-2000, accessed 30 June 2005).

European Council. 2002. *Good practice guide to mitigate the effects and eradicate violence against women.* Brussels.

European Foundation for the Improvement of Living and Working Conditions. 1997. *Second European Survey on the Work Environment, 1995–96.* Luxembourg, Office for Official Publications of the European Communities.

—. 2000. *Working conditions in atypical work*, TJ-39-01-619-EN-C. Dublin.

—. 2001. *Third Survey on Working Conditions in Europe.* Dublin (see: fr.eurofound.eu.int/publications/files/EF02109EN.pdf, accessed 17 Oct. 2005).

—. 2003. *Violence, bullying and harassment in the workplace.* Dublin (see: eurofound.eu.int/ewco/reports/F10406TR01/F10406TR01.pdf, accessed 10 Jan. 2006).

—. 2005. *Work-related stress.* Dublin (see summary at eurofound.ie.ewco/reports/ NL0502TR01/NL0502TR01.htm, accessed 10 Jan. 2006).

European Industrial Relations Observatory; European Foundation for the Improvement of Living and Working Conditions. 2005. "Industry sector social partners reach agreement on psychological working environment", Dublin, EIRO on-line (see: www.eiro.eurofound.eu.int/print/2001/06/feature/dk0106124f.html, accessed 2 Jan. 2006).

European Parliament. 1989. "Council Directive 89/391/EEC of 12 June 1989 on the introduction of measures to encourage improvements in the safety and health of workers at work", in *Official Journal of the European Communities* (Brussels), Vol. 32, Art. 6, pp. L183/3 to L183/14, 29 June.

—. 2000a. "Council Directive 2000/43/EC of 29 June 2000 implementing the principle of equal treatment between persons irrespective of racial or ethnic origin", in *Official Journal of the European Communities* (Brussels), L.180/22, 19 July 2000.

—. 2000b. "Council Directive 2000/78/EC of 27 November 2000 establishing a general framework for equal treatment in employment and occupation", in *Official Journal of the European Communities* (Brussels), L.303, 2 Dec. 2000, pp. 0016-0022 (see: europa.eu.int/eur-lex/pri/en/oj/dat/2000/1_303/1_30320001202en00160022.pdf, accessed 27 Nov. 2000).

—. 2001a. *Bullying at work*, Working paper, Social Affairs Series, SOCI 108 EN. Brussels.

—. 2001b. "Resolution on harassment at the workplace" (2001/2339(INI)), session doc. A5-0283/2001. Brussels.

—. 2002a. "Council Directive 2002/73/EC of September 2002, amending Council Directive 76/207/EEC, implementing the principle of equal treatment for men and women as regards access to employment, vocational training and promotion, and working conditions", in *Official Journal of the European Communities* (Brussels), L.269/15, 5 Oct. 2002.

—. 2002b. "Council resolution of 3 June 2002 on a new Community Strategy on health and safety at work", in *Official Journal of the European Communities* (Brussels), C161, 5 July 2002, pp. 001–004 (see: europa.eu.int/eur-lex/pri/en/oj/dat/2002/c_161/c_16120020705en00010004.pdf, accessed 6 Jan. 2006).

—, Committee on Employment and Social Affairs. 2001. *Report on harassment at the workplace* (2001/2339(INI)). FINAL A5-0283/2001. Brussels.

European Trade Union Confederation (ETUC). 1993. *Tackling violence at work*, background report for the ETUC Health and Safety Forum. London, Feb.

—. 2003. *Risks 128*, 18 Oct. (see: tuc.org.uk/h_and_s/tuc-7217.f0.pdf

—. 2004. *Risks 180*, 30 Oct. (see: tuc.org.uk/h_and_s/tuc-8894.f0.pdf

—; Union of Industrial and Employers' Confederations of Europe (UNICE); European Association of Craft Small and Medium-sized Enterprises (UEAPME); European Centre of Enterprises with Public Participation and Enterprises of General Economic Interest (CEEP). 2002. *Work programme of the European social partners 2003–2005*. Brussels, Nov. (In view of a European agreement on stress, including "Stress at Work: Seminar in view to negotiate a voluntary agreement", p. 2 (see: europa.eu.int/comm/employment_social_news/2002/dec/prog_de_travail_comm_en.pdf, accessed 22 Sep. 2005).

Family Violence Prevention Fund. 2002. "Corporate awareness of domestic violence", in *NewsFlash* (San Francisco), 12 Nov. (see: endabuse.org/newsflash/index.php3?Search=Article&NewsFlashID=389, accessed 23 June 2005).

Farrugia, S. 2002. "A dangerous occupation? Violence in public libraries", in *New Library World*, Vol. 103, No. 9, Sep., pp. 309–319.

Federal Aviation Administration. 2003. "Incidents of passenger misconduct, 1995–2002", in H. Kern: *The faces of air rage*, FBI Law Enforcement Bulletin, Vol. 72, Issue 8. Washington, DC (see: fbi.gov/publications/leb/2003/august2003/aug03leb.htm#page_7, accessed 18 Nov. 2005).

Federal Bureau of Investigation (FBI), United States. 2005. *Bank robbery in the US*. Uniform Crime Reporting (UCR) Program, Special Report, data collections for years 1990 and 2001 (see: fbi.gov/ucr/cius_02/pdf/5sectionfive.pdf, accessed 18 Nov. 2005).

Ferrinho, P.; Antunes, A.; Biscaia, A.; Conceição, C.; Fronteira, I.; Craveiro, I.; Flores, I.; Santos, O. 2002. *Workplace violence in the health sector: Portuguese case studies*, ILO/ICN/WHO/PSI Joint Programme on Workplace Violence in the Health Sector (see: icn.ch/SewWorkplace/WPV_HS_Portugal.pdf, accessed 18 Oct. 2005).

Le Figaro. 1996. "Les dix-neuf mesures arrêtés. Le plan de prévention de la violence à l'école se présente en trois grands axes et dix-neuf mesures", 21 Mar., Paris, p. 9.

Fisher, B.; Jenkins, E.; Williams, N. 1998. "The extent and nature of homicide and non-fatal workplace violence in the United States: Implications for prevention and security", in M. Gill: *Crime at work: Increasing the risk for offenders*, Vol. 2, pp. 65–82. Leicester, Perpetuity Press.

Fitzgerald, L.; Shulman, S. 1993. "Sexual harassment: A research analysis and agenda for the 1990s", in *42 Journal of Vocational Behavior*, Vol. 5, No. 7, cited in Murray, 1998. "Psychology's voice in sexual Harassment law", in *APA Monitor* (American Psychological Association), Vol. 29, No. 8, Aug. 1998, p. 1 (see: www.apa.org/monitor/aug98/law.html, accessed 17 June 2005).

Fitzpatrick, J. 1999. "Challenging boundaries: Gendered aspects of migration". Unpublished document submitted to the Special Rapporteur, United Nations, Economic and Social Council, 1999, p. 9.

Flores-Oebanda, M., et al. 2001. *The Kasambahay – child domestic work in the Philippines: A living experience*, Visayan Forum Foundation/ILO. Makati City, Philippine Institute of Development Studies.

Food and Agriculture Organization of the United Nations (FAO). 2003. "Policy on prevention of harassment", administrative circular No. 2003/17, 26 June.

Forastieri, V. 2002. *Child labour: Health and safety risks*. ILO, Geneva, 2nd edition.

Frascheri, C. 2003. *Mobbing: Guida alla tutela*, pp. 69–72. Rome, Edizioni lavoro.

Galli, R. 2001. *The economic impact of child labour*, discussion paper for the International Institute for Labour Studies at the ILO, University of Lugano. Geneva, ILO, Decent Work Research Programme.

German Foundation for International Development. 2000. *Public service reforms and their impact on health sector personnel*. Round Table, Berlin, 13–15 Oct. 1999.

Giga, S.; Hoel, H. 2003. *Violence and stress at work in financial services*, ILO Sectoral Activities Programme, Working Paper No. 210. Geneva, ILO.

—; —; Cooper, C. 2003a. *Violence and stress at work in the performing arts and journalism*, ILO Sectoral Activities Programme, Working Paper No. 201. Geneva, ILO.

—; —; —. 2003b *Violence and stress at work in the postal sector*, ILO Sectoral Activities Programme, Working Paper No. 200. Geneva, ILO.

Gill, M. (ed.) 1998. *Crime at work: Increasing the risk for offenders*, Vol. 2. Leicester, Perpetuity Press.

Global Alliance for Workers and Communities (GAWC). 2001. *Workers' voices: An interim report of workers' needs and aspirations in nine Nike contract factories in Indonesia*, prepared for the GAWC by the Center for Societal Development Studies, Atma Jaya Catholic University, Jakarta (see: theglobalalliance.org/pdf/indonesia-needs-assessment-full.pdf, accessed 7 Nov. 2005).

—. 2003. *Improving working conditions and future perspectives for factory workers in Indonesia: A report on workers' views on the improvement in the workplace*, prepared for the GAWC by the Center for Societal Development Studies, Jakarta. Final report, 15 May (see: theglobalalliance.org/pdf/indonesia-needs-reassessment-2003.pdf, accessed 7 Nov. 2005).

Globe and Mail. 1993. "Statistics Canada Survey (Canada First National Survey on Violence Against Women)", based on telephone interviews with 12,300 women (Montreal), 19 Nov.

Goldberg, R. 1997. "Victims of criminal violence in the workplace: An assessment of remedies in the United States and Great Britain", in *Comparative Labor Law Journal*, Vol. 18, No. 3, Spring.

Grainger, C. 1996. "How controllable is occupational violence?", in *International Journal of Stress Management* (New York), Vol. 3, No. 1, p. 17.

Hadland, A. 2002. *In terror and in silence, an investigation into crime and safety at petrol stations*. Petrol Station 5 Safety Project, Social Cohesion and Integration Research Programme. Cape Town, HSRC Press, Dec., p. 26.

Haspels, N.; Kasim, Z.; Thomas, C.; McCann, D. 2001. *Action against sexual harassment at work in Asia and the Pacific*. Bangkok, ILO.

Health and Safety Authority, Ireland. 2001. *Dignity at work: The challenge of workplace bullying*, Report of the Task Force on the Prevention of Workplace Bullying. Dublin, Stationery Office, Mar.

—. 2002. *Code of practice detailing procedures for addressing bullying in the workplace*. Dublin (see: entemp.ie/publications/employment/workplacebullying.pdf, accessed 6 Dec. 2005).

Health and Safety Commission (HSC), United Kingdom. 1990. *Violence to staff in the education sector*. London.

Health and Safety Executive (HSE), United Kingdom. 1991. *Violence to staff*. London, HMSO.

—. 1993. *Prevention of violence to staff in banks and building societies*. London, HMSO.

—. 1995. *Preventing violence to retail staff*. London, HMSO.

—. 1997a. "Review of workplace-related violence", in *Contract Research Report* (London), No. 143.

—. 1997b. *Violence at work: A guide for employers*. London, HMSO.

—. 1997c. *Violence in the education sector*. London, HMSO.

—. 2003. *Work-related violence – lone workers case study: Summary of key points*. London, 15 Oct. (see: hse.gov.uk/violence/conclusion.htm, accessed 30 June 2005).

—. 2005. *Statistics: Violence at work* (see: hse.gov.uk/statistics/causdis/violence.htm, accessed 11 Jan. 2006).

—, Health and Safety Laboratory. 2005. *Work-related violence – Lone workers' case study: Summary of key points*, HSE Infoline (see: hse.gov.uk/violence/conclusions.htm#4, accessed 4 Jan. 2006).

Health Services Advisory Committee. 1997. *Violence and aggression to staff in health services*. London.

Heitmeyer, W.; Hagan, J. (eds). 2003. *International handbook of violence research*. Dordrecht, Kluwer Academic Publishers.

Henk Schrama, C.; van der Sluys, R. 2004. *Monitoring the impact of anti-violence legislation in the Netherlands. The three waves*. The Hague, Ministry of Social Affairs and Employment.

Hiley-Young, B.; Gerrity, E. 1994. "Critical Incident Stress Debriefing (CISD): Value and limitations in disaster response", in *NCP Clinical Quarterly*, Vol. 4, No. 2, Spring (see: ncptsd.va.gov/publications/cq/v4/n2/hiley-yo.html, accessed 30 Nov. 2005).

Hoad, C. 1996. "Violence at work: Perspectives from research among 20 British employers", in *Security Journal* (London), Vol. 4, pp. 64–86.

Hoel, H.; Cooper, C. 2000. "Destructive conflict and bullying at work", Manchester, University of Manchester Institute of Science and Technology; unpublished report, Apr., cited in Rayner et al., 2002.

—; Einarsen, S. 2001. *Violence at work in hotels, catering and tourism,* ILO Sectoral Activities Programme. Working Paper No. 211. Geneva, ILO.

—; Rayner, C.; Cooper, C. 1999. "Workplace bullying", in C. Cooper and I. Robertson (eds.): *International Review of Industrial and Organisational Psychology*, Vol. 14. Chichester, Wiley.

—; Sparks, K.; Cooper, C. 2000. *The cost of violence and stress at work and the benefits of a violence- and stress-free working environment*. Manchester, UMIST. Report commissioned by the ILO (see: ilo.org/public/English/protection/safework/whpwb/econo/costs, accessed 1 Nov. 2002).

Homel, R.; Clark, J. 1994. "The prediction and prevention of violence in pubs and clubs", in *Crime Prevention Studies* (New York), Vol. 3, pp. 1–46.

—; Tomsen, S.; Thommeny, J. 1992. "Public drinking and violence: Not just an alcohol problem", in *Journal of Drug Issues* (Florida, Tallahassee), Vol. 22, pp. 679–697.

House of Representatives Standing Committee on Employment, Education and Training. 1994. *Sticks and stones: Report on violence in Australian schools*. Canberra, Australian Government Publishing Service.

Hudson, M. 1998. "Domestic violence isn't just domestic: sometimes it spills over into the workplace", in *Roanoke Times and World News*, Metro Edition, 19 Mar. p. C1, cited in Johnson and Gardner, 2000, pp.197–202.

Human Rights Watch, 2001. *Scared at school: Sexual violence against girls in South African schools*. New York (see: hrw.org/reports/2001/safrica/index.htm#TopOfPage, accessed 4 Jan. 2006).

—. 2004a. "Bad dreams: Exploitation and abuse of migrant workers in Saudi Arabia", in *Human Rights Watch* (New York), Vol. 16, No. 5, July (see: hrw.org/reports/2004/saudi0704/7/index.htm, accessed 4 Jan. 2006).

—. 2004b. "Help wanted: Abuses against female migrant domestic workers in Indonesia and Malaysia", in *Human Rights Watch* (New York), Vol. 16, No. 9(c), July (see: hrw.org/reports/ 2004/indonesia0704/index.htm, accessed 4 Jan. 2006).

—. 2004c. *Stop the use of child soldiers*. New York (see: hrw.org/campaigns/crp/index.htm, accessed 28 Sep. 2005).

Hurrell, J.; Worthington, K.A.; Driscoll, R.J. 1996. "Job stress, gender, and workplace violence: Analysis of assault experiences of state employees", in G. VandenBos and E. Bulatao (eds.), 1996.

Iannacone, N. 2003. *Azienda sanitaria e della regione* (see: digitaleterrestre.rai.it/news/articolonews/0,9217,73988,00.html, accessed 9 Nov. 2005).

IG Metall; FRAPORT AG. 2001. *Regelungsabrede über Parnterschaftliches Verhalten am Arbeitsplatz*. Frankfurt/Main (see: igmetall.de/betriebsraete/betriebsvereinbarungen/fraport.html, accessed 12 Dec. 2005).

Imbusch, P. 2003. "The concept of violence", in Heitmeyer and Hagan (eds.), 2003, pp. 13–14.

Incomes Data Services Ltd. 1997. *Violence at work*, IDS Study 628, June. London.

—. 2003. *Violence against staff*, IDS Study 749, May. London. (see: incomesdata.co.uk/studies/violence.htm, accessed 30 June 2005).

Infoplease. No date. "Terrorist attacks (within the United States or against Americans abroad): September 11, 2001 victims" (see: infoplease.com/ipa/A0001454.html; and also september11victims.com/september11victims/STATISTIC.asp, both accessed 27 Sep. 2005).

Institute for Security Studies, South Africa. 2003. "Bank robbery in the RSA for the financial years 1994/1995 to 2002/2003" (see: iss.co.za/CJM/stats0903/bankrob2.htm, accessed 4 Jan. 2005).

Instituto de la Mujer and Complutense, U. o. M. 2002. *Spanish Presidency: Good practice guide to mitigate the effects and eradicate violence against women*. Brussels.

International Air Transport Association (IATA). 1999. *Guidelines for handling disruptive/unruly passengers*. Geneva.

International Confederation of Free Trade Unions (ICFTU). 1995. *Trade Union Action Programme on Violence against Women*. Brussels.

—. 2004. *Annual Survey of Violations of Trade Union Rights: Americas*, p. 2 (see: icftu.org/displaydocument.asp?Index=9912194158language=EN, accessed 18 Oct. 2005).

International Council of Nurses (ICN). 1999. *Guidelines on coping with violence in the workplace*. Geneva (see: icn.ch, accessed 15 Nov. 2000).

International Federation of Journalists. 2003a. "A survival guide for journalists: Live news", Mar. (see: ifj.org/hrights/safecontexts.html, accessed 10 Jan 2006).

—. 2003b. "Journalists and media staff killed in 2003: an IFJ report on media casualties in the field of journalism and newsgathering" (see: ifj.org/pdfs/killreport2003.pdf, accessed 27 Sep. 2005).

—. 2004. "Global journalists call for government to act as media killings cast shadow over human rights day" (see: ifj.org/default.asp?index=2843&Language =EN, accessed Dec. 2004).

International Labour Organization (ILO). 1987. "Alcohol and drugs", *Conditions of Work Digest*, Vol. 6, No. 1. Geneva.

—. 1992. "Preventing stress at work", *Conditions of Work Digest*, Vol. 11, No. 2. Geneva.

—. 1993a. "Workers' privacy, Part II: Monitoring and surveillance in the workplace", *Conditions of Work Digest*, Vol 12, No. 1. Geneva.

—. 1993b. "Workers' privacy, Part III: Testing in the workplace", *Conditions of Work Digest*, Vol. 12, No. 2. Geneva.

—. 1995. *Occupational stress and stress prevention in air traffic control*, CONDI/T/W.P.6/1995. Geneva.

—. 1996a. *Bus drivers: Occupational stress and stress prevention*, CONDI/T/W.P.2/1996. Geneva.

—. 1996b. *Child labour: Targeting the intolerable*. Geneva.

—. 1996c. *Stress prevention in the offshore oil and gas exploration and production industry*, CONDI/T/W.P.1/1996. Geneva.

—. 1996d. *Work-related stress in nursing: Controlling the risk to health*, CONDI/T/W.P.4/1996. Geneva.

—. 1997a. *The ILO, standard setting and globalization*, Report of the Director-General, International Labour Conference, 85th Session. Geneva.

—. 1997b. *Stress prevention for blue-collar workers in assembly-line production*, CONDI/T/W.P.1/1997. Geneva.

—. 1999a. *Annotated bibliography on sexual harassment at work*. Geneva.

—. 1999b. *Decent work*, Report of the Director-General, International Labour Conference, 87th Session. Geneva.

—. 1999c. *Sexual harassment – An ILO survey of company practices*. Geneva.

—. 2001a. *Action against sexual harassment at work in Asia and the Pacific*, technical report for discussion at the ILO/Japan Regional Tripartite Seminar on Action against Sexual Harassment at Work in Asia and the Pacific, Penang, Malaysia, 2–4 Oct. (see: ilo.org/public/english/protection/condtrav/publ/hvs-sh-tr-01.htm, accessed 30 Nov. 2005).

—. 2001b. *Report on the ILO/Japan Regional Tripartite Seminar on action against sexual harassment at work in Asia and the Pacific, Penang, Malaysia*, 2–4 Oct.

—. 2002a. *A future without child labour*, Global Report under the Follow-up to the ILO Declaration of Fundamental Principles and Rights at Work, International Labour Conference, 90th Session, Report IB. Geneva.

—. 2002b. *Combating child labour: A handbook for labour inspectors*. Geneva.

—. 2003a. *Equality in employment and occupation*, General Survey of the Committee of Experts on the Application of Conventions and Recommendations, International Labour Conference, 91st Session, Report III (Part 1A). Geneva.

—. 2003b. "Violence at work", in *Labour Education* (ILO Bureau for Workers' Activities), 2003/4, No. 133.

—. 2004a. "Collective agreement on conflict prevention and resolution between the International Labour Office and the ILO Staff Union", Circulars 6/648 and 649. Geneva.

—. 2004b. *Workplace violence in services sectors and measures to combat this phenomenon*, ILO code of practice. Geneva.(see: ilo.org/public/english/dialogue/sector/ techmeet/ mevsws03/mevsws-cp.pdf, accessed 14 Oct. 2005).

—. 2005. *336th Report of the Committee on Freedom of Association*, Governing Body GB.292/8, 292nd Session, Geneva, Mar. (see: www-ilo-mirror.cornell.edu/public/ english/standards/relm/gb/docs/gb292/pdf/gb-b.pdf, accessed 10 Nov. 2005).

—; International Council of Nurses (ICN); World Health Organization (WHO); Public Service International (PSI). 2002. *Framework Guidelines for Addressing Workplace Violence in the Health Sector*, ILO/ICN/WHO/PSI Joint Programme on Workplace Violence in the Health Sector, Geneva (see: ilo.org/public/english/dialogue/ sector/papers/health/guidelines.pdf, accessed 24 Nov. 2005. See also: icn.org.).

International Maritime Organisation. 2003. "Right to work in a harassment free environment", Interoffice memorandum, 14 May. London.

International Monetary Fund (IMF). 1998. "Code of conduct". Washington, DC.

—. 2003. "Discrimination Policy". Washington, DC.

Iraq Body Count. No date. "A dossier of civilian casualties, 2003–2005" (see: reports.iraqbodycount.org/a_dossier_of_civilian_casualties_2003–2005.pdf, accessed 27 Sep. 2005).

Ireland, Department of Enterprise, Trade and Development. 2002. *Procedures for addressing bullying in the workplace*. Dublin.

Irish Equality Authority. 2002a. *Code of practice on sexual harassment and harassment at work*. Dublin.

—. 2002b. *Code of practice: Prevention of workplace bullying*. Dublin.

—. 2002c. *Guidelines on the prevention of workplace bullying*. Dublin.

Isaksson, K.; Hogstedt, K.; Eriksson, C.; Theorell, T. 2000. *Health effects of the New Labour Market*. New York, Kluwer Academic/Plenum Publishers, pp. 183–506.

Isolatus, N. 2002. "Prevention of physical violence at work", in *African Newsletter on Occupational Safety and Health*, Vol. 12, No. 1, Apr., pp. 13–15.

Italian Institute of Statistics (ISTAT). 2004. "Molestie e violenze sessuali, Italia" (see: eurofound.eu.int/ewco/2005/03/IT0503NU03.htm, accessed 17 Oct. 2005).

Japan Labor Flash. 2003. No. 5, 1 Dec. (see: jil.go.jp/foreign/emm/bi/5.htm, accessed 27 Sep. 2005).

Johns, M. 2003. "Wanted: Freedom from workplace bullying", 18–24 Oct. (see: RedBankLocal, American Postal Workers Union, AFL-CIO, redbanklocal.com/zero.htm, accessed 18 Nov. 2005).

Johnson, H. 1996. *Dangerous domains – Violence against women in Canada*. Scarborough, Ontario, Nelson Canada.

Johnson, P.; Gardner, S. 2000. "Domestic violence invades the workplace: Strategies for the global business community", in *Women in Management Review*, Vol. 15, No. 4, pp. 197–203.

Johnstone, R. 1997. *Occupational health and safety law and policy: Text and materials*. Sydney, LBC Information Services.

Kern, H. 2003. "Federal Aviation Administration: Unruly passengers, calendar years 1995–2002 (The faces of air rage)", in *FBI Law Enforcement Bulletin*, Vol. 72, No. 8 (see: fbi.gov/publications/leb/2003/august2003/aug03leb.htm#page_7, accessed 5 Jan. 2006).

Kershaw, C., et al. 2000. *British Crime Survey, Home Office Statistical Bulletin 18/00*. London, Research, Development and Statistics Directorate.

King, A.; Peart, M. 1992. *Teachers in Canada: Their work and quality of life*. Kingston, Ontario, Queen's University.

Kivimaki, K.; Elovainio, M.; Vathera, J. 2000. "Workplace bullying and sickness absence in hospital staff", in *Occupational and Environmental Medicine* (BMJ Journals), Vol. 57, No. 10, pp. 656–660.

Kuzmits, F. 1990. "When employees kill other employees", in *Journal of Occupational Medicine* (Arlington Heights, Illinois), Vol. 32, No. 10, pp. 1014–1020. With permission.

L'observation des nouveaux risques sociaux. 1998. "Transports urbains – Un terrain possible par les travailleurs et les intervenants sociaux", No. 13, Nov.

Labour Research. 1994. *Bargaining report*. London.

—. 2003. "Can zero tolerance deliver?". London, May.

Lamnek, S. 2003. "Individual violence justification strategies", in Heitmeyer and Hagan (eds.), 2003, pp. 1113–1127.

Lanza, M. 1996. "Violence against nurses in hospitals", in VandenBos and Bulatao (eds.), 1996, pp. 189–198.

Levin, L. 1995. "When domestic violence shows up at work", in *National Business Woman*, Vol. 76, No. 1, pp. 11–13, cited in Johnson and Gardner, 2000, pp. 197–203.

Leymann, H. 1990. "Mobbing and psychological terror at workplaces", in H. Leymann (ed.): *Violence and victims*, Vol. 5. New York, Springer Publishing Company, p. 119. Used by permission from Springer Publishing Co., Inc., New York, 10012.

Liberty Internet Magazine. 1999. "Courage at Columbine High School", 7 July.

Lim, L. 1996. *More and better jobs for women: An action guide*. Geneva. ILO.

Lim, V.K. 1996. "Job insecurity and its outcomes: Moderating effects of work-based and nonwork-based social support", in *Human Relations* (New York, Sage), Vol. 49, No. 2, pp. 171–194.

Littler, Mendelson, Fastiff, Tichy, & Mathiason, Inc. 1994. *Combating workplace violence: The New California Requirements Task Force Report*. San Francisco, California.

Lösel, F.; Bliesener, T. 1999. "Germany", in Smith, P.K., et al. *The nature of school bullying: A cross-national perspective*. New York, Routledge.

Long Island Coalition for Workplace Violence Awareness and Prevention. 1996. *Workplace violence awareness and prevention: An information and instructional package for use by employers and employees*. New York, Long Island (see: osha-sle.gov/workplace-violence/wrkplaceViolence.intro.html, accessed 1 Mar. 2001).

London Transport Occupational Health. 1997. *Report to Staff Assaults Working Group: Quantitative analysis of staff assaults*. London, Trident Consultants Ltd., J2909 Mar. Reproduced by courtesy of Mr. C. Lipscomb, Business Manager, London Transport Occupational Health, and Mr. S. Harris, Business Manager, London Transport Working Group, London Underground, 1997. Information provided 2 Apr. 1997.

London Underground. 2004. Press release, 6 Dec. 2004.

Loomis, D.; Wolf, S.; Runyan, C.; Marshall, S.; Butts, J. 2001. "Homicide on the job: Workplace and community determinants", in *American Journal of Epidemiology*, Vol. 154, No. 5, pp. 410–417.

Mantell, M.; Albrecht, S. 1994. *Ticking bomb: Defusing violence in the workplace*. Illinois, Burr Ridge, Irwin Professional Publishing. Reproduced with permission from The McGraw-Hill Companies, from M. Mantell and S. Albrecht.

Manufacturing, Science, Finance Union (MSF). 1993. "Prevention of violence at Work: An MSF guide with model agreement and violence at work questionnaire", in *MSF Health and Safety Information Sheet* No. 37. Hertfordshire, Bishop's Stortford.

—. 1994. *Working alone: Guidance for MSF members and safety representatives.* London.

Martine, M. 1994. *La situación de las mujeres, docentes en centroamerica: Hacia la igualdad de oportunidades y de trato.* Geneva, ILO.

Maticka-Tyndale, E.; Lewis, J.; Clark, J.; Zubick, J.; Young, S. 2000. "Exotic dancing and health", in *Women and Health*, Vol. 31, No. 1, pp. 87–108, cited in Giga, Hoel and Cooper, 2003b.

Mayhew, C. 1999. "Occupational violence: A case study of the taxi industry", in *Occupational Health and Safety in Australia: Industry, Public Sector and Small Business.* Sydney, Allen and Unwin, pp. 127–139.

—. 2000a. *Preventing client-initiated violence: A practical handbook*, Research and Public Policy Series, No. 30. Canberra, Australian Institute of Criminology.

—. 2000b. *Preventing violence within organisations: A practical handbook*, Research and Public Policy Series No. 29. Canberra, Australian Institute of Criminology.

—. 2000c. "Violent assaults on taxi drivers: Incidence, patterns and risk factors", in *Trends and Issues in Crime and Criminal Justice* (Canberra, Australian Institute of Criminology), Vol. 6, No. 178, p. 178.

—. 2002a. "Occupational violence in industrialized countries, types, incidence patterns and 'at risk' groups of workers", in M. Gill, B. Fisher and V. Bowie (eds.): *Violence at work: Causes, patterns and prevention.* Cullompton, Devon, Willan Publishing, pp. 21–40.

—. 2002b. *Violence in the workplace – Preventing commercial armed robbery: A practical handbook*, Research and Public Policy Series No. 33. Canberra, Australian Institute of Criminology.

—. 2003. "An exploration of the links between workplace stress and precarious employment", in C. Petersen (ed.): *Stress: Content and context.* Amityville, Baywood, pp. 203–219.

—. 2004. "Occupational violence risk for precariously employed adolescences: Multiple vulnerabilities to multiple risk factors", in *Policy and Practice in Health and Safety*, Vol. 2, No. 2, pp. 75–94.

—. 2005a. "Occupational violence in the health care industry", in C. Mayhew and C. Peterson (eds.): *Guide to managing OHS risks in the health care industry.* Sydney, CCH, pp. 121–153.

—. 2005b. "Violence in the workplace", in D. Chappell and P. Wilson (eds.): *Issues in Australian crime and criminal justice.* Sydney, Lexis Nexis Butterworths, pp. 392–408.

—; Chappell, D. 2001. *Prevention of occupational violence in the health workplace*, Working Paper Series, No. 140. School of Industrial Relations and Organisational Behaviour and Industrial Relations Research Centre, discussion paper No. 2 for the Taskforce on the Prevention and Management of Violence in the Health Workplace (NSW Health Department). Sydney, University of New South Wales (see: unsw.edu.au, accessed 14 Nov. 2005).

—; —. 2002. *Occupational violence in the NSW health workforce: Establishment of baseline data*, final research report to the Taskforce on the Prevention and Management of Violence in the Health Workplace. Sydney, Department of Health.

—; —. 2003. "The occupational violence experiences of some Australian health workers: An explained study", published as a monograph in a special issue of *Journal of Occupational Health and Safety: Australia and New Zealand*, Vol. 19, No. 6, pp. 3–43.

—; McCarthy, P. 2004. "Occupational violence: A pilot study of workers in a juvenile detention centre", in *Journal of Occupational Health and Safety: Australia and New Zealand*, Vol. 20, No. 6, pp. 511–521.

—; —; Chappell, D.; Quinlan, M.; Barker, M.; Sheehan, M. 2004. "Measuring the extent of impact from occupational violence and bullying on traumatized workers", in *Employee Responsibilities and Rights Journal,* special issue focused on "The traumatized worker", Vol. 16, No. 3, pp. 117–134.

—; Quinlan, M. 1999. "The relationship between precarious employment and patterns of occupational violence: Survey evidence from thirteen occupations", in Isaksen, Hogstedt, Eriksson and Theorell, 1999, pp. 183–205.

McCann, D. 2005. *Sexual harassment at work: A review of preventive measures*, Conditions of Work and Employment Series No. 2. Geneva, ILO.

McCarthy, P.; Mayhew, C. 2004. *Safeguarding the organisation against violence and bullying: An international perspective.* Basingstoke, Hampshire, Palgrave-MacMillan.

McDonald, D.; Brown, M. 1997. *Indicators of aggressive behaviour: Report to the Minister for Health and Family Services from an Expert Working Group*, Research and Public Policy Series, No. 8. Canberra, Australian Institute of Criminology. Reproduced with permission.

McNally, R. 2004. "Psychological debriefing does not prevent posttraumatic stress disorder", in *Psychiatric Times*, Vol. XXI, No. 4, Apr. (see: psychiatrictimes.com/p040471.html, and also i.cmpnet.com/cme/pt/content/p040471.jpg, accessed 11 Oct. 2005).

McSherry, B. 2004. "Risk assessment by mental health professionals and the prevention of future violent behaviour", in *Trends and Issues in Crime and Criminal Justice* (Canberra, Australian Institute of Criminology), Vol. 281, July.

Menckel, E.; Viitasara, E. 2002. "Threats and violence in Swedish care and welfare – Magnitude of the problem and impact on municipal personnel", in *Scandinavian Journal of Caring Sciences*, Vol. 16, pp. 376–385.

Meschkutat, B.; Stackelbeck, M.; Langenhoff, G. 2002. *Der Mobbing – Report, Eine Repräsentativstudie für die Bundesrepublik Deutschland.* Dortmund/Berlin, Bundesanstalt für Arbeitsschutz und Arbeitsmedizin.

Ministère de la Jeunesse, Education et Recherche, France. 2004. "Les actes de violence à L'école recensés dans SIGNA en 2002–2003", Information note, Feb. (see: trf.education.gouv.fr/pub/edutel/dpd/ni0404.pdf).

Ministry of Education, Culture, Sports, Science and Technology, Japan. No date (see: mext.go.jp/b_menu/houdou/15/12/03121902/002.pdf, accessed 10 Jan. 2006; in Japanese).

Ministry of Health, Labor and Welfare, Japan. 2003. *Japan Labor Bulletin,* Vol. 42, No. 7, July.

Ministry of Human Resources, Malaysia. 1999. *Code of practice on the prevention and eradication of sexual harassment at the workplace.* Kuala Lumpur.

—. 2001. *Guidance for the prevention of stress and violence at the workplace,* by V. Di Martino and M. Musri. Kuala Lumpur (see: ilo.org/public/english/protection/ safework/papers/malaysia/guide.pdf, accessed 1 Dec. 2005).

Ministry of Land, Infrastructure and Transport, Japan. 2004. "Enforcement of the revised Aviation Law to prevent acts causing a public nuisance aboard aircraft" (see: mlit.go.jp/koku/kinaimeiwaku.htm, accessed 2 Dec. 2005).

Mitchell, J.T. 1983. "When disaster strikes: The critical incidence stress debriefing process", in *Journal of Emergency Medical Services,* Vol. 8, No. 1, pp. 36–39.

—; Everly Jr., G.S. 2001. *Critical Incident Stress Debriefing: An operations manual for CISD, defusing and other group crisis intervention services.* Ellicott, City, MD, Chevron Publishing, 3rd edition, cited in McNally, 2004.

MMR Weekly. 1994. "Occupational injury deaths of postal workers – United States, 1980–1989", Vol. 43, No. 32, pp. 593–595.

Monahan, J. 1986. "Dangerous and violent behaviour", in *Journal of Occupational Medicine* (Arlington Heights), Vol. 1, pp. 559–568. Reproduced with permission.

Morita, Y.; Soeda, H.; Soeda, K.; Taki, M. 1999. "Japan", in P.K. Smith, Y. Morita, J. Junger-Tas, D. Olweus, R. Catalano and P. Slee (eds.): *The nature of school bullying: A cross-national perspective.* New York, Routledge. Cited in Verdugo and Vere, 2003, p. 15.

Muratore, M.G. 1999. "The 1997–98 Survey on Citizens' Security" (section on sexual violence). Rome, ISTAT, special tabulation for the ILO.

Murray, B. 1998. "Psychology's voice in sexual harassment law", in *APA Monitor,* Vol. 29, No. 8, Aug., pp. 1–2 (see: apa.org/monitor/aug98/law.html, accessed 17 June 2005).

Musri, M.; Daud, R. 2002. "Violence at work – Occupational safety and health perspective", in *Asian-Pacific Newsletter on Occupational Health and Safety* (Bangkok), Vol. 9, No. 1, Mar.

National Clearinghouse for Legal Services, Inc. 1994. "Do you know the effects of violence on your clients?", in *Special Issue of Clearinghouse Review* (Chicago), Vol. 28, No. 4.

National Commission on Terrorist Attacks upon the United States. 2004. *The 9/11 Commission Report, Final Report of the National Commission on Terrorist Attacks upon the United States* (the Commission closed on 21 August 2004) (see: 9-11 commission.gov/report/911Report.pdf, accessed 5 Jan. 2006).

National Committee on Violence (NCV), Australia. 1990. *Violence: Directions for Australia*. Canberra, Australian Institute of Criminology (see: aic.gov.au/publications/vda/, accessed 11 Nov. 2005). Reproduced with permission from the Australian Institute of Criminology, National Committee on Violence (NCV).

National Health Service (NHS), United Kingdom. 2000a. *Managing violence in ambulance trusts: We don't have to take this*, Resource Sheet Update. London, Department of Health, NHS Zero Tolerance Zone.

—. 2000b. *Stopping violence against staff working in the NHS: We don't have to take this – Managers' guide*. London, Department of Health, NHS Zero Tolerance Zone, p. 6.

National Institute for Industrial Accidents and Occupational Diseases (INAIL), Italy [Istituto Nazionale per l'Assicurazione contro gli Infortuni sul Lavoro]. 2003. "Office Circular No. 71", 17 Dec. 2003.

National Institute for Occupational Safety and Health (NIOSH). 2002. *Occupational hazards in hospitals: Violence*. Cincinnati, Centers for Disease Control and Prevention, DHSS (NIOSH) publication No. 2002-101, 1 Apr. (see: cdc.gov/niosh/2002-101.html, accessed 5 Jan. 2006).

—. 2004. *NIOSH Update: Most workplace bullying is worker to worker, early findings from NIOSH study suggest*. Atlanta, 28 July (see: cdc.gov/niosh/updates/upd-07-28-04.html, accessed 8 Aug. 2005).

National Occupational Health and Safety Commission (NOHSC). 1999. *Program One Report: Occupational violence*, discussed at the 51st Meeting of the NOHSC, Hobart, 10 Mar. (see: aic.gov.au/research/cup/occupational/index.html, accessed 27 Sep. 2005).

Nation's Business. 1995. *Creating a violence-free company culture*. Washington, DC, p. 22.

New South Wales (NSW) Health. 2003. *Zero tolerance: Response to violence in the NSW health workplace – Policy and framework guidelines*. Sydney, NSW Department of Health, July (see: health.nsw.gov.au/pubs/PD/2005/pdf/PD2005_315.pdf, accessed 1 Dec. 2005).

News Telegraph. 2004. "Doctors and nurses want more protection from assault", 20 Dec.

Nogareda Cuixart, C.; Nogareda Cuixart, S. 1990. "Valoración de la carga mental en el servicio de urgencias de un hospital", in *Salud y Trabajo* (Barcelona), No. 2, p. 11.

Nowak, A.; Dekena, B.; Cukur-Kunz, C.; Yakan, E.; Engelberg, R.; Lühr, S. 2002. *Prima-Projekt der Bremer Straßenbahn AG*. Bremen, BSAG Geschäftsstelle; unpublished material cited in Di Martino, Hoel and Cooper, 2003.

L'observation des nouveaux risques sociaux. 1998. « Transports urbains – Un terrain possible pour les travailleurs et les intervenants sociaux », No. 13, Nov.

Oberhardt, M. 1998. "Worker awarded $550,000", in *Courier-Mail*, 24 Apr., p. 1.

Occupational Safety and Health Service, New Zealand. 1995a. *A guide for employers and employees dealing with violence at work.* Wellington.

—. 1995b. *Guidelines for the safety of staff from the threat of armed robbery.* Wellington.

Office of the Ombudsman, United Nations. 2002. "Appointment and terms of reference of the Ombudsman", in *Secretary-General's Bulletin.* New York.

O'Gloff J.; Davis, M. 2005. "Assessing risk for violence in the Australian contexts", in D. Chappell and P. Wilson (eds.): *Issues in Australian crime and criminal justice.* Sydney, Lexis Nexis Butterworths, pp. 301–338.

O'Loughlin, E. 2001. "Slavery in the 21st century: Descent into lives of silent servitude", in *Sydney Morning Herald*, 6 June.

O'Neill, A. 2005. "The evolving nature of international terrorism and Australia's response", in D. Chappell and P. Wilson: *Issues in Australian crime and criminal justice.* Sydney, Lexis Nexis Butterworths, pp. 377–391.

O'Neill, D. 2001. *Non-fatal workplace violence: An epidemiological report and empirical exploration of risk factors.* Nebraska, University of Nebraska, PhD dissertation, funded by the US Department of Justice.

Organisation for Economic Cooperation and Development (OECD). 2002. *Preventing and dealing with harassment at the OECD – Policy and guidelines*, C(2002)141. Paris.

Ortega, R.; Mora-Merchan, J.A. 1999. "Spain", in P. K. Smith, Y. Morita, J. Janger-Tas, D. Olweus, R. Catalano and P. Slee (eds.): *The nature of school bullying: A cross-national perspective.* New York, Routledge. Cited in Verdugo and Vere, 2003, p. 15.

Palácios, M.; Loureiro dos Santos, M.; Barros do Val, M.; Medina, M.; de Abreu, M.; Soares Cardoso, L.; Bragança Pereira, B. 2002. *Workplace violence in the health sector – Country case study Brazil*, ILO/ICN/WHO/PSI Joint Programme on Workplace Violence in the Health Sector. Geneva.

Palmieri, P.; Harned, M.; Collinsworth, L.; Fitzgerald, L.; Lancaster, A. 2003. *Who counts? A rational empirical algorithm for determining the incidence of sexual harassment in the military,* DMDC Technical Report, 2000. Urbana/Champaign, University of Illinois, in Einarsen et al., 2003a, p. 85.

Paoli, P.; Merllié, D. 2001. *Third European Survey on Working Conditions 2000.* Dublin, European Foundation for the Improvement of Living and Working Conditions. Luxembourg, Office for Official Publications of the European Communities (see: eurofound.eu.int/publications/htmlfiles/EF0121.htm, and also ilo.org/public/english/protection/safework/violence/eusurvey.htm, both accessed 17 Oct. 2005).

—; Parent-Thirion, A. 2003. *Working conditions in the acceding and candidate countries*. Dublin, European Foundation for the Improvement of Living and Working Conditions (see: eurofound.eu.int, accessed 9 Jan. 2005).

Pérez, N.; Valera, C. 1995. *Impacto socio-economico de las maquiladoras y las zonas libres en Honduras*. Geneva, ILO.

PERSEREC (Defence Personnel Security Research Center). 1995. "Guidelines for employers", in *Combating workplace violence*. Washington, DC.

Philbrick, J.; Sparks, M.; Hass M.; Arsenault, S. 2003. "Workplace violence: The legal costs can kill you", in *American Business Review* (Connecticut, University of New Haven), Vol. 21, No. 1, Jan., pp. 84–90.

Pierce, R. 1985. "Alternative compensation schemes and tort theory: Institutional aspects of tort reform", in *California Law Review*, Vol. 73, pp. 917–937.

Piñuel, I. 2004. *Mobbing in Spanish public administrations*, Report CISNEROS V, 18 Sep.

—; Zabala, I. 2002. "La incidencia del mobbing o acoso psicológico en el trabajo in España." Alcalá de Henares, Universidad de Alcalá de Henares; unpublished report.

Pizzino, A. 1994. "Report on CUPE's (Canadian Union of Public Employees) National Health and Safety Survey of Aggression Against Staff". Ottawa, p. 15.

Popma, J.; Schaapman, M.; Wilthagan, T. 2002. "The Netherlands: Implementation within wider regulatory reform", in D. Walters (ed.): *Regulating health and safety management in the European Union: A study of the dynamics of change*. Brussels, Arbetslivsinstitutet, SALTSA joint programme for working life research in Europe, National Institute for Working Life, pp. 177–209.

Poyner, B.; Warne, C. 1986. *Violence to staff: A basis for assessment and prevention*, Health and Safety Executive. London, HMSO.

—; —. 1988. *Preventing violence to staff*, Health and Safety Executive. London, Tavistock Institute of Human Relations.

Pryor, J.; Fitzgerald, L. 2003. "Sexual harassment research in the United States", in Einarsen et al. (eds.), 2003a, p. 79.

Publiweb. No date. "La voce ai lettori: Sondaggi-fai sentire la tua opinione" (see: publiweb.com/sondaggi/pag31.shtml, accessed 28 Sep. 2005).

Rail Safety and Standards Board, United Kingdom. 2004. *Annual Safety Performance Report* (see: rssb.co.uk/pdf/ASPR2004-rwk.pdf, accessed 9 Jan. 2006).

Rayner, C., et al. 2002. *Workplace bullying*. London, Taylor and Francis.

Reinhart, A. 1999. *Sexual harassment: Addressing sexual harassment in the workplace – A management information booklet*. Geneva, ILO.

Reiss, A.; Roth, J. (eds.). 1993. *Understanding and preventing violence*. Washington, DC, National Academy Press, 4 vols.

Rennison, C.M. 2003. *Intimate partner violence, 1993–2001*, Crime Data Brief. US Department of Justice, Office of Justice Programs, Bureau of Justice Statistics, NCJ197838, Feb. (see: ojp.usdoj.gov/bjs/pub/pdf/ipv01.pdf, accessed 23 June 2005).

Richards, J. 2002. *Management of workplace violence victims*, ILO/ICN/WHO/PSI Joint Programme on Workplace Violence in the Health Sector; working paper. Geneva.

Richardson, S.; Windau, J. 2003. "Fatal and nonfatal assaults in the workplace, 1992 to 2001", in *Clinics in Occupational and Environmental Medicine* (London, Elsevier), No. 3, pp. 673–689.

Rigby, K. 2004. *Stop the bullying: A handbook for schools*. Melbourne, ACERE Press. Cited in Verdugo and Vere, 2003, p. 15.

—; Slee, P.T. 1999. "Australia", in P.K. Smith, Y. Morita, J. Junger-Tas, D. Olweus, R. Catalano and P. Slee (eds.): *The nature of school bullying: A cross-national perspective*. New York, Routledge.

Rogers, K.; Chappell, D. 2003. *Preventing and responding to violence at work*. Geneva, ILO.

Rosskam, E. 2001. "Perils of the check-in desk", in *Transport International* (London), No. 5, pp. 19–20, cited in Essenberg, 2003, p. 19.

Royal College of Nursing (RCN). 2000. *Challenging harassment and bullying: Guidance for RCN representatives, stewards and officers*. London.

Sadler, A.; Booth, B.; Cook, B.; Torner, J.; Doebbeling, B. 2001. "The military environment: Risk factors for women's non-fatal assaults", in *Journal of Occupational and Environmental Medicine*, Vol. 43, Issue 4, Apr., pp. 325–334.

Santana, S.; Fisher, B. 2002. "Workplace violence in the USA: Are there gender differences?", in M. Gill, B. Fisher and V. Bowie (eds.): *Violence at work: Causes, patterns and prevention*. Cullompton, Devon, Willan Publishing, pp. 90–113.

Saskatchewan Teachers' Association. 1994. "Survey finds teacher abuse growing", in *Saskatchewan Bulletin*, May, p. 3.

Schwid, H.; Duchin, J.; Brennan, J.; Taneda, K.; Boedeker, B.; Ziv, A. 2002. *Bioterrorism simulator*. Washington, Issaquah, Anesoft Corporation (see: anesoft.com, accessed 9 Jan. 2006).

Scialpi, D. 2004. *Violencias en la administración pública. Casos y miradas para pensar la Administración Pública como ámbito laboral*. Buenos Aires, Editorial Catálogos.

Scottish Office. 1996. *The Public Inquiry into the Shootings at Dunblane Primary School on 13 March 1996: The Government Response*, CM. 3392. Edinburgh.

Sczesny, S.; Stahlberg, D. 2000. "Sexual harassment over the telephone: Occupational risk at call centres", in *Work and Stress*, Vol. 14, No. 2, Apr.–June, pp. 121–136.

Sharp, S.; Smith, P. 1991. *Tackling bullying in your school: A practical handbook for teachers*. London, Routledge. Cited in Verdugo and Vere, 2003, p. 15.

Shaw, M. 2001a. *Promoting safety in schools: International experiences and action (report)*, Crime Prevention Services No. 3 (complete report). Washington, DC, US Department of Justice. Cited in Verdugo and Vere, 2003, p. 14–15.

—. 2001b. "Promoting safety in school: International experiences and action", *Crime Prevention Services*, Bulletin No. 3, May. Washington, DC, US Department of Justice (see: crime-prevention.org, accessed 20 Jan. 2006).

Sheehan, M.; McCarthy, P.; Barker, M.; Henderson, M. 2001. *A model for assessing the impacts and costs of workplace bullying*, paper presented at the Standing Conference on Organizational Symbolism (SCOS), 30 June–4 July 2001. Dublin, Trinity College.

Silva, N. 2004. "Braving mob mayhem and danger", in *NSW Police News*, Vol. 84, No. 4, pp. 7–9.

Sinclair-Bernadino, L. No date. *Negligent hiring doctrine opens more doors for pre-employment screening: Pimall, Private Investigator Network*, Island Investigations (see: pimall.com/nais/n.hire.html, accesssed 30 Nov. 2005).

Smith, P.; Singer, M.; Hoel, H.; Cooper, C. 2003. "Victimization in the school and the workplace: Are there any links?", in *British Journal of Psychology*, Vol. 94 (Pro Quest Medical Library).

Society for Human Resource Management (SHRM). 1996. *Workplace Violence Survey 1996*. Alexandria, Virginia. Reproduced with permission.

Sonoma State University. 1998. "Policy: Violence free campus". Sonoma, California (see: sonoma.edu/UAffairs/policies/violence.htm, accessed 30 June 2005).

South Africa, Department of Labour. 1995. *Code of practices on the handling of sexual harassment cases* (appended to the Labour Relations Act 66 of 1995).

South African Institute of Race Relations. 2000. *Fast Facts – National Crime Trends*. June.

Sripichyakan, K.; Thungpunkum, P.; Supavititpatana, B. 2002. *Workplace violence in the health sector – A case study in Thailand*, ILO/ICN/WHO/PSI Joint Programme on Workplace Violence in the Health Sector. Geneva.

Standing, H.; Nicolini, D. 1997. *Review of work-related violence*, Tavistock Institute for the Health and Safety Executive, Contract Research report for the Health and Safety Executive, report No. 143/1997. London.

Statistics Finland. 1997. *Quality of Work Life Surveys 1997*. Helsinki, special elaboration for the authors.

—. 2003. *Quality of Work Life Surveys 2003*. Helsinki, special elaboration for the authors.

Statistics Sweden. 1999. *The Work Environment 1999*, Supplement to the Statistical Report AM 68 SM0001, p. 24 (see: av.se/statistik/dok/0000085.pdf, accessed 10 Nov. 2005).

Steinman, S. 2002. *Workplace violence in the health sector – Country case study: South Africa*, ILO/ICN/WHO/PSI Joint Programme on Workplace Violence in the Health Sector. Geneva.

Streetnet International. 2004. *First International Congress*, Seoul, Republic of Korea, 16–17 Mar. (see: 77streetnet.org.za/English/congrepen.htm, Annexure 6, accessed 18 Oct. 2005).

Subedi, G. 2002. *Trafficking and sexual abuse among street children in Kathmandu*, Report No. 1. Kathmandu, ILO, International Programme on the Elimination of Child Labour (IPEC).

Suzy Lamplugh Trust. 1994a. *Personal safety at work: guidance for all employees.* London (see: suzylamplugh.org/home/index.shtml, accessed 25 Oct. 2005).

—. 1994b. *Violence and aggression at work: Reducing the risks. Guidance for employers.* London.

Swanton, B.; Webber, D. 1990. *Protecting counter and interviewing staff from client aggression*. Canberra, Australian Institute of Criminology.

Swedish National Board of Occupational Safety and Health. 1993. *Statute Book of the Swedish National Board of Occupational Safety and Health containing Provisions on Measures against Victimization at Work, Ordinance (AFS 1993:2) on Violence and Menaces in the Working Environment, 14 Jan.; and Ordinance (AFS 1993:17) on Victimization at Work, 21 Sep.* Stockholm.

Talli, R. 2003. "Growing fears for safety of people working alone in the service sector", in *Helsingin Sanomat*, International edition, 5 Aug. (see: helsinginsanomat.fi/english/archive/news.asp?id=20030805IE16, accessed 2 Nov. 2005).

Taylor, N. 2002. "Robbery against service stations and pharmacies: Recent trends", in *Trends and Issues in Crime and Criminal Justice* (Canberra, Australian Institute of Criminology), No. 223 (see: aic.gov.au/publications/tandi/ti223.pdf, accessed 3 Nov. 2005).

Tessari, R. No date. "Il pg militare: è un allarme sociale : Un fenomeno diffuso e preoccupante" (see: triesterivista.it/cultura/Tessari/nonnismo.htm, accessed 28 Sep. 2005).

TNO Arbeid. 2002. *Gewenst beleid tegen ongewenst gedrag: voorbeelden van goed beleid tegen ongewenste omgangsvormen op het werk*, TNO-rapport 9619/3510153/vri/yuk, 18 June, pp. 36–38 (see: arbo.nl/content/network/tnoarbeid/docs/beleid_ongewenst_gedrag.pdf, accessed 9 Jan. 2006).

Tomev, L.; Daskalova, N.; Ivanova, V. 2002. *Workplace violence in the health sector – Country case study: Bulgaria*, ILO/ICN/WHO/PSI Joint Programme on Workplace Violence in the Health Sector. Geneva.

Tondreau, J. 2000. *Inventaire d'outils sur la violence.* Montreal, Centrale des syndicats de Quebec. Cited in Verdugo and Vere, 2003, p. 14.

Toohey, J. 1993. "Corporate culture and the management of violence", unpublished conference paper presented at the "Occupational violence: Were you threatened at work today?" seminar series, University of Queensland, Australia, 10–12 Feb. Brisbane.

Toshiba Group CSR. No date. *Social and environmental activities: Corporate and individual relationships*, Ch. 2 (see: toshiba.co.jp/csr/en/soc/ch2.htm, accessed 30 June 2005).

Trades Union Congress (TUC). 1992. *Guidelines: Sexual harassment at work*. London.

—. 1993. *Racial harassment at work: Guidance for safety representatives and members on bullying at work and how to prevent it*. London.

—. 1999. *Protect us from harm: Preventing violence at work*, report by Julia Gallagher. London, TUC Health and Safety Unit.

—. 2002. "Bus crime crackdown launched", in *Risks*, No. 69, 31 Aug.

—. 2003. *Risks 128*, 18 Oct. (see: tuc.org.uk/h_and_s/tuc-8894-f0.cfm#i4, accessed 2 Jan. 2006).

—. 2004. *Risks 180*, 30 Oct. (see: tuc.org.uk/h_and_s/tuc-7217-f0.cfm#i6/, accessed 2 Jan. 2006).

Transport Salaried Staffs' Association (TSSA). 2001. *Health and Safety News*, "Annual safety performance report". London.

UNICEF, International Child Development Centre. 1999. "Child domestic work", in *Innocenti Digest* 5. Florence, May.

Uniform Crime Reporting (UCR) Program. No date. *Special Report: Bank robbery in the United States*, 1990 and 2001 (see: fbi.gov/ucr/cius_02/pdf/5sectionfive.pdf, accessed 9 Jan. 2006).

Union des Transports Publics, France. 2003. *La sécurité dans les transports urbains 2002*, Rapport de branche sur l'état de la sécurité dans les entreprises de transports urbains en 2002, Sep., p. 7 (see: utp.fr/documents/telecharger/rapport_de_branche_securite _2002.pdf, accessed 27 Sep. 2005).

UNISON. 1992. *Violence in the National Health Service*. London.

—. 1993. *Working alone in safety: Controlling the risks of solitary work*. London.

—. 1996. *Bullying at work: Guidance for safety representatives and members on bullying at work and how to prevent it*. London.

—. 1997. *Violence at work: A guide to risk prevention for UNISON branches, stewards and safety representatives*. London.

United Nations. 1992. "Report of the Committee on the Elimination of Discrimination against Women: Eleventh Session, General Assembly", *Official Records*, 47th Session, Supplement No. 38, A/47/38. New York.

—. 1993a. "Declaration on the Elimination of Violence against Women, General Assembly", *Official Records*, 48th Session, A/RES/48/104. New York.

—. 1993b. "Special measures for protection from sexual exploitation and sexual abuse". New York.

—. 1995. "Report of the Fourth World Conference on Women, Beijing", 4–15 Sep.

—. 2003. "ILO survey of United Nations System of Organizations and Directory of Senior Officials". New York.

—. 2004. *UN action against terrorism.* Geneva (see: un.org/terrorism, accessed 20 Nov. 2005).

—, Commission on Human Rights. 1997. "Further promotion and encouragement of human rights and freedoms …", *Report of the Special Rapporteur on violence against women, its causes and consequences*, Ms. Radhika Coomaraswamy. Geneva, E/CN.4/1997/Add.4, 12 Feb.

—, —. 1999. "Integration of the human rights of women and the gender perspective: Violence against women", *Report of the Special Rapporteur on violence against women* …. Geneva, E/CN.4/1999/68, 10 Mar. Add.1; see also "Report of the mission to the United States of America on the use of violence in state and federal prisons", Add. 2.

—, —. 2000. "Integration of the human rights of women and the gender perspective: Violence against women", *Report of the Special Rapporteur on violence against women* …. Geneva, E/CN.4/2000/68, 29 Feb.

—, —. 2002. "Anti-slavery", submission to the UNHCR, Sub-Commission on the Promotion and Protection on Human Rights, Working Group on Contemporary Forms of Slavery, 27th Session, Geneva, 21–31 May (see: antislavery.org/archive/submission/submission2002-childlabour.htm, accessed 6 Jan. 2006).

—, —. 2003. "International, regional and national developments in the area of violence against women, 1994–2003", *Report of the Special Rapporteur on violence against women.* … Geneva, E/CN.4/2003/675, Add.1, paras. 182 and 382.

—, Division for the Advancement of Women. 2000. "Optional protocol entered into force 22 Dec. 2000". New York, press release (see: www.un.org/womenwatch/daw/, accessed 6 Dec. 2005).

—, Office of the Ombudsman. 2002. "Appointment and terms of reference of the Ombudsman", Secretary-General's Bulletin, 15 Oct.

—, —. 2003. "Special measures from sexual exploitation and sexual abuse", Secretariat, 9 Oct.

United Nations Development Fund for Women (UNIFEM). 2003. "Not a minute more: Progress on ending violence against women", speech by J. Sandler, Deputy Director, 47th Session of the Commission on the Status of Women, New York, 3 Mar. (see: unifem/org/news_events/storydetail.php?StoryID=160, accessed 5 Dec. 2005).

United Nations Industrial Development Organization (UNIDO). No date. "Guidelines on sexual harassment" (available but being reviewed).

United States (US), Bureau of Justice Statistics, Department of Justice. 1998. *Workplace violence, 1992–1996: National Crime Victimization Survey.* Special Report. Washington, DC, June.

—, —. 2002. "Preventing school shootings. A summary of a US Secret Service Safe School Initiative Report", in *National Institute of Justice Journal*, No. 248, Mar. pp. 10–15 (see: ncjrs.ord/pdffiles1/jt000248c.pdf, accessed 18 Nov. 2005).

—, Bureau of National Affairs. No date. *Fair employment practices.* Washington, DC.

—, Centers for Disease Control and Prevention (CDC), National Center for Injury Prevention and Conflict, Department of Health and Human Services. 1994. "Occupational Injury Deaths of Postal Workers – United States, 1980–89", in *US Postal Service; A violence free workplace*, 19 Aug. Bureau of Statistics, US Department of Labour (see: www.cdc.gov/mmwr/preview/mmwrhtml/00032345.htm, accessed 1 Jan. 2006).

—, —, —. 2005. "Intimate partner violence: Fact sheet". Atlanta (see: www.cdc.gov/ncipc/factsheets/ipvfacts.htm, accessed 21 Nov. 2005).

—, Department of Labor, Bureau of Labor Statistics (BLS). 2001. *Number of nonfatal injuries and illnesses.* Washington, DC (see: bls.gov/iif/oshwc/osh/case/ostb1182.pdf, accessed 9 Jan 2006).

—, —. 2002. *Annual Survey of Occupational Injuries and Illnesses.* Washington, DC (see: bls.gov/iif/oshwc/osh/case/ostb1182.pdf, accessed 9 Jan. 2006).

—, —. 2003. *Census of Fatal Occupational Injuries.* Washington, DC (see: bls.gov/iif/oshwc/osh/case/ostb1260.pdf, accessed 6 Jan. 2006).

—, Departments of Education and Justice. 1999. *A guide to safe schools: Published guidelines on violence – A selection*, Ch. 5. Washington, DC. Cited in Verdugo and Vere, 2003, p. 14.

—, Equal Employment Opportunity Commission. 2002. "Sexual harassment charges. EEOC and FEPAs combined: FY1992-FY2002" (see: eeoc.gov/stats/harass.html, accessed 17 Oct. 2005).

—, Merit Systems Protection Board. 1995. *Sexual harassment in the federal workforce: Trends, progress, and continuing challenges*, No. 13.

—, Office of Personnel Management. 1997. *Dealing with workplace violence: A guide for agency planners.* Washington, DC.

—, Occupational Safety and Health Administration (OSHA). 1995. *Draft guidelines for workplace violence prevention programs for health care workers in institutional and community settings.* Washington, DC.

—, —. 1998. *Recommendations for workplace violence prevention programs in late-night retail establishments.* Washington, DC.

—, —. 2004. *Guidelines for preventing workplace violence for health care and social service workers*, OSHA 3148-01R. Washington, DC.

—, Postal Service. 1998. *Going postal: A violence free workplace*. Publication 45, Nov., p. 2 (see: crimelibrary.com/notoriousmurders/mass/workhomicide/4.html?sect=8, accessed 27 Sep. 2005).

University of Iceland, Social Science Research Institute. 1996. *Violence against nurses and other personnel working in health and social services in Iceland*. Reykjavík.

University of Illinois. 2000. *DMDC Technical Report*. Urbana, Champaign. Cited in Einarson et al., 2003a, p. 85.

Upson, A. 2004. *Violence at work: Findings from the 2002/2003 British Crime Survey*, Home Office Online Report 04/04. London (see: homeoffice.gov.uk/rds/pdfs2/rdsolr0404.pdf, accessed 27 Sep. 2005).

US/LEAP. 2002. "Violence against Colombian trade unions", in *Bulletin Issue* No. 3, Apr. (see: usleap.org/Colombia/VACTUBIssue3.html, accessed 12 Dec. 2005).

VandenBos, G.; Bulatao, E. (eds.) 1996. *Violence on the job: Identifying risks and developing solutions*. Washington, DC, American Psychological Association.

Vartia, M. 1993. *Psychological harassment at work*, OECD Panel Group on Women, Work and Health: National Report. Helsinki, Institute of Occupational Health, Ministry of Social Affairs and Health.

—. 1994. "Bullying at workplaces" in *Research on violence, threats and bullying as health risks among health care personnel*, proceedings from the Workshop for Nordic Researchers, Reykjavik, 14–16 Aug., p. 29.

—. 2001. "Consequences of workplace bullying with respect to the well-being of its targets and the observers of bullying", in *Scandinavian Journal of Work and Environmental Health* (Finnish Institute of Occupational Health), Vol. 27, No. 1, pp. 63–69.

—; Hyyti, J. 2000. "Violence in prison work", in J. Rantanen, S. Lehtinen and K. Saarela (eds.): *Safety in the modern society*, proceedings of the European Conference on Safety in the Modern Society, Sep. 1999. Helsinki, Finnish Institute of Occupational Health, People and Work Research Reports No. 33, pp. 144–48.

Verdugo, R.; Vere, A. 2003. *Workplace violence in service sectors with implications for the education sector: Issues, solutions and resources*, Sectoral Activities Programme, Working Paper No. 208. Geneva, ILO.

Victorian Community Council against Violence (VOCAV). 2004. *Family violence is a workplace issue: Workplace models to prevent family violence*. Melbourne.

Victorian WorkCover Authority. 2003. *Prevention of bullying and violence at work – Guidance note*. Melbourne, Feb. (see: www.workcover.vic.gov.au for future updates on the references used).

Walby, S. 2004. *The cost of domestic violence*. London, Department of Trade and Industry, Women and Equality Unit (see: womenandequalityunit.gov.uk/domestic_violence, accessed 22 June 2005).

Walters, D. (ed.). 2002. *Regulating health and safety management in the European Union: A study of the dynamics of change*, SALTSA Joint Programme for Working Life Research in Europe. Brussels, Peter Lang.

Waters (A.P.) v Commissioner of Police for the Metropolis. 2000. *All England Law Reports*. 4 All ER, pp. 934–947.

We! 2002. "WHO suggests new ways to address VAW problem", No. 4 (see: isiswomen.org/pub/we/archive/msg00097.html, accessed 6 Dec. 2005).

Weber, T. 2004. *Monthly Newsletter* (CEEP), Issue 1, June (see: ceep.org/en/themes/SocialAffairs/SANCNewsletterJune2004.doc.).

Wenn, B. 1989. "Violence in sport", in *Violence Today* (Canberra, Australian Institute of Criminology), No. 4.

Wijayatilake, K.; Zackariya, F. 2000. "Sexual harassment at work – Sri Lanka study with focus on the plantation sector", ILO working paper (unpublished). Colombo.

Wikipedia. 2004. "Madrid train bombings". 11 Mar. (see: en/wikipedia.org/wiki/March_11_2004_Madrid_attacks, accessed 27 Sep. 2005).

—. 2005. "West London bombings", 4 Oct.

Williams, C. 2000. "A pain in the neck: Passenger abuse, flight attendants and emotional labour", in *Australia and New Zealand Journal of Occupational Health and Safety*, Vol. 16, No. 5, pp. 429–435.

Wiskow, C. 2002. *Guidelines on workplace violence in the health sector – Comparison of major known national guidelines and strategies: United Kingdom, Australia, Sweden, USA*, ILO/ICN/WHO/PSI Joint Programme on Workplace Violence in the Health Sector. Geneva.

Women and Equality Unit (WEU), Department of Trade and Industry, United Kingdom. 2004. *Domestic violence* (see: womenandequalityunit.gov.uk/domestic_violence/index.htm, accessed 15 Nov. 2005).

WorkCover Authority of New South Wales. 1994. *Armed hold-ups and cash handling: A guide to protect people and profits from armed hold-up*. Sydney.

WorkCover Authority of New South Wales (Inspector Pompili) v Central Sydney Area Health Service [2002] NSWIR Comm 44, pp. 10–12. IRC 1509 of 1999, Justice J. Schmidt (see: aostlii.edu/cases/nsw/NSWIRComm, accessed 28 Mar. 2002).

— (Inspector Ankucic v Drake Personnel Ltd.) [1997] 89IR374.

WorkCover Corporation of South Australia. 1996. *Guidelines for aged care facilities*. Adelaide.

Workers' Compensation Board of British Columbia, Canada. 1995. *Take care: How to develop and implement a workplace violence programme – A guide for small business.* Vancouver.

Working Women's Centre. 1994. *Stop violence against women at work.* Adelaide.

Workplace Health and Safety, Queensland. 2004. *Guide to personal security in the retail industry.* Brisbane, Department of Industrial Relations.

WorkSafe Victoria. 2003. *Prevention of bullying and violence at work: Guidance note.* Melbourne, Victorian WorkCover Authority.

WorkSafe Western Australia. 1999a. *Code of practice: Workplace violence.* Perth, Department of Consumer and Employment Protection.

—. 1999b. *Guidance note on working alone.* Perth, Department of Consumer and Employment Protection.

World Food Programme. 1999. "Policy on the prevention of harassment", HR99/002. Rome.

—. 2004. "Special measures for protection from sexual exploitation and sexual abuse", internal doc. ED2004/001. Rome.

World Health Organization (WHO). 1996. *Prevention of violence: A public health priority*, 49th World Health Assembly Resolution WHA 49.25. Geneva, May.

—. 1999. *Violence against women fact sheets.* Geneva (see: who.int/frh-whd/VAW/infopack/English/VAW_infopack.htm, accessed 22 June 2005).

—. 2002a. *Global Campaign for Violence Prevention.* Geneva (see: who.int/violence_injury _prevention/violence/world_report/wrvh1/en, accessed 22 June 2005).

—. 2002b. *World Report on Violence and Health*, edited by E.G. Krug et al. Geneva (see: www.who.int/violence_injury_prevention/violence/world_report/wrvh1/en/, accessed 22 June 2005).

—. 2002c. *Youth violence facts.* Geneva (see: www.who.int/violence/violence-injury-prevention/violence/world_report/factsheets/en/youthviolencefacts.pdf, accessed 16 Aug. 2005).

—. 2004. *The economic dimensions of interpersonal violence.* Geneva.

—, Executive Board. 1997. Provisional Agenda Item 13, "Prevention of violence", doc. EB99/INF, Doc/3. Geneva.

World Intellectual Property Organization (WIPO). 2003a. "Harassment at work", Office Instruction No. 09. Geneva.

—. 2003b. "The Office of the Mediator", Office Instruction No. 20. Geneva.

World Meteorological Organisation (WMO). 2003. "Prevention and resolution of harassment", Service Note No. 26/2003. Geneva.

World Trade Organization (WTO). 2002. "Procedures for dealing with staff members' complaints and grievances", Administrative memorandum No. 941. Geneva.

Worsfold, P.; McCann, C. 2000. "Supervised work experience and sexual harassment", in *International Journal of Contemporary Hospitality Management*, Vol. 12, Issue 4, pp. 249–255.

Wynne, R.; Clarkin, N.; Cox, T.; Griffith, A. 1997. *Guidance on the prevention of violence at work*. Luxembourg, European Commission (see: wrc-research.ie, accessed 11 Oct. 2005).

Yamada, D. 2003. "Workplace bullying and the law: Towards a transnational consensus?", in Einarsen et al., 2003a.

Yamakawa, R. 2001. "Prevention and remedies regarding sexual harassment in Japan", ILO working paper (unpublished). Tsukuba.

Zaitun, K. 2000. *Baseline research on racial and gender discrimination towards foreign domestic helpers in Hong Kong*. Hong Kong, China, Asian Migrant Centre and Coalition for Migrants' Rights (see: asian-migrants.org/resources/99950665938152.php).

—. 2001. "Action against sexual harassment in the workplace: Asian women's perspective", working paper for the ILO and the Committee for Asian Women (CAW). Kuala Lumpur, unpublished.

Zapf, D.; Einarsen, S.; Hoel, H.; Varta., M. 2003. "Empirical findings on bullying in the workplace", in Einarsen et al., 2003a.

INDEX